Poet of Expressionist Berlin

□

The Life and Work of Georg Heym

□

⌐Poet of Expressionist Berlin⌐

□

The Life and Work of Georg Heym

□

Patrick Bridgwater

LIBRIS

First published 1991
Copyright © Patrick Bridgwater, 1991

Libris
10 Burghley Road
London NW5 1UE

*A catalogue record for this book is available
from the British Library*

ISBN 1 870352 75 0

Designed and produced by Cinamon and Kitzinger, London
Typeset by Wyvern Typesetting Ltd, Bristol
Printed in Great Britain by Billing & Sons Ltd, Worcester

Contents

Illustrations

between pages 146 and 147

Hermann Heym, Georg's father, *c.* 1905 (Private Collection, Hamburg)
George Heym in Würzburg, 1907/8 (Private Collection, Hamburg)
Ernst Balcke (Private Collection, Hamburg)

Simon Guttmann (drawing by Ludwig Meidner, 1912)
(Private Collection, Kuppenheim)
Jakob van Hoddis (Arche Verlag, Zurich)
Georg Heym, *c.* 1905 (Arche Verlag, Zurich)

Robert Jentzsch (Private Collection, Hamburg)
Hildegard Krohn (Private Collection, Hamburg)
Erwin Loewenson (Private Collection, Hamburg)

Ernst Ludwig Kirchner's engraving 'For the Poet Georg Heym', 1923
(Private Collection, Lugano)

Facsimile of a fair-copy made by Heym of his poem 'Berlin II'
(Private Collection, Hamburg)
p. 204

Preface

Georg Heym belonged to that generation of brilliant, semi-mythical young men who died in the trenches fighting for 'civilization' as they understood it. He was an exact contemporary of Rupert Brooke; indeed, one of his favourite haunts was the Café des Westens, known to English readers from Brooke's 'The Old Vicarage, Grantchester'. In literary terms he was a member of the brilliant 'Expressionist' generation which came of age creatively in the years immediately preceding the First World War. Those with whom he has most in common are the poet Georg Trakl and the painters Ernst Ludwig Kirchner and Ludwig Meidner. He is currently less well known than any of them. Now that he has lain graveward with his furies for well over two generations, it is time that he received greater recognition, for there are few more eloquent and passionate monuments to twenty-four years of life than Heym's diaries, poetry and tales.

The Germany in which Heym lived and died was a hidebound, conservative state of stifling pomposity, complacency and hypocrisy, the combined result of two generations of bourgeois materialism, an industrial revolution that took place in the course of a single generation, and a victory in the Franco-Prussian War of 1870/1 which was popularly regarded as the crowning glory of the new state, although the philosopher Friedrich Nietzsche considered that statehood, achieved at the expense of the German spirit or collective better self, to be in some ways an unmitigated disaster. In artistic terms this was a philistine society whose herds of sacred cows were anathema to Georg Heym's generation. When the son of a highly conservative judge advocate declares himself a would-be terrorist, there is clearly something wrong, but Heym's revolt against everything his father believed in was typical of his generation.

The effect of the over-speedy industrial revolution was unsettling and, eventually, revolutionary. It led to urbanization, urban sprawl, and urban discontent. Heym's adopted home town of Berlin, which practically doubled in size in his short lifetime, displayed all the inherent tensions and contradictions of the time in exaggerated form; they are to be seen in the paintings of Ludwig Meidner and Ernst Ludwig Kirchner. The 'Weltstadt', as Berlin liked to be called at this time, was famous for the fevered, febrile, frenetic pitch of life there, particularly the nightlife, which revolved around the cafés of the west end, notably the raffish Café des Westens at Kurfürstendamm 18/19, which Heym took to frequenting in 1911 as a reaction against the legal apprenticeship which threatened to transform him into a member of the establishment which he despised and detested. The establishment, for its part, regarded the Café des Westens as a den of iniquity, the home of undesirable elements.

Whether or not human nature changed in December 1910 or thereabouts, as Virginia Woolf later claimed (to the Cambridge undergraduate audience of her lecture 'Mr Bennett and Mrs Brown' in 1924), 1910 – the pivotal year of Heym's life – was later justifiably described by Gottfried Benn as 'the year when all the timbers started creaking'. Individually the timbers in question had been creaking for some time as the inadequacy of one shibboleth after another was revealed: the inadequacy of materialism as a way of life, of *sauve-qui-peut* capitalism, of the military caste system, of the self-regarding and self-congratulatory historicism of the *ancien régime*, and of an educational system which at times had little to do with education and much to do with brainwashing, to say nothing of the perceived inadequacies of Christianity, systematic metaphysics and dogmatic morality. It was not for nothing that Nietzsche spoke of the destruction of idealism, meaning the destruction of the idealist tradition on which German classic–romantic culture had been based. The men whose names were in the air in the first decade of the once brave new twentieth century (Nietzsche, Freud, Strindberg, Wedekind, Whitman) were all revolutionaries in their way, as were the major artists of the day, the founding fathers of modern art (Munch, Van Gogh, Matisse), which in Germany means Expressionism.

The present biographical and critical study tries to do justice to Heym both as man possessed and as poet of extraordinary power; in other words, it seeks to give a comprehensive survey of his life and work, including aspects of it which have yet to receive their critical due (notably the so-called 'Novellen' or tales), and to give a coherent interpretation of it. The book does not, however, aim for comprehensiveness in the sense of including every last available detail of the life or an exhaustive treatment of the poems (which would be merely exhausting). I have no axe to grind, although I confess to an admiration for my subject and to a wish to rescue Heym from the context of Expressionism, in which he has become too unthinkingly embedded; his relationship to Expressionism is discussed in a Postscript.

In organizing the book I have opted for a subject-based structure within an overall chronological framework. A straight chronological approach would have made the book of less use to students and of less interest to general readers. The book is addressed to both groups, and will succeed only if it appeals to both. For the sake of the general reader Heym's poems, which are quoted in the original, are followed by a plain prose translation; his other work appears only in English.

Acknowledgements

I am grateful to the following publishers for their permission to use material which first appeared in an earlier form in *The Poet as Hero and Clown* (Durham Modern Languages Series, 1986), *The Expressionist Generation and Van Gogh* (New German Studies, University of Hull, 1987), *The Poets of the Café des Westens* (Leicester University Press, 1984), and *Twentieth-Century German Verse* (Penguin Books, 1963).

It is a pleasure to acknowledge the debts incurred in preparing this book: to C.H. Beck Verlag, Munich, for permission to quote from Heym's work (whose publication they took over from Verlag Heinrich Ellermann, Hamburg); to the German Academic Exchange Service for a generous grant which enabled me to spend some time in Hamburg going through Heym's papers; to Frau Nina Schneider for reading and much improving the manuscript, locating many of the pictures, and for much kindness and inspiration besides; to Professor Gunter Martens and Professor Günter Dammann for kindly making available their then unpublished genesis of Heym's poems, and to Dr Peter Lewis for kindly lending me his unpublished D.Phil. thesis; to Dr Harald Weigel and Frau Marion Sommer of the Staats- und Universitätsbibliothek Hamburg for much help and kindness; to Dr Ron Mannheim for valuable help regarding early Van Gogh exhibitions in Berlin; to David Meidner (Kibbutz Shluchot, Israel) for kind permission to reproduce Ludwig Meidner's drawing of Simon Guttman; to Frau Margarete Heym and Frau Waltraut Härtel for kind permission to reproduce the hitherto unknown photograph of Hermann Heym; to my publisher for his enthusiasm, expertise and patience; to Christine Shuttleworth for compiling the index; and to Kathleen Lowson for word processing with her usual accuracy and cheerfulness.

Abbreviations

In referring to the four volumes of Georg Heym's *Dichtungen und Schriften*, edited by Karl Ludwig Schneider (Heinrich Ellermann, Hamburg, 1960–8), the following abbreviations are used:

D	*Dokumente zu seinem Leben und Werk*
L	*Lyrik*
PD	*Prosa und Dramen*
T	*Tagebücher, Träume, Briefe*

The abbreviation SUB, used in the Notes, stands for Staats- und Universitätsbibliothek.

Van Gogh's works are denoted by F followed by the number of the work in J. B. de la Faille, *The Works of Vincent van Gogh*, Amsterdam and London, 1970.

Life, 1887–1909

□ EARLY LIFE

Georg Theodor Franz Arthur Heym was born on 30 October 1887 at Hirschberg (now Jelenia Góra) in what was then German Lower Silesia and is now Poland; he was the eldest child of Hermann Heym and his wife Jenny (*née* Taistrzik). His sister Gertrud (1889–1920) was an epileptic and a sad, timid creature; but brother and sister were, although opposites, fond of one another. Gertrud often tried to pour oil on the troubled waters between her father and brother. Georg's last poem ('Die Messe') was written, on the day before his death, as a result of finding his sister crying. For all the individual, social and cultural differences, Georg Heym's relationship with his parents is reminiscent of Franz Kafka's relationship with his parents; in Heym's case, too, his domestic life was dominated by a father whom he professed to hate. In 1906 he noted: 'I consist of two quite different people, this presumably being explicable in terms of my ancestry: the sober Heyms and the more spiritually inclined Taistrziks ... Sometimes I am totally carried away by enthusiasm and filled with contempt for the down-to-earth, sober-sided type; sometimes I am only the latter (and a pretty rotten example of the type at that), mocking the dreamer (*T* 72).'

Hermann Heym (1850–1920), whose own father was, in English terms, a country gentleman, was a professional civil servant and a temperamental conservative. After taking part in the Franco-Prussian war, in which he won the Iron Cross (Second Class), he studied law at

Heidelberg and Berlin. At Heidelberg he belonged to the duelling corps Vandalia from 1870 to 1874. After qualifying in 1879, he married Jenny Taistrzik (c. 1855–1923). He worked as a counsel in the government prosecution service, a position involving frequent moves. Georg Heym's childhood was thus far from settled; at five he moved to Posen (now Poznan), at seven to Gnesen (now Gniezno), at twelve back to Posen, and at thirteen to Berlin; five years later he was exiled to Neuruppin in Mark Brandenburg (so far as young Georg was concerned, it might as well have been in Siberia). His associate David Baumgardt described Heym's father as 'the typically energetic "Prussian" civil servant of Wilhelmine Germany', but there was more to it than that, for this conscientious civil servant was brought to the point of breakdown by his job, which involved being present when death sentences were carried out; as a result he became unstable and in 1899–1900 was obliged to spend almost a year in a sanatorium. Rudolf Balcke, elder brother of Georg's closest friend, who knew the father from 1904, described him as 'very melancholy and very religious' (D 91); his son, on the other hand, described him (in 1910) with characteristic outspokenness as suffering 'a kind of religious mania and manic sense of sin' (T 140). As a reserve officer Heym père took part in the First World War, which caused a further breakdown; Rudolf Balcke last saw him, in 1916, as a patient in the maison de santé in Berlin-Schöneberg. His son's rowdiness, revolutionary proclivities and tragic death, and his daughter's epilepsy, must have taken their toll too, given that from October 1900 he was a judge advocate attached to the Reichsmilitär-gericht (military court) in Berlin and, as such, a pillar of the Wilhelmine establishment.

Inevitably the relationship between conservative father and revolutionary son was uneasy. That Georg was not lacking in good will towards his father is shown by an early diary entry:

How I should like to get on better with my father, seeing, as I do, that my behaviour pains him, but he simply cannot get it into his head that I shall be destroyed if I do not continue to reject these pettinesses. I cannot live as others do; either I must ride the fate which I daily challenge, becoming great and famous in the process, or it will do for me (T 25 May 1906).

In June 1908 (T 110) Georg described his father as 'very kind'. Unfortunately Hermann Heym became more and more seemingly petty as his nervous condition deteriorated. When Georg said, 'I should have been one of the greatest of poets if I had not had such a swine of a father. At a time when I needed care and understanding, I had to devote all my energy to keeping this blackguard off my back' (*T* 171), he no doubt thought that his father was too busy being petty-minded, self-righteous and sanctimonious to give him the support he so badly needed, but he probably also had something more specific in mind. Heym *père*, described by his son as consisting of nothing but skin and bone (*T* 11), regarded poetry and art as useless and therefore unnecess-ary, so much self-indulgence, an attitude that was tantamount to a red rag to a bull, given that Georg Heym lived for poetry (and girls). It is clear that his father's dismissive attitude towards his poetry got Georg's goat and that he overreacted in a way which was typical of him.

That relations between father and son were at one stage reduced to such a level was the result not only of increasingly serious differences about religion and poetry. More generally, Georg's conflict with his father revolved around convention, for Hermann Heym was totally conventional, a man who would have been unthinkable without his innate conservatism, which is what generally held him together, whereas his son was radically opposed to 'compromise' in any shape or form.

Hermann Heym, born in 1850, was very much a man of the nineteenth century. He was also, thanks to his position as judge advo-cate, a pillar of Wilhelmine society; the title of 'Geheimer Rat' (privy councillor), awarded to him by the Kaiser, was the outward recognition of that fact. His social position necessitated conservative attitudes and a conservative life-style. To make matters worse, the fact that he was the victim of a nervous constitution and was frequently ill meant that his family had, as it were, to creep around on tiptoe. Georg Heym therefore grew up in a narrow, oppressive, 'boring' family atmosphere; no wonder he was so impressed when he came across Schopenhauer's brilliant description of the boredom of life. Georg Heym's passionate aversion to Wilhelmine society and all its political, moral and cultural works was no doubt partly occasioned by his reaction against the atmosphere in which he grew up; as his aversion became more articulate, it inevitably became directed against his father as the very embodiment of that society.

As that happened, the good will which each bore towards the

other had little chance to surface. The tense relationship was probably inevitable, given the absolute difference in personalities and values, but Georg knew perfectly well in his calmer moments that he was making life difficult for his father, who was worried by his son's attitudes, activities and life-style. Heym *père*, for his part, continued to do everything in his power to further his son's various proposed careers; though often exasperated by Georg's unruly genius, he was proud of him.

It therefore seems clear that the conflict between father and son was based on an inevitable, but none the less tragic, misunderstanding. Rudolf Balcke said that if Heym had not been so upset at the time, he would have spoken of his father not as 'schweinern', but as 'ledern' (tedious). In fact Hermann Heym's behaviour was not so much tedious as tactless, for nothing could have been better calculated to make his son turn violently against his own values. We need look no further for an explanation of Georg's hatred of pettiness. Everything in which he so passionately believed was the diametric opposite of what his father believed in. More particularly, the father's religiosity turned the son against religion, with the result that in 1909 he sought to set up a new, humanistic religion to replace the Christianity which he had come to regard as a sham; but long before 1909 Georg's Helios-cult had been the opposite of his father's gloomy religious mania.

If Georg Heym inherited his extreme sensitivity (and illegible handwriting!) from his father, his romanticism came from his mother's side of the family, which originally came from the Polish/Ukrainian border region. Like Kafka's mother, Heym's loomed less large in his life and development, although he, too, was very fond of her. She was, according to Rudolf Balcke, 'a taciturn, reserved woman who was never on the same wavelength as her son' (*D* 39). David Baumgardt found her 'a good deal more feeling, but also rather more sentimental and conventional than the father' (*D* 86). No doubt the conversation between mother and son recorded in Heym's diary is fatally accurate:

My mother: 'You have no soul. I can't read things like that. Who is going to read things like that? People with noble, tender souls don't buy such things.' ... My objections ... 'But, Georgie dear, Goethe and Schiller managed to write differently. Why don't you write for *Daheim* or *Gartenlaube*?' (*T* 175).

Daheim was a family magazine ('Ein deutsches Familienblatt'), as was *Die Gartenlaube*: just the place for nice, safe, conservative, middle-class verse. He had to promise to write only 'noble, tender poems' in future (and that in December 1911, just weeks before his death).

All members of the Heym family had their crosses to bear, but the mind boggles at the gulf of incomprehension and censure that separated Georg Heym from his parents – truly a hawk in a sparrow's nest.

Apart from the fact that he attended the Gymnasium in Gnesen from Easter 1896 to July 1899, and the Friedrich-Wilhelms Gymnasium in Posen from August 1899 to October 1900, little is known of the detail of Heym's earliest life beyond the fact that he was emotional, shy and given to occasionally wild behaviour. His great love was, and remained, the world of nature. Born in Hirschberg in the Giant Mountains (Riesengebirge) of Silesia, his early life was dominated by mountains:

I was born in a small town leading an isolated existence in the mountains. In my childhood I never got to cross the mountains cutting us off from the outside world, but even as a small boy I knew my way around the mountain valley.

Early in the morning I would accompany the shepherd to the high pasture, where I roamed around all day. I was always afraid of returning to the musty streets of the town. I knew every bush and tree and would talk to them and hear them answering in the wind.[1]

Being often and easily bored, he lived largely – and increasingly – in his imagination, hence the appeal of Karl May's adventure stories (favourite reading of German youth from Einstein to Hitler), which left their mark on his imagination. Learning to read was as much of a red-letter event in his life as it was for the solitary, imaginative hero of Carl Philipp Moritz's late eighteenth-century psychological novel *Anton Reiser*.

Heym moved to Berlin with his family in autumn 1900, at the age of thirteen. That October he entered the Königlich Joachimsthalsches Gymnasium in Wilmersdorf, where he stayed until 1905. He met Ernst Balcke, the friend with whom he was to die, and his brother Rudolf at the Tennisklub Blau-Weiß in 1904; later, as a university student, he was a member of the Tennisklub Kaiserallee (Grün-Weiß); his interest in tennis revolved around the fact that girls play it. From 1905 Georg and Ernst saw one another mostly in vacations, for they attended different

[1] See Notes on pp. 283–91.

schools and mostly different universities. Ernst Balcke was similarly banished in 1905 (in his case from the Falk-Real Gymnasium in Berlin to the Saldern'sches Institut in Brandenburg, where he was involved in the production of a duplicated magazine entitled *Kreissende Sonnen*, in which some of Heym's early poems appeared; Balcke was himself no mean poet). Balcke went on to study French and English at Munich, Berlin, Besançon and Edinburgh. Heym no doubt owed to him his knowledge of the English and (to a lesser extent) French poets who were to loom so large in his inner life from mid-1909 (at which time Balcke was in Edinburgh). Ernst Balcke was his best friend.

In 1902/3, at the age of fifteen, Heym wrote an autobiographical sketch which is couched in astonishingly general terms:

I once planted hope in my poor tormented heart. It flourished there, nourished by my tears. It grew and turned into a great tree in the shadow of which I would recover from the troubles of the day. In this way I was happy and content. Then one day I fell asleep again beneath the tree, and dreams of a happy future were clustering mask-like around me when I was awoken by a deep roll of thunder. The sun had gone and the sky was filling with a livid grey; a gull fled from the coming storm with a shriek of terror. The earth rumbled and shuddered. Looking up, I saw a huge wheel coming towards me with terrifying speed. It came nearer and nearer, blood dripping from its spokes as it careered over broken bodies. Someone was sitting astride the wheel. He was motionless; not a muscle of his face so much as twitched, for he was blind. I begged and beseeched him, I wrung my hands, I threw myself down before him, imploring him to save my beautiful tree. A cruel laugh came from the mouth of the god, freezing the blood in my veins. The wheel reached my tree and smashed it. I lost my senses. When I came to, my tree was lying there a broken thing, and the onward rumble of the wheel was drowning my sobs. I buried my tree and tottered towards the pit of despair.[2]

There is not a little of the later Heym in this extraordinary sketch with its ruthless objectivity and sense of fate; most fifteen-year-olds would have produced something much more mawkishly subjective. His earliest extant poem ('Die Quelle') dates from 1899, when he was twelve. In 1902 he began a noteboook in which he recorded the poems written since 1899, to which he gave the collective title *Jungfernlieder* ('Maiden Songs'), the markedly old-fashioned title being a reflection of the fact that his early poetry is, until late 1904, essentially neo-romantic. By the age of fourteen he had, however, written a brilliant and extraordinarily prescient poem, 'Lied des Gefangenen' (*L* 532f.), ending 'Im Sterben hab ich meine Heimat gesehn' ('Dying I have seen my homeland').

The early poetry is considered in Chapter III. More relevant in the present context is the diary which he resolved to keep in December 1904, 'perhaps in order to be the ideal observer of my self, as I read somewhere or other, or for other reasons. It must bear the stamp of truth. I will leave nothing out. It must be my mirror' (*T* 6). The diary is peculiarly inward, the past in which he dwelt in his imagination (Greece in the sixth century BC; Renaissance Italy; revolutionary France) being in some ways closer and more important to him than the present, and his self-identification with dead writers substantially more significant than his friendship with live ones. The diary is important because it is so honest. It reveals 'the higher self concealed beneath the outer shell of my childishness' (*T* 18). It is often amazingly revealing, showing, for instance, an extraordinary and ever-increasing degree of self-knowledge; it leaves one in no doubt at all that Heym possessed a volatile temperament. He was given to hyperbolic extravagances. The immediate subject of the early diary is 'love'. In his imagination the borderline between reality and fantasy is blurred, so that one of his early girlfriends is named after the heroine of Eugenie Marlitt's novel *Goldelse* (1866). He had been writing poems about girls for several years already, but at this time he had a hunger for experience at once existential and poetic. Each girl yielded a couple of poems; the last thing he wanted was a steady girlfriend. However, the early diary is more than a fascinating study of adolescence; within a week he is noting his 'presentiment of never getting anywhere' and is quoting Hölderlin's 'Hyperions Schicksalslied' with reference to himself. A self-satire, 'Ach nun seht doch den Heym' (see Chapter III), also written in December 1904, signals his discovery of Hölderlin. It is with this passionately enthusiastic discovery that his poetically significant life begins. On 2 January 1905 he confided to his diary that what he needed was 'humanity, confessions' (*T* 8). This was always to be the centre of his interest in other writers. By this time he was seventeen.

The diary is the most important source for the inner events of Heym's early life; the later life is more fully documented in his work and letters. When he began keeping a diary in December 1904 he had been living in Berlin-Schöneberg (Martin-Luther-Straße 5) for four years; the Heyms were to remain there until February 1909, when they moved to Berlin-Charlottenburg (Neue Kantstraße 12 – a somewhat ironical address for one who took Georg Heym's scabrous view of transcendental logic).

As a result of 'idleness' (i.e. putting girls and poetry first), he failed to get into the upper sixth at the Joachimsthalsches Gymnasium; in the normal way he would have had to repeat his fifth-form year, but a silly prank (burning a skiff) meant that he was obliged to leave the school; he retained fond memories of it, particularly of the headmaster's classes on Homer and Sophocles, to which he owed his love of the classical world. On 26 April 1905 he was transported to the novelist Theodor Fontane's birthplace, Neuruppin in Mark Brandenburg, where he joined the lower sixth at the Friedrich-Wilhelms Gymnasium, a reputable, if less popular, grammar school which his father had been able to persuade to accept his unruly son. Neuruppin was rightly supposed to offer fewer distractions than Berlin, although this was not the point, for it still offered his favourite distractions: girls and drinking.

□ BANISHMENT

The diary which he now keeps more assiduously than at any other time – a sign of unhappiness and boredom – speaks of his 'banishment', his 'exile'. What it records is mostly not outer, but inner events. He lived a very quiet life, which was part of the trouble. The boys boarded out with local families; Heym boarded with the pastor, Superintendent Schmidt, with whom he got on well enough, but he was bored and lonely. He took to going for long country walks, his head full of poems, dramatic projects (these taking their starting-points from his study of the classics, which he loved, despite the pedantic way in which they were taught at his new school), and thoughts of the lives of his poetic heroes. He had discovered Hölderlin shortly before going to Neuruppin; while a pupil there he discovered Dmitry Merezhkovsky (June 1906), Alfred Dove (August 1906), Nietzsche (February 1906) and Christian Dietrich Grabbe (October 1906); some months after leaving school he discovered Kleist. His relationship to these writers is discussed presently. He seems to have first come across Schopenhauer in 1906, when he read the essay on death ('Über den Tod'); in the school year

1906/7 one of his French set texts was Edouard Pailleron's *Le Monde où l'on s'ennuie*, an amusing satire on Parisian *schopenhauerisme* in the eighteen-eighties which will have caught his interest.3 What these writers gave him was the courage to be himself. He published his first poems and wrote his first drama at this time. His school essays, which were not particularly good and were apt to be slapdash and misspelt, were also strangely impersonal, which points forward to the monumental impersonality of his poetry. When an essay on Goethe's *Hermann und Dorothea* (the title of which he mis-spells even in his diary) was returned with the comment 'Poor: words are no substitute for thoughts', he was furious ('What torture it is to be taught by such a pedant': *T* 10). It was a criticism which was to dog him; in 1946 Kurt Hiller, one-time 'eternal president' of the Neue Club, was still saying what he must have said to Heym's face: 'The non-thinking poet, however eminent he may be in visionary and formal terms, struck us as essentially second-rate.' At his previous school Heym had been known for his slapdash work; in the *Fest-Zeitung der Joachimsthaler Abiturienten 1906*,4 produced by those who were his classmates until the previous year, he appears briefly as having made twice as many mistakes as anyone else. He remained slapdash to the end – this is shown by his publisher's exasperated letters. He was above all unsystematic: he could take great care, and on the whole did so with his poems, especially when writing out final drafts, but at times he simply didn't bother.

He went in for rowing, drinking, chasing girls and flouting authority. He was already very much the rebel. He went around with an enigmatic smile on his face; in part intended to draw attention to himself, this was essentially the mask which he wore to hide his suffering from an indifferent world: 'I am strong,' he later wrote in his diary, 'because I display the opposite of my real characteristics (*T* 149).' He knew very well that Nietzsche had said that the man with any pretensions to profundity or intellectual nobility loves a mask. The only decent things in Neuruppin, he said, were the trees and the sunsets. He loved sunsets, though he did not always get to see them; he missed one glorious one because at the time he had to write out one hundred lines of Homer for some peccadillo or other; on another occasion he got detention for trying to enjoy a fine moonlit night. He was always unusually moonstruck; a note dating from January 1911 reads 'Unfortunately caught sight of the moon. Had to write instead of working.'5 Such are the tribulations of romantic young poets. Like Kafka he was disposed to the view that the real and the true were opposites. He was young, he was lonely, he needed support, but did not receive it. It was because he received no encouragement from the living that he sought it from the dead. He needed heroes and was inclined to worship them. He wrote rather pathetically of a friend of his housemaster that he would have made a good 'paternal friend' (T 65), underlining what he missed in his own father (who wrote him 'painful, horrible letters': T 49) and headmaster. Like Hölderlin, with whom he identified so passionately, he lived more in an ancient Greece of his imagining than in the everyday world; in a sense Marathon was more 'real' to him than Mark Brandenburg. He believed in and with the ancient Greeks, addressing his *alastor* (avenging demon) and praying to Helios for the 'daughter of the Sun' of whom he dreamt. He knew perfectly well that 'to trumpet one's melancholia at the age of seventeen is preposterous' (T 12), and yet that was the age at which he wrote of 'brazen-faced infinity staring down at us with thousand upon thousand of starry eyes' (T 20); eighteen months later, in November 1906, he said that the ancient Greeks seemed to have got it right with their 'pitiless gods' (T 76). His view of 'our terrible inscrutable destiny' is Hölderlinian–Greek, as he himself recognized: 'If anyone understands the pessimism of the Hellenic world, it is me (T 126).' This is the measure of the impact on him of Hölderlin and Nietzsche. It is true that his early diary is not lacking in self-irony and self-mockery, to say nothing of self-knowledge; thus he dismisses his own lucubrations on the subject of death as 'childish self-intoxication' (T 26). It is also true that he was often desperately unhappy. Had he not been, he would hardly have developed as he did in the time available.

Outwardly very little was happening, but inwardly these were momentous times, for it was now that he discovered his early poetic heroes and with them his poetic self and personality. We shall see in the next chapter how very seriously he took his heroes and how much they meant to him; it was not for nothing that he (who occasionally stammered in the heat of the moment) was known among his school-fellows as 'Gra-gra-gra-grabbe' – an allusion, to his enthusiasm for the German Romantic dramatist Christian Dietrich Grabbe, which is discussed later. If he discovered himself in his diary, which is so important at this time because of its self-absorption and obsessively recurrent themes (love, beauty, sun-worship, pessimism), he defined himself largely through identification with (and worship of) his poetic heroes. Surprisingly perhaps, his poetry ran ahead of his enthusiasms, for while his romantic enthusiasms reflect the romantic nature of his earliest poetry, by late 1904 his poetry was changing as a result of his discovery of contemporary (*fin-de-siècle, Jugendstil*) poetry. That said, he always remained a romantic; all that changed was the kind of romanticism in question.

Rudolf Balcke, who knew Heym well, though he had little in common with him, later said that he was relatively happy in Neuruppin (*D* 40). The evidence of the diary suggests, on the contrary, that he was often bored and desperately unhappy. What he enjoyed most was walking in the surrounding countryside; his love of nature is an important and constant feature of his life. Even before going there he had determined 'to appear in Neuruppin as the complete pessimist'; in the event he was so miserable that he threatened to commit suicide – but, as he admitted in his diary, 'it was probably mainly a matter of words intended to make me seem big and to make Neuruppin seem like a lesser Siberia' (*T* 17). He was given to heroics and self-dramatization, as his so-called 'dramas' clearly show (they are in reality self-dramatizations); his headlong flight back to Berlin to see his girlfriend of the moment (Nelli), after promising his father that he would not do so, was very much the dramatic gesture. The idea of suicide, on the other hand, was partly serious; he toyed with the idea throughout much of 1905, and in August 1906 addressed (but did not send) to the provincial board of education in Berlin a letter purporting to be written from Hades following his suicide (see pages 22–4 below). The letter was above all a bitter denunciation of his Neuruppin headmaster (Dr Begemann), whom he came to loathe and despise because he saw him – not entirely fairly – as crass (a *Geistesprolet*) and dishonest. There is venom as well as high spirits in the parody of the German Christmas carol 'O Tannenbaum' in which he apostrophized Dr Begemann:

O Begemann, du Rabenaas
Du wirst nun bald krepieren,
Man schleppt dich zum Schindanger raus
Pennäler lebt in Saus und Braus.
O Begemann ...[6]

O Begemann, you silly ass, you'll kick the bucket one day soon, they'll take you to the knacker's yard, no one will stop us boozing then. O Begemann...

Headmaster and rowdy pupil were on totally different wavelengths, the headmaster being a 'well-meaning' martinet who was as sadly lacking in imagination as Heym's own father; he advised young Georg to give up writing poetry because he could not spell, which did not go down well. Not surprisingly Heym described the school as the 'prison' of his youth; he was to graduate from it into what he saw as the prison of the world.

At Neuruppin, as at home, Heym felt that there was no one interested in or capable of understanding him. He put little effort into his schoolwork, which was therefore perceived to be unsatisfactory. The only things that kept him going were what he referred to in the language of the day as dallying with young ladies ('Poussieren [mit höheren Töchtern]') and tippling ('Kneiperei'). These were to remain his favourite activities. Both were, of course, forbidden at Neuruppin – a fact which he inevitably regarded as a challenge.

However, we should not be misled by his pranks while at Neuruppin into thinking that he was not serious about girls, for in fact he was deadly serious; he lived for love, 'eternal, redeeming, all-conquering love' (T 16 December 1906), and for the concomitant passion of creativity. He made a cult of love – 'to me, perhaps more than to anyone else, love is a religion' (T 26 October 1906) – and worshipped Woman well on the other side of idolatry; he apostrophized his first recorded girlfriend as an 'emblem of divinity' (T 6), and shortly afterwards declared 'I am inclined to see woman as a goddess' (T 15 May 1905). Being in love, or thinking himself in love, was for him a necessary condition; without it he would become melancholy, even suicidal. He had only to catch sight of a beautiful girl to be quite carried away. He loved Hölderlin as much for the depth of Hölderlin's love for Diotima (Susette Gontard), as for the beauty of his tragic poetry; he envied him the depth of his experience, envied him the happiness of experiencing such deep sorrow! He dreamt of a 'grande passion', and if he experienced mostly 'kleine Liebeleien', this did not really worry him, for being in love mattered to him more than the object of his love ('I cannot be without a girl to love' – T 10 March 1905). He asked himself: 'Am I one of those who love love more than its object?' (T 2 April 1905), and in his heart he knew that he was. It was the idea of love that mattered. The girls with whom he was forever falling in love belonged more to dream than to reality. When he writes in his diary: 'He was going his way again when he came across a girl who was as beautiful as she was good. Once again his heart caught fire' (*T* 17 June 1905), this is pure fairy-tale, the myth of *Brüderlein* and *Schwesterlein*. It was no doubt because, like Baudelaire before him, he needed love more than he needed any given object of it, that his numerous *affaires de cœur* ended in disenchantment.

If girls were, in 1905 (as at all other times), an essential part of the ideal life for which he longed, and of which he dreamt, there were several reasons for this. He already had a keen sense of the passing of time; in his essay on Lessing in the school-leaving examination (*Abitur*) he made clear his view 'that the domain of poetry is Time' (*D* 381), this being powerfully reinforced by the leitmotif of Merezhkovsky's *Leonardo da Vinci*,[7] which he quoted in his diary in June 1905: 'Youth is a beautiful time but quickly past; happiness means seizing its hours while they last.' No less important is his awareness that he needs 'love' in order to trigger his creative powers: 'All my dormant powers would be awoken if I could only find my *grande passion*' (*T* 12 April 1906), and 'Oh, I need love if I am to become great' (*T* 8 July 1906). This is why Hölderlin is ever-present in his mind in 1906: he longs for his own Diotima to trigger the poetry which is now beginning to come in earnest. Reading between the lines of his diary we can see that he often fell between the Scylla of his desire for love and the Charybdis of his evident intention of using love-engendered sadness as the trigger to his work. In other words, he both passionately desires to live in the present, and is temperamentally (because of his *Angst*) and poetically (because he writes best on the downbeat passion) unable to do so. In August/ September 1904 he wrote of this in a poem addressed to his girlfriend of the moment, Else M.:

Du fragst, warum ich dir nicht nah,
Wo du doch für mich blühen willst?
Ich habe Furcht vor dir,
Weil du zu schön bist.
Auch rollt mein Blut zu schwer
Durch meine Adern.
Ich kann nicht, wie die andern
Leichtsinnig sein
Und nur genießen.
Sieh, wenn die andern lachen
Dann muß ich weinen

Mitten im Genuß
Der großen Leidenschaft,
Da ahne ich das Ende
Das vergällt mir alle Freude.

Sieh, meine Tränen werden dich betrüben,
Drum will ich lieber abseits stehn
Und von fe ne in Schmerzen
Deine junge Schönheit sehn (*L* 557).

('You ask why I do not come closer to you') You ask why I do not come closer to you now that you are waiting for me. I am afraid of you because you are too beautiful. And my blood courses too slowly through my veins. I cannot be like the others and just enjoy life. Others laugh; I have to go and weep in the middle of my *grand passion* for I sense the end, which destroys my joy.

My tears would only distress you, therefore, I would rather stand aside and, in my grief, enjoy your young beauty from a distance.

He is forever quoting Hölderlin's 'Hyperions Schicksalslied' with obvious reference to his own fate. On 25 August 1906 he notes that he is beginning to write real poems ('ganz schöne Gedichte'); the following day he records a significant change in their generation:

Briefly, what occurred to me today was this. Previously I used to make my poems out of vague moods which only became clear to me as they turned into poems. They were all in me for a long time; I felt their presence in me before I was able to shape them. Today it occurred to me that the two poems I have written today, and yesterday's poem too, resulted from the sudden, chance appearance of their subject ... before my eyes. Yesterday I saw a branch of a tree laden with fruit, today I suddenly heard the rain on the trees, and then saw the vine shooting up out of the earth. Three poems resulted automatically. I enjoyed it more the way it was before, for I had to struggle to produce the poem. It is almost as if I am going to have to give away whatever I possess in order that my death shall not find me unprepared. I am convinced that I shall die soon.

This is pretty remarkable self-knowledge for an eighteen-year-old poet. What he needs in order to write in this increasingly inspirational manner is intensity of feeling/experience; thus he noted on the previous day: 'Just when I am feeling quite prostrated again, I find myself writing lyrics expressing love of life.' Nothing worried him more than 'the fear that my poetic vein may dry up for want of any great joy or great sorrow' (*T* 4 September 1905). That 'poetic vein' was the core of his being.

Central both to his being and to his work is imaginative passion. He believed with Diderot that only passions, great passions, can lift the soul to greatness. His poetry is the product of a blessedly powerful imagination that needed to be fuelled by extreme feelings. He was frequently reduced to tears by the very vehemence of his emotions. He loved 'les extrêmes' and hated mediocrity in every shape and form. Niggardliness was not in his nature. His work is dramatic, emblazoned with the whole panoply of death's images, yet throbbing with life. He hates compromise and those (particularly poets) who compromise. This is one of his many Romantic characteristics. As an out-and-out Romantic he had a violently contradictory personality. If it seems strange that such a furious rebel and zestful, exuberant individualist should also have been a 'poet of bile and brainstorm',[8] a 'poet of the most macabre visions and miasmic scenes',[9] it is a fact that 'Heym's sombre meditations on death provide the foil to his yearning for glory, enjoyment, and triumph, his dream of a wild exuberant life in years to come. This brooding introvert is at the same time possessed by a fierce vitality, a hunger for love, experience, physical and emotional fulfilment.'[10] Heym himself comments on the struggle within him of the 'luminary' and the 'boozer' (*T* 22 December 1905) and later adds: 'Enthusiasm and disgust, confidence and despair alternate within me' (*T* 31 October 1906). He was fully aware of what he called, in a phrase worthy of Hölderlin, 'this unholy dichotomy within me', adding, 'prosaic and poetic selves coexist within me. They coexist; they do not coalesce. I am a base creature today and tomorrow a god' (*T* 16 July 1905). Indeed, he was alarmed at the extent of the division: 'The schism is becoming too pronounced. On the one hand my passionate love of beauty, on the other hand my absolute uselessness and lack of any *savoir vivre*' (*T* 20 September 1906). He saw that 'in the long run my pedestrian and poetic selves cannot coexist' (*T* 13 October 1906). Shortly after this came the final split; it was on 26 October 1906 that he noted that he consisted of two quite different people. Even his favourite colour is a reflection of this split self: 'Golden brown is surely the most beautiful colour: *joie de vivre* combined with melancholy (*T* 101).' The totally different forms of handwriting which appear in his diaries and manuscripts at the same time are the outward sign of this dichotomy.

While poets almost necessarily suffer from a genial tension between self and anti-self, they rarely combine introvert and extrovert to such a degree, and rarely do self and anti-self see one another so clearly. The struggle between earthling and poet ended in victory for the poet, for it was the articled clerk who died, while the poet lived on; but even if Heym's destiny had been different, the outcome of this particular struggle would probably have been the same, for Georg Heym was nothing if not a poet, even if he did once say that poetry was no substitute for life and that he would cheerfully give a hundred poems for one moment of excitement. In his diary he wrote of his condition as a 'disease', listing some possible cures, such as fame, the applause of a large audience, a *coup d'état*, a great revolution, a new Hellenic war, a journey across Africa (*T* July 1909). It was at about the same time that he wrote the 'Versuch einer neuen Religion' (*PD* 164f.), which is partly about the fame which he craved (see *PD* 172): the poet as hero. More generally the 'Versuch' proposes hero-worship as the new religion. Two years later, in 'Eine Fratze' (*PD* 173f.), he spelt out what he called 'our sickness', but it is immediately obvious that it is *his own* condition that he is describing in some detail. The fact that he was dissatisfied with the recognition that came his way only underlines his essential romanticism and the hopelessness of his case. Death was the only real cure for such a radical condition.

His diary shows him forever slipping from elation into wild sorrow. Paradoxically, the poet who produced some of the most violent poetic imagery ever was the most sensitive of individuals, ashamed of the delicacy of his own feelings, afraid to wear his heart on his sleeve for fear of being rebuffed or ridiculed; in his diary he spoke of being 'ensconced behind ditch and rampart' – it is a remark which one needs to remember, for there is no doubt that he was as sensitive as D'Annunzio's Andrea Sperelli, the sensibility of whose nerves was 'so acute that the most trivial impression conveyed to them by external means assumed the gravity of a wound'.[11] At times he felt that he was not a real person at all: 'I am not a real person. I am a kind of mirror taking in other people's feelings and reflecting them back again; I dare not allow myself feelings of my own' (*T* 20 July 1906); he was sometimes frightened of the vehemence of his own feelings. He already sees nature as 'the enemy of genius' (*T* 21 July 1906), and thus illustrates as well as anyone the 'incompatibility of talent and life' of Goethe's Tasso, later signalling his awareness of the fact by noting in his diary: 'At least it is given to me to express my suffering' (*T* 5 September 1909), which is an echo of Goethe's 'Und wenn der Mensch in seiner Qual verstummt, /Gab mir ein Gott zu sagen wie ich leide' ('If other men must suffer in silence, a god gave me the power to voice my suffering'). Like Dylan Thomas he was 'lashed to syllables'.

Seeing everything as grey against a background of grey (*T* 20 May 1907), he needed a 'ray of hope' (*T* 24 May 1905) to lighten his existence, and therefore became a sun-worshipper. He was a pagan whose prayers were directed to Helios. His main source of this spiritual light was beauty, in which he believed quite passionately: 'I believe we have no greater god than Beauty' (*T* 13 August 1906). He, who needed beauty as much as he needed love, was no 'aesthete' as such, although it is understandable that his publisher, Ernst Rowohlt, should have expected him to be one and was surprised to find instead someone looking more like a 'butcher's assistant'; but he was serious about beauty in a way in which few self-proclaimed aesthetes are.

His Neuruppin landlady said that he always seemed disgruntled. He was deeply unhappy there, not only because no one understood him or even made an effort to try to understand him, but because he already felt himself to be a marked man – this is shown by the Hölderlinian poem 'Manchem Menschen', written in spring 1905, which begins:

Manchem Menschen meisseln die Parzen
Schon in der dämmernden Wiege
Den harten Spruch auf die kindliche Stirne (*L* 590).

Many there are, still slumbering in the cradle, whose brow is clearly marked by the Fates with their harsh judgement.

In biographical terms the whole poem is important. Heym said of it: 'I wonder whether it does not contain a presentiment of my fate' (*T* 18), qualifying this a month later: 'In the poem "Manchem Menschen" I recognized my fate; but whereas those in question know the happiness of love, I am obliged to look on from the sidelines (*T* 25).' The fullest account of his life at this time, however, is an obviously autobiographical fragment in the diary, dated 17 June 1905, in which he writes of himself under the well-worn guise of a 'friend':

17 June. I once had a friend who was very talented. From his earliest childhood he felt and lived in the world of nature. The sound of trees rustling in the

woods and of streams cascading over stones filled him with a longing which he never lost. When it was never fulfilled, he became more and more depressed and anxious. Oh, he would have come to such rich fruition if only his delicate life, which craved love and never found its ideal, had been placed in understanding hands from childhood onwards.

His father was well-meaning but dreadfully irascible, which made such a deep impression on the child that he began to be afraid of him. His mother meant well too. And the child loved her with all his heart and would run to her to escape from his father. But as the boy grew up, she could no longer understand him. She worried about him not confiding in her, for she had nothing to give him but love. The boy was deeply grateful for this, but since she could not keep up with him on his way to knowledge, a gulf opened up between them.

Now the boy was lonely, for those whom he called his friends were even less capable of telling him which way to go. It was at this point that woman first entered his life. He fell victim to a wild sensuality which made him bay for woman in his sleep. Eventually he got over it.

Then he turned to the ideal in woman, seeking for the love which would understand him and was willing to go with him. He found it one evening. His heart was so full of joy that he could not put it into words. The next day the girl left him. He put up with it and pinned his hopes on the future.

Then one day he was deceived by a girl to whom he had bared his soul.

At about this time he found a friend who consoled him, and to this friend too he opened his heart. Then he went out looking for love again. At first he was lucky; but he had been deceived too often, and therefore clung to her too closely and plagued himself and her with his jealousy. That caused her to leave him too, but she did not go with anyone else, though many asked her to do so.

He was going his way again when he came across a girl who was as beautiful as she was good. Once again his heart caught fire. And she was willing to fit in with all his plans. Then he had to move away and leave the girl. In the place to which he went he was lonely, for those with whom he wanted to be friends either did not understand him or laughed at him. Away from her his love grew more and more restless. He could stand it no longer and went to see her, only to discover that by then she was in love with someone else.

That was the fourth such blow. He realized now that it was possible to exist without love, as animals do, but he also began to be afraid of life.

For to him love was a religion. Yet when he wished to pray in its holy of holies, he found it barred to him. And slowly the holy voices of his longing for the great and the noble died within him.

For he was obliged to walk in darkness and could not see the light, which he learnt to conceal from himself, behaving like a shallow, commonplace person, in order that the others should not scoff at him and his sufferings.

He decided to embrace knowledge instead, but his teachers were pedants and pettifoggers, long since dead on their feet. He never found the teacher who would befriend him. He, with his fervent desire to drink at the very source of knowledge, had to be satisfied with geometrical formulae, for his teachers laughed at him and even hated him.

Still he did not renounce love; he clung to his last girlfriend, even though she could offer him no more than friendship.

Then he decided to see his beloved once more and die with a kiss of sympathy on his lips.

That's how it is with him. I hope that he may yet catch sight of the light again and will not therefore have to commit a sin against humanity. I call it a 'sin against humanity' because it would be robbed of a human being who had great potential.

This is a wholly accurate picture of Heym's Hölderlinian self (in his diary he quotes Bethge as saying of Hölderlin 'For him love was a religion': *T* 72). He was an extraordinary young man: self-absorbed, lonely, obsessed with beauty, love, evil and death. In 1906 one of his proudest possessions was an old skull which he found in the churchyard of the old Klosterkirche in Neuruppin and which he crowned with a wreath of vine leaves. To it he devoted a remarkable ode entitled 'An meinen Totenkopf' (December 1906):

Lieber, einst werd ich, wie du vor Jahrhunderten einstens,
In die Stille des Grabs zu langem Schlafe gelegt.
Nicht mehr schau ich das Licht und nimmer hör ich die Lieder,
Die der Wald und das Meer dem einsam Wandernden singt.
Nimmermehr trink ich den Wein aus hell erklingendem Becher
Bei der Freunde Gelag in abendlich dämmernder Laub.
Nimmermehr schau ich die Sterne in lauen Nächten im Sommer
Stille im Reigentanz gehn, die Freunde heimlicher Lieb.
Nimmer grüß ich am Morgen von einsamem Berge die Sonne,
Wenn über Wäldern und Seen glänzet das goldene Rund.
Nein, ich wohne im Dunkel, im engen Bette des Sarges
Und Erinnerung spielt schmerzlich in Träume hinein.
Niemand wecket mich mehr, der gern ich wieder erwachte,
Wenn ich der Freunde Mund über dem Grabe vernähm.
Doch das dumpfe Falln der Scholln auf den Deckel des Sarges
Ist ja der letzte Ton, den ich entschlafen noch hör.

Und nach manchem Säkulum wohl, wenn längst ich vergessen,
Wirft den Schädel empor des Landmanns wuchtiger Pflug.
Und es kränzet vielleicht ein Mädchen mit Efeu und Weinlaub
Mir auch einmal das Haupt, wie ich sooft dir getan
Und wie ich dir sooft von meiner Hoffnung erzählte,
Raunt dem schweigsamen Freund sie ins verschwiegene Ohr,
Welch ein selig Geheimnis sie tief in dem Busen sich heget,
Das doch der Glücklichen Herz nimmermehr trägt nur allein.
Und so sagt sie's dem Freund, doch droht sie schelmisch, daß nimmer
Er durch ein Lächeln verrät, was ihm zu sagen vergönnt (*L* 641).

('Ode to my Skull') Friend, one day I too, like you centuries ago, shall be laid in the silence of the grave to sleep the long sleep. No longer shall I see the light or hear the songs which the woods and the sea intone for the lonely wanderer. Never again shall I drink my wine out of a cheerfully clinking glass when carousing with my friends in the darkening summerhouse at dusk. Never again shall I see the stars, those friends of clandestine love, performing their round dance on mild summer nights. Never again shall I greet the rising sun from a solitary hilltop when that golden ball shines forth over woods and lakes. No, I shall be dwelling in darkness, in my coffin's narrow bed, remembrance of time past featuring painfully in my dreams. No one will wake me, who would be so glad to re-awake when I hear my friends' voices passing over my grave. But the dull thud of earth landing on the lid of the coffin will be the last sound I hear as I depart this life.

And maybe centuries later, when I have long since been forgotten, the farmer's ponderous plough will bring my skull to the surface. And perhaps a girl will one day crown my head with ivy and vine-leaves, as I have so often done with you; and as I have so often told you of my hopes, so perhaps she will whisper into her silent friend's ever discreet ear, telling him what a blissful secret she is cherishing, which the happy girl's heart can no longer contain. And so she will tell it to her friend, warning him archly not to betray by so much as a smile what she has forbidden him to reveal.

Foreseeing his own early death and its hideous nature, he had a passionate appetite for life. He longed for a life of infinite glory and was therefore engrossed by the lives of men like Leonardo da Vinci, Van Gogh and Hölderlin. He also envisioned a dramatic, heroic death: 'With my funeral wreath on my head I should like to ride the evening sea. Of course, it would need to be a beautiful autumn day' (*T* 18 October 1905). The diary contains other, similar versions of 'his' death, and there is also the early poem 'Wunsch' (June 1905):

Nach einer Stunde höchsten Glücks
In Grabesnächte sicher schreiten
Und ausgelöscht sein in der Zeiten
Vergilbtem Buch. So spurlos gehn,

Wie Atemhauch am Wintermorgen,
Wie Wölkchen in den blauen Weiten
Sanfter verwehn.
Wie süßer Nachtigallen Lied,
Das in den dunklen Büschen klang
Und dann verschied (*L* 597).

('Wish') After one hour of perfect happiness to walk boldly into that good night and be expunged from Time's yellowing book. To vanish as utterly as breath on a winter morning, as little clouds gently disappearing into the blueness of space. Like the Nightingale's sweet song which was heard in the darkness of the bushes and then fell silent.

Another version of his ideal was the death of Leonardo as described by the Russian poet Dmitry Merezhkovsky in his novel *Leonardo da Vinci* (1896), which moved Heym to tears every time he read it – and he read it repeatedly; but he will also have noted and applied to himself the words spoken by Niccolò Machiavelli: 'My friend, there is naught more terrible than to feel in yourself the power to do something, and to know you will perish and die without ever having accomplished anything whatsoever',[12] for ever since 1904 he had had 'a presentiment of perpetual failure' (*T* 7). As a romantic, he was not only fully conscious of the 'gulf between ambition and achievement' (*T* 25 May 1906), but was also haunted by the fear that death would rob him of his fame. An early sonnet, 'O meine Seele ist in Angst gefangen...' (February 1906), voices that fear:

O meine Seele ist in Angst gefangen,
Daß sie die großen Höhen nie erreiche,
Und ewig fern und ferner nur entweiche
Der Jugendtraum dem heißen Herzverlangen.

O welch ein Schrecken, welch ein tiefes Grauen,
Nach Jahren wie ein Tier dahinzukriechen,
Von einem Tag zum andern hinzusiechen,
Selbst ohne Scham auf meine Jugend schauen.

O Hände, Hände, daß sie mich befreien,
Daß dieser Fluch mir von den Augen falle,
Daß meine Toten nicht den Geist entweihen,

> Daß nicht das Tier in mir mich ganz umkralle,
> Und Geist und Herz sich ganz der Tiefe leihen,
> Und das Erhabne schnell in mir zerfalle (*L* 611).

('Oh, my soul is beset with fear') Oh, my soul is beset with fear that it may never reach those great heights, and that life's young dream may more and more lose sight of my heart's burning desire.

Oh, what a horrible prospect, what a terrible thought, after years to creep away like a dog, dying slowly day by day, even looking back on my young years without shame.

Oh for hands, hands, to free me, that this curse may be lifted, that my deeds may not desecrate my spirit,

That the brute within me may not master me completely, and heart and soul ally themselves with baseness, and all nobility be swiftly destroyed.

No wonder he wrote: 'How little resemblance my life bears to the ideal life for which I long' (*T* 10 June 1906). Even his death was to fall appallingly far short of the ideal death of which he dreamt, heroic though it certainly was.

The *ennui* which he came to see with Schopenhauer and Baudelaire as the curse of the human condition first became an ever-present condition of his own life in Neuruppin, where everything to which he attached importance was either forbidden or misprized. This made him concentrate obsessively on himself and his unhappy lot. Inevitably he took the extreme view, seeing himself as 'hated by the gods'. Although a diary entry dated 28 November 1905 shows that this feeling was exacerbated by an obsession with his own 'ugliness', it outlived that teenage obsession and became a permanent feature of his view of life. It were better, he argues, perhaps after reading Schopenhauer, not to have been born at all, for 'I do not believe that there are people who suffer as I do' (*T* 6 November 1906); two weeks later he writes that he could not imagine himself without the belief in his own (implacably hostile) fate. Now, of course, a portion of self-dramatization comes into all this; but the pessimism is palpably real. And lest there be any doubt about it, there is his letter to the provincial board of education (*Provinzialschulkollegium*):

I, Georg Heym, sixth-former, son of imperial judge advocate Hermann Heym, Berlin W 30, Martin Lutherstr. 5, born on 30 October 1887 at Hirschberg (Riesengebirge), pupil at the Ruppiner Gymnasium since Easter 1905, having taken my own life on   at   , beg leave to address the Provincial

Board of Education from Hades, in the following terms, in order that this tragedy may not lack its concomitant comedy:

The Provincial Board of Education is obliged to keep a record of all pupils committing suicide; of course in the present writer's humble opinion such inappropriate persons as yourselves ought not to be allowed to form conclusions about the reasons for such suicides; these are mostly attributed to failure to make the next grade, but the reasons naturally run a good deal deeper and inevitably involve the pupil's whole unhappiness at school; indeed, in so far as the school, instead of taking special care of the unhappy young person, rejects him out-of-hand, this latter reason is often decisive; but ... given that it is the custom to go into the dead person's state of mind, I will save the Provincial Board of Education the trouble of doing this in my case by myself reporting briefly on the reason for, and purpose of, my death.

At Easter 1905, then, I left the Joachimstal Gymnasium in Berlin – which I take this opportunity to thank again for all the fine things which I was privileged to learn there, especially at the Headmaster's (Dr Barth's) classes on Homer and Sophocles – for a dump called Neuruppin am Rhin. I was received (pardon the expression) by the local despot, Dr Heinrich B[egemann] (generally known as 'Bloodhound') in an uncommonly boorish way, something which would never have happened at my old school, and which therefore promptly made me fear the worst. On the following day we had to parade in Hall under the command of B. ..., like so many rookies. After he had dismissed the lower classes, he turned to us with a few vigorous words of greeting which included – verbatim – the following: 'How few of you look fit. That comes from drinking, from smoking and particularly from something one does not talk about. Just look at Rademacher and at Moritz – yes, Moritz may look fit enough, but he's rotten inside, a moral hooligan.' He said that in front of fifty pupils. He knew very well that there were reasons why those two had no choice but to remain at his institution. The beginning of this term had a very strange effect on me. My fellow-pupils on the other hand were evidently already used to such things; in particular that taboo subject left them quite unmoved. 'He often refers to it', one of my fellow-pupils (whose name I shall not reveal, in order to spare him unwelcome attentions) told me. I have myself heard B. use similar words on several other occasions.

In the course of the summer term, which began with twenty-three or twenty-four pupils, six whose parents were in the fortunate position of being able to accommodate their sons elsewhere left the school in order to get away from B., one of them, von Kräntzki, after he had been insulted in the grossest way.

Having reached the Upper Sixth I too wished to pack it in and leave – after all he had often enough advised me to get packing – but when I was finally on the point of escaping from this prison of my youth, he told me in a personal audience: 'If you leave now, I will do all I can to stop you taking your leaving examinations at Michaelmas 1906.' This civilized statement left me with no choice but to stay put ... In the winter term there were further instances of his unacceptable behaviour. Thus he once struck me on the arm with his clenched fist. My father, to whom I complained, naturally allowed himself to be brought round to B.'s side. In the summer I had another row with him, about a girl from a very respectable local family, with whom he forbade me to go out. In this case, the Board's views may correspond with B.'s, but I would remind the Board that it too was young once. At all events, my dear Councillor Lambeck, B. is certainly not a 'very distinguished educationalist'.

But I too have now had enough of this record of my unhappy schooldays; perhaps this tirade against B. will be instrumental in driving him out of Ruppin, or perhaps everything will, as so often, remain exactly the same, and I shall in vain have paid the highest price I could pay (my life) for ridding Ruppin of B.

At any rate I shall have done my duty by those who survive me in attempting to rid them of B.

The other thing which drives me to my death has nothing to do with your forum, for, alas, in Prussia's schools a teacher has never yet been the best and closest friend of one of his pupils. And with that I close my

'j'accuse'

with Apollo's deadly arrow already in my hand.

Just one other thing. That B. is not fit to be a teacher is shown by the following: on the occasion of an investigation of his, B., in front of the whole class, promised those concerned that they would not be punished if they owned up. They owned up and were promptly punished. I mean to say, a liar is hardly an exemplary model. In England the man would have been dismissed with ignominy on the spot. In this case, too, B.'s jesuitical sophistry will probably procure him a way out; on the other hand perhaps no one will believe him this time (T 194f.).

The fundamental complaint here is that the school, 'instead of taking special care of the unhappy young person, rejects him out of hand'. In Heym's case this hurt all the more in that it was precisely what his father had done. In their different way his early diaries are no less clear an indictment of the German educational system of the time, although this does not mean that 'Heym's diary reads like the autobiographical record of the harm done to him by a callous, philistine educational system',[13] for it is significant above all as showing the inner development of a writer of genius; the education to which he was subjected becomes important only in so far as a better, less intolerant form of education would have given him less against which to react, and might therefore have slowed down his extraordinarily rapid poetic development. That said, Heym's ideals at this time (greatness, nobility, beauty, love) are – in part – deliberate 'perversions' of the narrow conformist ideals of the Wilhelmine school system as interpreted by Dr Begemann. Heym's experiences and reactions, although extreme, were typical of his generation, as a number of famous and once-famous novels show. Whereas the reactionary 'system' is concerned only to produce the 'useful citizens' who were to die in their millions in 1914–18, Heym is concerned (like Nietzsche, Hesse and others) to discover his own ideal self. The two ideals have nothing whatsoever in common.

His non-academic priorities, which had caused him to be sent to Neuruppin in the first place, caught up with him again in autumn 1906, when his first application to be allowed to take the *Abitur* was turned down. His second application was successful, and he took it in February/March 1907 (in German, Greek, Latin and Maths). His final report was not good, and a note in the school's register of *Abiturienten* reads 'behaved in an uncouth way on numerous occasions; became known as a young poet' (*D* 385), the wording managing to imply both that allowing oneself to become known as a poet is also pretty uncouth, and that this was only to be expected of him.

Heym referred to his teachers (while thinking of Begemann) as the 'murderers of his youth' (*T* 79). His release from the 'prison of his youth' in Neuruppin is recorded in one word: 'Free' (*T* 20 March 1907). However, as Kafka once remarked, 'People often deceive themselves about freedom'.[14] The idea of freedom with which Heym fled from Neuruppin was certainly chimerical. The following day honesty compelled him to admit as much ('I am not really very happy'). This instant disillusionment was inevitable, given that the pessimism with which he left Neuruppin went far beyond a mere dissatisfaction with school life. If, as a university student, he was to be much freer in many ways than he had ever been before, he was never to be free of the view of life as 'our terrible inscrutable destiny' (*T* 16 November 1906) which he acquired at Neuruppin. His determination to play the pessimist there had backfired in the most tragic way, for he left school as desperate a pessimist as one is likely to meet. It is only a few months later – at a time when he has just recorded the view that love is the measure of all things – that the diary records one of the most memorable of all his images: 'Suffering is like a roof over the world. In individuals it builds itself pillars which enable it to span the whole of life' (*T* 13 March 1908).

□ UNIVERSITY

At home in Berlin a cloud of indifference descended upon him, especially when, to his utter fury, 'they' (i.e. his parents?) removed and destroyed his treasured skull. He realized that he had reached the end of his youth: 'My childhood is over – quant' è bella giovinezza ... Childhood and schooldays are over. My university days are beginning. I have found myself to have a good deal of imagination and passion. I have experienced many more sad days than happy ones' (*T* 14 April 1907). The leitmotif from *Leonardo da Vinci* was forever running mockingly through his mind, reminding him that his own youth had been a pretty unhappy affair. He had, of course, had good experiences as well as bad; on 12 October 1907 he lists them: 'I am thinking of my childhood. Of the day when I saw in the sky the inscrutability of all things, of the walk by the churchyard, of falling in the river, and above all of two paintings: *Mühle im Schwarzwald* and *Kleine Seestadt in Holland*, this old picture.' Rereading his diary, what struck him was the lack of any sustained highlights ('Every day virtually the same. Just occasionally some short-lived joy, otherwise everything grey against a background of grey' – *T* 30 May 1907).

By this time he was already in Würzburg and feeling particularly sorry for himself, for he had not wanted to go there. On Christmas Day 1907, when home for the vacation and feeling maudlin, he quotes (in German) from the first page of Oscar Wilde's *De Profundis* the words 'Suffering is one very long moment ... We can only record its moods'. He quotes the pessimistic tag, 'It is best never to be born, and next best to die young', and a year later records his wish to have been born a century later because: 'Then we shall have taken over space and will be greater than the gods' (*T* 17 April 1908); this is unusual, for he mostly wished to have lived in the past. Nor can it be argued that he was born at the right time but died in the wrong way, for while he always wanted to die a hero's death, Wilhelmine Germany was the last thing he would have chosen to die for had he survived until 1914. Or would his craving for excitement have overcome even that revulsion?

In Würzburg that first summer of 1907 he wrote: 'Why are we so unhappy? What have we done to deserve it?' (*T* 7 June 1907). However, if his 'pleasures' had been mostly pretty ephemeral, he also knew, increasingly, moments of poetic inspiration and enthusiasm, which he no doubt connected with Hölderlin:

It is quite extraordinary, enthusiasm sometimes hits me like a storm. My heart suffers a spasm; I go cold. Tears come unbidden and will not be held back, and a longing for the Unknown will not let go of me. It is like an acute ailment of the soul, or like the final convulsion of a tortured soul (*T* 23 June 1907).

If only, he later wrote, this enthusiasm were a permanent condition, there would be no limit to what he might achieve ('If only I could be in a state of continuous enthusiasm, how much I should be able to achieve': *T* 16 October 1911). Of course, it is in the nature of such creative mania to be sporadic, but however this mania is assessed, it is clear that Heym is a marked man, someone who is unlikely to fit into the bourgeois conventions of contemporary student life.

After a month at home in Berlin, he had proceeded to Würzburg on 25 April 1907. Würzburg was his father's choice; Georg had wanted to go to Heidelberg and was under the illusion that he might have become 'a good citizen and a useful human being' (*T* 125, 132) had he done so. Perhaps he wanted to belong to his father's Heidelberg Corps (student fraternity) in order to prove himself and appease his father who, for his part, was afraid that his son's behaviour would cause him to lose face among the senior members of his Corps. Arrived in Würzburg, he began studying law and became a member of the duelling fraternity Rhenania. At school in Neuruppin he had been a founder-member of the banned junior fraternity Rhinania, and in summer 1907 he had founded another fraternity in Berlin to which he gave the Neuruppin name Rhinania; originally it had fifteen members, but by 1912 there were only seven left in Berlin. It seems extraordinary that Heym (who, as in Neuruppin, went under the name of Brutus) took this particular initiative and kept it up even after Würzburg, for at Würzburg neither law nor Corps life agreed with him. His comments on law and on what he saw as the criminal folly of wasting his time in studying it, became more and more Rabelaisian as time went on.

Though possessing many of the qualities necessary to the Corps-student (he was a first-class fencer), he had the fatal weakness of intelligence. As a result, he found his Corps-brethren and their antics unbelievably tedious. He had no time for such 'deadly dull people' (*T* 16 October 1907): 'To be together with such people the whole day and to have to humour them, who can understand what agony this is? So much for carefree student days' (*T* 21 October 1907). He despaired of finding 'like-minded, idealistic souls' in Würzburg (*T* 19 January 1908), expressing himself most fully in a letter to his friend Balduin Fischer dated 21 October 1907:

To be honest, it is terribly boring here and always was. For among my Corps-brethren there is not one with whom one can hold a conversation that is not confined to the most banal subjects. It may be that among them there is the odd one who would not be averse to speaking an occasional rational word, but the whole Corps ethos discourages this. It is regarded as un-Corps-like to indulge in intellectual conversation ... I have positively craved the company of someone whose head is not full of gambling, boozing and duelling ... The superficiality of it is mind-numbing. I don't know how long I'll be able to stand life. I'd like to be an officer, but fear the army would be just the same, except that one would have more free time. There are people for whom there is simply no [appropriate] career. I count myself among them (*D* 500).

The very fact that he reacted so strongly to the beer-swilling mindless-ness of Corps life, shows how far removed he was from the 'boozing student' for which it is easy to mistake him. It is, however, easy to mock the Corps and all its conventions and prejudices; what is necessary is to realize its strength as a force for conventionalism and conservatism. In many ways the Corps is Wilhelmine Germany *in nuce*. Heym would have found it impossible, given his family background, not to become a Corpsstudent; that said, he did not become himself until he ceased to be one in November 1908.

In the meantime, he fought his duel on 30 October 1907, although he much preferred to spend his time chasing girls (there is said to have been hardly a pretty girl in Würzburg whom he did not know) or drinking schnapps and playing cards ('schwarze Sau') in his preferred non-Corps pub (Beisels). As for 'working', the only work worthy of the name was his writing, which at this time meant above all drafting plays rather than poems.

His time at Würzburg, where he spent three terms, falls naturally into two halves, the first from 25 April 1907 to 26 April 1908, when his diary is almost entirely negative (the number of dreams recorded in the diary in summer 1907 suggests that he had fled into his inner world), and the second from 27 April 1908 until 5 August 1908, when he left Würzburg. The latter was the first and main part of what the diary grandly if inaccurately calls his 'Year of Love' (in reality it amounted to three months plus aftermath). He wrote in his diary that 'It is perhaps a poet's privilege to love again and again with the same intensity' (T 21 July 1907), and knew very well that 'One often writes best after a good dose of unhappiness' (T 11 November 1907), the truth of this being borne out by his own elegiac gift; but his love for Hedi Weißenfels was a revelation, one of the high points of his life.

She came providentially, 'wie gerufen' (a month before meeting her he had a presentiment that things were going to get better, which must have come as a relief, for he was as superstitious as a cat): on 26 April 1908 the diary records his misery ('I am the most wretched of mortals ... afflicted with a hunger for life and a love of death. Ye gods, help me'), and on 27 April his joy ('auspicious day. I stepped into a church and found love'). By 2 May he was describing himself as the happiest of mortals ('perfelix'). Eighteen months later he added a note to the effect that he had been kidding himself, but at the time Hedi was the answer to all his prayers; their love brought together everything that mattered to him – love, beauty, enthusiasm, superstition, love of nature, love of the classical world, love of Hölderlin, and so on. It was too good to be true, hence his superstitious 'Days such as I never experienced before. Do not take them from me, o gods' (T 1 June 1908). 'Avert your gaze, o gods' (T 23 June 1908). They walked everywhere together, one of their most magical days (Hedi wearing a poppy on one shoulder, a wild rose on the other) being recorded in a poem:

> Roten Mohnes Blüten nahmst du viele.
> Schöne Blumen, die der Sommer gab.
> Brachst mit feiner Hand die feinen Stiele
> Aus der Woge grüner Garben ab.

> In die Schluchten hingen Rosen nieder,
> Die sich willig deinem Wunsche boten,
> Glänzten in den hohen Farben wieder,
> Da sie nun an deinem Herzen lohten (L 661; T 111).

Many red poppy flowers you took, beautiful flowers which summer gave. With your delicate fingers you broke the delicate stems from among the wave of green young shoots.

Roses hanging down into crevices gave themselves to you, wearing their true high colours again once they were glowing next to your heart.

On another occasion he drank from her hand at a brook before they read Hölderlin together. They were partly playing Hölderlin and Diotima, but other parallels also came to his mind, especially when he thought of the future: 'Sometimes I suffer in the same way as the hero of the novel *The Child of Pleasure*' (T 1 July 1908). No doubt D'Annunzio's novel came to his mind because with Hedi he was at last experiencing that intensity of aesthetic living which is put forward as an ideal there, and which had long been his own ideal. And all too soon he found himself in the same position as Andrea Sperelli, for Hedi, like Maria, was gone. Or rather he had himself gone back to Berlin. He was desolated on his return there: 'Under which unlucky star was I born? ... All my days are spent alone ... Not a day passes without thoughts of death (T 115f.).' He went back to Würzburg in November to spend a few days with Hedi. They revisited the scenes of their summer love, knowing that 'it is foolish to place one's hopes in Fate'. There was a terrible scene when Hedi's mother, a widow worried by her daughter's wild boyfriend, struck her. The Hölderlinian lines in which Heym records their parting show that he was keenly aware both of the tragedy and of the drama of the situation:

> Ihr zerreißt nicht Herzen, wie Ihr schiedet
> dies und das in Euren Prunkgeweben.
> O, sie sind zu fest in eins geschmiedet,
> daß sie je getrennet können leben.
> Ach, was wißt ihr, die im Lichte schweben
> von dem Gram, der unter Wolken wohnet.
> Unser Schmerz ist Euch ein leichtes Beben
> durch die Freude, die im Äther thronet (T 121).

You do not break hearts by decreeing this or that in your finery. They are too closely joined together to be able to live apart. Oh, what do you know, living in the light, of the sorrow of those dwelling beneath a cloud. For you our grief is but a tiny disturbance of the serenity prevailing in the ether.

He left Würzburg feeling defeated, quoting 'Hyperions Schicksals-lied'. His despair was both real *and* stagey. It lasted a long time too (the following August he was to write 'Ye gods, deliver me from this love!' – *T* 20 August 1909). His naïve prayer of 27 March 1907 ('I would have liked to experience the grief of a lovers' parting') had been answered with a vengeance. Looking back we can see that the experience helped to make him the great elegiac love poet that he is, but to him, at the time, things looked very different. He was wild with unhappy love: 'I am like a madman. I cannot bear this love' (*T* 5 August 1908). If he were a sculptor, he said, he would portray Love as 'A youth standing there as though poleaxed, like a madman, like a wounded man' (*T* 21 August 1908).

He parted from Hedi not once, but three times (on leaving Würzburg on 5 August, and again on 5 and 11 November after paying her flying visits). From November to January the question 'what am I going to do about Hedi?' is recurrent in his diary. He toyed with the idea of marriage, recognized that it was out of the question, and blamed himself for not making a clean break since break there had to be. Instead he broke with the Corps on 2 November.

That he continued his study of law at the University of Berlin at this time (he matriculated there on 25 November 1908) is not men-tioned in the diary, which is very sparse throughout late 1908 and 1909. It is not just that his shattered love-life was foremost in his mind; the part one or probationer's exam was too far away to call for any serious action (such as working), and in any case he now had two new interests of very different kinds, both of them of great significance for his poetry. The first of these was connected with his study of law, which currently involved visits to local prisons and the morgue. Rudolf Balcke, who accompanied him, wrote:

The official visits of this time, especially those to prisons and mortuaries, left an indelible impression on Heym. His poems about prisoners, madmen, sui-cides, the drowned, and so on, are the direct outcome of what he saw on those visits. He was particularly fascinated by the suicides' graveyard at Schildhorn (Grunewald) with its little mortuary to which bodies found in the water or in the woods were first brought. In January 1912 Heym and my brother lay there (*D* 40f.).

The other new interests were literary: his discovery, in January 1909, of Büchner, and then, in summer 1909, of Rimbaud, Baudelaire, Verlaine and Byron. These are all poets with whom he immediately identified; most of them were to be major influences. This was perhaps the first real sign that the emotional turmoil was over. His last literary enthusiasm had been for Kleist, in October 1907. If Büchner belongs, with Kleist and Grabbe, among his early heroes, his other discoveries signal the fact that he is now in a different phase with different heroes. The turmoil of his love for Hedi, combined with his discovery of some of his most important poetic models, produced some of the key features of his 1910–11 poetry, features which begin to appear from November 1908 onwards. A diary entry dated 3 September 1909, by which time the making of his best-known style was well under way, illustrates very clearly his attitude to law on the one hand and poetry on the other: 'I've just been reading a life of Byron and now have to crawl into the dusty mouse-hole of [my law books]. Who could make sense of this turn of events without doing himself an injury?' He himself never had any doubt as to his priorities.

If he was in a demoralized state by the time he left Neuruppin in March 1907, he was in an even worse state by the time he became a member of the Neue Club in late spring 1910, for the so-called year of love, which had taught him to love life (T 118), had been followed by eighteen months of real despair; the loss of that love left him convinced that life had little to be said for it. It is this that lies behind a diary entry dating from late December 1909: 'If the demon who let the world slip through his hands could be captured, he should be placed in irons and flogged to prevent him from perpetrating any further cosmic cock-ups.' Apart from the characteristic use of the word 'demon', this is a reference to the story of Brahma creating the world by mistake, mentioned by Schopenhauer in the Appendix to his On the Sufferings of the World. At very much the same time the diary contains the words: 'Suffering, suffering, suffering, suffering wherever one looks'. The Neue Club came not a moment too soon.

II

Romantic Hero

□ HÖLDERLIN

Heym is self-engrossed to an extraordinary degree. He is forever exploring himself, forever interpreting himself to himself; his work is a continual essay in self-definition. He reads everything subjectively; it is one
of his most pronounced characteristics that he identifies with his
favourite writers and their fictional self-projections. Greulich noted
long ago that Heym consorted with the heroes of some novels as with
real people,[1] and the same goes for his poetic heroes. Friedrich
Hölderlin, for instance, was more real to him than were most of his
contemporaries; for all the depth of his abhorrence of Wilhelmine
Germany, it was his imagination in which he lived. In a letter to one of
his girlfriends we find the revealing comment, 'We will recognize ourselves in our heroes' (D 507); Heym not only recognized, but found
himself in that way. Hölderlin is a case in point. It is not that Heym was
similar to Hölderlin to the point of identity, for he certainly was not – in
important ways he was the opposite of his ascetic idol – but he identified with Hölderlin absolutely, envied him, learned from him, adopted
some of his attitudes, beliefs and poetic forms, and so on. It is thus with
all his poetic heroes.

Hölderlin was his first poetic – and human – idol. His first
reference to Hölderlin, in a diary entry for 2 January 1905, puts the
emphasis on Hölderlin's life: 'I need the human touch, confessions.
That is why ... it is Hölderlin who is closest to me (T 8).' This sets the

pattern for his attitude towards his poetic heroes, his interest in all of whom is biographical and therefore subjective: he looks in their lives for confirmation of his own validity as a writer and hence as a human being. He defines himself by means of this self-identification with other writers and artists, just as he does subsequently by his identification with the characters of his own plays and tales. For all its seeming objectivity and impersonality Heym's work is unusually self-referential. In 1905, when he is only seventeen, he is quite simply self-obsessed, something which can (and occasionally does) lead to mawkishness for precisely the reason spelt out by Keats in the Preface to 'Endymion':

The imagination of a boy is healthy, and the mature imagination of a man is healthy; but there is a space of life between, in which the soul is in a ferment, the character undecided, the way of life uncertain, the ambition thick-sighted: thence proceeds mawkishness...

Some of his early verse is not free of the insipidity that comes from callowness, although he does not normally suffer from a mawkish over-sweetness. More often the young poet's self-obsession causes him to appear in a wholly unintended comic light, as he occasionally does in the present chapter.

An extreme type himself, Heym was drawn towards other extremes, which includes Hölderlin as described by one of his most stylish biographers, Hans Bethge: '*Les extrêmes* ... I forgot Bethge's Hölderlin. He must have been very similar to Leonardo da Vinci' (*T* 17 July 1905). He can pay Hölderlin no greater compliment than this. At this time he is using Bethge's *Hölderlin* in the same way that he uses Merezhkovsky's *Leonardo da Vinci*: as a guide to himself and the life for which he hopes. It was from Bethge's and Merezhkovsky's subjects that he acquired his super-ego, his ideal of the poet as Hero. Both Bethge and Merezhkovsky see their subjects in heroic, superhuman, quasi-divine terms; it is hard to imagine two biographies more likely to make an impressionable young poet dramatize himself, let alone one growing up when the very air was full of echoes of Nietzsche's Superman and therefore of inflated self-projections.

Heym's main source of information about Hölderlin's life was Hans Bethge's *Hölderlin*, which he read shortly after it appeared in 1904; it became one of his favourite biographies. Reading Bethge, it soon becomes clear why Heym identified so absolutely with Hölderlin; in the first half of the book most pages contain remarks that are immediately and intimately applicable to Heym:

He is highly sensitive and easily provoked ... from the beginning he lacked equilibrium. He was one of those people who, being over-endowed in terms of feeling, have nothing wherewith to counter it ... His view of nature is ... not dependent on particular images, but is a general or cosmic one ... He longs to become one with Sun, Ether, Moon and Earth, for these great universal concepts are dearer to him than red roses or the silver ripple of a stream ... With the enthusiast's passion which is so characteristic of him he seeks to embrace not only nature, but the ancient Greeks too ... To him, as to most mortals, it was given to know no repose, so that he stumbled, suffering, from one hour to the next ... [His] letters .. are feeling and only feeling; factual information is almost entirely lacking ... Being parted from his beloved makes him feel like a prisoner desperately rattling at the bars of his cell. He experiences a constant, nagging alternation of joy and anguish. One moment all exultation, the next totally dejected ... He speaks of early death, of freedom and his love of nature ... his mystical devotion to the mysterious unity of nature and the whole chaos of his fretful youthful emotions ... All his life he craved recognition, seeking it again and again and always in vain ... His ever more violent aversion to his job makes his moods even more irritable and melancholy ... at night he dreams of poetic fame ... of being crowned laureate, of wonderful days of creative joy. All of them things which he was not to be granted ... The pain of love, unsatisfied ambition and the melancholy recognition that he will never gain a firm foothold in life, combine to undermine his delicate health in an ever crueller way.[2]

Reading this Heym evidently felt that he was reading about himself; for us, reading it with all the facts of Heym's life known, the parallel is startling. Given that this is the description of his country's greatest romantic poet, it is no wonder that Heym idolized him and loved him so deeply.

Proof that it was Bethge's Hölderlin with whom Heym identified is the fact that, when, on 17 June 1905, he wrote a piece of stylized autobiography (quoted on pages 17–18 above), describing himself as a 'friend', this 'friend' bore a striking resemblance to Hölderlin as described by Bethge. Thus the words 'From his earliest childhood he felt and lived in the world of nature. The sound of trees rustling in the woods and of streams cascading over stones filled him with a longing which he never lost' echo Bethge's 'Nature he approaches with a love laden with dreams. To nature he gives himself with all his tenderest feelings, with all his vague longing, as a lover gives himself up to the thought of his beloved',3 as, more obviously, does a passage in the diary for 23 June 1907: 'With nature he is happy, pursuing her like a lover.'

On 10 September 1905 he writes (first covertly, and then openly) about his enthusiasm for Hölderlin, and what he chooses to stress tells us much about himself:

Oh, I so long for a great sorrow. To him whom they love the gods give great joy and great sorrow. And in addition they give him great beauty in order that their gift may be clothed in beauty. Where is any of this in my case? I know that beauty is the sign of happiness.

And it is written: Keep thy body pure, for it shall be a temple of the spirit. It is easy for those beloved of the gods to keep their beauty pure, for in great joy and in true sorrow one shrinks from baseness and vulgarity. For me it is not easy, but so far I have managed it.

When I am tempted to fall, I think of my beloved Hölderlin and how he was vouchsafed such great suffering. And then I return to waiting for my great sorrow, and turn away from vulgarity. For through ignoble behaviour I should only become further removed from my ideal. Oh, how I love Hölderlin. When he walked through the streets it was as though Apollo were passing by. I love him because of his great beauty, and because he was blessed with the greatest happiness and *the* greatest sorrow (*T* 36f.).

The qualities which he admires in Hölderlin are precisely those stressed by Bethge, whom he paraphrases in his diary. Thus Bethge wrote: 'His Tübingen fellow-students related in their old age that when the poet walked up and down the refectory before dinner, it was as though Apollo were striding through the room. Such was his beauty.'4 Heym idolizes Hölderlin for his personal beauty (he at this time is worried about his own supposed ugliness, and so passionately and platonically is he committed to beauty at this stage of his life that he identifies moral goodness with physical beauty), for his nobility of mind, his moral purity and hatred of vulgarity. The quotation (from Hölderlin's 'Emilie vor ihrem Brauttag') in the diary for 27 November 1905 ('For the good are often surrounded by an aura of light and happiness throughout their lives'), which belongs in this same context, is clearly taken from Bethge, who uses the lines (admittedly in a marginally different form) as the motto for his study of Hölderlin. Other diary entries, too, reflect his preocccupation with Bethge's *Hölderlin*. On 10 February 1907 the words 'We wept together; it was a glorious hour' paraphrase Hölderlin's words in a letter to Immanual Nast, as quoted by Bethge ('In the course of one awful month I had but one blessed hour, when I wept with my Luise – and for this I thank God'5). Above all else Heym admires and envies the searing passion and tragedy of Hölderlin's life with its alternation of what Bethge calls 'Wonne' (ecstasy) and 'Qual' (agony); it is not chance that 'Qual' becomes one of Heym's favourite terms in relation to his own life.

The 'Schmerz' (pain) to which Heym refers is *Liebesschmerz* (pain of love), for Hölderlin's love of Diotima with its 'consuming happiness' and no less consuming despair is never far from his thoughts at this time: 'How fortunate Hölderlin was to be able to die of love. How beautiful his suffering must have been (*T* 8 May 1906).' An echo of this attitude is found five years later: 'My heart, crushed and annihilated for the ten thousandth time, happy to be so unhappy (*T* 156).' To Heym, as to Hölderlin, love is a religion; he writes of this in October 1906: 'Otherwise I am in precisely the position described by Bethge in his *Hölderlin* ... For him love was a religion, yet he was driven out of its temple and foundered. To me love is more of a religion than it is to perhaps anyone else (*T* 72).' He does not actually quote Bethge's words, but the words which gave him so much cause for reflection are these:

His holiest feelings were a religion for him, and above all this is what his love for Diotima was. His love had been destroyed. He had been driven out of its temple and knew that he would never be able to return to his love's shrine.6

Heym's reaction to these words means that even in the most personal aspect of his life he is identifying unreservedly with his idol. For him, as for his 'friend', love is what Bethge described it as being for Hölderlin: a religion. Not surprisingly, Heym therefore identified with the Hölderlin of 'Diotima', the middle version of which was in his Reclam edition; on 27 November 1906 he quotes in his diary the lines 'O Begeisterung, so finden [Wir in dir ein selig Grab]' ('Enthusiasm, in thee we find [a happy resting-place]'); on 25 December 1906 and 8 January 1907 he alludes to the poem once again. On 25 December 1906 he quoted Hölderlin's 'An die Natur' with reference to his own need for love.

Hölderlin is so much in his mind at this time that it again comes as no surprise to find him noting, on 3 January 1907, with himself in mind, that Hölderlin was saved by Diotima. How often he must have thought of Hölderlin and Diotima in connection with his own love for

Hedi Weißenfels. He puts this into a Hölderlinian context on 1 July 1908:

Walking from early morning until midday. At a spring I drank out of her cupped hand. We walked through the beech wood near Zell ... And we saw the whole countryside as far as Spessart filled with warm sunshine. Then we lay down at the edge of the woods and read Hölderlin from a Reclam volume:

> Froh kehrt der Schiffer heim an den stillen Strom.
> Happily the boatman returns home to his peaceful river.

Then we descended into the valley and left paradise behind. carissima.[7]

Whenever he quotes from, or alludes to, Hölderlin's poems in his diary – no matter whether the poem in question is 'Brot und Wein' or 'Der Rhein' or 'Die Heimat' (*T* 81, 91, 115, 120) – it is always with reference to himself. Some poems lend themselves to this more readily than others; thus the lines in 'Der Rhein': 'Doch unverständig ist/Das Wünschen vor dem Schicksal' ('When faced with Fate, wishing is folly'), which he misquotes in the diary, are obviously applicable to his situation and his view of it, but it is as though he is, from 1905 to 1908, determined to define himself and his problems in Hölderlinian terms. The identification with Hölderlin is total.

The poem 'An Hölderlin' of June 1905 is, among other things, eloquent confirmation of the fact that he saw Hölderlin as transfigured by suffering:

> Und du starbst auch, du Sohn des Frühlings?
> Du, dessen Leben war wie lauter
> Strahlende Flammen in Nachtgewölben,
> Aus denen die Menschen stets vergeblich
> Nach Ausweg und Befreiung suchen?
>
> Du starbst. Denn diese griffen töricht
> Nach deiner reinen Flamme aus
> Und löschten sie, denn immer ward
> Das Große diesem Tier verhaßt.
>
> Dir senkte die Moira
> Unendliches Leid auf den zarter schwingenden
> Geist herab,
> Da hüllte der Gott seinem frommen Sohn
> Dunkelnde Binden um das gemarterte Haupt (*L* 596f.).

('To Hölderlin') And you died too, Son of Spring? You whose life was as pure radiant flames in Night's vault, from which men always seek escape and liberation in vain.

You died because they foolishly reached out for your pure flame and quenched it, for greatness was ever hateful to the human brute.

The Moira sent so much suffering down on your more sensitively vibrating soul that the god swathed his pious son's tormented head in darkness.

This is why Hölderlin is his ideal and his idol. On 14 September 1906 he refers to him as his model, and goes on: 'I am coming to believe more and more firmly in Helios, in the light, the sun, the whole holy universe.' A few weeks later he writes: 'I read Hölderlin again and was amazed by the beauty of the sunset; I prayed to Helios for beauty (T 71).' His prayer comes, at least figuratively, straight from Plato: 'Beloved Pan, and all ye other gods who haunt this place, give me beauty in the inward soul; and may the outward and inward be at one.'[8] Such prayers underline the fact that Heym's view of nature is close to Hölderlin's in being, although expressed in vivid, concrete images, essentially a general, 'cosmic' view. If it is to Hölderlin and Merezhkovsky that Heym owes his view of the Greek gods, it is to Hölderlin more than anyone else that he owes his cult of Helios, his cult of beauty, his religion of love, and, above all, his sense of destiny.

When he read 'Hyperions Schicksalslied', he was deeply moved to find there the love of the gods that he had made his own, together with a view of destiny – and indeed a view of life – that helped to form his own, all expressed in a memorable poetic form:

Ihr wandelt droben im Licht
Auf weichem Boden, selige Genien!
Glänzende Götterlüfte
Rühren euch leicht,
Wie die Finger der Künstlerin
Heilige Saiten.

Schicksallos, wie der schlafende
Säugling, atmen die Himmlischen;
Keusch bewahrt
In bescheidener Knospe
Blühet ewig
Ihnen der Geist,
Und die seligen Augen
Blicken in stiller
Ewiger Klarheit.

Doch uns ist gegeben,
Auf keiner Stätte zu ruhn,
Es schwinden, es fallen
Die leidenden Menschen
Blindlings von einer
Stunde zur andern,
Wie Wasser von Klippe
Zu Klippe geworfen,
Jahrlang ins Ungewisse hinab.

You walk above in the light on easy ground, blessed Genii. Heavenly breezes touch you lightly, as the harpist's fingers touch holy strings.

Fatelessly as a sleeping infant do the Heavenly Ones breathe; chastely preserved in its modest bud their spirit blossoms eternally, and their serene eyes gaze with calm, ever-lasting clarity.

But to us it is given to find no resting-place; suffering mortals dwindle and fall blindly from one hour to the next, like water tumbling from rock to rock, downwards for years to an uncertain future.

'Hyperions Schicksalslied' became one of his favourite poems, his own 'song of fate'; he quotes it no less than four times in his diary, as well as alluding to it. Having previously (mis)quoted the last lines of the poem ('Es schwinden, es fallen/die leidenden Menschen...': 'Suffering mortals dwindle and fall...') in relation to his own sufferings (T 7), he proceeds to say of his 'friend' that 'he was obliged to walk in darkness and could not see the light' (T 29), an allusion to the opening lines of 'Hyperions Schicksalslied', which he is forever quoting (T 76, 78, 121). Heym identifies himself no less clearly than his friend with man as seen by Hölderlin, the restless wanderer on earth whose lot is so different from that of the 'blessed Genii'. In December 1906, after quoting from 'Hyperions Schicksalslied', he added: 'Nothing can distract us from our terrible secret destiny but love, eternal, redeeming, all-conquering love (T 76).' Presently he goes beyond his idol; in the unfinished 'Odysseus' he sees the gods – with Heine now – as having become maliciously indifferent to humanity. The sun of romanticism having long since set, Heym shares with Hölderlin the soul-destroying sense of living in a period of night.

Hölderlin is, with Merezhkovsky, Nietzsche and Grabbe, one of the four heroes (T 86) of Heym's youth; more particularly he is the most important formative influence on his early and very late poetry. Heym retained his love of Hölderlin throughout the changing and often violent enthusiasms of his later years; on 13 September 1908 he lists Hölderlin first in a list of 'poetae Germaniae', and again and again he compares himself with Hölderlin, for instance on 19 July 1907 ('Although I am made of different stuff than Hölderlin and lack his purity, I am like him in not knowing where to lay my head'), on 15 March 1908 ('I know my fate now. To go mad like Hölderlin. But under different circumstances, after a life without love'), on 4 July 1910 ('What advantage do I have over ... Hölderlin? The fact that I am far more vital. In both a good and a bad sense'). Such references show the extent to which his identification with Hölderlin has helped him to self-knowledge. On 10 December 1911 he identifies with Hölderlin as a non-compromiser; this, the last reference to Hölderlin, takes us back to one of the earliest – that is, to his identification with Hölderlin as an extremist. Perhaps the most explicit of all his comments was made, however, on 20 July 1909, when he wrote 'I love all those who suffer torment, I love ... Hölderlin ... I love all those who are not worshipped by the Mob. I love all those who often despair of themselves as much as I do daily.' This is almost certainly an echo of Hölderlin's 'Menschenbeifall', the second stanza of which reads:

Ach! der Menge gefällt, was auf den Marktplatz taugt,
Und es ehret der Knecht nur den Gewaltsamen;
An das Göttliche glauben
Die allein, die es selber sind.

Alas, the crowd likes what sells in the market-place, and the menial honour only men of violence; only those who are themselves as gods believe in gods.

In a technical sense Heym returned to Hölderlin in the end, for he uses the form of 'Hyperions Schicksalslied' not only in some of his early, perhaps over-Hölderlinian poems, but also in his most significant work, the late elegies that are in effect a monument to his love of the greatest of his predecessors. Hölderlin is the inspiring genius behind the suddenly almost ethereal beauty of Heym's final poetic mode, which reduces much of the poetry of the intervening century to insignificance. It is where he is greatest that Heym owes most to his poetic idol, model and master.

☐ DOVE, D'ANNUNZIO, NIETZSCHE AND MEREZHKOVSKY

From 1905 onwards Heym's favourite books were two historical novels: 'My favourite books are *Caracosa* and *Leonardo da Vinci*. Without them I should be badly off indeed ... Ognibene ... Caracosa!' (17 August 1905: *T* 33). He is referring to Alfred Dove's *Caracosa* (1894) and Dmitry Merezhkovsky's *Leonardo da Vinci* (1896; first German edition, 1903).

Alfred Dove (1844–1916) is a little-known figure. An academic historian, he was Professor of History in Breslau (1874–84), Bonn (1884–91), and Freiburg im Breisgau (1897–1905); from 1891 to 1897 he was editor of the *Allgemeine Zeitung* in Munich. His main work was *Das Zeitalter Friedrichs des Großen und Josephs II* (1883); otherwise he published mainly essays. He was essentially a biographical writer. His historical novel *Caracosa* lives on in Heym's enthusiasm for it.

Caracosa is the story of a love which is doomed not to be. The appeal of the novel was clearly Ognibene and Caracosa themselves (it is they who feature five times in Heym's diaries over a five-year period), although the times in which this two-volume historical novel is set (the mid-thirteenth century) are also stirring.[9] Heym was absorbed by the unhappy lives of Ognibene and Caracosa because he felt so close to both of them. Ognibene is in many ways so like himself that Heym could not have helped seeing himself in him, in his sensitivity, his fervid imagination, above all in his enthusiasm and (figurative) blindness; but also in his sense of being a prisoner, his 'Gefangener-Schicksal' (*Caracosa*, I, p. 286), his fatalism, his pessimism. No doubt he over-looked Ognibene's fanaticism and self-centredness because he was so struck by the affinity between himself and this noble-born Franciscan friar:

Else – Else, there was a time when I might have won you, but *I was wearing Fate's blindfold over my eyes* and turned to D. instead. Stenzi, you too I might once have won, but *I was blinded by the Moirae* and went to D., whom I was not even able to win over as a slight recompense for the loss of the two queens of my heart, [but especially] for the loss of the eternally beautiful Goldelse. A related mood, which served to calm me a little, I find only in the unhappy lives of Ognibene and Caracosa. Whenever I am once again really unhappy I hear those doleful tones – Ognibene ... Caracosa ... Why do I not die yet? Because

I am condemned to go on waiting for some great happiness in love (*T* 25 December 1906; PB's italics).

The italics underline Heym's obvious self-identification with Ognibene. The fundamental connection is 'Fate's blindfold' over their eyes, the fact that both men are 'blinded by the Moirae'; it is this that causes Ognibene to lose the love of his life (as Heym was to do with Hedi), to say nothing of his worldly position, fulfilment and peace of mind.

Caracosa, for her part, is the heroine of the tale in a double sense. One thinks of her beauty, her clear mind unclouded by religiosity, her paganism and Nietzschean cheerfulness (*Heiterkeit*), and also of her heroic courage and imperious nature. It is no wonder that Heym loved her too, for she, rather than the doomed worldly monk, embodies the virtues and qualities which Heym recognized as pre-eminent; besides, it is her life which points to the tragedy of Heym's own life. Well might he ask 'Which of them do I love most?' (*T* 132), for they are both embodiments of his deeply held belief that 'It is not possible to be happy' (*T* 27 December 1909). His passionate devotion to Dove's and Merezhkovsky's novels shows how much he lived in his imagination.

Heym saw himself not only in Ognibene, but also in the hero of a similar novel, Gabriele D'Annunzio's *Il Piacere* (1889; *The Child of Pleasure*, translated by Georgina Harding, 1898; in German, *Lust*, translated by M. Gagliardi, Berlin, 1898): 'I sometimes suffer in the same way as the hero of the novel *The Child of Pleasure*' (*T* 114). This was written on 2 July 1908, when he was 'head over heels in love' ('grenzenlos verliebt': *T* 114). The novel is about what Heym in his diary (in March 1908) calls 'lust, that painful surrogate for love' (*T* 104). Andrea Sperelli, a writer of sonnets of haunting intensity, is the voluptuary, the hedonist pure and simple to whom moral qualities are to be judged by aesthetic rules; what makes him suffer is above all his own weakness. In other words, Heym identified with D'Annunzio's hero in moments of passion, of weakness, self-indulgence and self-criticism, and while this novel of excessive romantic individualism did not have the appeal of a *Caracosa*, it left its mark on Heym, who was still quoting from it in summer 1911. In 1908 he could link Hedi Weißenfels with the Elena Muti of the novel; in 1911 he could see his then girlfriend Hildegard Krohn as Maria Ferrès. At the end of the novel Andrea was in love with two women at the same time, as Heym was in summer 1911, and if Andrea Sperelli and Maria Ferrès regarded Shelley as 'their' poet – Maria quotes Shelley's 'Death' of 1820 by heart – Georg Heym and Hildegard Krohn regarded Keats as theirs. The fact that D'Annunzio himself 'knew glory at an age when others only dream about it, knew love at an age when it is for most only romantic imaginings, and had money in abundance at a time when it is apt to be only a hope'[10] would, if Heym was aware of it, have predisposed him in D'Annunzio's favour.

Dove, D'Annunzio and Merezhkovsky are linked by Nietzsche, who left his mark on all three men, as he did on Heym, whose first and most revealing reference to him takes the form of a diary entry dated 17 February 1906. The philosopher Friedrich Nietzsche (1844–1900), the self-styled 'first immoralist', was the great experience for Heym's generation throughout Europe, but especially in Germany, England, France and Russia; his influence was at its height from the eighteen-nineties to the outbreak of the First World War. What was so influential was Nietzsche's call for a great liberation from the trammels of the past, his 'transvaluation of values', his campaign against morality and call for a new subjectivism in art, his aristocratic individualism and aggressive elitism, his declaration that God was dead and that therefore the individual had to develop the strength to become his own god, and his gospel of strength (designed to replace the Christian gospel which he saw as having made a virtue of weakness). There is no doubting the fact that Nietzsche was the greatest popular success of any philosopher of modern times, and that it was the quasi-biblical *Also Sprach Zarathustra* (*Thus Spake Zarathustra*) which accounted for much of the spell which his work exercised over so many readers, Heym included. The diary entry for 17 February 1906 shows that Nietzsche had been on Heym's mind for some time, and that up to then he had fought shy of *Thus Spake Zarathustra*:

And yet. His teaching is great. Whatever people may say against it, it gives our lives a new meaning: that we should be arrows of longing for the Superman, that we should develop any potentially great or sublime qualities within ourselves and thus become rungs on the ladder to the Superman. Was not Goethe one such? O to ... learn to see ever more farsightedly, to turn away from the present, and to live for the Superman [ideal], that is what Zarathustra teaches us. And this teaching can make us totally self-reliant.

I read him and was captivated, I who had previously been afraid of this book. One passage has become my favourite and a signpost on my way, which

I had been losing as I strayed into ignobility. Oh, may I succeed in reforming my life in order to become an arrow on its way towards the Superman. But this is the passage:

> The new would the noble man create, and a new virtue. The old is what the good man wants, and that the old should be conserved. But the danger facing the noble man is not that he may become a good man, but that he may become a blusterer, a scoffer, or a destroyer. Ah! I have known noble men who lost their highest hopes. And then they disparaged all high hopes, living shamelessly in temporary pleasures, and beyond the day they had hardly an aim. 'Spirit is also voluptuousness', they thought. Then they broke the wings of their spirit ... *Once they intended to become heroes; but sensualists are they now. A trouble and a terror is the hero to them.*

(This from the man who is said to have preached unbridled sensuality.)

That is my fear. For I am very lonely here. And my spirit has no kindred fellow-spirit. And spring is still a long way off. [The italics are Heym's.]

What Heym read was *Thus Spake Zarathustra*, to various sections of which ('The Spirit of Gravity', 'The Friend', 'The Tree on the Hill', etc.) he here alludes. On a highly personal level it is obviously Zarathustra's warning against 'living shamelessly in temporary pleasures' that has spoken to Heym, for whom hedonism (or *Wollust*, as he calls it, following Zarathustra) was an ever-present temptation. Zarathustra is, as it were, urging him to devote himself single-mindedly to his wish to become a hero. It is a message that goes right to the heart of Heym's existence.

When he made up his mind to read it, Heym clearly found – like so many others – that the most influential book of the decade seemed to be addressed to him personally. More particularly, Zarathustra's Prologue[11] told him that it was time to 'launch the arrow of his longing', for 'one must have chaos in one, to give birth to a dancing star'. He was clearly convinced that the earth had 'become small'; he was already passionately devoted to the idea of greatness; the myth of the superman told him that it was up to him to create the missing greatness, that he should devote his life to it. What evidently impressed him most of all was Zarathustra's eighth discourse, 'The Tree on the Hill', and more especially the passage in which Nietzsche seemed to appeal to him to cultivate his own 'nobility'. He was so impressed that he wrote it out in the form of verse. Coming on top of Hölderlin and

Merezhkovsky, Nietzsche reinforced Heym in his determination to eschew mediocrity and pettiness, and cultivate the heroic. In other words, Nietzsche brought out the heroic instinct (as he did time and again, even in the most unheroic of men); after reading *Thus Spake Zarathustra* nothing came more easily than to fancy oneself 'A Hero of Our Time' (without, of course, the Lermontovian connotation of superfluity). Schopenhauer, whose work Heym did not read until later, put it most clearly: 'A happy life is an impossibility: the most that man can achieve is an heroic life.'[12] The upshot was that Heym saw himself as Zarathustra; it was with reference to himself that he wrote in his diary on 11 July 1906: 'So Zarathustra's downfall has begun.' His final school report put it much more drily in connection with his viva voce examination in Greek: 'Heym spoke about the significance of the Sophists; he knows that they are to be compared with Nietzsche (D 379).'

The next reference to Nietzsche in the diary is an indirect one. On 18 August 1906 Heym writes: 'Pity for man is the death of the gods.' This is an echo of Zarathustra's twenty-fifth discourse ('God is dead: of his pity for man hath God died'), but it is an indirect echo, for Heym is actually quoting from Dmitry Merezhkovsky's novel *Julian Apostata* (*Julian the Apostate*):

Julian, Julian! ... Your gods, seduced by the faith of the fisherman from Capernaum, are meek, mild, sickly shadows dying for their pity for man – for, mark my words, their pity for man will prove the death of the gods![13]

Merezhkovsky, Heym's favourite novelist, was an important intermediary of Nietzschean ideas, so that it is appropriate that a diary entry in May 1907 refers to 'Hölderlin, Nietzsche, Merezhkovsky, Grabbe, the 4 heroes of my youth' (T 86); it is precisely the theme of heroism by which they are joined. The diary shows that Heym identified with Merezhkovsky's Julian ('I should have liked to stand at Julian's side in those days': T 60), just as he did with his fictionalized Leonardo da Vinci; this is a subject to which we shall shortly come.

The next reference to Nietzsche in the diary comes on 19 October 1907, when he writes: 'It will soon be time to follow Nietzsche's example. Only it was much easier for him, for at home I am living in Corps circles and amid Corps views. Simply to get out, to break off everything – To be regarded as a coward, to be generally despised, would be too much.' He is referring to Nietzsche's resignation from the Burschen-

schaft Frankonia in Bonn after one year's membership; he himself left
the Corps Rhenania a year after this, on 2 November 1908, so it did take
time and courage to do so.

The only other reference to Nietzsche in the diary dates from 4
July 1910: 'What advantage do I have over Nietzsche, Kleist, Grabbe,
and Hölderlin? The fact that I am far more vital. In both a good and a
bad sense.' By this time he had written (on Christman Eve, 1909) the
somewhat Nietzschean 'Versuch einer neuen Religion' (PD, 164–72),
which sounds more interesting than it is. Unpublished in his lifetime,
this so-called 'draft lecture' is a half-baked utopian fragment which
shows nothing more clearly than the occasional folly to which the
extreme enthusiast is prone. The 'new religion' is a mixture of hero-
worship and nature-worship inspired, if that is the word, by Heym's
love of ancient Greece and of the work of Hölderlin, Nietzsche and
Merezhkovsky, who appear among his personal *penates*:

In my shrine I will hang pictures of poets (Grabbe, Byron, Büchner, Renner,
and Hölderlin), philosophers (Heraclitus, Plato, Schopenhauer, Nietzsche),
painters (Lionardo [sic], Michelangelo), and the composer Offenbach. In every
niche one picture with its own little candle. A work lying open on a lectern.
How the aspirant will be stimulated to know that after his death people will
worship him as a god (PD 172).

Though Merezhkovsky is not named, it is his Leonardo and
Michelangelo that Heym has in mind, just as it is his Julian whose
religion was Heym's model. It is impossible to take the document
seriously. The most charitable explanation is that its author was suffering from a mixture of family Christmas and alcohol. He was, creatively
speaking, having a bad spell; the poems written at that time are little
better than the 'Versuch einer neuen Religion', with which they belong.
The most obviously Nietzschean of them are 'Dionysos' (L 14–17) and
the less poetic but more shocking 'Ich verfluche dich, Gott...' (L 18).

When Simon Guttmann introduced him to the Neue Club in
April 1910 Heym was in need of fresh inspiration. One of the things he
got from his membership of the Neue Club was a renewed interest in
Nietzsche, on whom the vitalism which the members of the club
variously espoused was inevitably based. Thus the first Neopathetisches
Cabaret attended by Heym, on 1 June 1910, featured a reading from
Nietzsche entitled 'Rausch und Kunst'. It was at about this time that

Heym borrowed Nietzsche's *Zarathustra* from his new friend David Baumgardt, who later wrote:

When before going for a walk with him I stuck the pocket edition of *Zarathustra* in my coat pocket, he said in a rather superior way: 'What's in there is long familiar to me.' 'You don't say,' I replied. 'So give it here,' he said, taking my *Zarathustra* and keeping it for weeks (*D* 9).

He decided to seize the opportunity to reread *Zarathustra* (he was notorious for 'borrowing' books and returning them either in a shocking condition or not at all), presumably because he found Nietzsche so much on people's lips in Neue Club circles. Later that year (1910) he borrowed *Menschliches Allzumenschliches* (*Human, All Too Human*) from an acquaintance, Friedrich Schulze-Maizier, making such a mess of it that Schulze-Maizier declined to receive it back. In spring 1911 Heym made the following note of titles for reading:

3) Götzendämmerung (*The Twilight of the Idols*)
1) II. Unzeitgem[ässe] Betrachtung (*Thoughts out of Season, II*)
2) Jenseits von Gut u[nd] Böse (*Beyond Good and Evil*)
4) Fr[öhliche] Wissenschaft (*The Joyful Wisdom*)
5) Ecce Homo[14] (*Ecce Homo*)

While there is no reason to suppose that he did read them, it is interesting to find the second of Nietzsche's *Thoughts out of Season*, 'On the Advantages and Disadvantages of the Study of History', at what one assumes to be the top of the list (the peculiar numerical order is Heym's), particularly since he had by then virtually finished writing dramatic fragments on historical subjects. If he read it, we can be sure he would have approved Nietzsche's view that history is of value only in so far as it serves life. He would have been familiar with *Beyond Good and Evil*, for it is essentially an elaboration of parts of *Zarathustra*; judging by the already quoted diary entry for 17 February 1906, he would have been particularly drawn towards the ideal of 'nobility' and the concomitant dual morality of the strong and the weak. It is less likely that he read the other works; he had too many new interests for that, and by this time his view of life had taken on a pessimistic, fatalistic tinge which was fundamentally at odds with the heroic superman ideal.

The echoes of Nietzsche which exist in Heym's poetry at this time are reflex echoes of his past rather than necessary components of his present view of life, which comes to owe more to Schopenhauer than to Nietzsche. Shortly after borrowing *Zarathustra* from David Baumgardt in spring 1910 Heym borrowed 'the whole of Schopenhauer' (*D* 9).

Given that Heym had two phases when Nietzsche was on or near the surface of his mind (in 1906–7 and 1910–11), it may seem surprising that he was not more strongly influenced by the philosopher under whose spell so many writers throughout Europe were wallowing. Many minor 'Nietzscheans' took a few of Nietzsche's ideas over lock, stock and barrel. That was not Heym's way. He was far too much of an individualist to be unduly influenced by another man's ideas. Indeed, he was, on the whole, more hypnotized by ideas than influenced by them. He used Nietzsche as he used other writers: to clarify his own position. He identified with Zarathustra until increasing pessimism made that identification difficult to sustain. He was more strongly influenced by all his other early heroes, most of whose ideas overlapped with Nietzsche, and in the last analysis was no Nietzschean because – for all his passionate enthusiasms and self-projections – he was nothing if not independent-minded. Indeed, in his fatalistic heart he was thoroughly unNietzschean: far from loving his fate, he raged against it.

Dmitry Merezhkovsky (1865–1941), who is known as a leader of the older generation of Russian Symbolist poets and for his part in the religious revival among Russian intellectuals during Heym's schooldays, was one of the main Russian Nietzscheans. In the present context it is his *Christ and Antichrist* trilogy of novels (1893–1902) that counts. Heym read all three novels: *Julian the Apostate* (*Julian Apostata*, translated by Carl von Gütschow, 1903) in 1906, *Leonardo da Vinci* (German edition, translated by Carl von Gütschow, 1903) in 1905 and frequently thereafter, and *Peter the Great* (*Peter der Große*, translated by Carl von Gütschow, 1905) in 1907. All three novels are closely connected: they are all historical' novels in the sense of having historical figures as their ficitional characters, and indeed fictional heroes, for these characters are all presented as Nietzschean supermen: they are men apart, superhuman beyond good and evil. Furthermore, they all embody the Nietzschean (and Hölderlinian) dichotomy of Christian and pagan attitudes, and therefore portray the Nietzschean dual morality or moral relativism. All this was bound to appeal to a young poet immersed in Hölderlin, especially when, as in the case of Leonardo da Vinci, it is combined with an extreme artistic gift and love of beauty.

Of the three novels it was therefore the second that most impressed and influenced Heym, for a reason which is immediately obvious: that in Merezhkovsky's Leonardo Heym found his own ideal, the artist as hero. Leonardo is a great artist, a freethinker, and a man who, like Heym himself (no doubt under Leonardo's influence), was given to seeing chimerical monsters in the outlines of clouds. It is in his diary for 17 July 1905 that we find Heym identifying with Leonardo: 'My favourite books are *Caracosa* and *Leonardo da Vinci*. Without them I should be badly off indeed ... I wonder whether I have the same character as, for instance, Leonardo as described by Merezhkovsky, or the opposite. Either would account for my love of Leonardo. *Les extrêmes* ... I forgot Bethge's Hölderlin. He must have been very similar to da Vinci.' Clearly it is as brilliantly gifted outsider that Leonardo appeals to Heym. He identified with Leonardo to the point where Leonardo became his super-ego.

His first allusion to *Leonardo da Vinci* foreshadows none of this, for the rhyming couplet in his diary for 18 June 1905 ('Schön ist die Jugendzeit, doch schnell verschwunden./Wer fröhlich sein will, nütze die Stunden') is a translation of that 'favourite air of Lorenzo dei Medici':

> Quant'è bella giovinezza
> Ma si fugge tuttavia;
> Chi vuol esser lieto, sia
> Di doman non c'è certezza.

Youth is a beautiful time but quickly past; happiness means seizing its hours while they last.

This was to be the leitmotif of Heym's life from 1905 to his death. He read the novel repeatedly, particularly the account of Leonardo's death. His last reference to it comes on 30 November 1910; at that time he probably reread it, for the account of a sermon by Savonarola in the first chapter of the novel (and of Leonardo's drawing of the hate-inspired monk) inspired the poem 'Savonarola', written on 18 November:

> Wie eine Lilie durch das Dunkel brennt,
> So brennt sein weißer Kopf in Weihrauchs Lauge
> Und blauer Finsternis. Sein hohles Auge
> Starrt wie ein Loch aus weißem Pergament.

Verzweiflung dampft um ihn, furchtbare Qual
Des Höllentags. Wenn er die Hände weitet,
Wird er ein Kreuz, das seine Balken breitet
Auf dunklem Himmel, groß, und furchtbar fahl.

Er flüstert leise. Übertönt vom Schrein.
Ein Riese tanzt, der mit den Geißeln fegt
Das Meer der Rücken. Blutdampf steigt wie Wein.

Und sein Gesicht wird von der Wollust klein,
Vom Schauder eines Lächelns sanft bewegt,
Wie eine Spinne zieht die Beinchen ein (*L* 159).

('Savonarola') Just as a lily burns through the darkness, so does his white head burn amid the acridity and blue haze of incense. His hollow eye stares like a hole in white parchment.

Despair swirls around him, the dreadful agony of a day in Hell. When he stretches out his arms he becomes a cross extending its arms against a dark sky, immense and fearfully pale.

He mutters softly. Drowned by the screaming. A giant moves up and down, running the scourge over a sea of backs. Steaming blood rises to the surface looking like wine.

And his face contracts with wanton pleasure, touched by the shiver of a smile, like a spider drawing in its legs.

The poem is an incidental result of Heym's reading. More important, the novel gave him the inspiration for the story 'Der Dieb' ('The Thief'), which has its starting-point in the theft of Leonardo's *Mona Lisa* from the Louvre in 1911; Heym uses Merezhkovsky's *Leonardo da Vinci*, and the connection made there between beauty and evil, to motivate the thief. At the end of his life we even find him planning to attend (in winter term 1911–12) Heinrich Wölfflin's lectures on Leonardo, evidence of his continuing fascination with this artistic hero and genius.

The references to Michelangelo and Raphael in Heym's diary in summer 1906 show that he also knew Merezhkovsky's *Michelangelo und andere Novellen aus der Renaissancezeit* (German edition, translated by Carl von Gütschow, Leipzig, 1905) although, partly because it is only a *Novelle*, *Michelangelo* impressed him less than *Leonardo da Vinci*. Thus the words 'the stepchild Michelangelo' (*T* 47) and the remark that 'Michelangelo Buonarotti's nose was broken' (*T* 55) both derive from Merezhkovsky's statement that 'a broken nose disfigured him most'.[15] Heym identified with Michelangelo because at the time he was concerned about his own supposed ugliness. His hostile view of Raphael also demonstrably derives from *Michelangelo*.[16] We shall see later (in Chapter VII) that the opposing views of war attributed by Merezhkovsky[17] to Leonardo and Michelangelo are relevant to Heym's most famous poem.

□ ROMANTIC SELF-IMAGES: GRABBE, BÜCHNER, KLEIST

If Nietzsche, with Hölderlin, occupied Heym's mind and enthusiasm throughout 1906, by the autumn of that year he also has a new idol, 'the glorious Grabbe' (*T* 32 October 1906). He proceeds to quote the line 'Adler im Haupt, die Füße im Kote' ('Head in the clouds, feet in the mire'), which suggests that his interest in Grabbe was again personal, for just five days earlier he had noted 'I consist of two quite different people' (26 October 1906: *T* 72). His next entry is confirmation of the personal nature of his interest: 'I am inclined, like Grabbe, to lead a wretched, cheerless life' (*T* 11 November 1906). He agrees with Grabbe's view of life as suffering ('Grabbe, that's the right medicine. "Suffering enobles the face. The features are transfigured ... etc." One reads it so often that finally one believes it', *T* 9 September 1907), and by 20 December 1907 has come to the view that 'Great artists create in their poetry what they are unable to experience in life. Proof: Grabbe.' It is no doubt because of this view, which he finds consoling, that he presently refers to Grabbe as a 'god' (*T* 29 January 1909). When he refers to him in his diary, he mostly does so in the context of his other household gods of the time (Hölderlin, Kleist and Byron), which shows that it was above all a sense of personal affinity with the romantic playwright that lay behind his enthusiasm. He related to Grabbe because he, too, knew self-despair. If one thinks also of the excitability of Grabbe's temperament and the violent changes of mood to which he was subject, his melancholy, his pessimism, the passionate bitterness with which he viewed the world, and his view of life as suffering and ennui, to say nothing of his early death and the fact that he was what Heym thought of himself as being, the son of a prison superintendent, then the self-identification was inevitable. Heym will have been impressed by Grabbe's obvious desire to shock, by the fragmentary, inchoate nature of his dramatic work, and by its passion and tragic intensity (something Heym also found and admired in Marlowe in 1909).

Heym's admiration was directed at two of Grabbe's works in particular: *Herzog Theodor von Gothland* and *Napoleon oder die hundert Tage*. He took from the former lines which he used as a motto for one of his most significant poems, 'Die Hölle' (discussed below in Chapter IV), for Gothland's words, 'Hell? At least it's something new', echo the craving for excitement and novelty which was a fundamental part of Heym's make-up; at the time of writing the poem, on 25 August 1911, he had just been granted leave from the District Court at Wusterhausen an der Dosse, having been driven almost out of his mind by the boredom which it embodied. Technically, *Gothland* was not a good model for an impressionable young dramatist, but Heym was interested not in the improbabilities and inadequacies of the play, but in the heroic passions and violent excitement which it embodies; his interest will have centred on two of his characters: on Berboa as proto-Nietzschean *Raubtier-Mensch* (man-of-prey), and on Gothland's pressimism, moodiness and boredom, for he was himself an amalgam of Berboa and Gothland. Admiring the heroism of Grabbe's heroes, their 'capacity for action and achievement',[18] he was deeply moved by the scene in *Napoleon oder die hundert Tage* where his idol breaks down: 'Where in the history of the world is there a drama that would carry one away so much and fill one with so much anger and revulsion at man's stupidity, as this scene in which Napoleon collapses?' (*T* 20 January 1907). In his imagination the scene was surpassed only by Merezhkovsky's description of the death of Leonardo da Vinci.

From *Napoleon oder die hundert Tage* Heym took material which he used in his dramatic fragment *Napoleon* and, to greater effect, in the 'Mont St Jean' sonnet cycle (*L* 42f.). Napoleon was for Heym the great man *par excellence*, the very embodiment of the Nietzschean superman. He worshipped him; he dreamt of him. His view of Napoleon comes from Grabbe's *Napoleon*, and nothing will have impressed him more deeply than Napoleon's recognition there (Act I, Scene 4) of his 'Fate' as described by Grabbe: 'Yes, it stood at my side in Corsica, the sea-girt cradle of all my endeavours, and will be found beside my coffin. In the flames of Moscow – having forgotten it for a long time – I saw it rising up over me with its wings – Neither nations nor armies have overcome me – It was Fate.' The dialogue between Napoleon and the Spirit of

History on this subject may have been omitted by Heym for the 1910 revision of his unfinished play *Der Tod des Helden* because he preferred to see Napoleon as riding his own destiny, but the winged figure of Fate/Death clearly etched itself on his imagination, for it becomes omnipresent in his work, assuming terrifying guise in the tales.

In March 1910 Heym both revised *Der Tod des Helden* (the first version of which dates from 1908, the time of his deification of Grabbe), and wrote the 'Mont St Jean' sonnets, based on Grabbe's description of the fighting at Mont St Jean in the last act of *Napoleon oder die hundert Tage*. These sonnets, which encapsulate the heroic life which Heym craved, are about the battle of Waterloo of 18 June 1815, in which Napoleon was defeated by the English and Prussian armies and was forced into exile at St Helena. Underlying the cycle is Heym's characteristic idea of dying for a great cause. Heym's greatest Napoleonic poem is, however, the sonnet 'Marengo' (December 1910), which is about Napoleon's victory over Austria on 14 June 1800. 'Marengo' (discussed later, see pp. 235–6), is an archetypal poem in the sense that it implies an elemental struggle of the kind depicted by the visionary painter Albrecht Altdorfer in his famous *Battle of Arbela* (or *Alexander's Victory*) of 1529; whether Heym already knew Altdorfer's work from reproductions when he saw it in the Alte Pinakothek in Munich in November 1911 is not known, but 'Marengo' strongly suggests that he did. There is, however, a major difference between Heym's poem and Altdorfer's painting, in that the former shows nature cowed and dominated by an invisible god-like Hero (Napoleon) dictating events,[19] whereas in the painting it is the titanic forces of nature which are dominant; Alexander the Great is implicitly reduced to relative insignificance. What is in question here is not merely the difference between sixteenth-century and twentieth-century attitudes to nature, but Heym's hero-worship of Napoleon.

Although Grabbe left a clear mark on his numerous poems and dramatic fragments connected with Napoleon and the Napoleonic wars, Heym's interest in the German romantic tradition is essentially non-literary, a matter of personal affinities. While his crowd scenes owe much to Grabbe, he was not, on the whole, inclined to model his dramatic work on Grabbe's. In general his dramas and dramatic fragments should therefore be seen in the context not of German nineteenth-century historical drama à la Grabbe, but of the historical tragedies produced by three of his favourite poets (Keats, Shelley and Byron). Heym's 'dramas' are lyrical monodramas; they are his attempts to stage his personal concerns in a way that is both more and less public than lyric poetry. They are not 'dramatic', but 'theatrical'. That said, it was the theatricality of Grabbe's life that caught Heym's attention. After 1909, when the accent of his work turns to poetry and he has other, greater gods to worship, we hear no more of Grabbe in his diary, although he is mentioned in a letter to Hildegard Krohn in June 1911, in which Heym urges her to read 'the sublime Grabbe' (*D* 507); in the meantime he was to discover Büchner and Kleist.

He discovered Georg Büchner in January 1909. In September 1908 his diary refers to 'Büchner, whom I barely know'; on 29 January 1909 it is a different story: 'Received [the] Georg Büchner and placed a new god beside Grabbe on my altar.' The altar on which Büchner now joins Grabbe is that dedicated to Heym's worship of Napoleon and the men of the French Revolution, but also that consecrated to his poetic heroes. Büchner's *Dantons Tod* was one of the works he read to fuel his enthusiasm for the French Revolution following the drafting of the fragmentary play *Der Sturm auf die Bastille* in autumn 1908. His reading of it is reflected in his notes for a drama involving Robespierre. Those notes, dating from 1909 to 1911, suggest that he accepted Büchner's characterization of Robespierre as a vain petit-bourgeois fanatic; indeed, if he saw Napoleon through Grabbe's and Hölderlin's eyes, he saw Danton and Robespierre through Büchner's. In general *Dantons Tod* left its mark on Heym's later fatalism. George Büchner, the revolutionary genius who died in 1837 at the age of twenty-three, but whose work only established itself on the German stage during the Expressionist era, was bound to attract Heym's attention, for the two men shared a not dissimilar tragic view of life as rooted in suffering and a soul-destroying boredom. The differences between them are, however, more significant than the similarities. Thus *Dantons Tod*, which shows Büchner's reaction to what he called the 'horrible fatalism of history', and which was regarded as subversive in Wilhelmine Germany (one editor was imprisoned in 1891 for reprinting it), is more revolutionary and more ruthless than anything by Heym. Heym's revolutionism is an emotional affair compared with Büchner's, Heym being too ready to compromise his revolutionary fervour in the name of hero-worship. Büchner has no heroes, and there is in his work a profound social compassion which is almost entirely lacking in Heym. As a dramatist Büchner is able to do full justice to opposing arguments; Heym is not, for he completely lacks Büchner's dramatic impartiality. This is why Heym is so unconvincing as a dramatist. The most fundamental difference between them is, however, the fact that Büchner's passion was for truth, Heym's for beauty.

Heym probably first came across Heinrich von Kleist in 1905–6, when one of his school set texts was *Prinz Friedrich von Homburg*, although it was not until 21 October 1907 that he noted in his diary: 'I am feeling closer and closer to Heinrich von Kleist.' A year later he included Kleist in his rather eccentric list of 'poetae Germaniae' (Hölderlin, Kleist, Grabbe, Büchner, Renner, Kotzebue, Sudermann, Blumenthal) in his diary (*T* 118), and a year after that he made his most revealing comment when he wrote 'I love all those who suffer torment, I love Kleist' (*T*: 20 July 1909). In summer 1909 he took to visiting Kleist's grave at Wannsee. His only other reference to Kleist dates from 10 December 1911, when he is listed together with other 'honest' writers.

What these sparse references show is that Heym's interest in and adulation of Kleist is rooted in the biographical. Kleist was what Heym was in process of becoming: a desperate romantic, a wild pessimist, and a tragic poet; like Heym after him, he believed that he was born at the wrong time. His life, which he once called 'a twenty-four-year-long affliction', was marked by mental stress and the search for some 'great deed' which would justify his existence; this deed he was able to find only in suicide, for he regarded death as preferable to remaining the puppet of his fate. Heym, who toyed with suicide for the same reason, also regarded fame as the greatest good. Kleist actually sought to serve in Napoleon's army,[20] as Heym would have liked to do. The facts are all so close to the salient facts of Heym's life and temperament as to ensure that Kleist held a magnetic attraction for him. Both men owe their allegiance to the irrational; with Kleist's 'O Reason, miserable Reason',[21] we may compare Heym's 'Good God, that damned transcendental logic' (*D* 9). Their views of life are similar: Kleist saw life as chaotic, tragic, subject to the arbitrary intervention of monstrous forces whose helpless, hapless victim man is. Here, too, the parallel is obvious; in a posthumous review of 1922 Heym's prevailing mood was recognized as being akin to Kleist's 'metaphysical sadness'.[22] And then there are Kleist's *Novellen*, which in some ways represent a model for

Heym, whose poetry, Alfred Wolfenstein noted in 1932, is essentially epic and possesses 'the descriptive tension of Kleist's *Novellen*'.[23] This is a point to which we shall return in Chapter VIII.

We have therefore seen that every single one of Heym's many poetic heroes was a romantic, indeed an extreme romantic, and that his interest in every one of them was either solely or primarily personal. That he was himself an out-and-out romantic goes without saying (it is a point to which we shall have to return), just as it goes without saying that he was a revolutionary.

This romantic revolutionary's basic philosophy was expressed in the famous 'Conclusion' to the first (1873) edition of Walter Pater's *The Renaissance*:

Philosophiren, says Novalis, *ist dephlegmatisiren, vivificiren*. The service of philosophy, of speculative culture, towards the human spirit, is to rouse, to startle it to a life of constant and eager observation. Every moment some form grows perfect in hand or face; some tone on the hills or the sea is choicer than the rest; some mood of passion or insight or intellectual excitement is irresistibly real and attractive to us, – for that moment only. Not the fruit of experience, but the experience itself, is the end. A counted number of pulses only is given to us of a variegated, dramatic life...

To burn always with this hard, gemlike flame, to maintain this ecstasy, is success in life ... While all melts under our feet, we may well grasp at any exquisite passion ... we are all *condamnés*, as Victor Hugo says: we are all under sentence of death but with a sort of indefinite reprieve – *les hommes sont tous condamnés à mort avec des sursis indéfinis*: we have an interval, and then our place knows us no more. Some spend this interval in listlessness, some in high passions, the wisest, at least among 'the children of this world', in art and song. For our one chance lies in expanding that interval, in getting as many pulsations as possible into the given time. High passions give us this quickened sense of life, ecstasy and sorrow of love, political or religious enthusiasm, or the enthusiasm of humanity. Only be sure it is passion – that it does yield you this fruit of a quickened, multiplied consciousness. Of such wisdom, the poetic passion, the desire of beauty, the love of art for its own sake, has most. For art comes to you, proposing frankly to give nothing but the highest quality to your moments as they pass, and simply for those moments' sake.

Had he known it, Heym would surely have been delighted by this statement of a philosophy so close to his own. Every page of his diary records his determination not to 'sleep before evening' on this 'short day of frost and sun'. He, more than most men, had what Pater calls 'this sense of the splendour of our experience and of its awful brevity'; none knew better than Heym the 'pagan sentiment' which 'measures the sadness with which the human mind is filled, whenever its thoughts wander far from what is here and now'. He is a pagan not just in the sense of cultivating a pagan Hellenism, but in the sense of seeing what Pater calls the 'bewildering toils' of life in primitive, mythological form: in the form of demons. He would have recognized Pater's statement of the Epicurean creed for the counsel of perfection that it is and would have recognized – like Pater himself – the peril of such a creed. By this I mean the fact that such a philosophy is purely self-regarding and involves, or at least does not preclude, the temptation of a gross indulgence in sensuous delights. Heym himself avoided neither of these dangers; but it is the poetic passion, the passion for beauty, that is the positive pole of his existence. He was in no doubt at all that 'Beauty and art alone give life value' (T: 6 August 1906).

III

Early Poetry and Drama

□ POETRY

Georg Heym began writing poetry in 1899, at the age of twelve. By the time he changed schools in April 1905 he had already written almost ninety poems. In all he wrote some 643 poems, 232 of which are 'early' poems predating spring 1910, while the other 411 are the 'later' poems to which he owes his reputation. His only non-posthumous collection, *Der ewige Tag*, appeared in 1911. His second collection, *Umbra vitae*, appeared posthumously in 1912. In 1914 an incomplete edition of the sonnet cycle *Marathon* appeared in A. R. Meyer's 'Lyrische Flugblätter' series. The first, incomplete collected edition of his work, *Dichtungen* (edited by Kurt Pinthus and Erwin Loewenson), which came out in 1922, included fifty previously unpublished poems under the title 'Der Himmel Trauerspiel'. It was finally superseded by the collected *Dichtungen und Schriften* (edited by Karl Ludwig Schneider), four of the projected six volumes of which appeared in 1960–8.

Heym's early poetry is, with his dramatic work, the least-known part of his œuvre. Tradition has it that it is 'immature' and 'unoriginal'; it is thought to be quite different from and to fall far short of his 'real' poetry, this being the 'Expressionist' poetry written from April 1910 onwards. All this is questionable, for even very early poems are not necessarily 'immature', and some of Heym's earliest poems show an astonishing degree of what most people would call maturity. Nor are most of these poems essentially 'unoriginal', although some of them are. Besides, what is originality, a refusal to copy others, or a refusal to copy oneself? Certainly it does not involve a refusal to learn. One could, no doubt, make out a case for the 'unoriginality' of not a little of Heym's work between spring 1910 and autumn 1911, in the sense that what he produces at that time are variations on a single unwritten poem, and therefore self-pastiches. I neither wish nor intend to make out such a case; it is sufficient to point to the folly of accepting received opinions when they involve sweeping generalizations about a whole decade of creative work.

Periodizing a writer's work means, by definition, establishing imaginary barriers within what is essentially a continuum. Always a dubious business, this becomes positively foolhardy when the writer in question died at the age of twenty-four. Even the major division between the poetry written before and after spring 1910 is not clear-cut, for by spring 1910 Heym had been writing (occasional) 'expressionist' poems for some time. Within the period 1899–1909 there is, however, a general development from a nineteeth-century type of poetry to a twentieth-century type. This development can be seen to fall into three basic stages, provided these are not understood to be sharply defined 'periods'. Thus the work written between 1899 and 1904 is mostly straight neo-romantic poetry, while that produced between late 1904 and late 1908 reflects Heym's discovery of and ambiguous reaction to contemporary (fin-de-siècle) poetry; between late 1908 and late 1909 most of the various elements that characterize his 1910–11 style enter his work. We need to look at these phases in some detail, while at the same time remembering that from 1907 to 1909 Heym was a good deal less interested in poetry than in drama.

The earliest poetic work (1899–1904) is comparable to Rilke's: it is subjective, sentimental, neo-romantic. It is good of its kind, without being either particularly original or as polished as the early work of Hofmannsthal. As with Rilke, visuality and visual clarity are its strongest qualities. On the other hand, one could no more have predicted that the author of this promising but unremarkable work would go on to produce the poems for which Heym is now known, than one could have guessed from the footling Mir zur Feier (1899) that Rainer Maria Rilke would go on to produce the greatest cycle of poems in German of modern times, the Duineser Elegien of 1912–23.

Heym's early work is theatrical in the sense that nature provides the backcloth, lit by the pale sun of the pathetic fallacy, against which the apprentice poet parades his youthful, romantic emotions (sadness, loneliness, longing for the ideal other) and his recurrent themes (love, love of beauty, love of nature, love of the classical world, and so on). The poet's ego – and it is a biographical ego rather than a transformed poetic one – is as yet very much in evidence; one of the many major differences between the early poetry and the later is the fact that, for all the total subjectivity of his work, Heym comes to eschew the word 'ich', preferring to wear a mask of objectivity.

Given that 'love' was Heym's main single preoccupation at this time, his poems on the subject provide a measure of his early work. They show that, for all his lack of experience both of life and of poetry, he is able, almost from the beginning, to produce love lyrics which have a remarkable freshness and power. A good example is 'Du bist so dunkel, als die Nacht...' of June 1904:

Du bist so dunkel, als die Nacht,
Wenn sternenlos sie ihren schwarzen Mantel breitet.
Das letzte Licht ertränkt in tiefstem Schacht;
Nein, dunkler noch, im grausten Dunkel gleitet
Dein weißes, bleiches Angesicht
Und mit geheimem Schimmer
Loht die Nacht vor dir
In magisch blaues Licht getaucht.

Komm, Königin der schwülen Nacht
Und lege deinen weißen, kühlen Arm
Um meine sonnverbrannten, heißen Schläfen,
Komm, führe mich in deinen marmordunkeln Tempel ein,
Den meine Liebe dir erhellen soll.
Dann soll nicht eine einzge Sonne mehr
Dann soll Sternensonnen uns ein Heer,
Die Hochzeitsfackel durch die Nacht entflammen! (*L* 539).

('You are as dark as the night') You are as dark as the night when, starless, it spreads out its dark mantle, and the last glimmer of light drowns in the deepest shaft. No, you are yet darker; your pale, white face passes through the deepest darkness, and with a secret splendour Night glows before you, bathed in a magic blue light.

Come, queen of sultry night, and lay your cool white arm around my fevered sun-burned brows; come, lead me into your dark marble sanctuary, which my love shall illumine. Then not a single sun but a host of starry suns will blaze forth through the night, our wedding torch!

This was the first of his love poems to go beyond general adolescent yearning. Though clearly indebted to Hofmannsthal's 'Freundinnen. Ein Spiel', which had appeared in *Das Magazin für Litteratur* just four months earlier, in February 1904, it stands out as being specific and serious, and as having a rhetorical power that holds out great promise for the future. Not all his early love poems are like this, however. 'In meinem Herzen steht ein Tempel...' of September 1904 is a lapidary, classical piece:

In meinem Herzen steht ein Tempel.
Der Schönheit hab ich ihn geweiht,
Der Göttertochter, die erhaben
Gebietet der Unendlichkeit.

Ihn deckten Staub und Spinneweben,
Lang stand er in die Nacht versenkt,
Da nahtest du, vor deinen Augen
Klafften die Tore, freigesprengt.

Ein Frührot strahlet meinem Tempel.
Herrin, du kommst, ich harre dein,
Der Göttin Tempel steht dir offen,
Willst du die Priesterin mir sein? (*L* 561)

('In my heart there is a temple') In my heart there is a temple. I have dedicated it to Beauty, daughter of the gods, who holds sway over eternity.

For a long time it had been shrouded in night, covered with dust and cobwebs, until you appeared and your eyes caused the doors to fly open.

My temple is bright with the rosy light of dawn. Lady, I await your coming. Aphrodite's temple is ready to receive you; will you be my priestess?

Another early love poem, 'Ach, du bist wunderschlank' of the same month (and, like 'Du bist so dunkel', addressed to Emma R.) is Heine-like and indeed Heine-derived. Between them these three poems illustrate Heym's range of styles at this time, which will come as a surprise to those who know only his monotone poems of 1910–11. If the satire is the least effective, partly because it is derivative, and partly because it is over-clever, it points forward to the 'subterranean' satirical vein in his work and, more specifically, to one of his most amusing satirical self-descriptions, 'Ach nun seht doch den Heym...', written in December 1904:

Ach nun seht doch den Heym, wie er schreitet mit wankendem
    Schritte
Nur begleitet vom Wind, dem gewaltigen Herrscher der Lüfte.
Abschied hat er genommen von Toni seiner Geliebten.
Ihm deucht, er kann nicht mehr leben ohn sie die herrliche Schönheit.
Als er nun biegt um die Ecke, ein Leuchten geht über die Züge des
    herrlichen Heym.
Die Else hat er gesehen, die er schon lange bewundert.
Dies deucht ihm ein Wink von Athene, der herrlichen Göttin.
Für die herrliche Toni, die er eben mit Jammern verlassen
Hab er Ersatz gefunden in der Else, der blauäugigen Schönheit.
Flüchtig kennt er sie schon, er beschließt sie näher zu kennen.
Rot bis über die Ohren, das Zeichen der keimenden Liebe,
Grüßend geht er vorüber an ihr, die huldvoll ihm lächelt.
Er der eben noch jammert, kehrt freudig nach Hause zurück jetzt.
Else, sie ist jetzt sein Sehnen, Else, sie sieht er im Traume.
Else, sie soll ihn beglücken.
Am Morgen, da sieht er sie wieder
Und herrlich in der Jugend Prangen usw. (*L* 581f.)

('Just look at poor old Heym') Just look at poor old Heym staggering along, accompanied only by the wind, the great ruler of the air. He's just taken leave of his beloved Toni. He's thinking he cannot live without her, magnificent beauty that she is. As the magnificent Heym turns the corner his face clears. He has caught sight of Else, whom he has long since admired. He takes this as a sign from Athene, the magnificent goddess. For the magnificent Toni, whom he has just left, feeling sorry for himself, he has found a replacement in Elsa, the blue-eyed beauty. He already knows her slightly; he resolves to get to know her better. Blushing furiously, sure sign of growing love, he greets her as he walks past her; she smiles at him graciously. He who only a moment ago was feeling sorry for himself returns home happy. Elsa is now his heart's desire, it is Elsa of whom he dreams. Elsa is the one to make him happy. The next day he sees her again, resplendent in youth's etc. etc.

Compared with the impersonal polish of much of his early neo-romantic verse, or with the impersonality and deadly seriousness of much of his later poetry, this is refreshingly different – it is good to find him using Hölderlinian rhythms in such a relaxed and self-mocking way.

Although nature is the subject of Heym's earliest work ('Die Quelle', 'Nebelschauer'), it is soon apparent that this is not adequately described as 'nature poetry'. It is rather 'romantic', not least in its preoccupation with death. One of the most remarkable of the many poems which could be quoted as examples of this is 'Lied des Gefangenen':

Ich steh auf der Spitze des Turms,
Der Qualm und Lärm der Gasse bleibt zurück,
Weit hinten seh ich meine Heimatsberge blauen,
Wenn in die Ferne schweift mein Blick.

Über mir fliegen die Wolken dahin
Dem Land meiner Heimat entgegen.
O, hätt ich die Flügel des brausenden Winds,
Wie wollte ich mich regen.

Ich will, ich kann,
Ich hebe mich, ich stürme in den Himmeln hin,
Hoch in die Lüfte schwinget mich der Sturm.
Mit wilder Freude sauset mir der Sinn.

Nun senk ich mich auf meinen Heimatsberg.
Ich hör es an der alten Bäume Wehn – –
– – – Ein Schrei; auf der Gasse ein dumpfer Fall. – – –
Im Sterben hab ich meine Heimat gesehn (*L* 523f.).

('The prisoner's song') I am standing at the top of the tower, the smoke and din of the street are left behind; when my gaze scans the horizon, I can see the mountains of my homeland beginning to appear out of the mist.

The clouds overhead are flying towards my homeland. Oh, if only I had the racing wind's wings, how swiftly I should go.

I will, I can, I rise up, I storm into the heavens; the storm lifts me high into the air. My senses rage with wild joy.

Now I am falling on my homeland. I recognize it by the movement of the old trees in the wind ... A cry; in the street a dull thud... Dying I have seen my homeland.

This is, surely, an extraordinarily mature poem to have been written by a fourteen- or fifteen-year-old boy. Here already, sometime in 1902, is the poet as prisoner of life; the very title points forward to the cycle 'Der Gefangene' of 1905, and more important, to the various late poems which bear the title 'Die Gefangenen'. Scarcely less remarkable is 'Das Totenschiff', written in 1903:

Die Sonne sank weit hinten ins Meer
Ein fahler Schimmer umsäumet die bleiche Stirn des Alls.
Ich steh auf einem Nachen morsch und leer
Ich steh und treib in die Nacht.

Da glimmt im bleichen Schein
Eine ferne Sonne auf.
Du sollst das Ziel mir sein,
Dir lenk ich den Nachen zu.

Zu dir, du Einer, will ich fahn
Du großer Geist des Alls.
Ich zieh auf leuchtender Sternenbahn
Ich zieh, ich zieh in die Ewigkeit (*L* 529f.).

('The ship of death') Faraway the sun sank into the sea, leaving a pale halo around the world's pallid brow. I am standing on an empty, rotting hulk, drifting nightward.

Suddenly a distant sun begins to glow in the half-light. You shall be my goal henceforth. It is towards you that I now steer.

It is towards you that I am heading, great spirit of life. I am moving on my shining starry way. I am moving into eternity.

Here we have not only the characteristic preoccupation with death, but something much more striking: the poet himself as Flying Dutchman or ship of death (a theme which receives its most grandiose and macabre treatment a decade later, in the story 'Das Schiff').

The landscape of this early poetry is the landscape of mood. The dominant mood is the longing or 'immer nach Hause' mood of German romanticism, in which love and death come together, as they do in the greatest of Heym's later poetry.

If Heym's first phase shows him running the gamut of German romanticism, his second phase, which begins in late 1904, shows him coming to terms first with Hölderlin and then with the contemporary poet whom he associated with Hölderlin – Richard Dehmel. There is relatively little connection between the poetry Heym had to read at school and the poetry he was writing at the time. In 1905–6 his texts included the *Gedankenlyrik* (reflective poetry) of Goethe and Schiller, nineteenth-century German poetry, and the mid-nineteenth-century French poets Victor Hugo and François Coppée. His diary has nothing to say of any of these poets except Goethe and Schiller; on 2 January 1905 he writes 'I like Göthe [*sic*] and Schiller too', but this is an afterthought (it is preceded by 'I am closest to Hölderlin and, of the moderns, Richard Dehmel'), and in the following months there are some other fairly neutral references to Goethe (and one to Schiller) which contrast markedly with the enthusiasm he shows for Hölderlin.

It is not until some years later that he becomes outspokenly critical of Goethe, and when he does it is under the influence of the Neue Club, some of whose members were very hostile towards Goethe. So far as German nineteenth-century poetry is concerned, there is more evidence of it in his work before 1905–6. Nor does the poetry written in 1906–7 show any real influence of Klopstock or of the sixteenth- and seventeenth-century poets Heym was reading; poems with suggestive titles such as 'Totenschiff' ('Death Ship') and 'Alles ist eitel' ('All is vanity') date from earlier, his considerable use of the seventeenth-century technique of 'accumulation' or the piling up of images (*Häufung*) from rather later. Nor have Coppée and Hugo left any obvious mark on his work, the evidence of which suggests that in his last years at school his real enthusiasm was devoted to Hölderlin, and that otherwise he was discovering contemporary German poetry (notably Richard Dehmel, Stefan George and Hugo von Hofmannsthal). He evidently also knew Heine.

As we have seen, from January 1905 onwards he was much preoccupied with Hölderlin, who was not only his poetic role-model, but an important model in a technical sense. Heym's early poetry is Hölderlinian in its diction, mythology and mythical view of nature, in its rhythms (cf. the alcaic ode 'Trost' of July 1906, and the many poems in Hölderlinian free rhythms), its syntactical tricks (the postponing of the subject, reduplication, intensification by means of the 'absolute' comparative, and so on). In addition Hölderlin gave him much of the basis of his poetry: his ideals of love, beauty, religion and poetry, his Hellenism, his cult of Helios and his concept of Fate. More generally, but no less importantly, Hölderlin gave him encouragement, enthusiasm and inspiration. Heym was, at this time, increasingly an inspirational poet, and Hölderlin remained the ultimate source of that inspiration by giving him the courage to ride his demon, which he presently apostrophizes in wholly Hölderlinian lines:

> Der du, ein Sturm, mich durchwanderst Tag und Nacht,
> Der du in meines Blutes dunkelen Gängen wohnst
> Der es brausen macht.

> Der dunkel und rätselvoll,
> Tief in mir thront.
> Ungerührter, der mich zu schauen heißt
> Wie nie ein andrer geschaut

Des Sommers Fluren, den Wald
Und die Städte,
Wenn dunkel der Abend graut.
Der du mich durch die Straßen reißt.

Der mein Herz zittern macht. Du.
Wie oft stand ich maßlosen Taumels voll
Wenn dein Fittich rauschte mir zu
'Den' Ton, den keiner vernahm.
Der du in meinem Herzen wohnst.
Wie lange noch?
Bis du ausfährst eines Tags,
Wie ein dunkeler Rauch,
Und mich verläßt,
Wie die bekränzte Tafel
Nach einem Totenfest (L 105).

('Dedication') You who, stormy spirit, possess me night and day, you who dwell in the dark ducts of my blood, making it pound.

You who are enthroned, darkly, secretly, deep within me. Unmoved one, commanding me to see summer's meadows, forest and city as never another has seen them, when night more darkly falls. You who drag me through the streets.

Making my heart palpitate. You. How often have I stood full of boundless ecstasy when your wing-beat brought me the tone that is mine alone. You who dwell in my heart. For how much longer? Till the day when you will vanish like a breath of dark smoke, leaving me behind, a gravestone wreathed with flowers after a funeral.

This poem, entitled 'Widmung', written in July 1910, at the very end of Heym's first period, epitomizes that period. Of course, these are the lines of a young poet who has discovered Hölderlin and has been carried away by his discovery, but the solemnity is entirely genuine and wholly justified. Heym knew perfectly well that he had poetic genius.

It is as tragic poet that Hölderlin is his model, for Heym's poetry is 'tragic' both in the sense of conveying an increasingly tragic view of human destiny, and in a more specialized sense. For all the depth of his emotion, and for all its concentrated verbal power, much of Heym's poetry is not 'lyrical' and needs to be distinguished from lyric poetry as such. The relevant distinction is not so much that between 'lyric' and 'reflective' poetry (which loomed large in Heym's lower-sixth poetry lessons), as the distinction between 'lyric' and 'tragic' poetry in Hölderlin's definition, whereby the 'lyric' poem is the continuous metaphor of a feeling, whereas the 'tragic' poem is the metaphor of an intellectual point of view (that intellectual point of view being the awareness of being at one with all that lives, which is hardly applicable to Heym). Though it is not sufficiently highly intellectualized ('ideelich') to pass as 'reflective' or – in English terms – 'metaphysical', Heym was quite convinced that his poetry had what he called 'Metaphysik', this being the quality which in his view separated the sheep from the goats poetically speaking. For Heym poetry had to have 'Metaphysik', the poet who lacked this being a mere 'Zeitdichter'. This is an entirely proper argument which serves to distinguish Heym from most of his fellow-members of the Neue Club. His poetry is 'metaphysical' poetry in the general sense of dealing with the essential nature of reality (cf. his definition of God as 'something metaphysical'). That said, 'tragic' poetry seems the most appropriate term for it. The bulk of Heym's poems obviously convey a tragic view of life, but what makes them tragic in the Hölderlinian definition which applies to them is the fact that for all their sensuous, visual quality, they are ultimately (like Dehmel's) the expression of a view of life. This is precisely why Heym regarded his work as being 'metaphysical' by comparison with that of the coffee-house poets. This is the most fundamental way in which Hölderlin has left his mark on Heym's poetry, and it is on the later poetry that Hölderlin left the most fundamental mark.

Heym linked Hölderlin and Dehmel in his mind because of the intensely human interest of their work. Poetically speaking they are, for all the obvious differences, including that of quality, linked in terms of the previous paragraph. Dehmel, who had the reputation of being at once the most thoughtful and the most passionate of contemporary poets, was one of Heym's earliest poetic heroes. On 2 January 1905 he wrote in his diary: 'I need the human touch, confessions. That is why, of the moderns, Richard Dehmel means most to me.' Like Heym after him, Dehmel was banished from a Berlin Gymnasium to a provincial school. He, too, left his Corps at university. He, too, was a man of passion with a sense, at Heym's age, of being pursued by the Furies; he, too, was a visionary poet and lyric genius with an 'instinct for the heroic and the monumental',[1] as well as being a Nietzschean revolutionary with a healthy disregard for conventional pieties and poetic forms; he had even tried his hand, unsuccessfully, at drama. Reviewing Heym's *Der ewige Tag*, the critic Julius Bab wrote: 'It could be said that since Richard Dehmel's *Erlösungen* there has been no volume of German poetry as bursting with sensuous power as these poems of Georg Heym.' What Bab missed in Heym, 'Dehmel's iconoclastic intellectual passion', is precisely what now seems to be one of his prime characteristics, although it is true that Dehmel was a visionary preacher, which Heym is certainly not. No doubt Heym's sense of affinity with him made Dehmel into a 'model' in a general sense, but was he an important 'influence' as such? The only poem by Dehmel which Heym actually names is 'Geheimnis': 'If only I could get Emmy into the mood which is expressed so marvellously in Dehmel's poem "Geheimnis". On listening to this poem one feels a positively physical grief that this mood can never be realized (T 11).' It was obviously the last four lines of 'Geheimnis' which impressed Heym, for they ('O Geliebtes –/deine höchste Wonne/und dein tiefster Schmerz/sind mein Glück –': 'Beloved, your greatest joy and your deepest sorrow are my good fortune') describe the intensity of experience, the 'grande passion', which was Heym's ideal and which he otherwise associated with Hölderlin; this is no doubt why Hölderlin and Dehmel are named together in the diary entry for 5 January 1905. Judging by the evidence of his early poetry, Heym appears to have acquired his enthusiasm for Dehmel's work in summer 1904, although it may go back to 1902/3 – if, that is, the parallels between his 'Hymnus' and 'Später Morgen' (L 525), and Dehmel's once-famous formula 'from dull desire to incandescent fire' are anything to go by; 'Sehnsucht' (L 533) of 1903–4 parallels Dehmel's 'Ausblick' (from *Weib und Welt*) in this respect. Quotations from Dehmel appear, with or without acknowledgement, in Heym's diary throughout 1905. In his last diary entry for 1905 Heym is still quoting Dehmel, again with obvious reference to himself: 'Greif zu und iß, dann dulde' ('Take what you want, consume it, and then suffer in silence') is a quotation from the poem 'Gottes Wille' (in *Aber die Liebe*), the theme of which is the craving for existential fulfilment which was so familiar to Heym. If these quotations have to do with Heym's ideal of living and loving, another diary entry ('I wonder whether I have the strength to be lonely': 2 April 1905), which echoes the ending ('Gieb mir die Kraft, einsam zu bleiben,/Welt!': 'Give me the strength to bear solitude, O world') of Dehmel's 'Die Harfe' (in *Weib und Welt*) is no less personal. Heym's concern is not the poetic expression, but what he will have thought of as the *Lebensweisheit* (or wisdom). This also applies to the poem most obviously indebted to Dehmel, 'Trinklied' (August

1904), which is, however, only a pale shadow of Dehmel's famous 'Das Trinklied'; Heym lacks the self-confidence to produce the kind of satirical version of Dehmel's poem that Jakob van Hoddis produced in 1902.[2]

Not surprisingly, most of these parallels involve the idea of intensity of experience; no doubt Heym put together Dehmel and his other enthusiasm of 1905, Merezhkovsky, as both pointing to the need to make the most of his youth. There are a number of parallels between Dehmel's work and Heym's early work, especially his early love poems: 'Endlich Licht' (L 544) of July 1904 appears to borrow from Dehmel's 'Venus Primitiva' the motif of a lovers' meeting in a hostile crowd; 'Läuterung' (L 547f.), also of July 1904, appears similarly indebted to Dehmel's 'Zwei Menschen'; a number of passages in 'Schwarzer Tag' of October 1904 appear to derive from Dehmel's 'Anbetung'. These are a poet's typical early 'borrowings'; as such they are much less significant than the numerous general parallels, which revolve around Heym's hunger for experience, to which the first two stanzas of Dehmel's programmatic 'Bekenntnis' (in his 1891 first collection, *Erlösungen*) are applicable:

> Ich will ergründen alle Lust,
> so tief ich dürsten kann;
> ich will sie aus der ganzen Welt
> schöpfen, und stürb' ich dran.
>
> Ich wills mit all der Schöpferwut,
> die in uns lechzt und brennt;
> ich *will* nicht zähmen meiner Glut
> heißhungrig Element.

I will experience every pleasure to the very depths of my desire. I will draw my pleasure from every quarter, even if I die of it.

I will do this with all the creative frenzy which pants and burns within us; I *will* not tame my ardour's burning hunger.

Dehmel's frenzied creativity and Heym's no less frenzied image-making are the poetic responses to lives of similar temperaments.

These parallels are, however, trivial compared with the fact that Heym's basic poetic technique is the same as Dehmel's: the projection of violent emotion into a visioned landscape. This means that Dehmel is a far more important poetic influence than has yet been realized. However, if Heym clearly admired Dehmel's brand of poetic self-projection and lightness of touch, his reasons for identifying with Dehmel more closely than with any other poet save or since Hölderlin were ultimately more personal than poetic. In the end this personal affinity explains the greater part of Heym's enthusiasm, for he cannot but have been struck by Dehmel's rebellious youth and conflict with his father, his social-revolutionary fervour, his Nietzschean affirmation of life and Zarathustran loyalty to the earth, his religion of love, and the whole tumult and passionate turmoil of his life – the way in which he exposed himself to every storm that came his way. Dehmel may have been twice Heym's age, though he was under thirty when his first three subsequently famous collections appeared; but there can be no doubt that Heym's vitalism was powerfully reinforced by Dehmel's example. Here, in Dehmel, are the vehemence, vigour and vitality that we associate with Heym and which we think of as being his prime characteristics.

Another contemporary poet to impress the young Georg Heym was Hugo von Hofmannsthal. Thus 'Manche laufen blindlings...' of November 1904 is a pastiche, a less elegant version, of Hofmannsthal's poem 'Manche freilich...'; unfortunately it lacks the most significant feature of the original – the poet's compassion for his less gifted fellow human beings. Hofmannsthal appears in Heym's diary on 23 April 1905, when the lines 'Und viel zu grauenvoll, als daß man klage,/daß alles gleitet und vorüberrinnt' ('And far too terrible for one to lament the fact that all things lapse and pass away') from the first of the 'Terzinen über Vergänglichkeit' are quoted with evident approval in the very personal context of Heym's determination to show up in Neuruppin as a 'dyed-in-the-wool pessimist' (and the suicide of an acquaintance of his). That same year we find him, like so many young poets of the time, paying the slightly older poet the compliment of imitating him (his 'Skizzen zu einem Drama' is based on Hofmannsthal's *Der Tor und der Tod*); he was still imitating him in 1908 ('Durch herbstliche Alleen' is based on Hofmannsthal's 'Vorfrühling'), and even in 1911, for 'Ein Herbst-Abend' (*L* 292) owes its 'irregular terza rima and mournful dignity'[3] to Hofmannsthal's 'Ballade des äußeren Lebens'. These are, however, no more than incidental echoes which simply show that some of Hofmannsthal's poems happened to catch Heym's poetic eye.

What, then, was Heym's attitude towards Hofmannsthal's two more famous contemporaries, Rilke and George? Rilke is, on the face of it, the contemporary German-language poet with whom Heym has most in common. They are both visually oriented, with a love of painting; both are romantics (albeit of different kinds) with an obsession with death. They share the same poetic heroes (Hölderlin, Keats and Baudelaire); their poetic development is similar, with a not dissimilar traumatic experience (military academy, Neuruppin) providing the spur to creativity. But this does not mean that they were poets of the same kind. The difference between them arises not so much because Rilke is the poet of inwardness, for in his own, very different (Prussian as opposed to Austrian) way, Heym was that too, but because Rilke was a metaphysical poet whereas Heym was not. Rilke wrote meditative, philosophical poetry; he was a man of ideas. Heym, for his part, produced tragic poetry and was a man of feeling. Nor does it mean that Heym was drawn to Rilke, for the fact is that he regarded both Rilke and George as 'sick' (D 507), a judgement which recalls Goethe's magisterially mistaken rejection of Romanticism (as 'sick'). For Heym Rilke was 'that tart Maria Rilke' (PD 181; the term he uses is 'überschminktes Frauenzimmer'), 'a sparrow dressed in peacock's feathers' (a phrase which clearly derives from Merezhkovsky's 'Crows in borrowed plumes' in Chapter 16 of Leonardo da Vinci), a compromiser, a poseur, someone who – in sharp contrast to himself – wore his sensibility on his sleeve, someone whose 'style' he found alien. They both wrote early poems entitled 'An Hölderlin', but whereas Rilke's poem is rhetorical, Heym's is classical. Not surprisingly there is little sign of Heym having been influenced by Rilke. His temperamental dislike of the 'effeminate' Rilke made him blind to the poetic virtues which Rilke was beginning to show at this time.

Whereas Heym's contemporary, the poet Ernst Stadler, was, in 1903-4, producing fin-de-siècle (Jugendstil) verse in all seriousness (his Praeludien came out in 1905), Heym at precisely the same time was producing pastiches of it. His 'Manche laufen blindlings...' of November 1904 is a case in point; but it is 'Der Modedichter' – a dig at George and Rilke – of August/September 1904 that is of more general interest and more immediate relevance:

> Und nun ist Herbst.
> Schon schleicht der Herbstpoet
> Durchs rote Land,
> Gehüllt in einem Kragenmantel,

Des Faltenwurf ein malerisch Gedicht.
Und mit tottraurigem Gesicht
Holt mit der schlanken, weißen Hand
Er hinterm Ohr
Den goldnen Bleistift vor.
Dann setzt er sich ins feuchte Gras;
Beileibe nicht, sonst würden ja
Am End die neuen Lackschuh naß.
Nein, auf der Holzbank kauernd
Und bang erschauernd
Im Vorgefühl des nahen, kalten Winters,
Starrt er die todesmüde Sonne an,
Die ihrem Grab entgegenhinkt,
Und kritzelt endlich sein Geschmier
Auf japanesisches Papier,
Das nach den letzten Rosen stinkt,
Und merkt nicht, wie die Kinder,
Die ihre Drachen
Hoch in den blauen Herbsttag steigen lassen,
Mit meiner alten lieben Sonne um die Wette
Den jämmerlichen Wicht belachen (*L* 551f.).

('The poet *à la mode*') And now it is autumn. Already the poet of autumn is creeping around the reddening countryside decked out in a cloak, the fall of whose folds is a picture. And with a look of deathly melancholy he takes the golden pencil from behind his ear with his slender white hand. Then he sits down on the damp grass – not on your life he doesn't, lest his new patent leather shoes get wet. No, huddled on the wooden bench and shivering all over in anticipation of the approach of a cold winter, he stares at the sun, which, deathly tired, is limping towards its grave, and finally scribbles his rubbish down on Japanese paper which stinks of the last of the roses; and does not notice that the children flying their kites high up in the blue autumn day compete with the dear old sun in laughing at the absurd creature.

Heym's target here is the fashionable poet in general and Stefan George in particular. The poem shows that by autumn 1904 he was already reacting both to and against contemporary German poetry, and that he was as irked by George as would be that other great satirist, Bertolt Brecht. He dubs George 'the resounding pagoda from Bingen am Rhein' (*D* 15), calls him a 'cloddish hierophant, crazy discoverer of lower-case letters and self-appointed laureate' (*T* 8 July 1910), and guys him in the satire 'November': 'stefan george steht in herbstes-staat./an seiner nase hängt der perlen helle' ('stefan george is in his autumn finery. the drip on the end of his nose has the luminosity of pearls'). However, if there was much about George and the George-circle of which the 'rowdy' Heym inevitably disapproved, there were also aspects of George's work which compelled his admiration. We need to remember that Heym was given to extreme – and contradictory – judgements, and that the poetic heroes of his youth were men whose honesty or ability to cope with difficulties similar to his own he admired; he had no time for those (including Goethe and George) whom he saw as compromisers. It is true that he was himself a little readier to compromise than he would have liked to think, and that his attitude towards George was ambiguous. Basically he regarded George as a poseur and a pompous ass, but this moral disapproval was tempered by aesthetic approval of the formal elegance of George's work, for here, despite the distasteful context, was the beauty which he admired above all else. In that sense Heym's work ran parallel to George's. Julius Bab rightly argues that 'Georg Heym had the ruthless concision, the taut rhythms and sensuous imagery which poets are apt to gain from George's example' (D 235f.), although it does not follow that the form of Heym's later work is therefore indebted to George, for while aspects of it doubtless are (e.g. his use of the initial 'Des' for 'Dessen'; his use of the 3 × 4-line stanza form), in general terms his *later* poetry is far more profoundly influenced by the poet to whom George owed so much of his own formal elegance: Baudelaire. What has been mistaken for the influence of George is in fact the influence of Baudelaire, whose work Heym knew partly in George's translation.

Heinrich Eduard Jacob summed up Heym's attitude to George with admirable clarity:

George – whom he detested, but subconsciously also admired, in much the same way that Kleist detested, admired and loved Goethe – was for Heym a kind of inevitable heritage. George not in terms of thought ... nor in terms of the full range of his poetry, which Heym certainly did not know, but rather in terms of the 'Latin' form and formal discipline which George had himself inherited from Baudelaire. Throughout his poetic life this form surrounded the raging genius like a layer of crystal (D 70).

Echoes of George are found, particularly, in Heym's poetry of the period August 1906 to January 1908, a fallow spell when most of his energies were being expended on his student life and dramatic work rather than on his poetry; because his mind was not really on what he was doing (poetically speaking), he was too ready at this time to echo the newly discovered *fin-de-siècle* poets. A case in point is his 'Im Herbst' (*L* 622), written in August 1906, which has its *point de départ* in the poem 'Was ich liebe' by the 'decadent' poet Felix Dörmann (pseudonym for Felix Biedermann, 1870–1928), author of the scandalous collections *Neurotica* (1891), *Sensationen* (1892) and *Gelächter* (1895). Dörmann's poem begins

> Ich liebe die hektischen, schlanken
> Narzissen mit blutrotem Mund;
> ich liebe die Qualengedanken,
> die Herzen, zerstochen und wund.

I love consumptive slim narcissi with blood-red lips: I love excruciating thoughts, hearts broken and bruised.

These lines were effectively parodied by Alfred Lichtenstein:

> Ich hasse die farblose Feinheit
> Erklügelter Nervenkultur.
> Ich liebe die bunte Gemeinheit
> Der schamlosen, nackten Natur.

I hate the bloodless elegance of artful intellectualism. I love the motley vulgarity of shameless nature in the raw.

Heym's reaction should have been on the lines of Lichtenstein's parody or of van Hoddis's parody (entitled 'Der Bindfaden' and addressed to Rilke).[4] As it is, he takes Dörmann (and himself) too seriously, producing a wishy-washy echo of the original 'Wir lieben das Vergehende und Müde,/Den letzten Glanz im Abendlande' ('We love sickliness and lassitude, the passing glory of the western world'). He has failed to take the opportunity seized by Lichtenstein. It is not a mistake he would have made two years later. Nor would he have made it now if he had been *sur le motif*.

Once he had come under the powerful influence of Baudelaire in 1909–10, it was Baudelaire who was Heym's real model, not George. While Baudelaire might have led him back to George, there is no evidence that this was the case. The evidence suggests, on the contrary, that it was Heym's friend Ernst Moritz Engert who caused him to

interest himself in George in summer 1911; at this time Heym was a
frequent visitor to Engert's studio. Engert was later quoted as saying:
'His attitude toward George is interesting too. Rilke he completely
rejected, as I also did. But so far as George was concerned, I tried – I
knew half of George by heart at the time – and managed to get him to
recognize George as a great poet.'5 Evidence of Heym's interest in
George at this time is a notebook dating from February–June 1911,
which includes references to 'Die 2 Jahrbücher',6 'Klages',7 'Wolters –
Buch über Lechter',8 and 'Maximin'.9 Whether these notes refer to
Heym's preliminary reading for the visit which he paid to Friedrich
Wolters (man of letters and member of the George-circle) in late 1911,
or whether the titles were recommended to him by the historian Kurt
Breysig (whom he met at this time through David Baumgardt), or by
Robert Jentzsch (with whom he must have discussed George, for
Jentzsch was a great admirer of George), is not clear. At all events he
apparently visited Friedrich Wolters in late 1911, which suggests either
a genuine interest in George, or a genuine curiosity, quite possibly the
latter. The fact that by December 1911 he was writing of 'the sacred
carcass of a Stefan George' and 'the resounding pagoda of Bingen',
suggests that he probably reacted in a typically robust way to the
pomposity of the George cult. In other words, if he approached Wolters
in a fairly respectful frame of mind, he evidently reverted pretty quickly
to his normal disrespect. And, of course, all this was happening very
late, at a time when Heym's poetry was changing away from the formal
style which had been associated with George, towards a freer style
reflecting his discovery of the French elegiac poet Albert Samain
(1858–1900) and his renewed enthusiasm for Hölderlin.

The three *fin-de-siècle* German poets by whom Heym was most
strongly influenced were Richard Dehmel (in 1904–5), Stefan George
(from 1904, but especially in 1906–8) and Gustav Renner (in 1908/9).
The independence of Heym's judgement is again in evidence, for
Gustav Renner (1866–?) was as little known as the painter Martin
Brandenburg and the novelist Alfred Dove; his *Gedichte* came out in
1896, his *Neue Gedichte* in 1898, and the *Gedichte* (collected edition) in
1904; all were privately published. He therefore belongs very much in
the context of Dehmel and George, and if his impact on Heym was later
than theirs, it will be convenient to consider him briefly at this stage,
for it was the example of this little-known Silesian poet of the previous

generation that helped Heym to move from the second to the third phase of his early work.

Gustav Renner appears to make his first appearance in Heym's diary on 13 September 1908, when, as we have seen, he is listed (with Hölderlin, Kleist, Grabbe and Büchner) as one of the 'poetae Germaniae'. It is, however, possible that Heym's splendid vision of death recorded in his diary on 13 August 1906 ('und dann den Totenkranz um die Stirne am Abend auf das Meer zu fahren und mit der sinkenden Sonne auch zu scheiden von aller Schönheit': 'and then with death's wreath around my brow to go to sea in the evening and with the setting sun take leave of all beauty') was indebted to Renner, whose poem 'Sehnsucht' includes these lines:

> Sterben möchte ich in Wohllaut, in Licht und Farben,
> Im Angesichte des Meeres, wenn Orgeltöne
> Die Wogen heben, auf denen in leuchtender Schöne
> Die letzten Rosen der scheidenden Sonne starben.
> So von der Erde, auf der wir kümmerlich darben,
> Wir, des Staubes stumpfgeborene Söhne,
> Möchte ich scheiden, daß mich dort oben kröne
> Jene Schönheit, um die wir in Sehnsucht warben.[10]

I should like to die amid sweet music, amid light and colour, in sight of the sea, when thundrous organ tones power the breakers on which the last roses of the setting sun passed away in radiant beauty. Thus would I depart this world in which we dull sons of the dust are so haplessly undone, crowned by the beauty for which we longed.

However, it is more likely that the influence of *fin-de-siècle* aestheticism is at work on both poets. What evidence there is suggests that it was not until two years later that Heym discovered Renner. His enthusiasm for Renner, recorded on 13 September 1908, is still in evidence a year later. On 16 September 1909 Renner is again listed, this time in the company of Byron, Kleist, Grabbe, Marlowe and Büchner, as an Olympian. Confirmation of this status comes on 24/25 December 1909, when – as we have seen – Heym, in the 'Versuch einer neuen Religion', lists Renner as one of his poet-idols, the others being Grabbe, Byron, Büchner and Hölderlin. Heym was given to violent and sometimes hasty enthusiasms, but in autumn 1908 to winter 1909 Gustav Renner was clearly in the forefront of his mind.

Renner wrote poetry, *Novellen*, tragedies and a novel, and was also a painter; it was his *Gedichte* (1904) that were the subject of Heym's enthusiasm. Heym will have found in Renner key aspects of his own philosophy of life (including the need for heroic self-assertion), a number of his own obsessive themes (particularly that of death), and a painterly use of imagery that evidently impressed him; the last two come together in lines by Renner which gave Heym a model for some of the most vivid images in his most famous poem, 'Der Krieg' (see Chapter VII below):

> Doch durch den Dämmer, riesengroß und schwer,
> Hochbeinig, schreitet dort der Tod einher ...
> Und wo er seine schweren Füße setzt,
> Da glühen knisternd rote Flammen auf
> Und schlagen, hoch und höher, ihm hinauf.
> So geht er um des Horizontes Rund, ...

But through the dusk struts Death, gigantic, ponderous, long-legged ... And wherever he places his heavy feet, red flames blaze up with a crackling sound and rise higher and higher up towards him. Thus he straddles every horizon...

If with these lines one compares, as Ronald Salter has already done,[11] some of the key lines in Heym's personification of War/Death –

> In der Dämmerung steht er, groß und unerkannt, ...
> Einem Turm gleich tritt er aus die letzte Glut, ...
> Über runder Mauern blauem Flammenschwall
> Steht er, über schwarzer Gassen Waffenschall. ...
> In die Nacht er jagt das Feuer querfeldein ...
> Und die Flammen fressen brennend Wald um Wald, ...
> Aber riesig über glühenden Trümmern steht
> Der in wilde Himmel dreimal seine Fackel dreht, ...

In the growing dusk he stands, tall and unknown ... Like a tower he tramples out the dying light ... Over the blue sea of flame from burning towers he stands, over black streets full of clashing weapons ... Into the night he drives the fire across country ... And the flames, burning, consume forest after forest ... But gigantic over glowing ruins he stands, thrice brandishing his torch at the livid heavens...

– it is impossible not to see Renner's lines as the source of Heym's. Both poems no doubt go back to one or more common visual models, but Heym clearly knew Renner's lines by the time he came to compose his own. Salter has pointed to other slightly less suggestive parallels, and has also made the point that what matters are not particular instances where Heym has fairly obviously borrowed from Renner, but the more general parallels between the two poets' 'ways of seeing and expressing things', for, 'in the majority of cases Renner's poems present constellations of objects, events or scenes which are distinguished by the sophisticated treatment of their concrete, visual details'.[12] Heym goes beyond Renner, for the older poet normally ends his poems with an interpretative comment, often in the form of the simile ('als ob') which is so typical of his generation of poets, whereas Heym leaves his images to speak for themselves.

The fact that Renner was so much in Heym's mind in 1908–9, when the elements of his later poetry were being formed, and that most of the interesting parallels between the poets concern Heym's later poetry, suggests that Renner helped him to move away from subjective emotionalism to the visual, painterly style and objectivity of his later poetry. In other words, Renner helped to initiate a change which, as we shall see, the painter Ferdinand Hodler was instrumental in completing.

The period August 1906 to January 1908 is, not surprisingly, an experimental, transitional stage in Heym's poetic work: it included his last months at school (including the school-leaving examination), transition to university and move to Würzburg. It is also, relatively speaking, a fallow spell when most of his energies were being expended on his student existence and his dramatic work rather than on his poetry. In poetic terms his mind was not really on what he was doing, so that he was ready at this time to echo the *fin-de-siècle* poets, for even as 'old-fashioned' and classically inclined a poet as young Georg Heym was bound to take an interest in contemporary poetry, and, given his religion of beauty, was bound to go through an 'aesthetic' phase; but the evidence of his second phase suggests that he soon realized that his poetic kingdom was not of the aesthetes' world. Elegance was one thing, aestheticism another. In late 1906/early 1908 a vitally important development was taking place, but as yet it was attested by the diary rather than the poetic work.

It was in August 1906 that Heym said (*T* 61) that he was beginning to write really good ('ganz schöne') poems; from his description of the genesis of his work it is clear that he is writing in an increasingly 'inspirational' way. Previously, he says, his poems were prompted by vague moods and were a long time in the making. Now they come unbidden at the sight of something that triggers them: 'Yesterday I saw a branch of a tree laden with fruit, today I suddenly heard the rain on the trees, and then saw the vine shooting up out of the earth. Three poems resulted automatically (T 62).' The poems in question are 'Der Winzerzug' (L 623f.), 'Herbststurm' (L 624) and 'Das Lob der Reben' (L 625). Although they are not bad poems, they are neither particularly good nor particularly original. All three of them suggest that he has been reading George; they are occasional poems, written in the style that comes most naturally at the time. Heym implies that he has grown out of the 'Stimmungslyrik' (poetry of mood) of his early work, and that his new work is better because more 'inspirationally' produced. Lest it be argued that he confuses inspiration and facility, inspiration as such being identifiable with the vague moods of his previous work, it is clear in retrospect that this diary entry marks the beginning of Heym's characteristic manner. When he writes that he has produced three poems 'as a result of the sudden, fortuitous appearance of their subject before my eyes' (T 62), he is saying that his poetry is coming to be phenomenological in the sense of recording not merely a thought or a feeling, but a sight – something he has 'seen'. This is the beginning of the end of his early 'Stimmungslyrik'. Only a year before he had written: 'From now on I shall see my mood in nature' (T 39); now he insists that his work 'has nothing whatsoever to do with moods' (T 96).

In the final phase of his early work, then, Heym turns away both from the neo-romantic stereotypes of his first phase and from the aestheticizing of the second phase; gradually he comes to put the emphasis on precision and compositional coherence.[13] His work accordingly acquires a painterly and indeed a post-impressionist quality, while at the same time his fast-growing pessimism means that his poetry, which is predominantly nature poetry, no longer merely expresses a personal mood, but rather a whole world which is dominated by death and is therefore both threatening and itself paralysed with fear.[14] The combination of the two points straight to the 1910–11 poetry, many of the themes of which (war, revolution, contrast of Utopia and negative reality, steadily increasing pessimism) now begin to appear; nature, and with it reality, is coming to be seen in negative terms. He is also beginning to cultivate the sonnet, which was presently to be a rather over-used form, and the way in which he uses it shows that 1908, the year that saw his love for Hedi Weißenfels and his final return to Berlin, also marks his re-emergence as a poet. The five-finger exercises in the manner of George are over now; he is once again writing strongly and classically, as is shown by an untitled sonnet written in October 1908:

> Die Schwäne kennen, nahn der Wandrung Tage,
> Nicht Ruhe mehr. An dem gewohnten Hügel
> Versammelt sich der Schwarm. Die schweren Flügel
> Erheben sich und prüfen sich zum Schlage.
>
> Es kommt die Zeit, da sie nicht mehr ermüden.
> Mit lautem Rauschen ziehn sie auf und fliegen.
> Im Winde sie die freien Schwingen wiegen
> Und heimwärts eilt der Zug zum sonngen Süden.
>
> Es wohnt in mir, wie in den stolzen Schwänen,
> Die Ungeduld, ich zähle jede Stunde
> Die langsam zieht, und messe sie mit Tränen.
>
> O käm der Tag, da in der Vögel Bunde
> Ich südwärts reiste. Die Gedanken wähnen
> Sich schon bei dir und deinem lieben Munde (L 666).

Swans know no repose when migration time is near. They flock together on their usual hill. They raise their heavy wings and test them for flight.

The time comes when they no longer tire. With loud wing-beats they rise into the air and fly off. With wings, free now, cradled in the wind, the flock speeds home to the sunny south.

In me, as in those proud swans, impatience dwells; I count every lingering hour and measure it with tears.

Oh if only the day would come when I could travel south in company with the birds. My thoughts are already with you and your dear lips.

The sonnet, which he uses now to express his longing to return to Hedi in Würzburg, was to be one of his preferred forms in 1910; it was because he had begun to specialize in it that it became the vehicle for the description of contemporary urban reality.

What happened in spring 1910 was that Heym was prompted by his membership of the Neue Club to drop the neo-romantic mode which in one way or another characterizes most of his 'early' work, in order to concentrate on the proto-expressionistic verse he had been producing, in an unsystematic way, for some time, the exact time depending on the feature in question. The point has been admirably made by Richard Sheppard:

It must not be assumed that Heym's style was only radicalized as a result of his experience of the Neue Club. If one considers 'Die weißen Wolken zogen übers Land...' (October 1907), or 'Viel runde Städte liegen an dem Strom...' and 'Nova vita' (April 1908) or 'Die grauen Wolken fliehn in großen Heeren' (January/February 1909) ... then one will find there the dynamic treatment of landscape, the abandonment of a positive attitude towards nature, images of the moribund city, the stringing together of images without logical connexion, the self-contained lines, the faceless crowd, the propensity for the surreal, grotesque, violent and sadistic, the beginnings of his simultanéiste, non-linear conception and treatment of time, the monotone, throw-away metres, and the vision of an impending catastrophe, which are so characteristic of Heym's 'expressionist' poetry.[15]

Notions of 'expressionism' still differ sharply, but what makes it doubly difficult to be precise about the beginning of Heym's 'expressionist' manner is the fact that there are many different factors or criteria involved. We must therefore go into detail. The throw-away rhymes and metres, which have nothing to do with expressionism as such, are present in Heym's work from 1903; all that happens is that they become more pronounced and, from spring 1910 to autumn 1911, a mannerism, and arguably a weakness. Otherwise most of the features listed by Sheppard are present in his last example, 'Die grauen Wolken...' of 15 February 1909, which is therefore the date which marks the beginning of Heym's move to 'expressionism'; seventeenth-century poetry with its 'juxtaposition' and 'accumulation', seems to have been an important influence. There are, of course, some elements missing as yet, one of them crucially important – the 'absolute metaphor' which appears for the first time in 'Den Wolken II' of April 1909. This is the most striking and attractive poem of this time:

Der Toten Geister seid ihr, die zum Flusse
Zum überladnen Kahn der Wesenlosen
Der Bote führt; eur Rufen hallt im Tosen
Des Sturms und in des Regens wildem Gusse.

Des Todes Banner wird im Zug getragen.
Des Heers carrocha führt die Wappentiere.
Und graunhaft weiß erglänzen die Paniere,
Die mit dem Saum die Horizonte schlagen.

Es nahen Mönche, die in Händen bergen
Die Totenlichter in den Prozessionen.
Auf Toter Schultern morsche Särge thronen,
Und Tote sitzen aufrecht in den Särgen.

Ertrunkne kommen, Ungeborner Leichen,
Gehängte blaugeschnürt, die Hungers starben
Auf Meeres ferner Insel, denen Narben
Des schwarzen Tods umkränzen rings die Weichen.

Es kommen Kinder in dem Zug der Toten
Die eilend fliehn, Gelähmte vorwärtshasten.
Der Blinden Stäbe nach dem Pfade tasten
Wo Abgrund rings an Abgrund dunkel drohten.

Der crucifixus ward einhergetragen.
Da hob der Sturm sich in der Toten Volke.
Vom Meere scholl und aus dem Schoß der Wolke
Ein nimmerendend grauenvolles Klagen.

Es wurde dunkel in den grauen Lüften,
Es kam der Tod mit ungeheuren Schwingen,
Es wurde Nacht, da noch die Wolken gingen
Dem Orkus zu und den geleerten Grüften (*L* 678f.).

('To the clouds, II') You are the spirits of the dead escorted to the river, to the ferry overladen with the lifeless; your cries re-echo through the raging of the storm and the rain's wild downpour.

Death's standard is carried in your procession. The *carrocha* bears the heraldic beasts of the army of the dead, and grimly white are the banners whose edges beat against the horizon.

Monks approach in procession, shielding with their hand the funeral candles. Rotting coffins are carried on dead men's shoulders, with dead men sitting bolt upright in them.

Drowned men appear, the bodies of the unborn, hanged men blue in the face from the rope, and those who starved to death on a far-off island, their groins garlanded with death's black stigmata.

Children appear in the legion of the dead, scurrying on; the lame come hastening onwards too. Blind men's sticks feel for the path amid the dark menace of abyss after abyss.

The crucifix was also carried in the procession. That was when a howling rose among the dead. From the sea and out of the clouds came a terrible never-ending lamentation.

The grey air darkened. Death came on gigantic wings; night fell as the clouds were still on their way towards Hades and the empty catacombs.

Particularly interesting is the development of Heym's metaphor: in 'Die Abendwolken' of September 1905 the clouds are explicitly likened to red horsemen; in 'Die grauen Wolken' (February 1909) and 'Den Wolken I' (March 1909) Heym uses implicit comparison; in 'Den Wolken II' the clouds are identified with, have become, supernatural beings. The other missing element, the urban-imagery subject-matter, duly comes into his poetry in September 1909, by which time he therefore has all the characteristic features of his 'expressionistic' poetry in place. Sheppard's conclusion is clearly correct:

Joining the Neue Club did not cause the radicalization of Heym's vision, but it did broaden and accelerate the process, developing and fusing into a coherent whole the formal and conceptual elements of his work which were clearly present in autumn/winter 1909/10 and which therefore anticipated his 'expressionism'.[16]

All Heym needs to do is to stop writing old-fashioned poems as such (which remain the rule until 1910; the forward-pointing, proto-expressionistic poems are exceptions) and to stop including old-fashioned elements in new-fashioned poems. In fact he lived only just long enough to get beyond the mishmash of old and new elements which is the prime characteristic of early Expressionism in all the arts.

His early poetry deserves to be better known, partly because it is more varied, and some of it is a good deal better, than its reputation, but mainly because there are to be found some of his most characteristic modes and forms, a number of proto-expressionistic features, and prototypes for his final manner.

Although almost a third of Heym's poetry was written in the decade 1899–1909, it must not be forgotten that from 1905 he put more effort into, and attached more importance to, his dramatic work. Obviously he would have been a different poet if he had squandered less of his poetic energy on the dramatic attempts to which we should now turn our attention.

□ DRAMA

It is a strange fact that about half of Heym's entire *œuvre* consists of unperformed and arguably unperformable dramatic fragments. He wrote two 'complete' plays, *Der Feldzug nach Sizilien* (1907–8; 1910) and *Die Hochzeit des Bartolomeo Ruggieri* (1908; 1910), the latter in two versions, the second of which – *Atalanta oder Die Angst* (1910–11) – is in some ways the most interesting of his dramatic works. The one-act *Antonius in Athen* (1908) he also regarded as complete. Otherwise he produced some sixteen fragmentary works, of which the most considerable are *Arnold von Brescia* (1905–8), *Iugurtha* (1908), *Die Revolution* (1908), *Grifone* (1909–11) and *Cenci* (1911); the rest, being very short fragments, are neither here nor there, although they do include some material for a satirical *Faust* which promised to be the most striking and original of all his dramatic works. In his lifetime he published only the first act of *Der Feldzug nach Sizilien* (*Der Athener Ausfahrt*, Würzburg: Memminger's Buchdruckerei und Verlagsanstalt, 1907) and excerpts from *Atalanta* (in *Die Aktion*, March 1911). In December 1911 he offered *Der Feldzug nach Sizilien* to S. Fischer Verlag, only to be turned down in no uncertain terms, and that same year Rowohlt had rightly declined to include *Atalanta* in a volume consisting otherwise of *Novellen*. All of this suggests that Heym's dramatic work is problematical. And so it is. His own attitude towards it is ambiguous. On the one hand, he took it barely less seriously than his poetry (in 1905–10 he actually took it more seriously!), and was anxious for it to be taken seriously by others; on the other hand, he knew in his heart that he was not a dramatist. From the reader's point of view there is a strong case for arguing that Heym's dramatic work falls so far short of his poems and tales that it is better forgotten; but if it is a failure, the nature of the failure, and the reasons for it, are revealing.

His first dramatic project of any consequence was the tragedy *Arnold von Brescia*. On 31 October 1905 he wrote in his diary: 'Yesterday, on my 18th birthday, I first thought of Arnold Brescia, but having to spend so much time on schoolwork is appalling (*T* 37).' He struggled with this unmanageable project, off and on, for two years, before finally giving up the struggle on 19 January 1908: 'Finally gave up *Arnold*, in which I had quite lost my way (*T* 101).' Arnold of Brescia (d. 1155), monk, reformer and outspoken opponent of the temporal power of the papacy, was precisely the sort of solitary idealist battling against the establishment with whom Heym liked to identify. He probably first came across him in Alfred Dove's *Caracosa*,[17] which he described as his favourite book on 17 August 1905 – just a few weeks before beginning to write his tragedy. The evidence of the play suggests that he turned to Adolf Hausrath's *Arnold von Brescia* (Leipzig, 1891) for further information. However, what makes this first tragedy of interest to us are the close parallels between Arnold and Heym. Arnold is seen as the idealist full of enthusiasm ... for all greatness and for all beauty' (*PD* 433) who is made to face 'torture, fear of death, and hell' (*PD* 507). There is as much of Heym in the doomed unworldly monk as there is in that doomed worldly monk Ognibene in Dove's *Caracosa*, to the final chapter of which the 'chorus of flagellants' in *Arnold von Brescia* points. As the passionate idealist brought down by his own daemon, Arnold is a prophetic projection of Georg Heym. The play failed partly because Heym was insufficiently experienced to stop it getting out of hand, but mainly for the same reason that virtually all his dramatic attempts were to fail: because he was interested in his hero only as a projection and mirror of himself. He is too much on Arnold's side, and even then his interest in his character is the wrong kind of interest. Where there should be dramatic conflict there is only a one-sided play of ideas; where there should be tragedy there is only introspection. *Arnold von Brescia* is therefore in effect a further essay in self-definition. It is only as that that it counts.

Heym considered the completed *Der Feldzug nach Sizilien* good enough to be offered to S. Fischer Verlag, who turned it down as being unsuitable for inclusion in their list. He could have been spared the disappointment if the polemicist Maximilian Harden, to whom he sent the MS in summer 1909, had been franker; to speak of 'many signs of talent', as Heym quoted Harden as doing (*T* 127), but not of the glaring weaknesses of the work, was hardly helpful. As it is, *Der Feldzug nach Sizilien* is derivative (much of the early part is based on Thucydides's *History of the Peloponnesian War*), unbalanced (the two long first acts relate the Athenians' Sicilian expedition of 415–413 BC in a rambling way, with insufficient emphasis on the tragic hero, Alcibiades) and, in addition, suffers from much the same generic shortcomings as *Arnold von Brescia*.

Alcibiades shares Arnold of Brescia's – and Heym's – thirst for fame and greatness; he is depicted as a hero, a superman. His heroism is, however, at odds with and finally negated by the fatalism of the tragedy; this is the unresolved dichotomy of Heym's inner life at the time. The intellectual kernel of the play should have been the dialogue between Socrates and Alcibiades (written rather earlier than the rest of the work, and based on Plato's dialogues and Hölderlin's ode 'Sokrates und Alcibiades'), in which Socrates argues that moral goodness must come before anything else, notably Alcibiades's amoral craving for fame. The potentially dramatic dialectic is allowed to peter out; instead of a full-scale dialectic clash with either good or evil triumphing, a wishy-washy and non-dramatic, non-tragic 'synthesis' is arrived at, with Alcibiades arguing that fame is 'good' for one. The trouble is that Heym is partial: believing that aesthetic values are good values, he is too obviously on Alcibiades's side.

Worse still, this Platonic dialogue is not even integrated into the play, in which Alcibiades's motivation is inconsistent; albeit essentially 'aesthetic' (or 'Nietzschean') rather than ethical, it is also highly subjective. Heym's diary reveals what happened. On 22 September 1907 he noted: 'Wrote my "Sicilian Expedition" in 4 days. By chance I came across the piece of paper on which I once, in Neuruppin, sketched the beginning of the dialogue between Alcibiades and Socrates (*T* 95).' In a typically impetuous way he simply inserted the dialogue in the second scene of the first act. Having the first act published as *Der Athener Ausfahrt* will not have helped to induce the necessary self-criticism; as it is, the point looms large in S. Fischer Verlag's highly critical reaction to the completed tragedy in 1911:

Dear Sir,

We are unfortunately obliged to return your tragedy *Der Feldzug nach Sizilien* on the grounds that it is unsuitable for inclusion in our list. We gained the impression from the piece that a very early draft had perhaps been taken up again and completed without the weaknesses of the original conception being overcome. With the sole exception of the passage concerning Nikias' death, nothing in the piece struck us as powerful and convincing; the whole thing is concerned with abstract issues, and the problem of Gylippos cannot disguise this fact. But what is most fatal for the play is the fact that you have made nothing of Alcibiades. In word and deed alike he is such a weak figure that your deviation from history seems arbitrary.

Yours faithfully, S. Fischer Verlag (*T* 283).

Reading the play it is impossible to disagree with this verdict, which, being dated 18 December 1911, shows that right to the end Heym was trying to place this play too. The tragedy has two overriding weaknesses. One is that Heym, as usual, is simply not thinking in dramatic terms, so that Alcibiades is unconvincing as a tragic hero; Heym's subjectivity, his closeness to his hero, is a major impediment. The other is that he is unable to resolve the problem of heroism versus fatalism. Alcibiades is the outsider, the exceptional man, motivated – initially – by his enthusiasm for the heroic values of beauty and good-ness; he seeks, in Nietzschean fashion, to become his own god, to become God, but without being struck down by the gods or by Nemesis for his hubris, partly no doubt because Heym is not prepared to see his hero destroyed for espousing the values by which he is himself motivated, and partly because in the latter part of the tragedy he – for this reason -- motivates Alcibiades by means of patriotism. The change of motivation is as unconvincing as Alcibiades's downfall, for he is destroyed by the sheer malevolence (based on envy) of Gylippos. In other words, Alcibiades's death is no more satisfactorily motivated than his life.

It may be that Heym saw Gylippos as Alcibiades's *alter ego* (his ugliness is continually contrasted with Alcibiades's beauty) and *daimon*, for Alcibiades is destroyed by his 'Schicksal' in the way that Heym knew he would be himself. All that is certain, however, is that Alcibiades's fate makes a mockery of his 'greatness' (not because Heym was as yet a thoroughgoing fatalist, but because he was not), and that this fate results from the extreme ill-will of another human being rather than from the malevolence of the Schopenhauerian Will. The tragedy shows that Heym was unable to reconcile Nietzsche and Schopenhauer. It shows, too, that he – at least as yet – lacked the intellectual grasp and stamina to see through a full-length work; his forte, certainly, is the brief *tour de force*, whether poem or *Novelle*. Above all, however, *Der Feldzug nach Sizilien* suggests that Heym was too one-sided and too partial to be able to write successful drama; whether this was the case, we shall be better able to judge after considering his other completed play as such.

In the meantime Heym wrote a scene for a projected play about the 'Prussian Alcibiades', Prince Louis Ferdinand, which is purely and simply a matter of self-projection. Inevitably Heym identified with the eccentric outsider who was a prey to ennui and therefore given to womanizing, fraternizing with French revolutionaries, and hero-worship of Napoleon; the work was presumably not finished because he knew that it would be a matter only of self-dramatization, not of drama as such.

Presumably, too, *Iugurtha* (1908) remained incomplete because Heym began writing it, on 19 January 1908, without any good reason: 'Rushed into *Jugurtha* casually, without any real motivation, just for the sake of doing something in this town of clodhoppers (*T* 101).' 'Jugurtha' was the subject of the Latin poetry prize which Rimbaud won at the age of fourteen. If Heym knew this, the choice of subject may signal his self-identification with Rimbaud, although Rimbaud does not feature in the diaries until later that year. It is more likely that Heym came across Jugurtha in Sallust's *Bellum Iugurthinum* while still at school. Be this as it may, Jugurtha's struggle against Rome in its decadence stands for Heym's attitude towards contemporary Germany, later documented in the essay 'Eine Fratze'. Bernd Seiler has argued that 'It is a matter not of an anticipation in historical disguise of Heym's criticism of the stagnation of Wilhelmine Germany, but ... of an example of how history provided him with models and slogans which he then applied to his own time',[18] but there is no reason why the play should not be seen as incorporating both. What is quite certain is that Jugurtha is a Heym-like 'hero' who has to struggle against his destiny in his attempt to achieve fame and greatness.

In March 1908, two months after impetuously starting *Iugurtha*, Heym produced a one-scene playlet, *Antonius in Athen*, which he regarded as complete: on 20 March 1908 he noted 'Just finished *Antonius in Athen*' (*T* 105). It carries as its motto the opening lines of Hölderlin's 'Lebenslauf' of 1800 ('Größeres wolltest auch du. Aber die Liebe zwingt all uns nieder. Das Leid beuget gewaltiger': 'You too sought greater things. But love brings us all down, and grief humbles us further'), which both signals his identification with Hölderlin, and shows that the scene is to be a dramatization of greatness versus love. Indebted, as it is, to Shakespeare's *Antony and Cleopatra*, the scene explores the idea that love, far from being a spur to greatness, may in fact be incompatible with it. This is also a theme of the diaries; as such it reaches a climax in October 1910: 'I can see that for me there is nothing more fatal than love (*T* 146).' In brief, *Antonius in Athen* is a dramatization of Heym's two 'contradictory' drives at this time, written in his usual neo-classical style, and is therefore a particularly clear example of what Heym's 'drama' is and is not.

A diary entry dated 13 September 1908 shows that Heym once identified with 'Spartacus's men' (T 117), but no longer does so. The outcome of that identification is the fragment Spartacus (1908), inspired by the gladiator scenes in Bulwer Lytton's The Last Days of Pompeii and, more generally, by Henryk Sienkiewicz's Quo Vadis. The gladiator Spartacus represents Heym's heroic ideal in general (which identifies him as 'Hellene'), and also reflects his membership of the Corps Rhenania, from which he resigned shortly after noting that he no longer identified with Spartacus and his men.

The Last Days of Pompeii is very much of a piece with those other early favourites of Heym, Caracosa and Leonardo da Vinci. The fact that it inspired the Spartacus fragment is largely incidental. In general terms the novel will have appealed to Heym as a 'ripping yarn' set in the classical world in which he lived in his imagination, but also as a work which 'spoke' to him in a number of different ways. He will have identified with Glaucus as lover (Glaucus and Ione are ideal figures from this point of view) and with Lydon and Olinthus as heroes (albeit of very different kinds). Then there is the idea of the world as 'one vast prison'[19] governed by necessity, which is finally identified with Death. Because life is short and the future dark, there is no wisdom like that which says 'enjoy'.[20] The novel therefore reinforces the leitmotif of Leonardo da Vinci: Lorenzo Il Magnifico's song composed for the 'Mask of Bacchus and Ariadne' ('Quant' è bella giovinezza/Ma sin fugge tutta-via?/Chi vuol esser lieto, sia/Di doman non c' è certezza'). Heym must have been entranced by the aesthetic paganism of Ione, the 'Graceful Superstition' that is so close to his own cult of Beauty. The destruction of Pompeii, foreshadowed by the cloud 'like some vast giant, with an arm outstretched over the city', probably contributed to the imagery of Heym's most celebrated poem, 'Der Krieg' (see Chapter VII), in which the modern city, like Pompeii, is seen as a New Gomorrah.

Die Hochzeit des Bartolomeo Ruggieri, written in twenty-four hours in April 1908, is not only Heym's only other completed play (it is a one-act tragic melodrama), but, more important, is the only one of his dramatic works to have been subjected to a proper revision. It is based on the story of the Baglioni family, which Heym knew from Emilie von Hoerschelmann's *Die Bluthochzeit des Astorre Baglioni in Perugia* (Munich, 1907; first published in 1903). The theme of the play is the Sturm and Drang theme of the hostile brothers, in this case Bartolomeo and Sigismondo Ruggieri, whose hostility has to do with their wish to make Atalanta their own, although they also represent opposing ideas (Bartolomeo stands for beauty and goodness, Sigismondo for ugliness and evil). Atalanta is seduced by Sigismondo, but marries Bartolomeo. After a bedroom scene worthy of the early nineteenth-century gothic novelette, Atalanta stabs herself, thus escaping the variously unwelcome attentions of the two brothers. It is pure gothic melodrama. The reader is left cold because Heym's characterization is so weak (Atalanta is hysterical, Bartolomeo wet and Sigismondo brutish). In other words, Heym in 1908 lacked the ability to bring out the dramatic potential of the situation, although the material clearly had possibilities, particularly since the Gothic was to be his chosen mode. Simon Guttmann, to whom Heym showed the play in April 1910, found it embarrassingly 'old-fashioned' and 'declamatory', a half-baked piece.[21] He was not wrong.

By late 1910, when he rewrote the play as *Atalanta*, Heym was a different person. It is therefore hardly surprising that *Atalanta oder Die Angst* is very different from *Die Hochzeit des Bartolomeo Ruggieri*. Atalanta is now the central figure, the play being about her weakness, her inner conflict, her possession by demons, her horrified remorse and fear of death. She is no longer a hysterical ninny, but a tragic character who is described sympathetically because Heym now identifies with her. Everything is seen through her eyes (and therefore through his own). Heym concentrates his now considerable poetic resources on describing her fear of death, which, like his own, accompanies a love of life. In doing so he creates a realm that is very much part of his poetic world. The most memorable section of the most memorable speech in the play, Atalanta's long soliloquy, is a detailed visualization of Hell that belongs together with Heym's Hell poems; it will stand comparison with Dante and Schopenhauer, Bosch and Brueghel. He had difficulties with the ending of the play, of which there are three versions; the final version, in which Atalanta becomes the embodiment of her *Angst*, is the most striking.

Atalanta oder Die Angst is therefore not a gothic melodrama, but a poetic tragedy which is gothic in the manner of Heym's tales. It belongs with the tales. By the time he wrote it Heym had grown up; above all he had learned how to write. There still remain two questions: how seriously should we take this one-act poetic tragedy, and how good is it? The first question is easily answered: we must take it wholly seriously. The second question is more difficult. It has been argued that: 'With *Atalanta* Heym has created a compelling and poetic Expressionist drama that ranks with the best of his poetry.'[22] This seems to me to be exaggerated, for while it is a great improvement on its predecessor, the play spends rather too long dwelling on Atalanta's nameless *Angst* to be effective as theatre. Nor can I see it as Expressionist, for it is written in a style which harks back to Schiller's *Die Braut von Messina* (which Heym studied at school in 1905–6) and the tragedies of the English Romantic poets. In other words, the style, far from being experimental in the Expressionist manner, is egregiously – and absurdly – old-fashioned; it is therefore arguably still the gothic realm to which the play belongs.

Heym's last dramatic fragment, *Cenci*, dates from 1911 and is strongly indebted to Shelley's *The Cenci*, which he had known since his discovery of Shelley in 1908. He read *The Cenci* (in G. H. Neuendorff's translation of 1907, a Reclam volume) in 1908, as we can see by the verbal echoes of it in *Die Hochzeit des Bartolomeo Ruggieri* (and, even more so, in *Atalanta*). The story is the 'eminently fearful and monstrous story' (Shelley) of Francesco Cenci, who rapes his daughter and is killed by her. Heym's notes for the play show that Beatrice was to have been the main figure, and that the play was to have been modelled on Shelley, modified by Stendhal's version of the story, which he had also known since 1908. In Stendhal's version Francesco Cenci is motivated by a desire to offend public opinion so deeply as to astonish the world. While there are some enigmatic reminders of this motivation in Heym's fragment, it is clear that he was not interested in the clash with bourgeois morality as such. Rather he seems to have been persuaded by Shelley to see Francesco Cenci as devoted to debauchery and wickedness for their own sake. However, he goes beyond Shelley, for his *Cenci* was to have been about a world governed by evil, in other words, a world in which people are either born evil or are doomed to fall victim to it; it is a deterministic world watched over by a God who is not merely indifferent, but satanic. The philosophy of the fragment was to have been that of the late Heym, but there is no reason to think that it would have had anything like the power of the bleak tales which give more appropriate expression to that world.

Heym seems to have begun work on *Grifone* in August 1909; he was working at it again in September 1911. Both occasions point to the personal nature of the work: on 3 August 1909 he wrote in his diary: 'The storm [of passion of the last three days] had one positive result: I was able to put Grifone Baglioni's jealousy into words. It is as though that is why it happened (*T* 129),' and on 11 September: 'And yet this girl loved me, so help me. Now I can write about Grifone (*T* 163).' Zenobia stands for all those girls by whom Heym sees himself as having been deceived.

The piece, a neo-classical five-act tragedy, remained incomplete; a number of scenes are missing, although three different endings are extant. Again strongly reminiscent of Schiller's *Die Braut von Messina* (neo-classical style; fate-tragedy; hostile brothers; curse; astrology; determinism; pessimism), it is a grimly powerful fate-tragedy in the manner of gothic melodrama, complete with murderous hostility between brothers, pandemic deception and the triumph of evil. Life is seen as determined, and Heym's brooding preoccupation with death is again very much in evidence.

Like *Atalanta*, *Grifone* is in many ways an advance on *Die Hochzeit des Bartolomeo Ruggieri*. Its most obvious features are its remarkably old-fashioned style with its echoes of Shakespeare, Schiller and Grabbe; its power; its genuinely dramatic nature; and its unevenness. Although one still has the impression that Heym is more interested in words than in dramatic effect, *Grifone* is more than a poetic tragedy; it is the genuine article and – despite the undue length of not a few speeches – a potentially stageable work.

If *Der Feldzug nach Sizilien*, *Arnold von Brescia* and all the mostly fragmentary shorter dramatic pieces suggest that Heym was wasting his time in persevering with the drama, *Atalanta* and *Grifone* suggest that he might, given the time, have developed into a dramatist of some power. *Grifone* is the only one of his dramas that is a genuine drama and therefore suggests that he might, after all, have been able to produce worthwhile work in this genre, work which would have had much the same characteristics, including characteristic strengths and weaknesses, as his poetic and prose work; *Grifone* is the exception that proves the rule that Heym's dramas are undramatic. On the other hand, it is the

Faust fragment (also dating from 1911) that points to the possibility of Heym having an *original* contribution to make, including an original contribution to Expressionist drama.

Faust, one of the dramatic fragments, consists only of notes, which do, nevertheless, give one a good idea of Heym's approach. His *Faust* would have been a 'sport', a spoof; in other words, it is in part the dramatic counterpart of his scatological poetic satires. Given his opinion of Goethe, this was bound to be the case. If in 1905–6 he idolized Goethe (*T* 8, 44), by 1910–11 he had come to see him as 'the Weimar courtier and part-time literary big-wig', as a 'puffed-up idiot and gross fathead', as a 'swine' (*T* 148, 170). What irks him is what he sees as Goethe's pomposity and damnable Olympian calm at a time when revolutionary fervour was called for. He was presumably influenced by the attitude to Goethe prevalent in the Neue Club – I am thinking of Jakob van Hoddis's statement that 'by the time I've finished I hope that Goethe's name will not be spoken without an ironical smirk' (*D* 29) and the poem in which he guyed Goethe, 'Doch ein Palast stand huldvoll in Florenz';[23] certainly Heym was regarded as having wiped the floor with Goethe following his reading on 15 May 1911. He was both too extreme a character to have time for the 'Olympian' Goethe, and too much the opposite of Goethe's Faust ('Faustianism in Goethe's sense is precisely what he lacked': Kurt Hiller, *D* 87) to be inclined to write a 'straight' *Faust*.

This helps to explain his apparent idea of using a *Faust* of his own as a vehicle for a satirical romp through the world, or at least through the world of pre-war Berlin. He transmogrifies Goethe's classic/romantic world into a contemporary, 'Expressionist' world, a satirical anticipation of what were to be the typical scenes and characters of Expressionist theatre. If it were a pastiche, written a few years later, it would be less interesting; as it is, Heym takes off 'Expressionist theatre' before it has even happened. His *Faust* was, however, to be more than just a double parody, for the evocation of a popular notion of Hell, familiar from puppet-plays, pantomimes, etc., introduces a further kind of parody (including self-parody – cf. Heym's deadly serious poems on the subject, like 'Die Hölle': *L* 327f.), while his notes also show that he planned to guy Goethe and his Faust's romantic idealization of Gretchen.[24]

The implication of the final comment ('Anyone who can mix

tragedy with comedy has a philosophy of life') is that Heym is a better man than Goethe because he is less earnest. Opinions of Heym's projected *Faust* will differ; some readers will find it typically 'over the top', others will welcome this evidence of his ability to take himself less seriously than he customarily does. What is arguably most impressive is the way in which he parodies not only 'old Goethe', but the Expressionist theatre which is supposed not to have arrived on the scene until the following year. This suggests that Heym, had he lived, might have found effective employment for his satirical self in the theatre.

To those who know only Heym's poetry and diaries, the subject-matter of the dramatic work comes as no surprise. About half of it (*Der Feldzug nach Sizilien* and six fragments) is set in the ancient Greek world, while slightly more than half is set in the Renaissance or the Napoleonic era. The settings reflect Heym's historical enthusiasms; they do not mean that what he writes are 'historical dramas', for they are not. Whatever the setting, his themes are always the same: 'Ever-present, either positively as a Utopian ideal, or negatively as a travesty of it, are "enthusiasm, greatness, heroism" ['Eine Fratze': *PD* 173] in their various historical guises, shown concretely in the form of exceptional individuals'.[25] Although Heym shared the late nineteenth-/early twentieth-century fascination with the past – particularly those periods of the past which most clearly embodied the qualities which his own time lacked (notably ancient Greece and the Renaissance) – and although he identified with a number of historical figures, he is not, dramatically speaking, interested in his historical characters. Indeed, they are not really historical characters at all; they are personifications of ideas ('typical figures embodying conflicting principles'[26]) and at the same time masks or projections of Heym himself. He is all his characters; all his characters are himself. This fact brings the plays close to the poems and rather closer to the tales, but in dramatic terms the obvious lack of interest in his characters as individuals in their own right is fatal.

Nor, it must be added, is Heym interested in history for its own sake. Hermann Korte has argued: 'This is the weakness of all Heym's dramatic pieces: that their historical subject-matter merely represents his own age in historical costumes.'[27] There is some truth in this, but it is not the whole truth, for the comment overemphasizes the social aspect of Heym's work at the expense of the personal. Of course, Heym detested his father's Germany; but it was himself in whom he was engrossed, himself whom he continually dramatized.

His dramatic works, complete and fragmentary alike, are examples neither of 'Expressionist theatre' nor of 'historical drama'. His work may be expressive, but its neo-classical style means that it cannot usefully be described as 'expressionistic', which implies a quite different style; in terms of content it is neo-romantic. Labels are, as usual, not particularly helpful. The crux of the matter is that his plays are fancy-dress treatments of some of the themes of his poetry; they should be seen in the context not of German nineteenth-century historical drama à la Grabbe, but of the historical tragedies produced by three of his favourite poets: Keats (*Otho the Great*), Shelley (*The Cenci*) and Byron (*Marino Faliero*; *The Two Foscari*; *Sardanapalus*). It is true that he greatly admired Grabbe at the time when he was writing most of his dramas and dramatic fragments, but his interest in Grabbe was mostly bio-graphical. Heym's 'dramas' are therefore lyrical dramas and, as such, extensions of his lyrical work (or, in the case of *Atalanta oder Die Angst*, of his prose work), major themes of which they share.

Karl Ludwig Schneider, writing in 1971, gave a balanced and judicious summary of Heym's dramatic work:

Although the number of his dramatic works and fragments is considerable and he spent many years seeking ... to prove himself in this field above all others, he never managed to produce a real Expressionist drama. He thought too much in terms of the historical drama for that, and kept too much to this traditional form to be able to achieve the kind of radically new structure which was to be introduced by the Expressionist playwrights. But he was on his way towards this goal, and introduced distinctly Expressionist themes into his historical subject-matter. The dramas and dramatic fragments thus often con-contain direct parallels to the themes of his lyric poetry – we see the turn to the dark side of life, to those domains which in *Der ewige Tag* are termed 'Umbra' and 'Dolores'...

It will not escape the reader's notice that in Heym's dramas there are passages which are the equal of the best of his poetry. Any assessment of Heym's dramatic work must not lose sight of the fact that it occupies a position of considerable importance within the development of his work as a whole. Between 1905 and 1910 he devoted more time and energy to the drama than to the lyric; the preliminary development of his mature poetry therefore takes place within his dramatic work. It was there that he developed the fascinating imagery of his later poetry, there that he gained experience in the use of the five-foot iambics he preferred, there that the basic features of his poetic world were sketched in.[28]

It is, however, arguable that what Heym never really achieved was the breakthrough to genuine drama as such, not just to Expressionist drama. Here too the issue of Expressionism only distracts attention from more fundamental matters. There may be 'distinctly expressionist themes' in some of these dramas, but more significant is the fact that at root the 'dramas' share the *personal* themes of the poems and tales; these personal themes are what matter. The fact that Heym took these 'dramas' so seriously does not mean that he was right to do so. Nor does it tell us why he did so. In fact Schneider himself implies the answer to this question: Heym used the 'dramas' (or dramatic fragments, as they mostly are) as a test-bed for the poetry. It would, I think, be both logical and sensible for criticism to deconstruct these pieces and exhume the lyrical 'arias' which are lost from sight so long as they remain embedded in a less-than-readable matrix.

Essentially, then, Heym's 'dramas' are not so much 'dramatic' as 'theatrical'. They are self-dramatizations, dramatic self-projections, and as such an extension of the diaries, too.

Doubtless Heym remained attached to his dramatic work as the first sign of his genius (cf. *T* 127). He was not unduly worried about their fragmentary nature, for 'I almost prefer fragments to complete dramas' (ibid.). He made much the same point about his poems: 'A poem only strikes me as being any good until I have finished writing it.... Afterwards they no longer interest me (*T* 151).' What counted for him was the intense self-engrossment involved in the writing of the dramatic fragments; after that they had in a real sense already served their purpose. Besides, he simply could not write dialogue, presumably because he was too egocentric to be able to see and express a point of view that was not his own, for his heroes are largely *personae*, versions of himself (the hero he wished to be, etc.). That is why they all speak in the same way: they are all zombies.

No doubt he finally stopped trying to write verse dramas because he recognized that his real art was fundamentally monologic. The only surprising thing is that he spent so long, so tragically long, on the futile attempt to establish himself in a genre which was not his because he was not willing or able to take it seriously (it is himself that he takes seriously in connection with his dramatic fragments). The tales, which largely superseded his dramatic attempts, were an easier proposition, for they depended not on dialogue, but on the descriptive writing which was his forte.

IV

Life and Death, 1910–1912

☐ THE NEUE CLUB

One can always argue as to the best point at which to divide a writer's life for critical purposes; in Heym's case that point lies between summer 1908 and Easter 1910. The break with Hedi Weißenfels in autumn 1908 was an important landmark in terms of his personal development, and his discovery of the modern French poets in summer 1909 (did Ernst Balcke bring news of them back from his French studies in Besançon?) a significant poetic watershed, although the effects of it are not really seen until 1910. In a letter to Rowohlt, Heym himself said that he had developed very considerably in the years 1909–10 (*T* 226). The logic of his personal and poetic development establishes spring 1910 as the most important single turning-point, for joining the Neue Club brought him, for the first time in his life, into contact with a group of people of his own age (many of them poets) who understood him, shared many of his ideals and admired his work, and was therefore to be a watershed in his poetic development. The very fact that he only included two isolated poems from before March 1910 in *Der ewige Tag* shows that he himself regarded March 1910 as the decisive turning-point in his life and work. It was now that he caught up with what has come to be known as Expressionism; more important, it was now that his tragically short career as a writer took off.

On 19 March 1910, when Heym had just completed his 'Marathon' cycle of twenty-two sonnets, a young art critic and literary entrepreneur named W. S. Guttmann placed in the *Berliner Tageblatt* an advertisement inviting young playwrights to submit unpublished work to the 'Neue Bühne', newly founded as a radical alternative to the 'Akademische Bühne' of the Rotter brothers. This was grist to Heym's mill, for he had been producing mostly fragmentary 'dramatic' work for some time, and was very keen for his work to be produced. He seized the opportunity and appeared before Guttmann in early April with his play *Die Hochzeit des Bartolomeo Ruggieri*.[1] Guttmann was surprised at this appearance of someone who looked much more like a Corpsstudent than a progressive young playwright à la Wedekind (which is what he had been expecting), and was also placed in a somewhat embarrassing position, for he saw at once that the play was 'old-fashioned, declamatory *Machwerk*'; it was therefore more suitable for the 'Akademische Bühne' than for the 'Neue Bühne' he envisaged. The long and short of it was that the play was unstageable, but also, in other respects, exceptionally interesting and powerfully written, the work of a real writer, though not of a real playwright. Guttmann, having made it 'inexcusably' (his word) clear to Heym that he had serious reservations about the play, therefore asked him whether he had written anything else. Heym said that he had written poems. On being asked whether he had them with him, he replied that he didn't need to carry copies about because he knew them by heart. Without further ado he proceeded to declaim the first line of one of his Berlin sonnets: 'Der hohe Straßenrand, auf dem wir lagen.' Before Heym had reached the end of the sonnet Guttmann knew that listening to it was one of the high points of his life; some seventy years later he was still describing it in the same way.

Heym, far from taking umbrage at Guttmann's outspoken (but very necessary and honest) criticism of the play, was delighted by his highly positive and understanding reaction to the poems. They met several times in order to amend the play together, but the project was soon abandoned. More significant was Guttmann's enthusiastic reception of the poems and his determination to do everything he could to help Heym. He wished to propose Heym for membership of the Neue Club, but he was only a new member himself and was in any case not sure whether Heym would fit in. Hence his reported reservations, which vanished when he discovered that Heym, for all his 'establishment' background and appearance, was as radical a critic of the

Wilhelmine state as any member of the Neue Club. Not long afterwards the diary records Heym's view that the Kaiser is a clown, and that his lackeys would be better employed as spittoon-holders. Guttmann therefore proposed him for membership of the Neue Club[2] notwithstanding the fact that Heym was, on the surface, a forceful, energetic, vehement character who would not leave unchanged any group into which he was released. Before going any further, let us therefore briefly consider the rather wild young man who presented himself first at Guttmann's flat and then at the Nollendorf Casino in late April 1910.

Most of those who have left descriptions of Heym knew him in these last two years of his life. To look at he was of average height, but was stockily built, 'musklig wie ein Panther' in Kurt Hiller's words (D 87). He looked, and indeed was, athletic (he went in for rowing, fencing, skating, swimming). He had a shock of brown hair, one streak of which was paler than the rest. He had a fresh complexion and was generally agreed to have been disgustingly healthy looking. He had a strong, slightly snub nose, full lips and a powerful 'metallic'-sounding voice which he was apt to raise. He was given to putting on a Berlin accent.

So much for the outer man. The inner man was a great deal more complex. Like the title-character of the sketch 'Bagrow' (see PD 155), he was a strange mixture of child, genius and hero. He was in some ways larger-than-life-sized, given to drinking water out of the jug, sitting in his room wearing nothing but his Jacobin sash, and to carrying girls around more often than most. One should not be misled, however, for he enjoyed being provocative and often put on a 'tough' act in order to hide his sensitivity.

He was a dreamer who lived for his dreams, which he cultivated to the point where they became visions. Like Georg Trakl, he was possessed by these visions, becoming almost demented when he was unable, for one reason or another, to record them: 'The agony, the misery of it: I have poetic images coming out of my ears, instead of being able to get them down on paper' (T 20 December 1910). Because he craved excitement above all else, his dreams were extraordinarily martial: he dreamt of military glory, of serving – and dying – with distinction in the armies of Napoleon, whom he idolized. His ideal was heroism in whatever form – in love, in battle, in death; but he was also a revolutionary and once said (in those far-off days before terrorism became so banal) that one of his selves would have liked to be a terrorist. He was more than a youthful rebel reacting against what he perceived to be the petty tyrannies of his father and of society, for he cultivated his revolt to the point where he could no longer conceive of himself without his Jacobin cap. On 3 August 1911 he was to write to Hildegard Krohn: 'If only I had been born at the time of the French Revolution. These days there's nothing to enthuse about, no cause to devote one's life to, it's worse than the plague and cholera combined (D 512).' A few weeks later he went further:

In my daydreams I always see myself as a Danton or someone manning a barricade; I cannot imagine myself without my Jacobin cap ... My God, if only I had been born at the time of the French Revolution, I should at least have known where to die (T: 15 September 1911).

The image of him sitting on the outside windowsill of David Baumgardt's flat in Charlottenburg singing the Marseillaise (D 11) is a startlingly vivid glimpse of the *real* Heym, as is that of him sitting writing poems like 'Ich verfluche dich, Gott' (L 18) in front of an open window, wearing only his Jacobin cap and sash.

Further evidence of his passionate interest in the French Revolution can be found in his diaries and in his work of every kind. That he identified with Robespierre – and with Danton – is also clear. His Jacobin sash is the outward sign of the revolutionary fervour which caused him to link the *ancien régime* with the Wilhelmine state which he so detested. Yet all this does not mean that he was a 'democrat' in the modern sense, for in fact he was the opposite: a Nietzschean individualist, pure and simple. His attachment to the French Revolution is more a matter of revolutionary enthusiasm than of reasoned political idealism; it is the 'greatness' of the events, the historic fervour of the times that means so much to him because he contrasts it with the banality of his own admittedly undemocratic age. Poetic 'Jacobin', yes; democrat, hardly – after all, did he not say: 'A republic is only the ideal form of state so long as no geniuses exist (PD 737).' In political terms he was a 'Nietzschean "aristocrat" '; but his rage is ultimately more metaphysical than political.

He was, then, a hothead: impetuous, reckless, headstrong, slap-dash, careless. He couldn't spell. He was vital, pleasure-loving; his zest for life was one of his most pronounced features. He was unanalytical, unphilosophical, essentially unintellectual: a sensation type. Those who knew him almost invariably refer to him as a natural genius and a natural phenomenon. He was naïve, sometimes childish. He was passionate (more passionate than anyone else has ever been was his characteristic way of putting it), vehement, open to a fault; but also shy, reserved, afraid of wearing his heart on his sleeve. A literary notebook known as the *Notizbüchlein* contains a relevant jotting – 'shyness concealed by poetic genius' – which clearly refers to himself. He was a dare-devil with a devil-may-care attitude, but also anxious, fatalistic, superstitious; the anxiety by which he had been ridden from an early age was in 1910 rapidly taking control of his life. He had a sunny, outgoing personality, but was also – increasingly – a prey to the blue devils (he knew the term and used it in his notebook) and to occasional tantrums. He had an extraordinarily strong visual imagination, in which he mostly lived (he told Hildegard Krohn that he lived 'for what he could see': *D* 508), and, as the critic Helmut Greulich first noted: 'He consorted with the heroes of certain novels as if they were real people.'[3] He rarely read *anything* without reference to himself; in a note he wrote: 'No one thinks about himself as much as I do', to which he added: 'Perhaps no one so misjudges himself (*T* 176).' He was highly sensitive, and therefore touchy, always liable to break into tears. A big softie, he also rightly saw (and drew) himself as Furor, for he was two persons in one; in a draft note addressed to Erwin Loewenson he wrote: 'I am very strong, and also very weak' (*T* 176), which was fundamentally true. Emmy Ball-Hennings, who met him shortly before his death, described him as half 'rowdy', half 'angel' (*D* 90). In many important ways he was the opposite of what he seemed – this is the most fundamental fact of all. It will not have taken the members of the Neue Club long to realize this.

The Neue Club developed, in autumn 1909, from a student society at the University of Berlin known as the 'Freie Wissenschaftliche Vereinigung'; this in turn had developed, in 1908, from an informal student debating society or discussion group apparently founded in 1907. The Neue Club as such was not a university society, although most of its members were university men. The president of the club was Kurt Hiller. Club members (initially Kurt Hiller, Jakob van Hoddis, Erwin Loewenson, Rudolf Majut, Erich Unger and John Wolfsohn; presently joined by David Baumgardt, Ernst Blass, Simon Guttmann,

Georg Heym, Robert Jentzsch, Friedrich Koffka and Friedrich Schulze-Maizier) used to foregather on Wednesday evenings, in the 'Fledermauszimmer' of the Nollendorf Casino (Kleiststraße) in order to discuss aesthetic and related questions. The club had no 'programme' as such, for it existed in order to further individualism; in a general sense, however, the members (who held different views on many subjects) came together in perceiving the need for change; their aesthetic and social views identified them as typical members of the Expressionist generation in today's terms. Erwin Loewenson summarized the nature and aim of the club in a letter to Frank Wedekind in which he described it as: 'An association of students and young artists who have vowed no longer to stand idly by, watching the obscenities of the age, but to make known their disgust at the pettiness of contemporary art and science and their admiration for exceptional individuals (D 394).' No doubt Loewenson described the club in similar terms to Georg Heym, who was the archetypal lone wolf, and as such already shared the club members' basically Nietzschean attitudes.

Kurt Hiller later related how Simon Guttmann – then eighteen or nineteen – one day appeared in the Nollendorf Casino café and announced that he had discovered a genius. The other members of the Neue Club naturally greeted the announcement with hoots of laughter. When Guttmann insisted that it was true, and that the genius in question was one 'Georg Heym with a y', Hiller said that in that case the said Heym should be dragged along to the next club evening and made to read some of his work. This duly happened in late April 1910, when Heym read his first two 'Berlin' poems. The members were impressed by his work and by Heym's openness and transparent honesty and good nature. It was the general view that this Georg Heym was 'a likely lad' (D 14) and quite possibly a genius. He was promptly invited to join the club, which he did on the spot.[4]

Erwin Loewenson presumably brought *Atalanta* with him to this meeting, it having been passed on to him by Guttmann. Heym appears to have read some of it to the club members; no doubt it was the subject of vigorous discussion. What mattered was that it had served its purpose in introducing Heym to what was to be in many ways his spiritual home. Loewenson then invited Heym to attend (as a spectator) the first cabaret evening on 1 June 1910. Heym responded to Loewenson's invitation by saying that he would be delighted to do so provided it did not cost him anything; he described himself as being 'as poor as a church mouse', and signed himself 'Georg Heym with a y, alias Robespierre on his cart' (T 203). At the second cabaret evening, on 6 July 1910, Heym gave the first public reading of some of his poems.

Loewenson was surely right when he said of Heym: 'The break with conventional ideas only came about once he belonged to a group which was in a continual flux and which was cheerfully furious [with the established order], sure of itself, and nothing if not independent-minded (D 391).' Rudolf Balcke later described Heym's attitude towards the Neue Club:

At first Heym could find no common ground with this highly intellectual group. But he was hoping that the Neue Club might be his springboard to poetic fame. To start with he felt that he had nothing in common with these people so much more rational and intellectual than himself. But once they had recognized him as a poet, he regarded himself as belonging to the group.[5]

Heym's closest friends in the club were Jentzsch, van Hoddis, Guttmann, Loewenson and Wolfsohn. Van Hoddis, who lived on his nerves, was the one who was always egging the others on;[6] at this time a most articulate critic of poetry, he became for Heym an absolute authority: 'Heym crossed things out when van Hoddis told him to do so.'[7] Heym's attitude towards van Hoddis was a mixture of respect and rivalry. He was, naturally enough, jealous of the extraordinary reputation of van Hoddis's 'Weltende', knowing that he was himself a far better poet than van Hoddis. On the other hand, he and van Hoddis clearly got on quite well on one level; when there was a major row following the discovery of a girl in Heym's room at home, it was van Hoddis who simply lent him the key of his flat until it had blown over. In some obscure way van Hoddis was to feel responsible for Heym's death, which was a contributory factor in his own nervous breakdown that year; although not able to carry it out, he later planned to write a tragedy entitled Der Tod Georg Heyms.

In the present context the tensions and conflicts within the Neue Club between big-enders and little-enders, alias voluntarists and ideologues, which were caused by a mixture of personal jealousies and aesthetic wrangles regarding the place of conceptualism in poetry, are unimportant because Heym had no part in them; all that matters is that, partly as a result of the split in the club, but mainly because of his genius and amiably forceful character, Heym soon became a central figure in it:

Anyone who knew him before his poems were published, anyone who heard him read his work, was conscious of listening to the eternal voice of a hurricane or surging sea. He embodied the idea of poetic inspiration ... and anyone who remembers the evenings on which this burly student declaimed his vivid, violent verses in that characteristic monotone of his, surging like the sea's own rhythms, had the tremendous, unforgettable awareness of listening to a great poet ... There he sat with us, reading from sheets of manuscript those grandiose poems which have nothing to do with literature, with any literary programme, with style or form, but which simply grew organically, assuming a shape which made discussion or diagnosis irrelevant. Never again were we so carried away, so deeply moved (Ernst Blass, in D 173, 177).

He features in all the 'Neopathetisches Cabaret' evenings organized by the club from the second evening onwards (with the exception of the seventh evening, when he was in Munich), but seems to have been very casual and relaxed about the central role his readings played in the club's programmes. In his diary he does not even bother to mention any meeting after the first two (not even the Georg Heym Evening on 15 May 1911); that this is not just because the diary rarely documents 'outer' events is shown by the fact that there is virtually no mention of these readings in his published letters. His main diary entry on the subject shows that after years of panting for fame, he had suddenly realized that what matters is not the applause of the unknowing, but his own awareness of a piece well written:

At a Neo-Pathetisches Cabaret yesterday I read some poems which received a lot of applause. But if that's fame ... All I know is that it suddenly seemed to me as though it was animals who were looking at me out of the darkness of the room and as though the goats [literally oxen] were sitting at the front bleating at me. I thought: the poems are too good for you, much too good (T 139).

The derogatory word 'beklatscht' (for 'applause') already implies the dubious nature of this success, but what is most remarkable is the Ensor-like way in which the audience is reduced to a sea of animal masks.[8] It looks as though he knew Ensor's work; although he could not have seen The Entry of Christ into Brussels in 1889 in the original, which was not exhibited until 1929, he could have seen reproductions of much of Ensor's work, for instance in the November 1898 number of

La Plume (also issued in book form in 1899), or – more likely – in Emile Verhaeren's *James Ensor* (1908). His account of his reading is provocatively reminiscent of Ensor's strange painting, with Heym playing the role of Ensor/Christ surrounded by the gaping, gawping crowd. The next day Heym was furious to find that the 'Preßhengst' (literally 'press stallion', in English 'press jackal' – a continuation of the Ensor-like metaphor) of the liberal *Berliner Tageblatt* (his preferred paper) had called him a disciple of Stefan George, a subject on which he was very touchy. It is as well that his response (*D* 604) was never sent, for it was seriously outspoken. For better or worse, then, from 6 July 1910 he was exposed to the gawping of the public and the bleating of the press.

After his second reading on 9 November 1910 he noted laconically: 'Reading yesterday. Audience rowdy. Armin Wassermann read my "Vorstadt". Spontaneous applause. The audience quietened down and listened (*T 149*).' In a letter to Ernst Rowohlt of *c.* 11 December 1910 he mentions that the Neopathetisches Cabaret meeting on 9 December, at which he again read some of his poems, was attended by Karl Kraus, Franz Pfemfert and Herwarth Walden; he adds that Kraus made a complimentary comment on his work. We, for our part, may add that Herwarth Walden showed uncommonly bad judgement when, a fortnight later, he rejected two of Heym's poems, one of them the masterpiece 'Der Hunger', for publication in *Der Sturm*. Presumably literary politics and cliquishness came into it, for by this time the Neue Club was closely associated with the rival periodical, *Der Demokrat*, which was shortly (in February 1911) to turn into *Die Aktion*.

That Heym plays down his Neopathetisches Cabaret readings is not surprising. The Neue Club was clearly important to him above all as a source of encouragement. His membership of it gave him a badly needed fresh start, prompting him to write kinds and forms and a style of poetry he had not written before. For this encouragement he must have been deeply grateful. On the other hand, what mattered to him was the actual excitement of writing the poem; knowing that he was writing better than ever, and that his work was appreciated and valued, will have enhanced that excitement; but he was curiously little interested in the finished object once it had gone cold: writing about this on 22 November 1910 he contrasts his attitude with that of Richard Strauss: 'I recently read that that musical idiot Strauss had let it be known that he was going to retire to spend a whole winter immersed in the beauties of the score of his *Elektra*. What a fool. Admiring the beauty of his reflection, just like a monkey, with life so short (*T* 151).' Obsessed as he is with the passing of time, Heym takes the view expressed by Nietzsche in the second of his *Unzeitgemässe Betrachtungen*, that loving the past means robbing the future. Reading his poems at Neopathetisches Cabaret meetings brought him momentary satisfaction, but more important was the recognition these readings helped to bring. The most significant and tangible outcome of his membership of the Neue Club was a contract from Ernst Rowohlt for the volume on which, more than on anything else, his name still depends.

It would, of course, be wrong to imagine that Heym spent the time between March and November 1910 (when his correspondence with Rowohlt began) exclusively in the company of fellow-members of the Neue Club. Apart from anything else, he was based in Jena from the end of April until early August. He matriculated at Jena on 4 May 1910, having gone there with Rudolf Balcke, because they had come to the conclusion that they would have more chance of passing their part one examination in Law if they took it not at the Supreme Court in Berlin but at the provincial Court of Appeal at Naumburg, which entailed spending two terms at Jena. It soon became apparent, however, that Jena was too congenial a place to enhance their chances of passing the examination. They therefore returned to Berlin after one term and went to a crammer.

Before going to Jena Heym could have seen the comet which appeared on 17 January 1910 as a trailblazer for Halley's Comet. It was, however, at Jena that he saw Halley's Comet on the occasion of its spectacular return in the early hours of the morning of 19 May 1910, for he was very likely among the crowds of people who stayed up to see it, its advent having given rise to what the *Annual Register* called 'the utmost alarm'. The poem 'Die Menschen stehen vorwärts in den Straßen' (*L* 440) represents such a belated reaction to Halley's Comet (it was written in late October 1911) that it could equally well have been inspired not so much by the comet itself as by F. S. Archenhold's book *Kometen, Weltuntergangsprophezeiungen und der Halleysche Komet*, which came out in 1910.

While living in Jena Heym travelled back to Berlin frequently, a journey of some two hundred kilometres; but he was in only sporadic touch with the Neue Club, and was therefore spared some of its time-consuming ideological vicissitudes. Not that he would have had much time for them anyway.

Having returned from Jena, he spent the second half of August on holiday at Swinemünde and at Sellin on the island of Rügen. It was at Sellin that he met Lily Friedeberg, who later wrote an account (D 34–8) of the rough-and-tumble of their boy-meets-girl brief episode, which Heym as usual took too seriously (cf. T 141). On 31 August he wrote Lily a letter which, as we shall see, is interesting for what he says about his career plans.⁹

Leaving aside the minor detail of his approaching part one law finals, involving a dissertation to be completed in September, we now come to the point at which his membership of the Neue Club bears fruit. On 1 October 1910, thanks to the mediation of a Neue Club friend, Heinrich Eduard Jacob, he published his first two poems, 'Laubenkolonie' (L 109, retitled 'Laubenfest') and 'Vorortbahnhof' (L 102), in the weekly Herold. In a general way the turn to subjects reflecting contemporary social reality was confirmed by his membership of the Neue Club, but these two poems owe a more specific, and in some ways more characteristic, debt to the work of the Berlin painter Hans Baluschek, whose Laubenfest Heym had seen at the last Secession exhibition. Ernst Balcke later wrote in his review of Der ewige Tag:

Occasionally the author turns his back on death and its attributes, and gives instead a description of simple events, such as a charabanc ride or a Berlin outdoor party [Laubenfest], the latter reminiscent of a painting by [Hans] Baluschek in the last Secession exhibition. My impression is that Heym is not really at home with such small-scale subjects. His preference is for the boundless, the gigantic ... with which an idyllic view of things cannot be reconciled. No doubt he feels that life in a metropolis cannot be adequately described in terms of the cosiness of a Laubenfest or of a Sunday-afternoon charabanc ride (D 194).

Seeing Baluschek's Laubenfest appears to have prompted Heym to write his 'Laubenkolonie', but he is no doubt also writing from experience, for the Berlin 'allotments' were well known. Of greater significance at this stage is the fact that on 23 November 'Berlin II' appeared in Pfemfert's Der Demokrat. Kurt Wolff read the poem there and drew Ernst Rowohlt's attention to it; Rowohlt (who, like Wolff, was Heym's own age) invited Heym to offer him a manuscript (either poetry or prose). Within rather less than six months of joining the Neue Club

Heym had thus reached the most important milestone of his poetic career. While it is possible to argue that in some ways his membership of the Neue Club had a deleterious effect on his poetry, there can be no doubt that he would have been extremely unlikely to have had a contract with Ernst Rowohlt in his pocket by this time if it had not been for Simon Guttmann, who was instrumental both in getting 'Berlin II' published in *Der Demokrat* and in getting Heym accepted as a member of the Neue Club. The next six months were spent preparing his first collection; before coming to this we need to go back, for on a day-to-day basis the Neue Club is less important than the inner events of the diary.

☐ DESTINY

On the very first page of the diary which we have now reached (the third, dating from 17 June to 7 December 1910) Heym wrote: 'I am starting my third diary under what may be more auspicious circumstances ... In general terms I am now happier and calmer than I used to be. *I am settling in to the robust style which surrounds me like a fortification*' (the italics are Loewenson's, who underlined the words when the diary was in his possession). This is true, for he has reached a new phase in his life, but it is also misleading, as he goes on to make clear when he writes 'Why doesn't someone assassinate the Kaiser or the Tsar? They are simply being allowed to go on doing harm. Why doesn't someone start a revolution? A craving for something to happen is the keynote of my present phase (*T* 135).' This craving for action, for excitement, for something to happen, no matter what, is a personal characteristic which was exacerbated as he became more outraged by his legal studies and anxious about the outcome of his forthcoming examination, and as his sense of time running out got sharper. It connects with his partly real, partly unreal plans for a future career (as cavalry officer; as dragoman; as revolutionary) which he must have known in his heart would never be. Above all, the craving for excitement represents a personal need to escape from a present and a future which are both perceived as intolerable: ennui, having to study law – while one has poems coming out of one's ears – to what end? To end up working for a state which one detests? To become a legal spittoon-holder? Ever since being transported to Neuruppin he had been praying for something to happen. At first this had been a matter of temperament. Now it was a matter of urgency, for unless something did happen, he would find himself working for the 'lousy rotten Prussian state' (*T* 146). While this was not the main reason for his depression at this time, it was unquestionably a contributory factor. And he was plagued not only by ennui, but also by fear of death, a need to forget the inexorably approaching future.

The apocalyptic mood which so many of his later poems explore has a terrifying personal dimension; the horrors and unhappiness of his life make the most complete and hideous sense once one realizes him to have foreseen how it would end. A few months before his death he wrote: 'It could perhaps be argued that my poems are the best proof of the existence of a metaphysical realm whose black tentacles stretch far into our fleeting days' (*T* 15 September 1911). It is typical of him that the image (it is a cloud image) preceded the thought. But this does not mean that he had any illusions about Art, for he also recorded his view that 'Poetry ... is a very poor substitute for action and life' (*T* 7 December 1910). He would not have been Georg Heym if he had taken any other view. There is a considerable difference between Heym's earlier and later diaries and the view of life which goes with them:

In the [later] diary one sees a man who is no doubt calmer than he was in his Neuruppin days, but who is also obsessed by the problem of existence, a man who seems to be forever brooding on this.[10]

While the idea of a hostile personal destiny runs right through the diaries, following the break with Hedi Weißenfels on his return to Berlin in late 1908, and more especially in the last eighteen months or so of his life, his view of life becomes radically pessimistic.

When Heym read his poems at a Neue Club meeting on 15 May 1911, he was compared to Dante. Poets' friends make extravagant comparisons, but this particular one forms a leitmotif in early reviews. Thus François Pauwels, reviewing *Der ewige Tag*, noted that Heym 'deploys images that are reminiscent of Dante in their originality and power' (*D* 244). What prompted such comparisons were, of course, his visions of purgatory and Hell. They are omnipresent in his work. He has three set-piece descriptions of Hell. The first, in May 1910, forms the first part of 'Styx'; it is spoilt by voyeuristic overwriting. The second is found in *Atalanta oder Die Angst* (late 1910–11), quite the most remarkable thing in which is Atalanta's vision of Hell, which is similarly Dantesque:

... Die weite Helle
Des bodenlosen Nichts. Die langen Ketten,
Daran die Geister wie ein Bienenschwarm
Mit Bergeslast sich schaukelnd hin und her
Mich niederzogen in den weiten Fall
Der hellen Klüfte, wo Gelächter rief
Von jedem Grat der Schlünde, jedem Karst,
Und großen Nestern, drin die graue Brut
Der Teufel saß, in schwarzem Federkleid,
Wie ungeheure Geier auf dem Horst.
Wo tief ihr Abgrund unermeßlich sank
In ungeheurer Räume hohlen Schall,
Da auf dem meilentiefen Grund die Flut
Des Riesenbottichs, wie ein Meer so weiß
Zum Horizonte schwamm, Verdammter voll,
Weißglühend, unersättlichen Geschreis (*PD* 381f.).

The bright expanse of bottomless nothingness. The long chains by means of which the spirits of the dead, struggling like a swarm of overloaded bees, were pulling me down into the great abysses, where laughter rang out from every ridge of those maws, from every plateau, from great nests in which nondescript packs of devils sat, dressed in black feathers, like great vultures on their eyries; while the abyss dropped down immeasurably far into enormous, hollow-sounding chambers, at the bottom of which, a mile down, the waters of that boundless basin flowed towards the horizon, white as an ocean, full of the damned, burning bright, full of their never-ending screams.

In calling such descriptions 'Dantesque', I mean both that they are, in general, comparable to descriptions in Dante (which makes them characteristically old-fashioned), and that they may derive their inspiration partly from Dante; no doubt they also owe some of their images to paintings of Hell which he had seen on his various visits to art galleries. Dante first appears in Heym's diary in 1905, in a biographical context ('Dante waited sixteen years for Beatrice', he writes apropos his own love-life); the last reference comes in a letter to Hildegard Krohn written in early June 1911, where he writes of 'the Dante' (which volume is in question is not recorded).

Whatever the extent to which these two visions of Hell are indebted to Dante, the third, which is the first poem in the cycle 'Die Hölle' (August 1911), was written shortly after Heym had been reading

Dante. Although in origin a satirical reaction to his experiences in the District Court at Wusterhausen an der Dosse, which he regarded as Hell, this is also one of his great set-piece poems. In it Hell is no longer Death. It is life; life is Hell:

> Ich dachte viel der Schrecken zu erfahren,
> Als ich an ihren hohen Toren stand
> Abgründe rot und Meere voller Brand
> Hinter den großen Riegeln zu gewahren,
>
> Und sah ein Land voll ausgespannter Öde,
> Und Monde bleich, wie ein paar starre Tränen.
> Man gab mir keinen Gruß zurück. Nur blöde
> Sahn mich die Schatten an mit lautem Gähnen.
>
> Die Unterwelt, sie gleicht zu sehr der Erde:
> Im Schlamm des Hades lag ein Krokodil.
> Man warf auch hier nach seinem Kopf zum Spiel,
> Vielleicht mit etwas müderer Gebärde.
>
> Wanderer gingen in den Sonntagsröcken,
> Sie sprachen von den Sorgen dieser Wochen
> Und freuten sich, wenn junge Falten krochen
> Aus ihrer Freunde Stirn wie Dornenhecken.
>
> Laternen wurden durch die Nacht geschwungen,
> Und einen Toten trug man uns vorbei.
> Er war im ewig grauen Einerlei
> Vor Langeweile wie ein Pilz zersprungen (*L* 327f.).

('Hell, I') I expected to experience many terrors as I stood at its great gates, expected to see behind those great bolts red abysses and seas of fire,

And saw instead a land of endless devastation, and pale moons looking like glassy tears. No one returned my greeting; the shades merely looked at me cretinously as they yawned out loud.

The underworld too much resembles the world: in the mud of Hades lay a crocodile. Here too they threw stones at its head for fun, perhaps with a somewhat wearier gesture.

Passers-by were dressed in their Sunday best; they spoke of the week's worries and were delighted when new wrinkles like thorn hedges appeared on their friends' foreheads.

Lanterns came swinging through the night, and a dead man was carried past us. In the never-ending grey monotony he had burst like a puffball, with ennui.

Though this final vision of Hell inevitably takes one back to Dante, the comparison brings out Heym's limitation – or his modernity – for with him there is no question of any compensating beatific vision. His inferno is, rather, like Baudelaire's and Schopenhauer's; both in 'Die Hölle, I' and in 'Die Vorstadt' (*L* 133f.) it is that described by Schopenhauer ('The world *is* Hell'). When he writes in his diary: 'Nothing befits man more than grief and tears. And in between the boredom, boredom' (*T* 27 December 1909), this could be Schopenhauer describing the burden of existence.

If Baudelaire is Heym's poet, his philosopher is Schopenhauer. His interest in Schopenhauer dated back to summer 1905, when he was pondering suicide:

I am afraid of life. There are hours when I feel immensely happy, but with how much suffering has this been bought. Gentle Nirvana, being absorbed into the universe. I too may say that 'Our existence is an act of folly committed by others', but for all that I still wish to live' (*T* 4 June 1905).

The definition of existence comes from Schopenhauer's 'The Vanity and Suffering of Life'. The determinedly pessimistic frame of mind in which he went to Neuruppin had got out of hand, had turned into the radical 'Weltschmerz' which was to dog him for the rest of his life. How much of Schopenhauer he read in 1905 is not clear; what is certain is that he read the essay on death in 1906, probably in a selection which also included the essays on the life of the species, heredity and, possibly, the metaphysics of love. In 1910 he borrowed the whole of Schopenhauer from David Baumgardt; when it was eventually returned, two blank pages of *Die Welt als Wille und Vorstellung* were adorned with a typical 'Heymerei'. We may safely assume that he read the famous Fourth Book of *Die Welt als Wille und Vorstellung*, which summarizes Schopenhauer's philosophy and contains much that parallels his own view of life (life as Hell on earth; the prison of life; ennui; the vanity and suffering of life; death; the suicide theme; etc.). In spring 1911 he made a note of 'Parerga [und] Paralipomena [.] Grundl[age] der Moral'.[11] If he read Baumgardt's Schopenhauer, he will already have known *Parerga und Paralipomena*, which contains much to interest him. He is unlikely to have read *Über die Grundlage der Moral*, Schopenhauer's least known and most academic work.

Just as some of Heym's most characteristic images are paralleled in

Van Gogh, so too a number of his ideas are in effect elaborated by Schopenhauer; but he was not, of course, a Schopenhauerian or even a thinker, as his reported reaction to the mention of Kant shows. His 'philosophy' was existential, visceral, beyond his control. He must have admired Schopenhauer, above all, as an artist in words, someone who said exactly what he thought both forcefully and with style. No doubt he was attracted by Schopenhauer's lucubrations on the subjects of time and death, and will certainly have approved the view of Art as man's momentary deliverance from the toils of life, but it seems doubtful that Heym, had he lived, would have come round to sharing the philosopher's view of the wisdom of renunciation; it is much more likely that he, like Verlaine, would have refused to learn from experience, would have scorned to subjugate his will-to-life, would have remained passionately in love with life until whatever other quietus it prepared for him.

By summer 1910 Heym is more than ever obsessed with the idea of a malign personal destiny, justifying his thoughts on the matter on 26 June: 'The idea of an amoral Fate is clearly more profound than that of a moral God, a God who is obliged to be moral.' He clearly regarded his work as having a 'metaphysical' depth which that of many of the Berlin poets lacked, and while his poetry is hardly 'metaphysical' in literary-historical terms, it is the product of a fully developed pessimistic *Weltanschauung*. In other words, it conveys not just a view of society, but a view of life, that view of life being bitterly pessimistic:

I can prove that no God exists, or at least no benign God. A widow loses all her children one after the other. Every night she prays for the last one to be preserved. It dies. Why? What moral idea is at work here? People resort to the pathetic argument that God's thoughts are loftier than man's, but what would be the use of any lofty thought which could not take on board this simple little request? If a benign God existed, his heart would have been torn by so much suffering; he would not only have kept his own Son alive, but would have commanded everyone else's dead sons to leave their charnel-houses. This so-called benign God just sits up there behind his clouds and never raises a finger. Everything about him is stone: he is deaf, hollow, empty.

The idea of a malign God or malign Fate has much more to be said for it, for everything that happens either is or becomes evil. Good fortune can no more be seen than can a grain of gold dust in the desert. Why does the lord of the universe always remain hidden, why does he never show any sign of life?

Because he is malevolent, cold and silent as the cloud-figures who always have their heads averted from the earth, as though they are privy to some terrible secret and have to carry it with them through all eternity to a destination that is dark, unknown and remote (*T* 26 June 1910).

His thoughts on the subject of God culminate two months later in the view that, if God existed, he should be hanged for his infinite cruelty (*T* 17 August 1910). While his wording implies a Nietzschean view of 'der alte Gott', his comment is far from being a satirical *bon mot*. In the poem 'Das infernalische Abendmahl' (*L* 231–5), which owes its atmosphere to the black mass celebrated in Merezhkovsky's *Leonardo da Vinci*, there is a similar identification of Christ and Satan (cf. the confusion in Giovanni Boltraffio's mind on this subject in Merezhkovsky's novel). Clearly Heym is well on the way to his characteristic late belief in the malignity of human destiny,[12] although his view of God remains essentially Greek:

It is far more ethical to have several gods than to have one. It is far more ethical to personify one's gods than it is to imagine a great bubble of nothingness havering around overhead. Why is it that ancient Greek religion is not only more aesthetic (which is obviously the case), but also more ethical? Because those suffering from the same disease – love, say – resorted to the same god. Because they sacrificed together, they came to know one another's troubles, and were therefore drawn closer together. And forging closer links between people is certainly the noblest function of the gods (*T* 31 December 1910).

In other diary entries at this time he relates his increasingly morbid view of life to his own situation, in which, as in his temperament, it has its origin:

I suppose I haven't really managed to come to terms with my sadness yet. Feelings often overwhelm me right out of the blue; I feel that I am simply getting older and older all the time without ever achieving anything. I have found neither fame nor love. It is terrible. It can't have been any worse even in 1820. Everything is always the same, so boring, boring, boring. Nothing ever happens, absolutely nothing. If only something would happen which would not leave this stale taste of commonplaceness. If I ask myself what the point of my life has been so far, I am at a loss for an answer. Nothing but agony, misery, wretchedness of every kind. You say, dear Wolfsohn, that no one has ever struck you as being as healthy as me. Alas, no, my dear fellow, ... What you see is only a mask which I wear with such skill. I am wretched with listlessness, cowardly for want of any danger to face. If only I could cut the cord which is keeping me tethered to the ground. If only something would happen. If only barricades were being built again. I should be the first to mount them; even with a bullet in my heart I should like to feel the intoxication of enthusiasm. Or even if someone would only begin a war, it need not be a just one. This peace is so rottenly oleaginous and greasy, like the surface of old furniture (*T* 6 July 1910).

All this speaks for itself. The only thing that needs underlining is its importance (including the importance of the mask, cf. *T* 155: 'Heym wears a mask, Hoddis does not'): it is this view of life that lies behind and explains those terrible black tales (discussed in Chapter VIII).

On 17 June he said that he would like to cut loose the balloon-man's balloons, just for the hell of it, but this new entry shows that the balloon stands for himself, for his wish to break free. The baroque metaphors which he uses in his diary ('One is the plaything of every breath of wind ... I am drifting like a ship [without a rudder]' – *T* 20 September, 26 October 1910) emphasize his wretched feeling of drifting out of control, the plaything of a malign fate. This was one of his strongest feelings, and was no doubt what caused him to rediscover the beauty of clouds at this time; reading Baudelaire and rereading Merezhkovsky will have confirmed him in his visionary and supersti-tious inclination to see cloud-patterns as portents.

The only things that kept him going that summer and autumn were his poetry, which was going extremely well, and his new enthusiasms (notably Van Gogh; Keats and Shelley; Rimbaud, Baudel-aire and Verlaine). He was particularly attached to 'the divine' Rimbaud whose portrait he had on the wall of his room; we shall see that his enthusiasm for his other private gods was scarcely less extreme. His 1911 *Notizbüchlein* shows that he was interested by what he had heard of Swinburne, Sterne and Swift.

On 23 November 1910 the sonnet 'Berlin II' ('Beteerte Fässer rollten') (discussed in Chapter VII below) appeared in Franz Pfemfert's *Der Demokrat*. Ernst Rowohlt, a go-ahead young publisher of Heym's own age, had his attention drawn to the poem by Kurt Wolff (who was to take over Rowohlt Verlag at the end of 1912), read the poem and was so impressed that he promptly wrote to Heym inviting him to submit work for possible publication. His letter, a landmark in Heym's life, was dated 30 November 1910; it read as follows:

Dear Sir,

Having had my attention drawn to you by your sonnet in No. 48 of the *Demokrat*, I take the liberty of inquiring whether you could not let me have a manuscript for consideration, either poetry or prose. I should be greatly interested to see such a manuscript, and hope that you may be able to satisfy my wish in the near future.

For the present I remain,
Yours very sincerely,
Ernst Rowohlt (*T* 222)

The letter was as flattering as it was encouraging. When he received it, via Franz Pfemfert, Heym lost no time replying: 'What I can offer you is a volume of poems which have been called quite new in German literature by a number of independent critics (*T* 224).' He sent in the poems he already had in typescript, plus a few others, and for good measure also mentioned *Atalanta* and 'ein anderes großes Drama' ('another major drama') on which he was working. He added: 'My prose is not suitable for publication since it is concerned almost entirely with the problems of love', an odd comment in view of the fact that his *Novellen* were neither concerned with 'dem Problem der Erotik' nor indeed written. This is, I think, the point: Heym is no doubt thinking of 'Die Novella der Liebe' (1907), but he is mainly flying a kite, hoping to interest Rowohlt in the tales which he is planning to write, and which were in fact mostly written between January and June 1911.

Two days later he sent Rowohlt two further consignments of poems, making a total of about forty. He said that he could have sent another thirty, but did not regard them as good enough. As title for the collection he suggested *Das Meer*; the following day (7 December 1910) he wrote again changing the title to *Die Wolken*; both sea and clouds were particularly important to him.

Like Baudelaire – and like the Romantic poets, who revered them as manifestations of 'energy divine' – Heym was fascinated by clouds. On 29 June 1910 he wrote in his diary that 'One ought to do nothing but watch the clouds, the faraway mysterious clouds', and in the poem 'O Wolkenland...' (*L* 699f.) he explains why:

O Wolkenland, zu dessen Küsten fliehen
Stets die Gedanken, suchen sie Vergessen.
O Wolken, die am Himmel einsam ziehen,
Ihr könnt allein die Einsamkeit ermessen (*L* 699).

O land of clouds, to whose coasts our thoughts forever flee, seeking forgetfulness. O clouds, sailing lonely through the skies, you alone can measure [our] loneliness.

This love of clouds, which is seen in poem after poem and is confirmed by the fact that his original title for *Der ewige Tag* was *Die Wolken*, goes right back to his childhood, as is shown by an autobiographical passage in the fragmentary drama *Die Revolution*, in which the revolutionary Mögling says:

How stormy and thundery it is outside, Marie. How the clouds are coming across the lake. The wild army of a March night. What sadness there is in the clouds. As a child I always wanted to play with them, to catch them. But they never came to me, they always stayed far away; my mother consoled me with my toy lamb; now no one consoles me for their sadness. I once knew a shepherd who has long been dead. When he lay on the mountain pasture and played his flute, all the clouds in the sky would come to him; they would sit down in a circle on the bare mountain peaks and would listen to his tune.

The little white cloud-children were always flying around his head. In his flute dwelt all the dead who had been struck by lightning on the moor and who had been drowned at sea on autumn nights. What a sad tune it was. And when it was over, all the clouds would begin to cry and it would rain day and night. Are they not beautiful when a storm blows them across the sea and they hang low over the breakers? Do they not look like the sails of the Spanish fleet which carried Columbus to the new world? Are they not freedom itself? (*PD* 688f.)

This memorable passage both confirms that there are passages of poetry waiting to be discovered in the dramas and dramatic fragments, and also shows that Büchner left his mark on Heym, for the preternatural clarity or naïvety here is all Büchner, from whose *Woyzeck* the name Marie may derive.

This passage shows that Heym associated clouds with 'infinite sadness' (*T* 136) and with the freedom that only comes in death. It was because of his childhood love of clouds that he was so moved in 1901 when he saw Martin Brandenburg's painting *Die Menschen unter der Wolke* at the Third Secession exhibition in Berlin.[13] This work, which he described as 'one of the few pictures I will never forget' (*T* 29 September 1909), is emblematic of his whole view of life. He was fascinated by clouds because of their beauty and ambiguity, and also regarded them as signs. Obvious symbols of the passing of time, of which he was so aware, clouds represent a higher realm of beauty and promise escape from earth-bound misery, but they also, and more often, mockingly mirror the scene below. Thus the first striking cloud-description in Heym's diary – 'In the East there was a great bank of cloud like a high mountain range with its rock walls and gullies lit by the setting sun' (*T* 14 April 1909) – is simply a reflection of the sublimity of nature, lit by the sun which he worshipped. A number of cloud-formations are animated. On 3 February 1908 he notes 'a big cloud shaped like a broad-necked bull's head looking down at the earth', and on 30 November 1910 he writes: 'I am watching the clouds, yellowish and white fish and pheasants, a mouse against a blue background. And on the right a marvellous phantom like a huge polyp with countless long skinny arms.' Such images illustrate the tendency of Heym's imagination to see objects in animal form (a tendency which he perhaps acquired from and certainly shared with Merezhkovsky), as well as recalling Nietzsche's *Thus Spake Zarathustra* (XLVIII: 'The passing clouds I detest, those stealthy cats of prey: they take from thee and me what is common to us').

Typical of Heym is a striking cloud-image noted in the diary on 20 September 1910:

Clouds: a huge black area like a gigantic black country is covering the southern sky. To the right, to the West, it is followed by a broad band of deep red spanning the whole sky. A number of long red streamers are hanging down from it, like the grapes on the brow of a crowned god.

Right on top, in the middle, looking like a huge spiral nebula, is a diaphanous red cloud which is slowly dissolving into the deep blue around it. When I saw this I was so giddy with delight that I almost fell down.

Once his imagination has seen it thus, the cloud-formation becomes a revelation, a sign to the poet from one of 'his' gods, while in poetic terms this remarkable image prefigures that of 'Der Gott der Stadt' elaborated two months later (see Chapter VII below).

Heym gave clouds darker associations than did Baudelaire and Brecht, for he connected them with the dead, writing in 'Den Wolken II' (*L* 678f.):

Der Toten Geister seid ihr, die zum Flusse
Zum überladnen Kahn der Wesenlosen
Der Boote führt...

You are the spirits of the dead being escorted to the river, to the ferry overladen with the lifeless.

In another poem, 'Die Stadt in den Wolken' (*L* 628f.), he writes of a cloud-necropolis. This in turn suggests that when he writes of his work as 'the best proof there is of the existence of a metaphysical realm which extends its black peninsulas deep into our fleeting days' (*T* 15 September 1911), he is developing what was originally a cloud-image; the 'metaphyscial realm' with its black peninsulas is a variant of the 'gigantic black country' noted above. It is therefore the realm of death whose fingers or tendrils stretch down into 'our fleeting days'.

On the same day (7 December 1910) as he wrote to Rowohlt changing the title of his collection to *Die Wolken*, Heym also sent in *Atalanta* and again mentioned his prose, this time in an even more intriguing and misleading way: 'My novellas, which I intend to take in hand at the end of January, will deal partly with problems of love, partly with various arcane cults – I am currently working in the Royal Library [in Berlin] on little-known areas of literature and clandestine publications (*T* 228f.).' Although it is true that Heym was interested in Indian religion and in Rudolf Steiner's thought at this stage, he exaggerates his interests and concerns; besides, the tales, when they came to be written, showed that what he had been reading was Poe.

Rowohlt evidently asked for more poems in order to give him some leeway. Heym replied on about 27 December promising some further poems and changing the proposed title yet again ('after consultation'), this time into *Der ewige Tag* (or *Der metallene Tag*) (*T* 233). Clearly the best title was finally chosen. On 31 December he duly sent in another twenty or thirty poems, together with an interesting letter, part of which reads as follows:

I would add that at the same time I am also sending you a collection of poems, among which are to be found those which I consider my best – 'Die Dämonen der Städte', 'Der Gott der Stadt', 'Die Wanderer', 'Nero', etc. Altogether you will now have some 60–70 poems – quite enough, I imagine, to fill a volume.

The poems in question, and a handful of others, I initially intended not to publish, on the ground that the time was perhaps not yet ripe for them or for a poem like 'Fieberspital'. However, prompted by my friends, I have now decided to publish them (*T* 232f.)

He was not always, it should be added, the best judge of his own work.

Rowohlt was satisfied with the poems he now had. Heym received the first proofs in mid-February and corrected them in such a slapdash way that the publication of the book was delayed; it eventually appeared on 20 April 1911, just a week after Heym had sent Rowohlt a first batch of 'Novellen'.

☐ CAREER

While this correspondence was going on (and it was a fussy and impatient one on his part), Heym was also busy studying with his crammer, one Dr Gebhardt – probably Richard Gebhardt, author of a Leipzig dissertation on *Der Erwerb des Eigentums an Fahrnis* ... (1909), and of *Römisches Recht. Ein Hilfsbuch für Studierende und Doktoranden* (Hanover, 1911) – for the 'erste juristische Staatsprüfung'. A necessary dissertation, 'Die Reform der Städteordnung durch den Freiherrn von Stein 1808', had been completed at the beginning of September (thanks, no doubt, to the assistance of Heym's friends), shortly before the publication of the two poems in the *Herold*; by late November Rowohlt had decided to offer Heym a contract after reading 'Berlin II' in *Der Demokrat*. In the meantime Heym had the first part of his law finals to prepare for. In order to see what they were up against, he and Rudolf Balcke attended some of the examinations, which were public, in November 1910. It is to this experience that we owe one of Heym's most famous satires, 'Die Professoren' (*L* 157), the first draft of which bore the title 'Das Examen', which made its personal relevance clearer. Max Liebermann's picture *Professorenkonvent* of 1906 provides an interesting parallel. At this time Heym's father seems to have been using the threat of a military career as a way of getting him to work at his law books; in a letter to Heym dated 13 November 1910 Simon Guttmann quoted himself as saying to Kurt Hiller: 'Heym is in a desperate state. Says he's bound to fail. His father has said that if he does he'll have him posted (as ensign) to Outer Pomerania. Heym has sworn that he'll shoot himself rather than rot in such a place!' (*T* 218)

In the event the need for such a drastic solution passed, for Heym passed his part one examination in mid-January 1911. Legend has it that he found an ingenious way of cheating by throwing the questions out of the window to a group of four lawyer friends, who sent in the answers to their long-suffering friend at the bottom of a bag of pears. Whether the story is true or apocryphal cannot be known, although

Heym was himself the source of a scarcely less preposterous story about the oral examination. He told his friends that this consisted of a single question. The candidate before him had been asked whether there was any difference between 'Besitz' and 'Eigentum'. The unfortunate candidate chose the wrong answer, saying that the difference was very small, which made the examiner so angry that he would not allow his victim to say another word. Instead he asked Heym the same question. Heym, who was not born yesterday, naturally replied that there was a very considerable difference between the two terms. He was not allowed to elaborate, but was passed. Heym drew the conclusion that the son of an Imperial Judge Advocate (*Reichsmilitäranwalt*) could not have been allowed to fail,[14] which did nothing to raise his opinion of the Wilhelmine state. Maybe this is why he was not very excited about passing; David Baumgardt reported him as appearing afterwards, wearing a top hat, but saying that he did not feel particularly excited ('Is mir jar nich besonders': *D* 12). He did, however, celebrate the occasion by ceremonially burning his hated law books (the 'Pandekten' of 'Die Professoren') and some of his lecture notes – others he had already used for poetic jottings – on a piece of ground opposite the family apartment (*D* 42) while local policemen looked on in horror.

Having passed his part one law examination (*Kammergerichtsreferendarexamen*) and begun his professional training at the District Court in Berlin-Lichterfelde, Heym shortly afterwards took a room of his own in 'Dichterstadt' Wilmersdorf (Spichernstraße 14/bei Kleinert); he moved back into his parents' house a month later. In order to compensate for the stultifying nature of his job, he took to frequenting the most Bohemian and raffish of cafés, the famous Café des Westens, the rest of the time. He was now, like many of the habitués of the café, publishing in Franz Pfemfert's *Die Aktion*.

No doubt his reaction to passing his legal examination was relatively muted because this marked the end of his real student days and therefore brought to the fore the vexed and vexing question of his career. What does a natural genius and born poet do in life? In contemporary Germany, at least, one answer was to become a freelance writer.

Heym never saw himself becoming a freelance writer, not because he did not wish to be one, but because he was nowhere near the stage when such a thing might have become possible; on the other hand, he does nearly always write as someone whose unalterable condition it is to be a poet. In some ways his talk about his career has to be taken with a pinch of salt. This possible career takes various forms. There is, first, the type of career which is implicit in his study of law, although the idea of following his father and ending up as a pillar of the society which he loathed is absurd, as he himself clearly recognized. On 29 November 1910 he wrote in his diary, with considerable feeling, that if he had had any money he would long ago have done something else. In early February 1911 he wrote asking Rowohlt to include in an epilogue in *Der ewige Tag* the words: 'I have recently passed my law exams and am now ready to let any wave take me where it will. I should like to see the world. Perhaps one of my readers will be sufficiently interested in me to make this possible (*T* 237).' Rowohlt dissuaded him from the epilogue idea, so he had little choice but to let events take their course, for on 8 February 1911 he had been assigned to the District Court in Berlin-Lichterfelde to begin his professional training (*Vorbereitungsdienst*). Three months later he was suspended for destroying a particularly boring and potentially time-consuming legal document by tearing it up and flushing it down the toilet, which unfortunately blocked, so that all was revealed. His immediate suspension was inevitable; but for his father's intervention he would have been dismissed.

Having been suspended from the District Court in Berlin-Lichter-felde on 22 May 1911, Heym had a three-month respite during which he worked on his Ph.D. thesis. On 18 July he was (thanks to his father's efforts to get his son's legal career back on the rails) posted to the District Court at Wusterhausen an der Dosse to continue his pro-fessional training; the posting was effective from 10 August. In the event he could only stand it for eleven days. On 21 August he returned home to Berlin. A month later, on 19 September, he belatedly obtained extended leave from his post at Wusterhausen in order to enrol at the School of Oriental Studies. That he only obtained leave shows how careful he was being not to burn any boats.

It was at this stage that Heym decided to apply for a place at the School of Oriental Studies in Berlin, run jointly by Berlin University and the German Chancellor's office, which trained young jurists for employment in the Interpreter and Colonial Service (*Dolmetscher- und Kolonialdienst*). His original intention was to study Chinese, English and French; in the event he read Chinese, English and philosophy. The several notebooks containing Chinese characters and vocabulary show that Heym took his Chinese studies very seriously, as indeed he took most things seriously at this stage. Greulich wrote rather fancifully of finding among Heym's papers 'slips of paper on which the fantastic, exotic-looking Chinese characters can barely be distinguished from his normal cramped handwriting'.[15] In fact the Chinese characters are quite unlike Heym's handwriting – they are as bold and clear as it is not. His English notes, on the other hand, are of interest mainly for a fascinating possibility raised by several book titles (*England and the English* by Bruce Collier; *New Canada and the New Canadians; British Citizenship* by Parker), namely that he might have chosen to take his abhorrence of contemporary Germany to its logical conclusion in leaving the country altogether; had he done so, he would have left Europe, for while the wording of his note in 'Zu den Wahlen' – 'The whole of Europe is deep in the same winter sleep' – may be partly Heine's, the sentiments are certainly Heym's. Whether this notion of himself as 'New Canadian' is serious cannot be known for sure, but it probably was, for the need for adventure, for new, wide-open horizons ran very deep. Be this as it may, he certainly took his philosophy lectures very seriously; this is a token of how much he has changed. His lecture notes[16] show that he was deeply interested in Georg Simmel's lectures on Johann Friedrich Herbart's account of the 'Ich' and on Friedrich Schelling's conception of God. As always, it is his own 'Ich' that is his ultimate concern, but his interests are now widening and changing; his *Notizbüchlein* of February–June 1911[17] shows that he was interested in mysticism and oriental asceticism as found in the series *Bibliotheka mystika et ascetiki*, and more especially in Theodor Benfey's translation of the ancient collection of fables embodying the wisdom of India, the *Pantschatantra* (2 vols, 1859).[18] He also appears to have been interested in the work of Rudolf Steiner, although it is impossible to be more specific (his *Notizbüchlein* merely includes the name Steiner).

Having discovered that he could not begin his language studies until the winter term, he applied for permission to resume his legal training on 14 July; the application was granted and he was posted to the District Court at Wusterhausen an der Dosse (near Neuruppin!) from 10 August to 1 October (1911). By 21 August he had already applied for leave, with the intention of not returning. He never did. By 21 August 1911 his legal career as originally envisaged was therefore over, which may seem to make it hard to credit the story that he took his Ph.D. at Rostock in late autumn 1911. It is true that on 7 July the University of Würzburg rejected his Ph.D. thesis (an expanded version of the thesis which he had written for his part one examination), giving him three months to revise it. However, given that he had burned his law books and some of his lecture notes back in January, and was furiously busy with his writing, he could only have resubmitted this thesis in a more or less unrevised form. No record of the award of a Ph.D. has been found.

He was now faced, in terms of external reality, with an increasingly urgent need to find an alternative career (in terms of inner reality the last thing he wanted was anything that would leave him less time for writing). There was, for instance, the military option, which had been at the back of his mind for several years. Ever since 21 May 1908 he had been toying with the idea of a military career: 'I am going to decide to be an army officer (*T* 108).' He was probably driven to the idea of becoming an army officer by despair of ever finding an appropriate career, but the idea was an obvious one, for his father was a reserve cavalry officer, and other members of the family also enjoyed the high social standing that went with holding a commission. At the same time the idea was no doubt also partly a romantic one, put into his head by Géricault, Delacroix and Stendhal, Grabbe and Kleist. Karl May's *Husarenleutnant* Hugo von Greifenklau may even have been a role-model.

Heym's admiration for Karl May is belatedly confirmed by a draft entitled 'Notizen zu einer Rezension' ('Notes for a Review') of 1911:

A man called Avenarius, by profession a guardian of art, has had the confounded cheek to attack the poet Karl May in his rag intended for the daughters of higher civil servants with literary leanings [*Kunstwart*] and to denounce him as a writer of trash. Karl May, whose magnificent imagination naturally cannot be comprehended by this purveyor of literary droppings.

The main reason he advances for Karl May's inferiority is the fact that he allegedly – ho! ho! – spent several years as a smuggler and bandit, something which ought to guarantee the poet the goodwill of every decent person (*PD* 181).

Even in translation it is clear that Heym is seriously annoyed at Ferdinand Avenarius's slur on a writer he has long admired. Because of the over-sharp distinction which German literary criticism makes between *Literatur* (high-class literature) and *Trivialliteratur* (popular or trashy literature), Heym's indebtedness to Karl May has largely gone unnoticed, as though the indebtedness of high-brow literature to low-brow literature was a taboo subject – unless, that is, German literary critics are unwilling to admit publicly to having read Karl May.

There are motifs from Karl May everywhere in Heym's work, but especially in his diaries, tales and dramatic work. The idea of being a dragoman, of travelling the 'endless desert', the 'endless savannahs' or the 'further reaches of Asia'; of sailing the seas, of crossing Africa; of being a hussar officer serving in the Napoleonic wars (the dying Emperor); the sun-god; the evil eye; the vultures; and so on – it is all there in Karl May. I do not mean to imply that Heym is egregiously indebted to May, just that May has clearly left his mark on Heym's imagination. In particular Heym's dreams of 1907–9 contain a number of parallels with May's *Der Weg nach Waterloo*; thus on 17 September 1907 he dreams that he is in a French inn, when in comes the King; in the same dream he is stabbed by a beggar, but the dagger glances off, as does Richemonte's dagger when he waylays Hugo von Greifenklau. On 10 March 1909 Heym dreams that it is the eve of a battle; he is wearing a French cuirassier-officer's uniform, as Greifenklau's grandson does in *Der Spion von Ortry*. And so on. No doubt these are all common motifs in blood-and-thunder literature, but there is, I think, little doubt that they go back to Heym's teenage reading of Karl May. Given that he lived in his imagination, that reading must have left an indelible mark – which is why it is even reflected in his essentially unrealistic career plans and plans for travelling the world with Lily Friedeberg. There is a dragoman in May's *Durch die Wüste*, although he is an unglamorous figure compared with the hero of the novel, the intrepid traveller Kara Ben Nemsi. Perhaps if Heym had not seen himself as Kara Ben Nemsi or Hugo von Greifenklau his career plans would have been more realistic.

The whole question of the mark left on him by his reading of Karl May is all the more important in that he also knew and read other comparable writers: Hanns Heinz Ewers (to whose *Das Grauen* of 1907 Heym's tales seem indebted), Robert Kraft and Balduin Möllhausen (senior).

A diary entry dated 22 September 1911 (and therefore written while he was staying with the painter Ernst Mortiz Engert) gives a clear summary of the pros and cons of a military career:

Where is the great panacea for all evils? Shall I become an officer or not? *Pro*: the glamour of the position (representing the possibility of happiness in itself) might reconcile the inner man (who has currently lost his way) with himself and thus restore him to his former strength ... *Con*: the appalling lack of freedom, the enormous expense, the so-called social life, one's superiors – indeed, the feeling of not being one's own man.

If only, he goes on to say, he could decide whether or not it would be good for his poetry. In wondering this he will have had in mind the fact that a fortnight earlier, under the influence of the Morocco crisis, he had written one of the best of all his poems, 'Der Krieg'. Novalis, as Heym knew, makes his Klingsor call war a poetic phenomenon; might it not therefore be good for his poetry? Good for it or not, Heym's father seems to have decided, when his son returned home, that the time had come to try to salvage a 'respectable' career. On 8 October 1911 he therefore wrote asking the officer commanding Feldartillerie-Regiment Nr. 72 to take his son on as ensign. The request was turned down, as was a similar request made by Heym himself a month later to a regiment stationed in Ulm. At the time of his death, however, he had been accepted (without knowing it) as ensign in the Lothringisches Infanterie-Regiment. Given his earlier attitude towards the Corps Rhenania, to say nothing of his threat to shoot himself rather than be posted to Hinterpommern, it is difficult to believe that he would have been able to stick a peace-time military career in an obscure regiment of the line. If only he had secured a cornetship in a cavalry regiment, the Napoleonic *chasseur* à la Géricault self-image might have been preserved!

The alternative was the idea of travelling the world, perhaps as a 'dragoman' or government interpreter. In the letter to Lily Friedeberg referred to above, he wrote:

I am potentially much better at living in distant parts, in the outer reaches of Asia, say, than at home. So I want either to work as an interpreter for our foreign and colonial service, or to try to get a job with an overseas branch of one of our big firms. My father is also keen for me to try for a consular career. But there's no great hurry.

How would you like me to take you with me out there?

Then we could ride together over the savannahs. Day and night. You could work out our position by the stars, for you balance azimuth and eclipse – things which still make my flesh creep – with astonishing ease (*D* 502).

A sketch beginning: 'Wir werden die Meere sehen' ('We shall see the oceans') (*PD* 160) belongs together with this letter, by the end of which Karl May seems to be taking over. Of course, the 'dragoman' notion is a vague one, but it is also serious, proof of this being the fact that he began courses in Chinese and English at the same time as applying for an ensignship. On 29 September 1911 we find him wondering (*T* 166) whether or not to pursue the officer idea; a fortnight later, on 8 October, he wrote a letter applying for an ensignship, but was evidently not sure whether that was what he wanted to be, or whether he would rather be a terrorist (*T* 168). On 19 October he began his courses at the School of Oriental Studies. It is reasonable to suppose that it was the 'dragoman' option that he himself preferred; in enrolling at the School of Oriental Studies he had already given his legal career a new turn, for the courses in question were intended as further, specialist training for law students wishing to enter the consular service. However, if this was a real alternative career which – to some extent, at least – had his father's blessing, it is likely that Heym also had the romantic aspects of a life à la Rimbaud or Gauguin at the back of his mind, but then travelled to Metz in the New Year (to apply for the ensignship which he was granted without living to know it) because he realized that he could not live on romanticism alone (or with his parents) for much longer. It could be said that death solved many problems; it had become a virtual necessity.

□ 'FUROR'

Outlining the most pressing external realities of the last year of Heym's life, which, as we have seen, tend to shade off into inner reality, has meant bypassing the all-important inner events from mid-January 1911. After the publication of *Der ewige Tag* in April 1911 the next most important event of his life was his meeting with Hildegard Krohn in summer 1911; before we come to that there are the events of early 1911 (as recorded in the diary) to be considered.

On the day before Rowohlt wrote inviting him to submit work for publication, Heym had been in a trough of frustration:

I feel as though I am wearing a strait-jacket. I am bursting at the seams mentally speaking. My drama should have been finished a long time ago. And now I'm having to stuff myself with ... jurisprudence, like an old sow being fattened up for slaughter; it's enough to make one vomit. I'd much prefer to spit on the stuff than to have to stuff myself with it. It's such a job to get anything creative done (*T* 152).

Of all his many laments, this is the most frequent and most palpably serious. Rowohlt's letter only aggravated the situation in that it gave him even more to do, while also giving him the encouragement and promise of recognition ('fame', he always called it, perhaps with Schopenhauer's essay on fame in mind), which he needed. Not that he had any illusions about literature; on 7 December 1910 he made it clear that his allegiance, like Nietzsche's, was to *Leben* rather than *Geist*:

Poetry seems pretty stupid, for it is a very poor substitute for any sort of action and therefore for life, but on the other hand it is the only substitute available to me, for what else am I to do, given that I haven't a bean?

It was in a 'Breviarium eines Wintertages' (*T* 154), written on 20 December 1910, when he was desperately trying both to get together the extra poems which Rowohlt had requested and to prepare himself for his forthcoming examination, that his inevitable frustration came to a head:

Ye gods, I am practically going out of my mind. Snowed under with work of a particularly ghastly sort, having to learn shoals of stuff by rote so that my head is at bursting point, bogged down with all sorts of minor troubles – Elsa K. insists on having her 10 M. back, – the agony, the misery of it, and all the time the poetic images are coming out of my ears instead of being got down on paper. – Stuffed full of pills. Hideous dreams. No place of my own to live. Sexual repression. In short, on the threshold of a nice bout of hysteria.

Even after he has passed his examination and published *Der ewige Tag*, the situation is no better, for every day there is the same conflict between law and poetry. Having to do what bores him out of his mind, for the sake of a career which he knows he could not stand, is to him a criminal waste of that most precious of all commodities, time, which he could be using to write what he alone can write, before it is too late. By 28 May 1911 he is even more desperate:

My brain is forever going round in circles, like a prisoner banging on his prison door. I need violent emotions, outbursts, anguish. No, I've got anguish enough. – I'm going mad.

It was at this stage that he destroyed the legal document, thus procuring a respite of a kind in terms of suspension from his legal traineeship. Not only did he feel that he was near to going out of his mind; he was considered 'mad' (*T* 157), and took the whole experience sufficiently seriously to explore it in his tales. He also found release from his frustration in a series of satirical poems which were written between May and November 1911. Some of these – 'Der Sonntag' (July: *L* 305), 'Fröhlichkeit' (September/October: *L* 389) – are straight social satires, in which the poet lets off steam by indulging himself at others' expense. More serious is 'Nachtgesang' (November: *L* 459), in which an officer – the career for which Heym was applying at the time – hangs himself with a hair-band, ending up not only dead but a figure of fun. Poems such as these show that Heym had a sense of humour and was perfectly capable of regarding anyone or anything in a comic, satirical light. We have, moreover, already seen a poem in which he satirized himself in 1904, 'Ach nun seht doch den Heym' (see page 63 above). At that time he was telling himself not to take himself too seriously. In mid-1911, when his situation had radically worsened, he was still doing the same, and at the same time taking his frustrations very seriously. This applies to 'Das Grundbuchamt' (May: *L* 265ff.) and, even more, 'Die Hölle' (August: *L* 327). 'Die Hölle', which has already been quoted, is a satirical poem based on his experiences in the District Court at Wusterhausen an der Dosse, which he evidently found hellish, but at the same time it reflects his reading of Dante and goes beyond the satirical to make a desperately serious comment on life. The combination is typical.

As before, Heym was saved by love, which was always the main single factor in his equilibrium. If Hedi Weißenfels came 'wie gerufen' – just when he most needed her – in April 1908, so too did Hildegard Krohn in June 1911. Or perhaps one should say Hildegard Krohn and Leni F. The main thing was, he was in love again and, in June, free from the shackles of the law. A few of his letters to Hildegard Krohn have been preserved; of these it is the first, dating from early June 1911, that is the most significant:

Give me the Dante. Let us steep ourselves in one another. If we read the same books, we will in course of time come to have the same ideas; we will share a love for the beautiful, we will merge into one another, recognizing ourselves in our heroes. Be my Alissa and Clara, then even in the grave we will think of one another on winter nights. Don't read those people, those idiots, George, Rilke, [Peter] Altenberg. They are all sick men who belong in hospital and who perform a lame St Vitus's dance on the crutches of their verse. I don't care for any of them ... Read Grabbe, sublime Grabbe, Büchner, Kleist. Read Rimbaud, Baudelaire, Samain, Keats. These are men with something to show for themselves. Read Mirbeau and André Gide, Shakespeare, Marlowe, Dostoyevsky and Zola (D 507).

The letter reveals that this was a literary sort of love (Alissa is the heroine of André Gide's La Porte étroite, Clara the heroine of Octave Mirbeau's Le Jardin des supplices), which helps to explain his simultaneous love for Leni F., and also points forward to his late elegies, both by linking love and death, and by its rather surprising reference to the French elegiac poet Albert Samain (1858–1900), whose work appeared in German (Gedichte, translated by Lucy Abels) in 1911.

Hildegard Krohn (born 18 April 1892), daughter of a Jewish businessman, was Heym's official girlfriend for the last six months of his life. Two poems dedicated to her, 'Deine Wimpern, die langen' and 'Ein Herbst-Abend', appeared in Die Aktion; Heym père, who did not approve of Hildegard Krohn, tried to prevent their reappearance in Umbra vitae. When 'An Hildegard K.' (i.e. the first five stanzas of 'Ein Herbst-Abend': L 292) appeared in Die Aktion on 19 February 1912, it was followed by a note in which Pfemfert quoted Heym as saying (in a letter dated 17 June 1911 which accompanied the poem) that for him art had become the mother of love.

It is mildly surprising to gather from the diary that in August 1911 Heym was also 'madly' in love with one Leni F.; but this late blossoming of his love-life combined with his feeling of helpless drifting, his premonition of death, and his reading of Samain, to produce the final elegies. It is for this reason that 21 August 1911 – the day on which he was granted leave from the legal treadmill, to which he had no intention of returning – was one of the most important days of his life: this liberation led to a spell of quite extraordinary creativity in which he produced his greatest poetry. Did he know, as he drowned, that he had secured his fame? I imagine he did.

The third diary ended, on 7 December 1910, with the poet bemoaning the limitations of poetry. He would have preferred to be a painter, for the images teeming in his head cried out to be painted. In July/August 1911, while bitterly lamenting not being a painter, he produced two crayon drawings which have been preserved, 'Furor' and 'Die Irren'.[19] From December 1910 to August 1911 he had been too busy to keep a diary as such, although scattered 'diary entries' are found elsewhere.

The fourth diary (1 September to 10 November 1911) opens with quotations from *Le rouge et le noir* which show him identifying with Stendhal (see Chapter V below); the emphasis is again on his personal fate. When he writes on 4 September, 'I have struggled heroically, but I suddenly feel as though I can't go on', he seems, on the face of it, to be referring to his heroic struggle with Leni's mother; but when read beside other entries dating from about the same time, it is evident that the remark has far wider application. He repeats what has already been said, that he cannot have a 'real job', although his reason is a novel one: 'for my real vocation is to be in love'. He reviews some of his past loves (*T* 163), making it clear that in some ways his love of the moment is Leni rather than Hilde, and that his real regret is that he ever allowed Hedi to slip away in summer 1908.

Heym was, of course, not only an *Augenmensch*, but an *Augenblicksmensch*, by which I mean that he lived for the present and was in constant need of excitement and new impressions; love was a part of that, proof of this being the very fact that his loves were so short-lived. He recognized this himself: 'But for my wild temperament I might have been all right ... but as it is, I can't be. I must "be in love" all the time. That's my fate' (*T* 10 November 1910). His diaries and tales alike show that travelling the world in search of ever-new sensations and 'experiences' or 'adventures' (the German word *Erlebnisse* denotes both) was the life-style that would have suited him best. On 15 September 1911 he returns to his most familiar and insistent lament: that he was born at precisely the wrong (because so boring) time. What follows is his most significant pronouncement on the subject:

My God, my enthusiasm having to lie fallow in this banal age of ours is stifling me, for I need violent external stimuli to keep me going. In my daydreams I always see myself as a Danton or someone manning a barricade; I cannot imagine myself without my Jacobin cap. Now I'm hoping for a war at least. Vainly, no doubt.

My God, if only I had been born at the time of the French Revolution, at least I should have known where to die, at Hohenlinden, say, or Jémappes.

All these people like Jentzsch and Koffka can get used to the age; being

... intellectuals, they could come to terms with any age, whereas I, a sensation type, a breaking sea, always storm-bound, I, the mirror of the outside world, as wild and chaotic as the world itself, I who am unfortunately so constituted as to need a large and enthusiastic audience, sufficiently sick never to be self-sufficient, should be suddenly cured, a god, redeemed, if I were to hear an alarm bell ringing somewhere, if I were to see people running around in circles with faces taut with fear, if the populace were to rise up and a street be seen bright with pickaxes, swords, fanatical faces and bare chests. What an easy time the contemplative types have of it. See how calm their faces look compared with mine, crossed as it is by anguish, debauchery, despair, enthusiasm, and lord knows what else, a thousand times an hour (*T* 164).

All this is absolutely fundamental to Heym and shows how personal a poem his impersonal-looking 'Der Krieg' is.

The following evening (16 September) he compares himself with Baudelaire in terms of his own mixture of enthusiasm, sensibility and melancholy. On 9 October he comes back to the extraordinary mixture that he is:

There has surely never been such a mixture before; strictly speaking it ought to result in madness. Today, imagine, I should most like to be a lieutenant of hussars; by tomorrow I'd rather be a terrorist. And now you have to imagine these things not nicely and tidily separated, but jumbled up together in a confused knot. There is only one position that would have suited me: I should have been an emperor.

I have a talent for the most hail-fellow-well-met kind of camaraderie, for the wildest boozing, and for chatting up girls, and then five minutes later I am desperately unhappy, empty, hollow, lonely; and then suddenly I am an artist again. And now I'm supposed to be deciding what is the best thing for me to do (*T* 163).

The extent to which he identified with Napoleon is now confirmed. 'Why,' he asks (still on 9 September), 'was life so crazy as not to have let me be born under Napoleon? Ye gods, with what fanaticism I should have yelled "vive l'empereur"!' When he agreed to let his father try to obtain an ensignship in an artillery regiment for him, he no doubt remembered that Napoleon started as an artillery subaltern.

This self-absorption is the keynote of these last months, dominated as they are by a feeling of having nowhere to go save into death. It is as though, knowing that Death was fast approaching, he was trying to establish what sort of person he had been ('I am the most passionate person imaginable': *T* 172). When he now ends 'Against whom am I struggling? Where is the horrible thing that never gives me a chance to fight it head-on?' (*T* 10 November 1911), the only answer is that the foul monster is Death, and that it is waiting for him beneath the waters of the Havel. Knowing this, Heym addressed an ode to his corpse ('An meinen Leichnam', September 1911: *L* 343f.) and then, at a long, late-night meeting with Loewenson, Jentzsch and Koffka on 28 December 1911, spoke of his forthcoming death and appointed the editors of his literary remains. Clearly he had had a premonition of what was to come, for otherwise things were looking up for him: he was gaining recognition, was negotiating with Rowohlt for *Morgue* to be published with illustrations by Ernst Mortiz Engert, and had succeeded in giving his career a not unpromising new turn. He did not yet know (and indeed never did know) that he had been offered an ensignship, but he did live to see the most positive of the reviews of his work published in his lifetime, that in the *Berliner Zeitung am Mittag* for 5 January 1912 in which Herbert Eulenberg greeted him as the most significant of the younger German poets.

Inner and outer reality finally coincided. On Tuesday, 16 January 1912, he left home early, having arranged to spend the day skating with Ernst Balcke on the river Havel. At midday they reached the island of Lindwerder off the east bank of the Havel. After visiting the café there to have a drink and warm up, they donned their skates and set off on the ice at about 2 p.m. About a thousand metres south of Lindwerder Ernst Balcke fell through the ice, it is presumed in one of the areas where holes had been made in the ice for the sake of the fish and waterfowl, and which had subsequently thinly iced over. Heym went in, too – deliberately or accidentally – in the attempt to rescue his friend. How quickly Ernst Balcke died, is not clear, but Heym is known to have wrestled with his fate for up to half an hour. His desperate shouts for help were heard by some forestry workers, whose account makes chilling reading:

they had ... watched two skaters who had fallen through the ice some 800–1200 metres away from where they were working, upstream, below Lind-werder, near the water-way, between 3 and 4 o'clock in the afternoon. For almost half an hour one of the skaters had shouted for help; they had been able to see him in the ice too, but since they had no ladders, poles and boats, they could do nothing to help. The holes in the ice on the Havel, which had been made for the fish and waterfowl, and which froze over again at night, made the ice unsafe to walk on. The two skaters must have fallen into one of them. No one else was around at the time. After half an hour, they said, it had gone quiet (*D* 459f.).

Heroic as was Heym's attempt to save his friend, this slow, slow, wholly conscious death was far removed from the heroic death he had so often envisioned, and far removed from the dream of 2 July 1910 (*T* 185), which had a happy ending. The morgue to which he was taken was one which he had often visited; Rudolf Balcke said that Heym was fascinated by the morgue, of which he wrote: 'They all come here before going their separate ways.'[20] He was, eventually, buried in the Luisenfriedhof in Berlin-Charlottenburg. His gravestone bore not the word KEITAI, as he had wished, but a religious text (Jeremiah XXXI,3: 'I have loved thee with an everlasting love: therefore with loving kindness have I drawn thee [to me]') which would have appalled him.

V

Tragic Poet

□ BYRON, KEATS AND SHELLEY

Prior to 1909 Heym's poetic models were mostly rather desperate romantics (e.g. Grabbe, Büchner, Kleist), although Hölderlin is better described simply as a tragic poet, for, however romantic his perceptions, his manner of expression was severely classical. From 1909 Heym continued to relate to poets of a similar kind, including the English romantic poets (and Marlowe), although, as we have seen, his great discoveries at this time were the modern French poets (Baudelaire, Rimbaud, Verlaine, Samain) and Stendhal. If his earlier and later self-images are thus linked by an extreme romanticism, there is a difference of emphasis: before 1909 the emphasis is on heroism, after 1909 it is on tragedy. Heym develops from neo-romantic to necromantic.

His later poetic heroes (or 'gods', as he called them) included Byron, Keats and Shelley. Given that he invariably identified with those whom he admired, and admired those with whom he identified, it follows that he was no less interested in these poets' images (and self-images) than in their works; after all, he himself combines the heroic cynicism of Byron, the haunted sensuality of Keats and the pessimistic idealism of Shelley.

Whether Heym read any of Byron, Keats and Shelley in English, and whether he read his favourite French poets in French, is not known. At school he got the same marks in Latin, Greek and French as in German (in the school-leaving examination he did better in Latin and Greek than in German). He knew Latin well enough to write letters in it, and is said to have been able to proclaim Latin hexameters spontaneously. In autumn 1911 he began to study English seriously, as part of his training for the government interpreter service (*Dragomanen-dienst*). His English notebook (of September–October 1911) contains these sentences: 'Do you speak English [?] I speak only a little. Do you read French [?] Yes, I read French.'¹ While these are English-language exercises, there is no reason to doubt the truth of what they say. Nor is there any reason to suppose that he was capable of reading the English romantic poets in English in 1909–10. It is likely that he owes his knowledge of Byron, Keats and Shelley partly to Ernst Balcke, and partly to the various translations that were available.

In 1909 Byron was, and had long been, by far the best known of the three poets in Germany. He was not only the only poet recognized as his equal by Goethe; his mood expressed and corresponded to the 'Weltschmerz', the disillusionment and despair rife in the early nineteenth century. A major influence on Heine, Byron was also admired by Heym's favourite philosophers, Schopenhauer and Nietzsche. Schopenhauer (an exact contemporary of Byron) felt a real sense of kinship with the English poet, whom he saw as having given expression to a philosophy similar to his own; in the fourth canto of his 'Grotto of Egeria' Byron expresses Schopenhauer's most fundamental belief, that our life is 'a false nature', something which ought not to be. Nietzsche, too, enthused over Byron, to whom his superman idea was said (by his sister) to be indebted. Byron therefore enjoyed, as it were, the *imprimatur* of some of the greatest German writers. In 1909 all his work had long been available in German, including a recent (1907) Reclam edition of his letters.

Heym's interest in Byron was biographical: on 3 September 1909 we find him (*T* 130) reading a Life of Byron, probably Emil Koeppel's *Lord Byron* (Berlin, 1903), or Richard Ackermann's *Lord Byron. Sein Leben, seine Werke, sein Einfluß auf die deutsche Literatur* (Heidelberg, 1901), or Karl Bleibtreu's *Byron der Übermensch, sein Leben und sein Dichten* (Jena, 1897). Two days later he quotes (in German), from 'Fare Thee Well' the lines 'Love may sink by slow decay,/But by sudden wrench, believe not/Hearts can thus be torn away'; the first line of the stanza, 'Yet, oh yet, thyself deceive not', is indicated only by a line of dashes, for Heym was at the time in the throes of self-pity following his 'betrayal' by a girlfriend. His interest persisted, though: two weeks later Byron is listed (together with Kleist, Grabbe, Marlowe and the incongruous Gustav Renner) as an 'Olympian'. For Heym Byron epitomizes the poet as hero; his life and (no less important) his death are Heym's ideal; indeed, when Heym envisaged an heroic death for himself, he may well have been thinking of Byron. The Byronic hero, the Byronic lover, Byronic despair – these are all key elements of Heym's self-image.

Heym's poetry, particularly that of 1910–11, is Byronic in being the expression of excited passion, just as it is 'Byronic' (among other things) in being romantic in theme but classical in technique. That the examples of both Byron and Baudelaire reinforce Heym's own classic/romantic inclinations is obvious. And then there is Byron's rhetoric, which is not without an element of theatricality – a feature both of Heym's self-image and of his satires. While his interest in Keats was serious and constructive, it is difficult to take too seriously Heym's passing enthusiasm for his famous fellow-iconoclast and pessimist, which is perhaps more a matter of histrionic *morbidezza* than of anything else. The main reason for saying this is the lack of evidence to the contrary (Heym's diaries, so revealing in some ways, are tantalizingly reticent in others). In general terms Byron's poetic example will have affected him in much the same way as Keats's, although it came to his attention at a less crucial time, but Byron's personal example was more important to him, for it embodied his ideal self-image (the poet as hero) in his preferred context (the Napoleonic wars) and with his preferred aura (romantic pessimism); it was a heady mixture.

In October 1910, by which time he was coming into his own poetically and was therefore less given to theatricality, we find him saying: 'I do not believe that there is a greater poet than Keats' (*T* 31 October 1910). A week later he is listing Keats (together with Shelley, Baudelaire, Verlaine and Rimbaud) as one of his 'gods' (*T* 5 November 1910). Unlike Byron and (to a lesser extent) Shelley, Keats was little known in Germany at this time. When Heym wrote in his diary that there was no German translation of Keats (*T* 147), he showed that he did not know Marie Gothein's *John Keats Leben und Werke* (2 vols, Halle, 1897), the first volume of which is a Life, and that he had not heard of Keats's *Gedichte* (translated by Gisela Etzel, Leipzig, 1910). It is therefore likely that his knowledge of Keats comes from Ernst Balcke, who was studying English literature in Edinburgh at the time. It was Ernst

Balcke who drew his attention to 'Isabella; or, The Pot of Basil' in October 1910. Keats clearly held his interest, for in June 1911 he wrote to Hildegard Krohn that he was on his way to Balcke's to talk about Keats (D 507). In his review of *Der ewige Tag* in May 1911 Balcke had commented: 'In his poems there is no sign of the incomparable restraint which Keats shows in "The Pot of Basil" in his description of the dead Lorenzo' (D 193), which may well have been what Heym wished to discuss. At all events he seems to have been undismayed by the 'inexperience', 'simplicity' and 'mawkishness' that Keats himself saw in his 'Isabella' – no doubt because, as always, he was reading subjectively, with emotional self-identification (and, in this case, love) uppermost in his thoughts.

There were particularly good reasons for his identification with Keats, as he will have realized from talking to Ernst Balcke. Heym was as much of a sensation type as Keats; he sighed, with Keats, for a life of sensation rather than thought. His work is no less sensuous, and indeed sensual. Both men express themselves in vivid concrete imagery; the pictorial splendours of Keats's work are no less evident in Heym's, for all its post-romantic nature. For Heym, as much as for Keats, holiness meant 'the holiness of the heart's affections'. Both are inspirational poets; what Robert Gittings has said of Keats ('Unlike most poets, whose method of composition fits better with Wordsworth's doctrine of "emotion recollected in tranquillity", Keats' writing is an almost instant transmutation of impressions, thoughts, reading and ideas into poetry'[2]) applies to Heym with the proviso that his work, unlike Keats's, is less philosophical than visual; its meaning resides in the painterly surface imagery, not in philosophical depth – great Socratic odes may be Keats's style but they are not Heym's. Like Keats, on the other hand, Heym was extremely impressionable, mercurial in temperament, the very embodiment of the chameleon-poet; his real living took place in the imagination, and 'his powers of imagination are so strong, that the poems are far from being a poetic diary of the life, and enrich their original impulse with a complete life of their own'.[3] Like Keats, Heym mostly described not what he saw, but what he imagined, so that his poems, too, are absolute creations. His work embodies the rampant subjectivism which is a fundamental characteristic of romanticism, although it is not a surface subjectivity. Like Keats, he was rarely relieved from the tensions of life and the nagging nearness of death, save when he was composing. Robert Gittings's comment on Keats, that 'in spite of his vitality, sense of fun and animal spirits, his personal view of life was tragic and heroic, but at the same time positive',4 is precisely applicable to Heym, who personified the passionate intensity which was Keats's prime characteristic. Both men knew despair; Heym was marked by Keats's 'horrid morbidity' of temperament; he, too, had an 'innate sense of the tragic',5 and in his case, too, this tragic view of life became obsessive. Both men were haunted by death and were hunted down by it at an early age (Heym at twenty-four, Keats at twenty-five).

There were, of course, significant differences, although these differences tend only to reinforce the similarities. If it is true, as Lionel Trilling has said, that Keats made an heroic attempt to solve the problem of evil by showing that life may be called blessed even when its circumstances are cursed, then his heroism goes beyond Heym's, although the common concern with evil remains. Heym had, like Keats, moments of 'vertical transcendence', although in his case it was mostly a downward transcendence (*Transzendenz nach unten*). He even modelled his epitaph on Keats's: with Keats's epitaph (written by himself) – 'Here lies one whose name was writ in water' – compare Heym's diary entry for 30 October 1910: 'When the time comes there should be nothing on my gravestone except the word ΚΕΙΤΑΙ. No name, nothing. κειται. He is sleeping, he is resting (*T* 147).' In other words, Heym went only slightly less far than Wilfred Owen, who kept Keats's death-day as a day of mourning.

That it was to Heym the romantic that Keats appealed is shown by the fact that we find him quoting from 'Isabella' the lines 'Love! thou art leading me from wintry cold,/Lady! thou leadest me to summer clime' in a letter to Hildegard Krohn. From Keats he will have gained, first, the encouragement that came from discovering a major poet with whom he shared so much (his friends called him 'Keats resurrected' and 'Keats's German brother'). For someone as uncertain of himself as Heym this will have been important, but we can be more specific and say that precisely because he was a similarly unrestrained personality, Keats will have confirmed him in his marked preference for restrained poetic forms, particularly since Byron, Baudelaire and Rimbaud (to say nothing of Hölderlin) used them, too. The crux of the matter is that Heym will have been encouraged by Keats's example to persevere with the sort of poetry that he had begun writing, much of it massively detailed, packed tight with images. Keats's influence was therefore in this respect much the same as Baudelaire's for, as Arthur Symons once said,

To 'load every rift with ore': that, to Keats, was the essential thing; and it meant to pack the verse with poetry so that every line should be heavy with the stuff of the imagination ... For as Keats, almost in the same degree as Baudelaire, worked on every inch of his surface, so perhaps no poets ever put so much poetic detail into so small a place...[6]

A poem like 'Der Krieg' is essentially Keatsian in this sense.

Shelley never achieved anything like Byron's popularity in Germany, partly because, having been admired in the eighteen-thirties and forties as a political prophet, he later came to be seen as naïve and indeed as over-English (as opposed to Byron, who was regarded, at least by Heine, as un-English). Shelley's work was translated from 1840 onwards, but it was not until the turn of the century that his fortunes revived, thanks above all to Helen Richter's full-scale *Percy Bysshe Shelley* (Weimar, 1898). After that there was something of a Shelley-revival, of which Heym's interest was part. Shelley was subsequently translated by Heym's fellow-Expressionist Alfred Wolfenstein (Shelley, *Dichtungen*, Berlin, 1922). *The Cenci*, the work of Shelley's which Heym knew best, was translated into German no less than four times between 1907 and 1924. So far as Heym is concerned there was not only *Die Cenci* (Reclam, 1907), which he knew and used, but also Shelley's *Sämtliche Dichtungen* (edited by G. H. Neuendorff, Dresden, 1909) and, potentially no less important, Richard Ackermann's *Percy Bysshe Shelley: der Mann, der Dichter und seine Werke* (Dortmund, 1906); there were also numerous academic works on Shelley, several of them published in 1906.

Although, as we have seen, he was sufficiently impressed by Shelley's *The Cenci* to write his own adaptation of it, Heym mentions Shelley in his diary (in October 1910) only in the context of Keats; it is Keats who is by far the more influential figure. Heym has, however, some significant characteristics in common with Shelley. Above all he shared Shelley's need to turn himself into a mythical figure. He will have sympathized with Shelley's self-image as a beautiful but vulnerable spirit; we should not be misled by Heym's surface rowdiness, for beneath the surface he was extremely vulnerable. Shelley was, like

Heym after him, a visionary poet; his thought, too, was peopled by monsters (cf. 'The Daemon of the World', the 'irresistible furies' of 'Alastor', etc.) which were so real to him that he was convinced he had been chased by a *Kakadaimon* at Tan-yr-allt in 1812. The demons by which the two poets were possessed were not the same ones (Shelley's were essentially Greek, Heym's part-Oriental), but they were equally vivid; both men were all too familiar with the sense of being hounded by the Furies. Heym identified with the Shelley of 'Alastor' (and it was Thomas Love Peacock who told Shelley that Alastor was an evil genius, a *Kakadaimon*) because of his own feeling of being hounded by the Furies to an early death (the 'untimely tomb' of 'Alastor'). The 'wide waste and tangled wilderness' of 'Alastor' corresponds with Heym's view of the wilderness of life. I doubt whether the references to 'alastor' in the diaries (*T* 76, 125) are references to Shelley, Heym's knowledge of whose work hardly goes back to 1906. Heym is using the word in its classical connotations: Fury, and he who is hounded by the Furies because he deserves to be, in other words himself. Thinking of himself as 'alastor', however, most likely led him to read Shelley's 'Alastor; or The Spirit of Solitude', in the preface to which he will have found a description of himself among the 'luminaries of the world' who are struck by the furies with 'sudden darkness and extinction'. Heym's only literary debt to Shelley is his dramatic fragment *Cenci* of 1911 (see Chapter III above), which is based on *The Cenci*: the 'eminently fearful and monstrous' story of which chimed in with his own increasing fatalism.

Whatever the precise extent of Heym's knowledge of the English poets – a rather old-fashioned interest in 1909/10, when there was more general interest in England's political position in the world, of which Germany was understandably jealous – it seems clear that his admiration for them was based more on their lives than on their works.

This enthusiasm for the English romantic poets was followed, in 1909–10, by his even greater enthusiasm for Baudelaire, Rimbaud and Verlaine. All three had only recently been translated into German: Charles Baudelaire, *Die Blumen des Bösen*, translated by Stefan George, second edition, 1908; Arthur Rimbaud, *Leben und Dichtung*, translated by K. L. Ammer, 1907; Paul Verlaine, *Ausgewählte Gedichte*, translated by Graf Wolf von Kalckreuth, 1906.

□ BAUDELAIRE

David Baumgardt found that Heym knew Baudelaire and Rimbaud better than he knew any German poets. Heym's allegiance to Baudelaire, like that of some of his English contemporaries, accounts for and signals his rejection of most of the post-Romantic poetry of his own national tradition. Reviewers generally regarded him as a German Baudelaire. This is appropriate, for he identified with Baudelaire more closely than he did with any other poet save Hölderlin (and in 1910 his enthusiasm for Hölderlin was less obvious than it had been), and more closely than did any other poet of his generation in Germany, although he was certainly not alone in his admiration for the French poet. Relevant here are Stefan George's fastidiously elegant versions of *Les fleurs du mal*, the fact that *Les fleurs du mal* was an early favourite of Georg Trakl (who, as a child, almost invariable spoke French to his brothers and sisters, which helps to explain the preternatural clarity of his work, its primitivism and naïveté), and Baudelaire's impact on Rilke and Alfred Lichtenstein.

Although he could read French, it is unlikely that Heym read the modern French poets (Baudelaire, Rimbaud, Verlaine, Samain) only in French. He clearly knew K. L. Ammer's Rimbaud translations, and undoubtedly knew Baudelaire's *Werke in deutscher Ausgabe* (translated by Max Bruns, 5 vols, Minden, J. C. C. Bruns, 19[01]–10), although it is worth remembering that Bruns's translation was very badly reviewed (e.g. in the *Literarisches Echo*, 1907/8, p. 1633), and that there were a number of other Baudelaire translations available, including Stefan George's 'Umdichtungen' (or reworkings) of *Les fleurs du mal*, which Heym must also have known; his knowledge of George's versions helps to explain the influence of Baudelaire being mistaken for that of George. However, the evidence of Heym's diary shows that he derived his knowledge of Baudelaire partly from Bruns. On 16 September 1911 Heym noted in his diary that Baudelaire embodied the 'combination of enthusiasm, sensibility and melancholia' which Poe described as characterizing genius, a combination which he himself embodied; this reflects his reading of Bruns, who says, 'For the temperament of the genius – says Edgar Allan Poe – combines melancholia, sensibility and enthusiasm' (Baudelaire, *Werke*, translated and edited by Bruns, vol. II:

Die künstlichen Paradiese, Minden, 1901, xxxii) and therefore points to one certain source of Heym's information about Baudelaire. Similarly, Heym's reference to 'those whom their philistine fellow-citizens contemptuously call "original"' derives from Bruns's version of a passage from the 'Le poëme du haschisch, IV' (ibid., II, 67). The Baudelaire quotation noted on 15 September 1911 ('Commonsense tells us that material things possess very little reality, and that true reality is to be found only in dreams') comes from the same source (p. 6). On the same day Heym had written: 'My God, my enthusiasm having to lie fallow in this banal age of ours is stifling me.' He saw his task, with Baudelaire, as the overcoming of the banality of the age. His knowledge of Baudelaire's poetry, on the other hand, probably derives from a variety of sources, including Stefan George's versions; he may well have attended a poetry reading at the Architektenhaus (Wilhelmstraße 92/93) on 26 February 1911 which included Baudelaire's 'L'Albatros', 'Chant d'automne', 'Don Juan aux Enfers', 'Spleen', 'La Béatrice', 'Abel et Cain', 'Le Revenant', and 'Le Voyage, VIII'. His knowledge of Verlaine's poetry probably came from Graf Kalckreuth's versions or from Verlaine's *Gedichte. Eine Anthologie der besten Übertragungen*, edited by Stefan Zweig (Berlin and Leipzig, Schuster & Loeffler, second edition, 1907). The work of Albert Samain, which was much on his mind in 1910–11, he may have read in French, perhaps with the help of Ernst Balcke whose French was better than Heym's because he was studying French and English, for the first German translation (*Gedichte*, translated by Lucy Abels) only appeared in 1911. However, these details are less important than what Heym found in these poets to enthuse about.

Poets, like painters, take from their predecessors what they need, so that a poet like Baudelaire is all things to all poets. In Heym, as in much contemporary English literature (e.g. Swinburne), Baudelaire is present as a 'suffused and multiply expressive intellectual and imaginative influence',[7] for if he is 'the great laureate of a collapsing civilization',[8] he is also 'the pivot around which European poetry turns to become modern'.[9] Heym, like Des Esseintes in Huysman's *A Rebours*, found in *Les fleurs du mal* the source of most that is expressive, significant and profound in modern poetry. Baudelaire did much to turn Heym into a modern urban poet and prophet of a collapsing order, and, more generally, helped him to become himself.

Heym possessed the immense passion and the formidable will which Baudelaire demanded of 'extreme genius', but if vehemence of feeling and imaginative passion are basic to his work, it is the *spleen*, which he, too, knew all too well, that is even more important, for Heym, like Ernest Dowson in a poem entitled 'Spleen', was 'troubled and torn/By ennui, spleen and regret'. Hugo Ball made an admirable comparison of Heym and Baudelaire from this point of view in 1924:

I am reading Georg Heym and Baudelaire at the same time. I am interested in why they are both subject to such hellish despair. In Baudelaire there is great fear of the horizontal dimension which consists of four planks and which in some place and at some time will be consigned to the earth. In his fear of death Baudelaire clings to form, to beauty. He too could well have written and cried out with Heym: 'Ye stars of heaven, I do not wish to die!' Heym's sorrow is even more uncanny than the great Frenchman's. With Heym it is accompanied by a pervading sense of the meaningless of existence. Baudelaire believes in art, in symmetry, in strict form, which cannot be eaten away by those worms without eye or ear. Heym does not even believe in that. Heym possesses artistry and a matchless, soaring imagination, but he drags his wings and his art gives him only a bitter aftertaste. His verses are written as though he were already beneath the ice.

What a great illusion! What a great, sublime illusion!

In Paris one can live with this. But in Germany? ... The perversities which Baudelaire collected are a trick. When one reads his poems one after another this perversity seems contrived. Baudelaire is driven to the infamous because there there are contrasts, gaudy images, sensations involving all five senses ... This is an invention, a technical device which he could have patented. With Heym it is different. He too finds the diabolical irresistible because the Devil keeps to the senses more than the Virgin Mary seems to do, and it seems that the poet cannot do without the sensuous. But Heym has no technique as such, no trick of the trade. Life affects him directly. He sees things as he describes them. He sees the abyss, but does not seek it out. He is drawn to the depths, to silence. His death was every bit as gruesome as his poems (*D* 170).

Though a great artist, Heym was artless in this sense. He suffered to a marked degree what Baudelaire called 'la fertilisante douleur'. He, too, 'cultivates his hysteria', although he does so far from calmly, for his work is inspired by rage against Dylan Thomas's 'dying of the light'. He, too, has a saturnine temperament. There is in Heym's and Baudelaire's work a pervading sense of tragedy, of loss, of absence.[10] The malaise of

Above Hermann Heym
(Georg's father), *c.* 1905
Above right Georg Heym
in Würzburg, 1907/8
Right Ernst Balcke

Above Simon Guttmann,
drawing by Ludwig Meidner, 1912
Above right Jakob van Hoddis
Right Georg Heym, *c.* 1910

Above left Hildegard Krohn
Above Robert Jentzsch
Left Erwin Loewenson

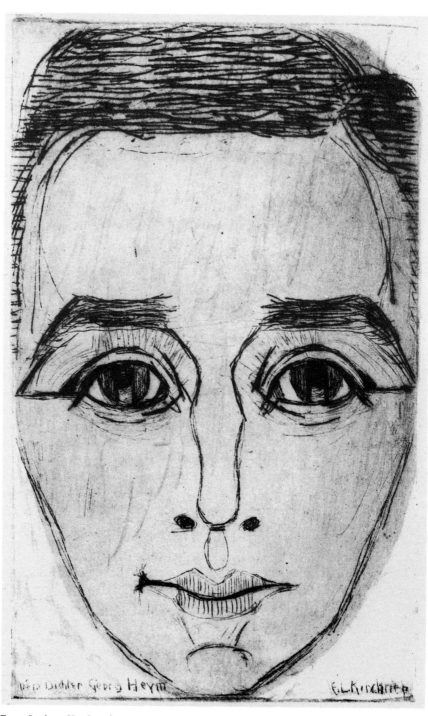

Ernst Ludwig Kirchner's engraving, 'For the Poet Georg Heym', 1923

Heym's later work, which goes far beyond the romantic-adolescent alienation of the early work, is Baudelairean in that, like Baudelaire, he objects to the suffering which Schopenhauer saw as fundamental to life; he is obsessed with suffering and with evil; 'everything that happens is either evil or turns to evil' (*T* 26 June 1910). If he knew it, he would have agreed with Baudelaire's statement that good – whether in art or morality – can only be achieved by conscious ... effort, by ... constantly battling against the powerful, but senseless and undirected impulses of Nature.[11] Heym's diary documents his own struggles against just those impulses.

Joanna Richardson's comment that 'Baudelaire shows a Romantic – indeed a Gothic – concern with death and corruption, as well as a Romantic interest in violence, a Romantic nostalgia for the past, and a Romantic longing for escape to eternity or to exotic climes'[12] is entirely applicable to Heym, who is a 'Romantic' of a similar kind and whose Romantic and Gothic proclivities can best be shown by a comparison with two of Baudelaire's preferred subjects: Delacroix and Poe.

Romantic in Heym are his restlessness, his energy (and the ends to which it is directed), his searching for something which, ultimately, does not exist. Romantic are his preoccupations (with love, death and the whole irrational world), his eccentricities, his egocentricity. His egregiously self-centred response to the world is characteristic of an extreme romanticism. He is the very embodiment of the cult of feeling, although what counts for him is not so much the 'intoxication of the heart' which Baudelaire followed Poe in spurning, as intoxication of the imagination. His longing for passion and glory is romantic because it puts the emphasis on the quality of the moment rather than its duration.

Heym's is, however, in many ways a 'negative' romanticism, for his work has a Satanic, Byronic or Baudelairean quality and is characterized by a feeling of desolation – a feature alike of German Romantic painting and of Baudelaire's poetry. That he was 'lured into nightmare's alley'[13] by the demons lurking on the nightside of nature is itself the sign of his romanticism, as it is of Poe's. Over his thoughts, as over Wordsworth's, 'there hung a darkness, call it solitude or blank desertion'. In Wordsworth's *Prelude* this feeling was mainly premonition; in Heym's poems and tales it has become stark fact. 'Der Krieg', for instance, welling up as it does from the depths of the unconscious, is the romantic vision *par excellence*, for it combines the dreadful desolation of Caspar David Friedrich's *The Monk by the Sea* with what Baudelaire called the 'Molochism' of Delacroix. It is with Delacroix that we come to the heart of Heym's romanticism and to an affinity no less striking than those which he himself noted in his diaries, for his later work as a whole is informed by this 'Molochism', in other words by the constant preoccupation with devastation, massacres and conflagrations that we find in Delacroix. Baudelaire described Delacroix's work as being 'like a terrible hymn composed in honour of destiny and human anguish'[14] – the constant subjects of Heym's diary – while the poetry features 'Ein Moloch, drum die schwarzen Knechte knien' ('A Moloch around which black bondsmen kneel': *L* 161).

At no time does Heym mention Delacroix, but it is virtually certain that he shared Van Gogh's admiration for the revolutionary romantic colourist whose famous *Journal* his own diary recalls. He cannot but have been struck by the description of Delacroix as having 'the sun in his head and a hurricane in his heart' when he read it in Margarete Mauthner's edition of Van Gogh's letters,[15] for this is a description of himself. Each man longed to be able to express himself in the other's medium (Delacroix: 'Why am I not a poet? How I long to be a poet!'[16] Heym: 'Satan has denied me the ability to paint. Why have the powers that be denied me the ability to draw?': *T* 158f.). For both men passion was the *sine qua non* of creativity (Delacroix: 'There is in me some black depth which must be appeased. Unless I am writhing like a serpent in the coils of a pythoness I am cold'[17]). Heym is a romantic in the grand style of a Géricault, a romantic in the classical mould of a Delacroix. In describing his friend Delacroix, Baudelaire also described himself; more important in the present context, his description of Delacroix is applicable to Heym. Thus the 'unique and persistent melancholy with which all Delacroix's works are imbued'[18] is everywhere in evidence in Heym, of whom it is no less true to say that his 'lofty and serious melancholy ... shines with a gloomy brilliance';[19] in his work, too, we see a 'fathomless limbo of sadness'.[20] In both cases this brilliant melancholy is allied with passion, for if Delacroix was 'passionately in love with passion',[21] this is no less fundamentally true of Heym, who shares not only Delacroix's vehemence, fervour and intensity, but also his subject-matter. Delacroix's imagination embraces the heavens, hell, war, Olympus and love – Heym's very themes. For him, as for Delacroix, the whole visible universe is 'but a store-house of images and signs'.[22] In the last analysis, however, it is the personal affinity that matters; it is this that Heym would have noted, for both men are hypersensitives with the most grandiose conceptions. For all the differences, Heym's diary is closer to Delacroix's journal than to any other.

Géricault's *Portrait of a Young Man* (c. 1818–19), that haunting picture of the young artist and sufferer from *mal de siècle*, with a skull among his possessions, invites comparison with Heym's self-image in the diaries. Heym is a romantic because the way of feeling in which romanticism is situated is his way of feeling, and yet in the last analysis the comparison with his spiritual predecessors fails because he was not only an extreme romantic, but a post-romantic, a man who knew that the sun of romanticism had set for ever, to be replaced by a Night blacker by far in its historical finality than that which Hölderlin knew. He is the heir to Baudelaire's 'Le coucher du soleil romantique' (from 'Les Épaves'):

Que le Soleil est beau quand tout frais il se lève,
Comme une explosion nous lançant son bonjour!
– Bienheureux celui-là qui peut avec amour
Saluer son coucher plus glorieux qu'un rêve!

Je me souviens!... J'ai vu tout, fleur, source, sillon,
Se pâmer sous son œil comme un cœur, qui palpite...
– Courons vers l'horizon, il est tard, courons vite,
Pour attraper au moins un oblique rayon!

Mais je poursuis en vain le Dieu qui se retire;
L'irrésistible Nuit établit son empire,
Noire, humide, funeste et pleine de frissons;

Une odeur de tombeau dans les ténèbres nage,
Et mon pied peureux froisse, au bord du marécage,
Des crapauds imprévus et de froids limaçons.

('The setting of the Romantic sun') How beautiful the sun is when it first rises, like a greeting to us from a distant explosion! Happy the man who is able to greet with love its setting, more glorious than any dream!
    I remember ... I have seen everything – flower, spring, furrow – faint beneath its cyclop eye like a palpitating heart ... Let us run towards the horizon, it is late, let us run swiftly, to catch at least one slanting ray!

But I pursue in vain the god who retires; all-powerful Night establishes its empire, black, inclement, baleful and full of terrors;

There is a graveyard smell in the shadows, and at the edge of the swamp my timid foot crushes unexpected toads and unresponsive snails.

Heym knew better than anyone else – Baudelaire alone excepted – those 'deux sentiments contradictoires: l'horreur de la vie et l'extase de la vie', although it must be added that his experience of the former outweighs that of the latter. *Spleen et Idéal* would be an appropriate motto for his work, were it not for the fact that *Spleen* is more in evidence there than *Idéal*, which for him has the connotation only of Beauty and Love. The basic polarity of his work – the tension between zest and disgust, excitement and ennui – is reminiscent of Baudelaire. He, too, is caught between contradictory and conflicting impulses; there is in his diary (and to a lesser extent in his work) the same oscillation between contrary states and moods. He is the poet as described by Baudelaire in 'L'Albatros': the monarch of the clouds who, living in the eye of the storm, scorns outrageous fortune's slings; exiled on earth amid the mocking crowds, he cannot walk for he has giant's wings. If it is also true that the 'romantic' Baudelaire had something classic in his moderation, this moderation becoming at times 'as terrifying as Poe's logic',[23] then here there is a difference between them, for Heym – despite the conventionality of form of so much of his work, the quality which caused critics to link him with Baudelaire and, to his fury, Stefan George (why not Byron? That would have been a comparison to relish) – was an outright enthusiast, with all the strengths and weaknesses of that ilk. He was no ascetic aesthete. He, who regarded moderation as an obscenity, was much more of a romantic than the fastidious Baudelaire. Divine fire, passion, was what he lived for; nothing else mattered to him. In one of his greatest poems, the sonnet 'Der Hunger' (quoted in the next section), he has given classical expression to the hunger for life of the being with death's mark on its brow; who, reading it, can doubt that Heym's dog stands for the poet himself, who heard too soon what his revered Keats called 'The thunder of the trumpets of the night'? This brilliantly stylized sonnet owes its inspiration to Rimbaud's 'Les effarés' and 'Fêtes de la faim', and its classical form and intensity to Baudelaire.

There are, of course, other differences both of degree and of kind between the two poets. If Baudelaire was the 'false monk' of his own sonnet 'Le mauvais moine', an ascetic of passion, then Heym was an unashamed hedonist. The only forms of perfection that mattered to him were perfect beauty and perfect love, but here we come back to the affinities between the two poets, who have a common craving for beauty, a love of art (they were both would-be artists), a romantic love of clouds, an idolatrous love of woman. There is much of Baudelaire in his comment on his friend Delacroix – 'No doubt he had loved woman greatly in the troubled hours of his youth. Who among us has not sacrificed too much to that formidable idol?'[24] – but it is also highly applicable to Heym, who said that he could not live without love; like Baudelaire before him, he needed it more than he needed any given object of it, needed it as a creative condition, the precondition for creativity. He has a thirst for glory and a diabolical thirst for fame which he shares with the French poet.

His hedonism and cult of love notwithstanding, Heym has nothing to do with the 'Fleshly School' of so-called Baudelairism; he saw too deeply into Baudelaire for that; one looks in vain in Heym for the 'Baudelairean flowers' of English *fin-de-siècle* poetry; his deepest concern is Baudelaire's 'révolte', his sense of life slipping away with his work unwritten. He was dogged by Baudelaire's 'Ennemi':

> O douleur! ô douleur! Le Temps mange la vie,
> Et l'obscur Ennemi qui nous ronge le cœur
> Du sang que nous perdons croît et se fortifie!

O sorrow, sorrow! Time devours our life, and the unseen enemy gnawing at our hearts grows bigger and stronger on the blood we lose!

His most real feeling was the 'tristesse étrange'[25] that comes from living in time, knowing that time is slipping away. His work is feral because he felt like a trapped animal, imprisoned in time; knowing intuitively that he had no future, he was unable to escape from the vicious circle of his own anxiety and ennui. For him there is no way, no escape save into death, around which all his deepest fears are clustered. His poetry, like Baudelaire's, reaches its climax in the theme of death. He devotes not a little of his descriptive power and imaginative energy to periphrastic descriptions of death, and while he no more knows what death holds than did Baudelaire, for him, too, it is, though terrible, less terrible than life in that, lacking all attributes, it necessarily lacks the negative attributes of life. He is obsessed by the way: 'I no longer know where my path is leading ... Everything is dark, disjointed, fragmented', he wrote in his diary on 9 October 1911. It was two months after this that he referred to himself as 'Georg Heym, who does not know the way'. What he meant was that he knew that for him there was no way to meaning, or fulfilment, or life. He was indeed the brother of Baudelaire, although this must not blind us to the differences between the two poets, particularly the fact that whereas *Les fleurs du mal* is the work of a Christian poet, *Der ewige Tag* is not.

'Why, this is Hell, nor am I out of it!' Arthur Symons imagined Baudelaire voicing to himself these words of Marlowe's Mephistopheles.[26] It is equally easy to imagine Heym voicing them for he, too, viewed life as Hell. In charting what he sees as Hell on earth, he writes with a cold chagrin reminiscent of *Les Litanies de Satan* and of *Spleen et Idéal*; his 'Ich verfluche dich, Gott' (*L* 18) parallels Baudelaire's 'Ô mon semblable, ô mon maître, je te maudis',[27] except that his agony is without any Christian solace. His 'Die Hölle I' (*L* 327f.) depicts a Dantesque Inferno in that he, too, 'took the raw material of his Hell from this world and yet made a very proper Hell of it';[28] otherwise his inferno is, rather, like Baudelaire's and Schopenhauer's in being characterized by what he, like Baudelaire, found to be, and what Schopenhauer described as, one of the main features of life: *ennui*. He can imagine nothing more hellish.

Baudelaire is the *éminence grise* behind the urban poetry that Heym took to writing in spring 1910, poetry that is inconceivable without the example of the *Tableaux parisiens*. If his evident sense of kinship with Baudelaire is explicable in terms of the affinity between the men and the correspondences between their views of life, there remain the connections between their poetry, some of them explicable in terms of influence. It is with temperament that we must start again, for Heym's work would no more have been possible without his morbidity of temperament than would Baudelaire's, since it is from that temperament that all its significant strengths and weaknesses derive. Heym has in common with Baudelaire a use of intensification (achieved by the use of plurals, personification, exaggeration, massed imagery, and so on) that reflects a similar creative temperament. His black visions (unlike George Moore's 'flowers of passion') are genuinely Baudelairean, with the qualification that it is the cycle of spleen, rather than the love cycles, of *Les fleurs du mal* that they recall. Whether Heym's expression of the *horreur de la vie* is as skilfully modulated as Baudelaire's, readers will judge for themselves; in doing so they will remember that moderation was not in his nature.

Baudelaire was a painter *manqué*; so, too, was Heym. Baudelaire's poetry is notable for its painterly qualities; so, too, is Heym's. In his *A Vision* W. B. Yeats saw Baudelaire as the archetype of 'the sensuous man'; Heym is another outstanding example of the type, although, that said, the beauty of his poetry – as Swinburne (whose name, as we have seen, appears enigmatically in Heym's 1911 *Notizbüchlein* on several occasions) said of Baudelaire's – is rather passionate than sensuous; in other words, it is above all a matter of intensity. His work has the tautness and bite characteristic of Baudelaire's, qualities which it owes partly to its high-key quality, and partly to its solidity and often monumental, monolithic manner. Both poets favour the grand manner, this being part of their classicism. That Heym's *grandezza* derives from Baudelaire will scarcely be doubted. In general terms his poetic work is less theatrical than Baudelaire's, though no less dramatic; but his despair has a theatricality that again points to Baudelaire. T. S. Eliot argued that Baudelaire's view of life has grandeur and exhibits heroism; Heym's view of life exhibits heroism, and his work, like Baudelaire's, is characterized by a grandiose mythicality.

While Heym and Baudelaire are both romantics, and indeed extreme romantics, they both prefer the classical manner when it comes to expressing their malaise; their poems therefore 'have the external but not the internal form of classic art'.[29] They are both opposed to realism on the grounds that without imaginative intensification there is no poetry. Poetry, for them, means intensity of language; it actually gains in intensity from being confined in such unadventurous forms. One of the conventional, classical forms they favour is the sonnet. Swinburne noted Baudelaire's 'mastery of the sonnet-form' and his 'natural bias towards such forms of verse as are most nearly capable of perfection',[30] and Eliot was inclined to think that 'the care for perfection of form' was 'an effort to support, or to conceal from view, an inner disorder'.[31] Heym's classicism hardly 'conceals' any 'disorder' as such, although it may be a way of dissociating himself from it; but whatever their psychological reasons for preferring the classical mode, there is, in both poets, a frequently pronounced disparity between classical form and romantic content. Indeed, the *frisson* which Heym's poetry conveys comes from our shocked recognition of the disparity between form and content, the 'spectacle of the individual and his world falling to pieces *inside the classical mould*';[32] it is this that makes him a quintessential modernist à la Baudelaire. Seen thus, those regular, 'classical' forms become both a lament for the classical world, a kind of poetic *recherche du temps perdu*, and at the same time a mockery of that world. During the period when he is most under Baudelaire's sway, Heym's work reflects the predomination of the will-to-form over the 'mere' will-to-self-expression, which is characteristic of Baudelaire's work – until, that is, the final months of Heym's life, when the will-to-self-expression takes over. Heym, too, was given to talking about beauty; in his poetry, too, beauty is equated not with romantic or otherwise conventionally attractive images (for his images are frequently grotesque), but with form, the superimposition of the poet's will upon life.

However, it is not only the 'square' forms of Heym's later poetry that are Baudelairean; so, too, are many of the images which those forms frame. In the *Salon of 1859* Baudelaire remarked: 'The whole of the visible universe is only a storehouse of images and signs to which imagination will give a place and a relative value.' The two men's poetic apparatus or stock of images is naturally different, Baudelaire's being more exotic and Heym's more gothic, but they have many images in common. Above all, they both use urban imagery in a similar way. Heym's Berlin poems are indebted to the imagery of Baudelaire's *cité fourmillante*, for Baudelaire

gave new possibilities to poetry in a new stock of imagery of contemporary life ... It is not merely in the use of imagery of common life, not merely in the use of imagery of the sordid life of a great metropolis, but in the elevation of such imagery to the *first intensity* – presenting it as it is, and yet making it represent something much more than itself – that Baudelaire has created a mode of release and expression for other men.[33]

This seems to me to apply exactly to Georg Heym who is, in 1910–11, an urban poet in precisely this sense of simultaneously seeing the megalopolis of Berlin realistically and symbolically; but not only is much of Heym's imagery a demonized urban imagery, he also shares with Baudelaire a sense of the unreality of this and any other reality. Without the influence of Baudelaire and Rimbaud the iconography of his work would have been quite different.

The form of much of Heym's best-known work is a reflection of Baudelaire's form, and a few of his poems actually echo poems by the French poet; thus 'Der Tod der Liebenden' (*L* 151, November 1910) was inspired by 'La mort des amants'. Heym's starting-point, in the first version of his poem ('Der Tod der Liebenden im Meer'), was the first two lines of Baudelaire's poem ('Nous aurons des lits plein d'odeurs légères,/Des divans profonds comme des tombeaux': 'We shall have beds full of light aromas, divans profound as sepulchres'), which gave him the opening lines of his first version ('Wir werden schlafen bei den Toten drunten/Im Schattenland. Wir werden einsam wohnen/In ewgem Schlafe in den Tiefen unten': 'We shall sleep with the dead down among the shades. We shall dwell in solitude, in eternal sleep, down in the depths'), which appear in the third stanza of his final version. As always, Heym strikes out independently, in this case both by assigning the lovers to a watery grave and by making death, like life, a domain of demons. He always goes beyond his starting-point, whether it be in Baudelaire, or Rimbaud, or elsewhere; thus 'Die Schläfer' (December 1910) was said by Hugo Ball to be 'a preposterously beautiful poem' which 'out-baudelaires Baudelaire' (*D* 170f.) for reasons which have already been given. By the same token his 'Hymne' is clearly indebted to Baudelaire's 'Hymne', his 'Der Tag' to Baudelaire's 'La fin de la journée'. The description of Paris in 'Der fünfte Oktober' as a 'sea of darkness' echoes Baudelaire's 'la mer des Ténèbres' in 'Le Voyage (VII)'. And so on. A list of parallels would be rather longer.

Like Baudelaire, Heym produced a variety of work other than poetry; but he, too, was above all a poet; if his other work were lost, his reputation would be relatively unaffected, for it rests, and will continue to rest, on two slim volumes of poems, together with the tales. His treatment of 'the horror' in the tales, like Conrad's in *Heart of Darkness*, goes back to Baudelaire. His tales in fact belong to the gothic tradition of Poe's tales, by which they are strongly influenced; it may well be that Heym had his attention drawn to Poe by Baudelaire, who himself belongs to that same tradition. By 1910 Heym's imagination had become genuinely 'gothic', so that he is never more himself than when he is closest to Poe and Baudelaire.

Most apprentice writers learn from other writers in a technical sense; in other words, they learn from them a technique or techniques which they themselves develop in some way. Heym learnt from

Baudelaire in this way (see his use of the plural, for instance), but Baudelaire provided him neither with a philosophical system as such (though he was steeped in the spirit of Baudelaire, who clearly helped him to form his own view of life) nor with a technique of 'correspondances'. The influence of Baudelaire is to be seen not so much in particular techniques, important though a few of these are, as in the overall form and style of the poetry of 1900–11 – its formality, density, elegance, impersonality, and so on. Heym would have been unlikely to play down personal emotion so much had it not been for the example of Baudelaire. As it is, his poetry, highly personal in its origins and neuroses, is almost totally impersonal in manner. Nor would he have produced that particular kind of urban poetry with its massed imagery and classical forms if he had not had Baudelaire in mind, and indeed if he had not looked up to him to such an extraordinary degree.

Baudelaire, Rimbaud and Verlaine, like the English Romantic poets, helped Heym to be himself: he studied their lives and measured himself against them. They taught him to bear the *malheur d'être poète*, to which he owed most of the little happiness he knew. His interest in other writers (Samain excepted) is invariably biographical and therefore subjective. He looks in their lives for confirmation of his validity as writer and human being; he defines himself by means of this self-identification with his poetic heroes, who are heroes for him because they were men of similar temperament who were able to triumph over difficulties similar to those which beset him. Baudelaire was therefore for Heym what he had been for Rimbaud: 'le premier voyant, roi des poètes, *un vrai Dieu*' ('the first visionary, king of poets, *a veritable god*').[34]

□ RIMBAUD AND VERLAINE

David Baumgardt was particularly struck by Heym's attachment to Rimbaud's 'Le bateau ivre'. This is appropriate, for with the divine Rimbaud, as he called him, Heym has much in common: 'I love anyone with a broken heart ... I love Rimbaud' (*T* 20 July 1909). When he writes in his diary on 26 October 1910 that 'I am quite lost, drifting like a ship [without a rudder]' (*T* 146), he has in mind not only the Flying Dutchman, but Rimbaud's *Bateau ivre*, which, according to Ernst Moritz

Engert, he began translating in 1911.[35] Like Rimbaud he rebelled against a strait-laced upbringing; he shared the French poet's contempt for philistinism (including bourgeois morality), his vehement nature, his desire to escape altogether from European culture, and so on. His idea, in September 1911, of studying Chinese and becoming a dragoman, is pure Rimbaud. What was Heym's life, marked, as it was, by the same abrupt transitions of mood as Rimbaud's poetry, but a brief Season in Hell? He, no less than Rimbaud, had a *fureur de vivre* (in a drawing he personified himself as Furor); he, too, sought to live with all his faculties all the time; he, too, was 'greedy as the sea' (Rimbaud) for the life that was to be but a dream, complaining bitterly of the monotony between the ecstasies – how often does he echo Rimbaud's words from a letter of 2 November 1870: 'I am dying surrounded by greyness.' For him, too, the work was nothing, the act of producing it, everything. If it is true that Rimbaud's mind was 'not the mind of the artist but of the man of action', and that 'To him it was an identical act of his temperament to write the sonnet of the *vowels* and to trade in ivory and frankincense with the Arabs',[36] then this applies in a general way to Heym too, though he was continually exasperated, as a poet, by the activities of his mundane alter ego. If it is true that Rimbaud brought into French verse something of that 'gipsy way of going with nature, as with a woman',[37] then something not so very different is true of Heym, for whom it is the *frisson*, of whatever kind, that counts. Many German poets have written more than their share of poems on death; none has written of it with greater erotic excitement. For Heym the aesthetic and the erotic are closely linked. Life, for him, is a matter of waiting for death *avec gourmandise*. No less than Rimbaud, he seeks always for the absolute and is content with nothing less. When he, too, feels contempt for the finished product, it is because it is by definition imperfect; the moment of consummation, whether aesthetic or erotic, is the beginning of disenchantment.

In general Rimbaud gave Heym the encouragement to ride his Fury. In poetic terms Heym's debt to his French idol is more specific. If Baudelaire gave his work of 1909–11 its classical, strophic structure and teeming imagery, Rimbaud gave that imagery its visionary content. He also gave Heym the starting-point for some memorable poems. A case in point concerns Rimbaud's 'Ophélie', the first and most relevant part of which reads as follows:

Sur l'onde calme et noire où dorment les étoiles
La blanche Ophélie flotte comme un grand lys,
Flotte très lentement, couchée en ses longs voiles...
– On entend dans les bois lointains des hallalis.

Voici plus de mille ans que la triste Ophélie
Passe, fantôme blanc, sur le long fleuve noir.
Voici plus de mille ans que sa douce folie
Murmure sa romance à la brise du soir.

Le vent baise ses seins et déploie en corolle
Ses grands voiles bercés mollement par les eaux;
Les saules frissonnants pleurent sur son épaule,
Sur son grand front rêveur s'inclinent les roseaux.

Les nénuphars froissés soupirent autour d'elle;
Elle éveille parfois, dans un aune qui dort,
Quelque nid, d'où s'échappe un petit frisson d'aile:
– Un chant mystérieux tombe des astres d'or.

('Ophelia') On the calm black water where the stars are sleeping, white Ophelia is floating like a great lily, floating very slowly, lying in her long veils ... In the distant woods one can hear them sounding the mort.

For more than a thousand years now sad Ophelia has been passing, a white ghost, down the long black river. For more than a thousand years now her sweet madness has been whispering its tale to the evening breeze.

The wind kisses her breasts and opens like a corolla those great veils cradled gently by the waters; the shivering willows weep on her shoulder, the rushes lean over her wide dreaming brow.

The water-lilies past which she brushes sigh all about her; from time to time she awakens, in a slumbering alder, a nest from which escapes the sound of startled wings; a mysterious music comes from the golden stars.

Heym's 'Die Tote im Wasser' (August 1910: *L* 117f.) and 'Ophelia' (November 1910: *L* 160ff.) are indebted to this poem (and to Baudelaire's 'Une charogne'); they invite comparison with Gottfried Benn's Heym-inspired 'Schöne Jugend' and Brecht's 'Vom ertrunkenen Mädchen'. The more memorable of Heym's two poems is 'Die Tote im Wasser':

Die Masten ragen an dem grauen Wall
Wie ein verbrannter Wald ins frühe Rot,
So schwarz wie Schlacke. Wo das Wasser tot
Zu Speichern stiert, die morsch und im Verfall.

Dumpf tönt der Schall, da wiederkehrt die Flut
Den Kai entlang. Der Stadtnacht Spülicht treibt
Wie eine weiße Haut im Strom und reibt
Sich an dem Dampfer, der im Docke ruht.

Staub, Obst, Papier, in einer dicken Schicht,
So treibt der Kot aus seinen Röhren ganz.
Ein weißes Tanzkleid kommt, in fettem Glanz
Ein nackter Hals und bleiweiß ein Gesicht.

Die Leiche wälzt sich ganz heraus. Es bläht
Das Kleid sich wie ein weißes Schiff im Wind.
Die toten Augen starren groß und blind
Zum Himmel, der voll rosa Wolken steht.

Das lila Wasser bebt von kleiner Welle.
– Der Wasserratten Fährte, die bemannen
Das weiße Schiff. Nun treibt es stolz von dannen,
Voll grauer Köpfe und voll schwarzer Felle.

Die Tote segelt froh hinaus, gerissen
Von Wind und Flut. Ihr dicker Bauch entragt
Dem Wasser groß, zerhöhlt und fast zernagt.
Wie eine Grotte dröhnt er von den Bissen.

Sie treibt ins Meer. Ihr salutiert Neptun
Von einem Wrack, da sie das Meer verschlingt,
Darinnen sie zur grünen Tiefe sinkt,
Im Arm der feisten Kraken auszuruhn.

('The dead girl in the water') The masts tower above the grey harbour wall like a forest of charred tree-trunks, as black as slag, rising up into the red morning sky, while the water stares listlessly at crumbling, decaying warehouses.

There is a dull sound the length of the quayside when the tide comes in. The town's dishwater from the previous night drifts around on the river like a white skin and rubs against the steamer lying in dock.

Dirt, orange peel, paper, in a thick layer: the filth comes out of its pipes. A white evening dress appears, and amid the oily sheen a bare neck and a chalk-white face.

The whole body heaves in sight. The dress catches the wind like a white ship. The dead eyes stare unseeingly at the sky, which is full of pink clouds.

The lilac-coloured water trembles with tiny ripples. – A crew of water-rats manning the white ship. Now it moves proudly away, arrayed with grey heads and black fur.

The dead girl sails blithely away, carried by wind and tide. Her great belly is above water, hollowed out and almost eaten away, echoing like a grotto with the sound of gnawing.

She drifts out to sea. Neptune salutes her from a wreck as she is swallowed up by the sea into whose green depths she sinks, coming to rest in the bloated Kraken's embrace.

The Kraken, a mythical sea-monster said to lurk in the waters around Norway, features in Rimbaud's poem, but is peculiarly at home in Heym's. In the last two quatrains, the girl's body, a white ship manned by water-rats – no less memorable an image than Rimbaud's 'il a vu sur l'eau, couchée en ses longs voiles,/La blanche Ophélie flotter, comme un grand lys' – becomes reminiscent of the *bateau ivre*; but while the poem thus reflects the influence on Heym of Rimbaud's poetry in general and 'Le bateau ivre' in particular, what it really demonstrates is the power of his visual imagination and the alchemical ability, which he shares with Baudelaire, to transmute dross into gold, horror into beauty. Other well-known poems indebted to Rimbaud include 'Die Toten auf dem Berge' (*L* 99ff.), cf. 'Le bal des pendus'; 'Der Schläfer im Walde (*L* 40f.) and 'Nach der Schlacht' (*L* 124), cf. 'Le dormeur du val'; 'Sehnsucht nach Paris' (*L* 227ff.), cf. 'L'Orgie Parisienne'; 'Das Lettehaus' (*L* 285), cf. 'Voyelles'; 'Die Professoren' (*L* 157), cf. 'Les Assis'; and 'Der Hunger' (*L* 158), cf. 'Fêtes de la faim' and 'Les effarés'. The list need not be extended, for what such comparisons show is that Rimbaud tends to spark Heym's imagination, giving him the starting-image for a poem which then outstrips the French poet. For instance, Rimbaud described the ecstasy of hunger of 'Les effarés' and personified his own hunger for life in 'Fêtes de la faim', but 'Fêtes de la faim' is a weak affair compared with Heym's brilliantly stylized sonnet 'Der Hunger', the imagery of which is a *tour de force*:

> Er fuhr in einen Hund, dem groß er sperrt
> Das rote Maul. Die blaue Zunge wirft
> Sich lang heraus. Er wälzt im Staub. Er schlürft
> Verwelktes Gras, das er dem Sand entzerrt.
>
> Sein leerer Schlund ist wie ein großes Tor,
> Drin Feuer sickert, langsam, tropfenweis,
> Das ihm den Bauch verbrennt. Dann wäscht mit Eis
> Ihm eine Hand das heiße Speiserohr.

Er wankt durch Dampf. Die Sonne ist ein Fleck,
Ein rotes Ofentor. Ein grüner Halbmond führt
Vor seinen Augen Tänze. Er ist weg.

Ein schwarzes Loch gähnt, draus die Kälte stiert,
Er fällt hinab, und fühlt noch, wie der Schreck
Mit Eisenfäusten seine Gurgel schnürt.

('Hunger') It passed into a dog whose red mouth it opens wide. The blue tongue lolls out. The dog rolls in the dust. Savours some dead grass which he pulls out of the sand.

His empty maw is like a great door inside which fire drips slowly, drop by drop, burning his belly. Then a hand pours ice down his red-hot gullet.

He staggers through steam. The sun is a patch of fire, a red oven-door. He sees a green half-moon dancing before his eyes. He's a goner.

A black hole yawns through which coldness stares. He falls into it and is just aware of the shock taking him by the throat in its iron grip.

This poems owes its inspiration to Rimbaud and its classical form to Baudelaire, but what it illustrates is Heym's poetic power and originality. The poem expresses his own passionate hunger for life, which is seen so absolutely that this is a – or the – poem about hunger. An enigmatic note at the beginning of his fifth diary reads 'Der Mensch als Hund'; in 'Der Hunger' the dog stands for Man. Whether the *donnée* comes from life or from art – and it is normally visual – Heym uses it to produce works of absolute authenticity. 'Der Hunger' is an appropriate point to leave our discussion of Baudelaire and Rimbaud, for it shows, as well as any other poem, that Heym combines the vision of Rimbaud with the intensity of Baudelaire. It is a powerful combination. 'Der Hunger' also leads naturally to the subject of Verlaine, who shared Heym's hunger for life.

Little is known of Heym's attitude to Verlaine, who is mentioned in the diaries only once (*T* 149, 5 November 1910: 'Baudelaire. Verlaine. Rimbaud. Keats, Shelley. I really think that I am the only German [poet] worthy to stand in the shadow of these gods'). This deification is explicable in terms of self-identification. Heym believed absolutely in Verlaine's maxim: 'The secret of art is to be absolutely oneself.' The two men were similarly saturnine in temperament; both were dual characters; both were men of feeling making up in sensitivity what they lacked in profundity. They both had a *fureur d'aimer* which left them at the mercy of the emotion or impression of the moment; having the child-like temperament to which love in the *sine qua non* of existence, neither could live without it. Both had a passionate hunger for life, which caused them to live with a similar intensity, giving absolute value to every moment; they had the same vital energy, the same sharpness of sensation, the same instant receptivity, the same fierce subjectivity. For both men every mood had the vehemence of passion, every sorrow the absoluteness of despair. Both were devoured by dreams. For both of them the visible world existed as vision, seeing and vision, by a strange alchemy of the mind's eye, being one. Both embody that 'pagan' sentiment which 'measures the sadness with which the human mind is filled whenever its thoughts wander from what is here and now';[38] but whereas Heym is 'beset by notions of irresistible natural powers' ranged against him, Verlaine is more conscious of the glory of the visible world, that is, conscious that these powers are 'the secret also of his fortune, making the earth golden and the grape fiery for him'. The difference is, however, only one of emphasis, for both men are so intensely aware of sunlight and beauty that they shudder before the descent into death and therefore exemplify the 'pagan' determination not to 'sleep before evening', the determination to 'get as many pulsations as possible into the given time'. In other words, they both exemplify the 'poetic passion', the desire of beauty, the love of art for its own sake which Pater described so memorably.

There were, of course, important differences between them, notably the fact that Verlaine, despite a series of disasters which made the outward pattern of his life more dire than Heym's, possessed a private cheerfulness which was denied to Heym, although Heym was outwardly gregarious, fun to be with. That point made, we come back to the fact that both men exemplify what has been called the fundamental abnormality of the artist. Both despised 'normality'; but it was the dying of the light against which they raged. When Heym sent a memorable postcard to his publisher – 'on a bender in Metz; sending of MS delayed' (T 286), he wrote in French – he was, among other things, on a pilgrimage to Verlaine's birth-place, making a last-minute obeisance to the Prince of Poets, to the example of whose elegance of expression and delicacy of feeling his own greatest poems (those elegies which he had just been writing) are as surely indebted as his preceding poems are indebted to Baudelaire and Rimbaud.

Baudelaire, Rimbaud and Verlaine, like the English Romantic poets, helped him to develop his work in decisive ways. There were also several other French writers whom he particularly admired, including Stendhal, Albert Samain, Octave Mirbeau and Villiers de l'Isle Adam. The last two belong in the context of the tales, and Samain in that of the later poetry. With Stendhal it is a very different matter.

□ STENDHAL

In summer 1908 Heym gave Hedi a copy of Stendhal's *Chroniques italiennes*. On 3 November 1908 he notes that he is rereading them; he probably first read them before summer 1908 since he will have given Hedi a copy of a book which he already knew and valued. There are verbal echoes of Stendhal's short story 'Les Cenci' in Heym's dramatic work from *Die Hochzeit des Bartolomeo Ruggieri* (1908) onwards; his main use of the story came in 1911, when he drafted his own *Cenci*. It was in 1911 that he read Wilhelm Weigand's *Stendhal* (Berlin, 1903) and, more important, Stendhal's *Le rouge et le noir*, which he read in the translation by Friedrich von Oppeln-Bronikowski (*Rot und Schwarz. Eine Chronik des XIX. Jahrhunderts*, second edition, Jena, 1907). His diary shows that he saw himself both in Stendhal (October 1910) and in his part-autobiographical 'hero' Julien Sorel (September 1911).

On 29 October 1910 Heym quotes a critic he has been reading as saying:

'Stendhal only seemed to be the cynical dare-devil and hussar who filled with moral indignation the society types who listened to his tall stories without having the psychological know-how to assess them for what they were worth; in reality throughout his life he was capable of the most delicate feeling, of that most private of passions which is happy to be allowed to enjoy its bitter-sweet secret in silence.' Stendhal?

As if it were not obvious that this passage is noted because it records a hidden sensitivity similar to his own, he later wrote in after 'Stendhal?' the word 'Ego'. The quotation is taken from Weigand's *Stendhal*, which thus becomes important as one confirmed source of Heym's view of Stendhal.

Of the five quotations from *Le rouge et le noir* noted by Heym on 1 September 1911,[39] the interesting ones are the three in which he identifies with the French novelist (the other two are merely *bons mots*).

After quoting the words, 'In those days a man's life was a succession of chances. Now civilization has driven away chance; nothing is unexpected any more', he says that they apply to his own time more than to Stendhal's, a comment behind which lies his whole view of the monotony of his age. The other two are related more directly to himself. He quotes: 'He was sick to death of all his own good qualities, of all the things he had once enthusiastically loved, and in this state of inverted imagination he was attempting to judge life,' and adds: 'Ego saepe.' Like Julien Sorel, Heym is an enthusiast who finds the world a miserable enough place when he is not fired up; and yet that is when he judges it in his diaries. Finally, he refers to his own feeling of being almost destroyed by fate when he notes: 'I swayed to and fro, I was shaken. After all, I was only a man. – But I was not carried away.' He comments in one word: 'Ego.'

In the course of the next few weeks there are further self-related references to Stendhal. On 13 September he notes: 'He was always in tumult. Stendhal on Sorel.' No one who has read the preceding diary pages could doubt the parallel in his mind. A fortnight later the reference to self is explicit: 'Stendhal. Danger gives a sensible person a touch of genius, may make him, as it were, superior to himself. The imaginative person it inspires with whole novels which are no doubt bold, but mostly nonsensical. Ego-Leni.' On 6 October 1911 he quotes Stendhal's 'Some situations are eternal', and adds: 'My constellation is also eternal.' The longest and most explicit of all such diary entries is the last, which is dated 16 October 1911:

'It reveals the secret of that small number of higher men who, too richly endowed for their century, almost at the first attempt take everything to its logical conclusion and drain everything down to the dregs ... They are filled with disgust at things, at the emptiness of everyday life, sick with the very richness of their own souls, and discover, in this atmosphere of aridity and egoism, within themselves an irresistible and elemental need to love ... to be churned up, to be moved, to be transported by passion ...' In a word, Stendhal anticipated me.

Reading these diary entries one can only agree with his friend John Wolfsohn, who quotes Heym's 'I am very strong and very weak, I torment myself, I suffer from self-torment', and comments: 'He quotes, often with almost pathetic reference to himself, a number of similar remarks made by ... Stendhal ... about his hero Julien (*D* 147).' This is true, although there is a good deal more to Heym's attitude towards Stendhal/Sorel than is revealed either by his own quotations or by Wolfsohn's comment.

Heym shares with Stendhal a passion for self-observation and self-analysis; his diaries are so many *souvenirs d'égotisme*. Like Stendhal, he tends to view himself as both subject and object, tends to view his life from the outside as a work of art. There are striking similarities between the two men. The three verbs in which Stendhal sought to summarize his life (I lived, I loved, I wrote) are surely those which Heym would also have used to describe his own life. Stendhal's career anticipates Heym's at every point (he was the officer of dragoons under Napoleon that Heym longed to be, even claiming – falsely – to have fought at Marengo; he was civil servant, amateur painter, student actor, consul, lover, writer). Like Heym after him, Stendhal was permanently unsettled, a prey to boredom; he was forever travelling (as Heym wished to do), forever falling in and out of love (his love affairs, like Heym's, were arguably his main single occupation, for there was nothing he needed more or took more seriously). Both men were aristocratic by inclination and Jacobinic by reaction. Both wore a mask to protect their inner being. It is this inner being that is so similar. Mérimée wrote that all his life Stendhal was governed by imagination; in everything he did he acted impulsively and enthusiastically. It might be Heym. In both men we find the same headlong enthusiasms, the recurrent thought of suicide, the constant rediscovery of despair. Both dreamed of glory, both went in for dramatic gestures. Stendhal noted the intimate details of his life on the same kind of scraps of paper on which Heym jotted down lines of poetry; much of Stendhal's work, too, is fragmentary.

Enough has been said to show that Heym's self-identication with Stendhal inevitably went far beyond the points which he notes in his diary. Nor is that all, for there is also his self-identification with Stendhal's part-autobiographical 'hero', Julien Sorel.

Heym sitting on the outside windowsill of David Baumgardt's flat singing the 'Marseillaise' is reminiscent of Julien Sorel sitting astride a roofbeam reading the *Mémorial de Sainte-Hélène*, that keystone of the Napoleonic legend. Like Heym, Sorel is a passionate and imaginative young man whose head is full of his cult of Napoleon and his enthusiasm for the French Revolution (he even identifies with Danton, as Heym does). His imagination, too, always runs to extremes, finally becoming his implacable enemy – surely Heym remembered this when he wrote 'Now I've got a struggle on my hands, for my imagination has turned against me' (*T* 174) – so that he needs the full energy of his character to maintain himself above the level of despair. This will all have been totally familiar to Heym. If it is true that Julien lives not so much his own life as a modified or counterfeit copy of another's, Heym does something similar, for he, too, seeks to define himself by conforming to borrowed models (he is now Hölderlin, now Leonardo da Vinci, now Ognibene, now Julien Sorel). His ambition, like Sorel's, is rooted in a chimerical fantasy. His fictional career as 'hussar officer' was as much a chimera as Sorel's. His real career, like Sorel's, was love. A diary entry dated 5 November 1911 shows that he has been reading Stendhal's *De l'amour* (*Über die Liebe*, translated by Friedrich von Oppeln-Bronikowski, third edition, Berlin, n.d., p. 299), the subject of which is close to Heym's heart. Both men are forever contemplating the possibilities of their destiny, Sorel ending up in the prison in which Heym had always felt himself to be incarcerated. When they die, the novel of their life begins. Heym was bound to recognize in Julien Sorel (and in Mathilde de La Mole) his own impassioned, beleaguered self; the diary shows that he did so. It was to be his final act of self-definition.

VI

Painter Manqué

□ VAN GOGH

While most of the 'heroes' and 'gods' in whom Heym saw his own image were poets or men of action, or both, others were painters. Given that his imagination was primarily and powerfully visual, and that he claimed (with his customary exaggeration) to write only because he could not paint, it was inevitable that he would identify with certain painters and would incorporate some of their images into his own work, which is very much of the post-Impressionist era.

From an early age Heym visited exhibitions; when in other towns, he would visit the local art gallery. He grew up, of course, at a time when painting in Germany was in ferment. He read the books that people interested in painting were reading at the time: Margarete Mauthner's selection of Van Gogh's letters (1906), Meier-Graefe's *Der moderne Impressionismus* (1903) and *Manet und sein Kreis* (1902), Worringer's *Formprobleme der Gotik* (1911), and so on. One of his closest friends – Ernst Moritz Engert – was a painter, and two other friends, Simon Guttmann and John Wolfsohn, were keenly interested in art history; indeed Guttmann was an art-critic, as was Heym's acquaintance Hanns Heinz Ewers. Engert had a large collection of reproductions, which Heym saw and used. Heym's mind worked iconographically; he made collections of images, these becoming the building-blocks of which his later poems were composed (interestingly enough, these images mostly involve similes). His notebooks contain a number of rather naïve, childish drawings, although Engert recalled one (lost) self-portrait which was 'completely amateurish' but also 'an amazing likeness';[1] Engert was clearly right to say that drawing (or painting) was 'quite beyond him', for this is precisely what his drawings prove. There is no doubt, however, that Heym had a clear preference for painting over poetry, this reflecting the argument which Merezhkovsky puts into Leonardo's mouth:

The eye gives a more complete knowledge of nature than the ear! Things seen are less to be doubted than things heard. Painting, which is silent poetry, comes nearer to positive science than poetry, which is invisible painting. Words give but a series of isolated images following one another; but in a picture, all the forms, all the colours appear synchronously, and are blended into a whole, like the notes of a chord in music; and thus both to painting and to music a more complex harmony is possible than to poetry. And the richer the harmony, the richer is that delight which is the aim and the enchantment of art. Question, say, any lover, whether he would not rather have a portrait of his loved one than a description in words of her countenance, though it were composed by the greatest of poets?[2]

Although, as we have seen, Leonardo was Heym's ideal of the artist as hero, his super-ego, in biographical and artistic terms alike he found it easier to relate to Vincent van Gogh, who from winter 1909/10 was one of his major enthusiasms. The five works by Van Gogh which he saw at the Third Exhibition of the Berlin Secession in May 1901 were the first such works he had seen, and indeed the first to be seen in Germany; we know from the diary (T 131) that he attended this exhibition, at which he was much impressed by Martin Brandenburg's *Die Menschen unter der Wolke*. From then on he had every opportunity to acquire a good knowledge of the whole range of Van Gogh's work. Between May 1901 and January 1912 there were no less than eighteen exhibitions in Berlin at which Van Gogh's work was shown, including six major exhibitions of the paintings at Paul Cassirer's gallery, in December 1901 (nineteen works), April 1905 (twenty-three works), March 1908 (twenty-seven works), October 1908 (seventy-five works), May 1909 (twenty works) and October/November 1910 (fifty-two works), and two of the drawings, at the Twelfth and Nineteenth Secession exhibitions in December 1906 (thirty works) and December 1909 (twenty-three works).[3]

Whereas in 1901 Van Gogh was little known in Germany, by

1910, when Julius Meier-Graefe's *Vincent van Gogh* first appeared, he had become one of the brightest stars in the Expressionist firmament, not least because he was himself a proto-Expressionist, someone whose work exemplified the passion which is so fundamental to Expressionism.

By the time Heym left school in 1907, the young artists of Die Brücke were so much under the influence of Van Gogh that Emil Nolde remarked that they should be known as 'Van Goghians'; indeed, Van Gogh was so much in the air that Kurt Hiller found it necessary to go on record as saying that 'some people go around saying "Van Gogh", thinking this shows how smart they are'.4 The appearance of Margarete Mauthner's one-volume selection of Van Gogh's letters (*Briefe*) in 1906 was a landmark in the reception of the Dutch artist in Germany, particularly in literary circles. Illustrated selections from these letters first appeared in the leading art journal of the time, Bruno Cassirer's *Kunst und Künstler*, in 1903–4. Whether Heym saw them there is not known; what is known is that in August/September 1910 he borrowed Margarete Mauthner's volume from John Wolfsohn. It is to this widely read volume that he is referring when he writes on 2 September 1910: 'Many thanks for the Van Gogh which I walked off with (*T* 205).' John Wolfsohn later said that this letter was written 'when he [Heym] had just been shaken by an exhibition of Van Gogh's paintings and by reading Van Gogh's letters' (*D* 144). But for Wolfsohn's statement that Heym (like so many other poets and painters) had been reading Van Gogh's *Briefe*, it might have been supposed that it was Julius Meier-Graefe's *Vincent van Gogh* that he had borrowed, for this book, which did so much to establish the myth and the mythology of Van Gogh, was published in 1910. Had Heym read the book – and while there is no proof that he did, it is most unlikely that he did not – he could not but have been 'erschüttert' (shaken or shattered) to discover how much he had in common with Van Gogh. As to the Van Gogh exhibition which Heym is said to have just attended in September 1910, Wolfsohn's statement, made ten years after the event, was not entirely accurate. Heym could not have 'just' attended such an exhibition in September 1910. If he had recently been deeply impressed by a Van Gogh exhibition by September 1910, then it must have been by the most striking Van Gogh exhibition of his lifetime, the one at Paul Cassirer's in October 1908. The evidence of the poetry, as we shall see, suggests that this was the case. The use of pure, expressive colour in his poetry dates from 1909,[5] and becomes a regular feature of it in January 1910; from then until October 1911 it is combined with clear visual echoes of Van Gogh's work.

No doubt Heym also attended the large one-man exhibition of Van Gogh's work at the Kunstsalon Paul Cassirer (where Neue Club meetings were held) from 25 October to 20 November 1910, by which time he was already full of enthusiasm for him; the evidence of the poetry suggests that this new exhibition renewed the flame of his enthusiasm. It was probably this exhibition that Wolfsohn had in mind.

When he wrote to John Wolfsohn on 2 September 1910 to thank him for allowing him to walk off with Van Gogh's *Briefe*, Heym went on to say of him:

He is perhaps even closer to me than Hodler, for he sees colours as I see them. On reading [his letters] I have again and again said, Good Lord, that is just how you would make a poem: The sailors seen against the disc of the sun. The lilac boats. The sower in a boundless field, etc. The difference is that painting is very difficult, whereas writing poetry is terribly easy provided one has eyes to see (*T* 205).

The motifs which Heym lists come from Van Gogh's letters. Van Gogh did not actually paint 'The sailors seen against the disc of the sun', but he did write of 'Sailors walking with their girlfriends towards the town with its drawbridge silhouetted in a remarkable way against the enormous yellow disc of the sun';[6] it is this image that Heym abbreviates. Nor did Van Gogh paint 'lilac fishing-boats', but Mauthner reproduced two paintings of small fishing-boats (Van Gogh's F413, which Heym may have seen at Paul Cassirer's in December 1901 and October 1908, and F426, which was shown at Paul Cassirer's in April 1905), and included Van Gogh's comment on the way in which an evening sky can give things 'a pale lilac tone'. Heym put the two together. The 'sower in a boundless field', is, of course, straight Van Gogh: Mauthner reproduces such a sower, together with Van Gogh's comment about 'longing for the infinite, to which the *Sower* and the *Sheaves* bear witness'.[7] By 1910 Heym had had several opportunities to see versions of Van Gogh's *Sower*.

Heym himself certainly had eyes to see ('Optik'); he saw everything in images, these immediately taking on a symbolical dimension in his mind. His later poems are brilliantly, vividly visual: they can always be seen and could easily be painted, for they are the work of a man with a painter's eye. His black visions have, often, an appalling clarity – for instance, the nightmare vision of a group of demons standing round a woman giving birth to a headless child. Such images burn themselves into the memory. Heym was in fact a painter *manqué*; even in this he resembles Baudelaire. In July/August 1911 we find him recording in his diary: 'Satan has denied me the ability to paint.' He proceeds to describe in detail four paintings that he would paint if he were able to do so, and cries out in exasperation: 'Why did Heaven deny me the ability to draw? I am plagued by images in a way that no painter ever was.' The 'Imaginationen' that fill his poems invite comparison with those of Bosch and Brueghel, Goya and Kubin. Thus the lines

> Licht. Taghell. Blutrot.
> Musik. Weiße Clowns
> Die Königsärge schwanken auf den Schultern.
> Strohköpfe auf langen Besen.
> Waffenröcke
> Der ganze... (*L* 515).

Light. Light as day. Blood-red. Music. White clowns [–] Kings' coffins swaying on shoulders. Straw heads on broom handles [.] Uniforms [,] the whole...

read like notes not so much for a poem, as for a painting. He would also have liked to paint the battle of Marathon (see *T* 28 August 1908). For a poet of his power, this is an extraordinary state of affairs, especially when one remembers that his 'Marathon' cycle of poems includes more images than most paintings. Unlike some of his contemporaries, he does not blame the language for his own inability to find the right words; but he does make it quite clear that he would have liked to be able to paint, and that he finds it very frustrating not to be able to do so.

No doubt many factors combined to make the experience of seeing a number of works by Van Gogh and reading his letters so 'shattering' for Heym. The fact that he was himself a painter *manqué* with a keen eye for colour and for the physical reality of the world was a major factor, but even more important will have been the fact that he perceived and found in Van Gogh a kindred genius with similar urges, obsessions and fears, for, in Albert Aurier's words, 'What distinguishes his [Van Gogh's] entire *œuvre* is its excess, excessive power, excessive nervousness, violence and expressiveness . . . He is one of the exalted, an enemy of bourgeois sobriety and meticulous accuracy, a sort of drunken giant.'[8] This could be a description of Heym, whose work has the same kind of dramatic intensity and expressive pathos as Van Gogh's. He, no less than Van Gogh, had a zest and a lust for life; he, too, suffered from ennui and melancholia. To Heym, too, applies what A. de Graaf wrote of Van Gogh: 'He walked naked in the world . . . He lay face downwards on the earth, and it scared him to death.'[9] John Wolfsohn could not have chosen a stronger word to describe the combined impact on Heym of Van Gogh's work and letters; the word 'erschüttert' implies that Heym was profoundly shaken, 'shattered' to the point of being upset. Even given Heym's volatile, mercurial temperament, such a reaction is only explicable if what he has seen, and read in the letters, has led him to identify with Van Gogh. We shall be left in no doubt that this was the case, for he was, like Van Gogh, an outsider uncertain of his own identity. Both men suffered, in different ways and to different degrees, from the problem of identity. There is a revealing parallel between Van Gogh's self-portraits and Heym's – relatively fewer – poems directly about himself, which are no less astonishingly objective. Both men had difficulty in defining themselves. Van Gogh describes his pictures as 'almost a cry of anguish',[10] which Heym's poems certainly are; but Heym lacks Van Gogh's saintly humility, he rages against his fate.

What struck Paul Klee most about Van Gogh was his 'exemplary tragedy'. By the same token we might speak of his exemplary heroism in always working and living at the limit, on the edge of the abyss, undaunted by the appalling implications of failure. His paintings represent a heroic victory over illness and therefore over life. The artist as hero, then, which brings us back to Georg Heym, for nothing was more basic to Heym's temperament and view of life than his belief in a heroism which consists in painting or writing in the teeth of potential tragedy.

Whether Heym was lucky to be spared Van Gogh's 'terrible need for religion',[11] or unlucky to lack the bedrock of the Dutchman's earlier religiosity, could be argued either way; there is a significant similarity and a significant dissimilarity between the two men at this point. Heym would never have seen Christ as *the* artist; he would have given that title to Leonardo da Vinci or, possibly, to Van Gogh; otherwise he would have invoked Helios. Both Van Gogh and Georg Heym are, of course, sun-worshippers; in many ways Heym is remarkably like the Van Gogh described by Meier-Graefe. In Van Gogh's *The Raising of Lazarus* (F677), which Heym may well have seen in December 1901, the rocks open to reveal not Christ, but blue hills and a yellow rising sun. Christ is displaced by the rising sun – the pagan divinity to which Van Gogh offered himself up as a sacrifice.[12] *The Raising of Lazarus* is an emblem not only of Van Gogh's heliocentric universe, but of Georg Heym's too.

Van Gogh's sunflowers are burning suns, for he 'saw the flaming face of Helios glowing in the orange of the sunflower',[13] but behind this crowning glory of the visible world lies the tragedy of what Carl Einstein called Van Gogh's 'manic identification with the sun':

Emphasis on light turns into identification with the sun. We note that Van Gogh exchanged a still-life, *Sunflowers*, with Gauguin, in return for a self-portrait. The male, fecundating sun shines behind the open, female drawbridge. His sower is identical with the sun in front of which he is striding. Van Gogh's signature coud be called positively solar. Van Gogh's situation becomes tragic not for any technical reason, but because this identification with the sun backfired.[14]

Heym was a sun-worshipper even before he came across Van Gogh; back in 1906 he wrote in his diary: 'I find myself believing more and more firmly in Helios, in the light, the sun, the holiness of the whole natural order (*T* 63).' It is their love of the sun, and of the colour which it reveals, that gives the work of Heym and Van Gogh alike its vitality and lyrical richness. But there is also a darker side to it, for night also fascinated both men, and autumn was the season most congenial to both.

Van Gogh was overwhelmed by the colours that were revealed when the snow first melted at Arles; Heym was no less sensitive to colour, as his diary reveals and as Heinrich-Wilhelm Keim noted in a review of Heym's work published in 1922:

Colour is the expression of his longing; it is what remains of the beauty with which life decks out its sad ruins of the ideal life. Heym loved colours – strong, pure, clear colours – every bit as passionately as Van Gogh. Such colours are to be found on rotting nature in great cities ... they rest like butterflies on life's depraved creatures, they even embellish the dead (*D* 296).

In his diary (25 October 1910) Heym writes: 'I am intensely aware of colours these days. I see a flower-bed full of red shrubs with a cool deep blue sky over it, and am delighted beyond measure (*T* 144).' This diary entry was written on the opening day of the second largest Van Gogh exhibition to be held in Berlin in Heym's lifetime,[15] at which he had seen fifty-two works including *Vincent's House at Arles* (F464), with its incredibly blue sky, and *Poppies in the Field* (F81).

The many likenesses between Heym's images and Van Gogh's show that poet and painter saw things in a similar way, and that similar things caught their eye. Even in the early poetry there are figures (e.g. the sower, 31 October 1907: *L* 653; the horizon figure, April 1908: *L* 656; the huge ball of the setting sun, 2 August 1906: *L* 619) which are reminiscent of Van Gogh and may conceivably go back to his work (thus Heym could have seen the sower in Van Gogh's F1441 and F690 at the Twelfth Secession exhibition in December 1906 and at Paul Cassirer's spring 1907 exhibition), although it is likely that some of them are merely parallels, for in September 1910 Heym was *surprised* to discover how much he had in common with Van Gogh. This does not mean, however, that he had been unaware of Van Gogh until then. The evidence suggests that he had known Van Gogh's work since May 1901, and that he had taken increasing interest in it since October 1908. Van Gogh-like images had been appearing in his work since 1906; they increase from late 1908 and increase again sharply following the 1910 exhibition, which he probably attended on the first day.

The 1909–10 Van Gogh exhibition at the Kunstsalon Paul Cassirer lasted from 27 November 1909 to 9 January 1910 and appears to have left an immediate mark on Heym's poetry. Thus in December 1909 he wrote a poem, 'Die Wiesen des Todes' ('The Fields of Death') (*L* 739f.), in which the treatment of the reaper figures is reminiscent of the Van Gogh reapers (F1317, F1318) which Heym could have seen at the Nineteenth Secession exhibition just days before writing his poem; there were similar figures (F618, F687) in the October 1908 exhibition. In January 1910 he wrote a triptych of poems, 'Abende im Vorfrühling I, II and III' (*L* 8, 9 and 13) which are word-paintings, two of them including Van Gogh-like images: 'Im Uferwalde brennt in gelbem Schein/Der Abendhimmel' ('In the woods on the bank the evening sky is burning with a yellow glow'), 'Am Horizonte in den Bergen weit/Ruht grün und rot der Abendwolken Saum' ('On the horizon, in the distant mountains, the evening clouds' edge is red and green'). The

second of these is particularly interesting in that it not only involves the
horizon image which becomes so ubiquitous in Heym's poetry following his exposure to Van Gogh, but also the discordant combination of
red and green, which may also derive from Van Gogh. Horizons, in
Van Gogh and Heym alike, represent the edge of the visible world and
therefore the limit of what can be painted or conveyed in words; but
they also mark the border between time and eternity, and are accordingly a *memento mori*, although they do not always carry such a weight of
symbolism. The sonnet 'Berlin I' (April 1910) ends with these lines:

> Doch westlich sahn
> Wir an der langen Straße Baum an Baum,
> Der blätterlosen Kronen Filigran.
>
> Der Sonnenball hing groß am Himmelssaum.
> Und rote Strahlen schoß des Abends Bahn.
> Auf allen Köpfen lag des Lichtes Traum.

But in the west, in that endless street, we saw tree after tree, the filigree of their leafless
branches.
     The great ball of the sun hung on the horizon. Evening's path emitted red rays.
Every mind was filled with the dreams of light.

While it is possible that the setting sun has reminded the poet of Van
Gogh's *Autumn Lane at Sunset* (F123), it is far more likely that this is
simply a typical Van Gogh motif.

     The discordant combination of red and green in 'Abende im
Vorfrühling III' (which Heym had used in a poem written in October
1907: *L* 654) was very much in the air at this time, partly because of Van
Gogh's use of this particular combination in *The Night Café* (F463), and
partly because of Van Gogh's comments on this in a letter of 8 September 1888, in which he wrote that he had 'tried to express the terrible
passions of humanity by means of red and green'. I am not suggesting
that the red and green in 'Abende im Vorfrühling III' have any such
connotation, just that their savage dissonance, which may derive from
Van Gogh in this case, is a major factor in Heym's poem. This combination of colours, which is a feature of the Van Gogh-inspired painting of the Fauves and of Die Brücke (in 1912 it was to be a positive
feature of the work of Heym's illustrator, Ernst Ludwig Kirchner), is
recurrent in Heym's work of 1910–11.

The horizon-figure is common in Heym's work following his discovery of Van Gogh. Another notable example is found in the poem 'Die Menschen' of October 1911:

Die Pappeln stehen gegen den Himmel still.
Die Menschen gehen schattenhaft im Kreise,
In leerer Wege ausgetretnem Gleise.

Stumm mit den Säcken gegen den Himmelsrand
Und heben ihre Arme in dem Späten,
Wortlos wie in der Tauben flachen Städten.

Und in die Starre der leeren Öde gepflanzt
Ein Leiterwagen steht im Felde groß
Und hält das letzte Rot in seinem Schoß (*L* 431).

('Humans') The poplars are still against the sky. Like so many shades, men tramp in a circle, in a rut worn in empty paths.
They walk silently with their sacks silhouetted against the horizon, arms pointing up into the late daylight, wordless as those in the stale, flat cities of the deaf.
And in the torpor of the empty countryside a rack-wagon standing in a field, cradling the setting sun in its lap.

This is practically a composite Van Gogh image: the poplars, the people (prisoners) on their daily round, the bearers of the burden, the rack-wagon – all are familiar from Van Gogh's work. The dominant image is that of the poplars, which stand for 'Die Menschen' of the title and second line. In his next poem, 'Die Nacht ist ohne Sterne...' ('The Night is without Stars'), Heym identifies the two: 'Die Menschen sind wie Bäume,/Die in dem Winter stecken' ('The men are like trees against the winter sky') (*L* 433). It may well be that he has been prompted by Van Gogh's flame-like trees to make the tree the symbol of man's brief appearance before the backcloth of eternity. The rack-wagon cradling the setting sun in its lap is a brilliant painter's image, albeit an ominous one (cf. the bloody head of 'Printemps', *L* 261).

Another interesting old-type poem written in October 1911 and related both to 'Die Menschen' and to 'Printemps' is 'Die Mühlen':

Die vielen Mühlen gehen und treiben schwer.
Das Wasser fällt über die Räder her
Und die moosigen Speichen knarren im Wehr.

Und die Müller sitzen tagein, tagaus
Wie Maden weiß in dem Mühlenhaus.
Und schauen oben zum Dache hinaus.

Aber die hohen Pappeln stehn ohne Wind
Vor einer Sonne herbstlich und blind,
Die matt in die Himmel geschnitten sind (*L* 416).

('The mills') The many mills are all working slowly. The water is falling on to the wheels and the mossy spokes are creaking in the weir.

And the millers sit there in the mill, day in, day out, white as maggots. Glimpsing the sky through the roof.

But the tall poplars, indistinctly silhouetted against the sky, stand becalmed in front of a blind autumn sun.

The mill in this case is a water-mill, another familiar Van Gogh motif;[16] the millers are reminiscent of Van Gogh's many studies of weavers. In Heym's poem the three basic images (mills, millers, poplars) all represent the monotony of life; wherever one looks, it is all the same, as life is to any powers that be, who are indifferent to Man's existence.

Having rediscovered Van Gogh's work in winter 1909/10, Heym proceeded, in the course of the next two years, to incorporate images from it into his own work, a feature of which, from summer 1910, is the use of intensified colour à la Van Gogh. He also wrote one poem which is, in the most literal sense, a verbalization and appropriation of a work by Van Gogh, that work being itself an appropriation of the work of another artist! The poem in question is 'Die Gefangenen, I', the most fascinating and compelling Van Gogh-inspired poem produced by Heym following the 1909–10 exhibition but before the exhibition of autumn 1910:

Sie trampeln um den Hof im engen Kreis.
Ihr Blick schweift hin und her im kahlen Raum.
Er sucht nach einem Feld, nach einem Baum,
Und prallt zurück von kahler Mauern Weiß.

Wie in den Mühlen dreht der Rädergang,
So dreht sich ihrer Schritte schwarze Spur.
Und wie ein Schädel mit der Mönchstonsur,
So liegt des Hofes Mitte kahl und blank.

Es regnet dünn auf ihren kurzen Rock.
Sie schaun betrübt die graue Wand empor,
Wo kleine Fenster sind, mit Kasten vor,
Wie schwarze Waben in dem Bienenstock.

Man treibt sie ein, wie Schafe zu der Schur.
Die grauen Rücken drängen in den Stall.
Und klappernd schallt heraus der Widerhall
Der Holzpantoffeln auf dem Treppenflur (*L* 122).

('The prisoners, I') They tramp around the courtyard in a narrow circle. Their eyes roam around their bare surroundings, searching for a field or a tree, and shrink back from the bare walls' whiteness.

The black circle of their footsteps keeps turning like the machinery in a mill, and like a pate with a monk's tonsure the centre of the courtyard is shiny and bare.

Thin rain is falling on their short jackets. Their eyes travel sadly up the grey wall to the tiny windows, with boxes outside, like black honeycombs in a beehive.

They are driven inside like sheep to the shearing. Their grey backs push their way into the stall, whence comes the clattering echo of their clogs on the stairs.

This is a verbalization of one of Van Gogh's most famous images. What makes it so interesting is the fact that Heym did what Van Gogh had done before him: he took an existing image and gave it a highly personal connotation.

While working as a bookseller's clerk in Dordrecht in 1877, Van Gogh came across some engraved reproductions of Gustave Doré's plates for W. B. Jerrold's *London, a Pilgrimage* (1872). One of the plates represented *Newgate – The Exercise Yard*. Although he never owned a copy of the Jerrold/Doré book, Van Gogh did collect the engraved reproductions from it which appeared in the Dutch periodical *Katholieke Illustratie* in 1877. These engravings included *Newgate*, a copy of which his brother sent to him on 25 January 1890.[17] Now at St Rémy, in February 1890, he copied Doré's drawing in oil, and indeed copied it so exactly that he clearly had the engraving in front of him at the time. The two versions are almost identical, but in copying Doré's image Van Gogh gave one of the prisoners (the one in front looking towards the artist) his own features; some of the others have typical features of Nuenen peasants. Van Gogh felt himself to be imprisoned in a vicious circle from which there was no escape. The men marching in a circle are therefore a 'translation into pictorial language of a poetic and metaphysical idea summed up by the artist himself in the extraordinary phrase, "Life is probably round"', for 'He too, like his *Prisoners*, was tramping in a circle behind the bars of his cell, round and round incessantly, a permanent captive.'[18]

This was also the dominant feeling of Georg Heym's tragically short life: 'My brain is forever going around in circles, like a prisoner banging on his prison door' (T 28 May 11). His work shows that he felt trapped, imprisoned in time. For him there was no way, no escape from the demon of a premature death by which he was dogged and which dragged him under at the age of twenty-four. This is why he was so impressed by Van Gogh's *The Prison Court-Yard* (F669), which he most likely saw in Meier-Graefe's *Vincent van Gogh* (1910), that he transposed it into words just two days after discussing Van Gogh with John Wolfsohn. The original title of the poem, 'Der Gefängnishof', points explicitly to Van Gogh (and Doré). The result is a painfully personal poem. Nowhere else is Heym's self-identification with Van Gogh so total. In this poem, as in Vincent's painting, the prisoners are the victims of a life represented by the bare walls, and in each case the prisoners represent the artist. In Vincent's case the bare walls and the bars were literal; in Heym's case they were figurative, but no less real. Reality, as almost every poet and painter of the time tells us, is what is inside a man's head.

In the course of the year following the 1910 exhibition Heym wrote two further poems entitled 'Die Gefangenen', one written in October 1911:

Vor ihren Spindeln sitzen sie, zu stecken
Ein jeder eng in seiner hohlen Kammer,
Und drehen ihrer Stunden weißen Jammer.

Wie Spinnen, die auf ihren Faden starren.
Und fahren plötzlich herum vor Schrecken
Wenn in der Tür die großen Schlüssel knarren.

Und wieder ziehn den Faden ihre Hände
Und machen ihn so lang wie ihre Jahre.
Und immer weißer werden ihre Haare,
Und leer die Spulen laufen noch zu Ende.

Ihr Leben ist wie ihre leere Zelle,
Ein hohles Etwas, einer Mauer Enge.
Nur manchmal gehen traurige Gesänge,
Und auf dem Hofe schreit die Totenschelle.

Dann halten sie den trocknen Hals erhoben,
Wie Gänse, die ein blasser Schreck erhebt.
Und sehen, wie in ihren Gittern oben
Ein kleiner Fetzen grauen Himmels klebt (*L* 412).

('The prisoners') They sit before their spindles, entombed in their empty hovels, spinning out the white wretchedness of their hours.

Staring at their thread, like spiders. And turn round terror-stricken when the great keys rattle in the door.

And once again their hands pull the thread and make it as long as their years. And their hair turns ever whiter, and finally the spools remain empty.

Their lives are like their empty cells. A hollow thing, a wall's confines. Only occasionally are sad songs to be heard, and in the yard the bell tolling for the dead.

Then they hold up their scraggy necks like geese startled by some pale terror. And notice that there is a little patch of grey sky stuck in the bars over their heads.

This is no subjective poem in which Heym reflects upon his own sense of being imprisoned in life, but an objective and compassionate study of a group of people whose lives were in most ways infinitely more wretched than his own. It is accordingly such an unusual poem for Heym that it seems entirely possible that its starting-point came not from life, but from Van Gogh. In a general sense Heym will again be indebted to Van Gogh's 'Doré' painting, to which his title points, but more especially to Van Gogh's studies of spinners and weavers working endlessly in the solitude of their cottage rooms.[19] Heym's 'spinners' poem is so atypical and, for all its no doubt perfectly genuine compassion, so literary, that I have no doubt that Van Gogh was the source of Heym's inspiration; he probably saw versions of Van Gogh's spinners in December 1909 (F1290a) and October/November 1910 (F36). Its objectivity also makes the poem exceptional in that, with most poets, it was the subjective strain that was nourished by Van Gogh.

Heym was not only 'shattered' by his discovery of Van Gogh, but proceeded, from January 1910 to October 1911 (when his last manner suddenly begins), to include a number of clearly recognizable Van Gogh motifs in his own work. Van Gogh himself always used a model and produced many works based on the work of other artists. It seems to me that Heym, too, may have used models more than has been thought, to provide himself with starting-points or seamarks in his poems. It is the final similarity between himself and the Dutchman. He was 'shattered' by his discovery of Van Gogh because he found in him so many of his own human problems and artistic solutions; if the power of Van Gogh's *daimon* will have been frightening, the example of his expressionism must have encouraged Heym to go on with what he had begun. It may be that some of the echoes of Van Gogh are tributes to one further along his own road; at all events, they show that Heym recognized a kindred spirit and a great artist when he saw one.

When Heym writes that Van Gogh is more congenial to him than Hodler is, he means that he has found in Van Gogh someone whose view of life and of art has much in common with his own. No doubt Salter is right in arguing that this fundamental agreement is rooted in their common phenomenological view of things.[20] This helps to explain the striking similarity between the portraits of individuals created by both men, who are equally at pains to cut out all extraneous detail in order to put the emphasis on a phenomenological examination of the individual. Heym knew at least some of Van Gogh's self-portraits.

Heym has not a little in common with Van Gogh as an artist, as Ronald Salter has convincingly shown. The most important point concerns the immediacy which the Berlin poet Ernst Blass associated with Van Gogh.[21] Such immediacy of expression is achieved by means of colour and abstraction, both of which are as fundamental features of Heym's work as they are of Van Gogh's. Abstraction as such means departing from any model by means of simplification and therefore of intensification; the forms of intensification involved are those appropriate to the genre. Both Heym and Van Gogh concentrate on the world of objects, while at the same time seeing through it to a visionary reality beyond. The visionary quality of both men's work has been the subject of frequent comment: in 1911/12, for instance, the Dutchman François Pauwels wrote, in one of the most penetrating early comments on his work, that Heym's vision, though expressed in a far more stylized way, had much in common with Van Gogh's (*D* 239f.).

However, while Van Gogh and his images clearly impressed Heym, in terms of technique he is closer to Hodler.

☐ HODLER, MUNCH AND OTHERS

Heym signalled his interest in and approval of the work of Ferdinand Hodler when he wrote to John Wolfsohn, in a letter dated 2 September 1910, that Van Gogh was even closer to him than Hodler. In his reply dated 4 September Wolfsohn, to Heym's evident delight, elaborated on the parallels between his work and Hodler's:

You and Hodler construct your worlds in a regular, consequential way. That world is an *unbroken unity* which cannot be broken down into its constituent parts. This mood is only made possible by the fact that the artist ... suppresses all particulars. Here there are no particulars contributing to a whole; all particulars have been eliminated and we see only a uniform whole. This whole is a fact of life – impassive, unchanging, dead – and there is nothing to deflect our gaze from it. Faced with this dead impassivity, this mere presence, a new, alien world rises before the spectator's eye: a self-contained reality which has no connexion with any other realities. And because there is thus absolutely no mediation, the perception of this reality is inevitably an overwhelming experience for the spectator, and a monumentality of feeling is made manifest such as is found in architecture after Michelangelo, and in poetry (to the best of my belief) only in Hölderlin and George. Do you see now how close Hodler is to you? It is a strange fact that as unique a temperament as the painter Hodler's should be found again at the same time in a young poet without there being any external connexion or influence involved. This affinity even extends to matters of technique. You have doubtless heard of Hodler's 'parallelism'. People point to it as a great innovation, although it is relatively unimportant from the point of view of Hodler's work; it is significant only as a symbol of his temperament. According to Hodler himself, 'parallelism' means any kind of reduplication. Through this reduplication Hodler manages to produce that powerful monotone and impassivity of which I spoke above. You too often use this 'parallelism', this being the first time it has been used in poetry.

You repeat yourself, you juxtapose all sorts of disparate things, giving each one the same status, and treating them all as equivalent. The effect is ... the same as with Hodler.

The many parallels with Hodler ... seem a little forced at this stage and refer less to the Heym of today than to Heym as he must and will become.

So much for temperament. I now come to perception. Here no one is as close to you as Van Gogh. Have you seen pictures by him? His letters, clear as they are, are no more than reminders of his work, and only the person who is familiar with the work will remember it and thus gain the right impression from the letters. Take a look at him, there is much that you can learn from this painter. For although you see things very clearly, that vision does not yet receive adequate expression in your poems. Have you seen one of Van Gogh's colours, one of his harsh, strong, deep, rich colours? Although you occasionally use colours, you really go in for colour as little as Hodler does. Hodler gets away without colour, for with him it is replaced by line, the creation of a surface, an elongated space, and a powerful regular rhythm which your work does not possess. You ought to use more colour, and there is no one from whom you could better learn the use of it than Van Gogh. Another point: in your work the individual expression still sometimes lacks the boldness for which you were presumably aiming, and which is essential for the effective realization of that aim. This boldness of treatment is something that Van Gogh can teach you. When he paints something like 'Matrosen vor der Sonnenscheibe' (not a painting I have seen), what he produces is not a round, flickering, moving something-or-other in front of which a restless crowd of people happens to be standing (which is how an Impressionist would do it), but, on the contrary, there is a round, full ball of the sun, something altogether substantial, and there in front of it, large as life, are the human figures. If you can get across this colour and boldness in your poems, then the as yet latent monumentality of your perception will be revealed and your work will be the equal of Hodler's.[22]

It is no exaggeration to say that this is the most important letter Heym ever received on an aesthetic matter. It is important in two ways: it takes him extremely seriously as a poet, and it encourages him to cultivate what quickly became the main features of his poetry for the next year (its impersonality and monumentality, its use of 'parallelism' and of colour). Delighted by it, he wrote to Wolfsohn at once: 'Many thanks for your kind and very valuable letter.' On 11 September he wrote again: 'I am delighted to have found in you the understanding which I so badly need (T 213ff.).'

Heym will have been all the more impressed by this view, so flattering to him, in that it was duplicated, in print, in an article by Simon Guttmann entitled 'Über Hodler', which appeared in Der Demokrat in November 1910. In it Guttmann wrote that Hodler's parallelism 'is to be found – independent of Hodler – in Georg Heym'. In 1976 Ronald Salter elaborated on the parallel between Hodler's 'parallelism' and Heym's 'accumulation' of images, and more especially between their landscapes. Hodler's grandiose formal rigidity – his monumentalism – will have been for Heym not a weakness but a strength, for it corresponded to the style which he was already developing; indeed, it was probably the flattering comparison with Hodler, by two of his best friends, that prompted him to persevere with his monumental, monolithic style for too long.

If Heym was keenly interested in what Wolfsohn and Guttmann

wrote about the parallel between Hodler's 'monumentalism' and his own peculiarly general (or 'cosmic' or 'monumental') view of nature, he will have been scarcely less struck by Hodler's view of life. Hodler's early work, like Heym's work, dwelt on the darker side of life, and more particularly on death and the fear of death. The singular romanticism of Hodler's early work is paralleled in Heym; painter and poet exhibit the same strange mixture of melancholy and vitalism. One can imagine Heym identifying with the youth-as-superman of Hodler's *Looking into Infinity*, just as one can imagine him being fascinated by *Night* and *The Disillusioned*. In *Looking into Infinity* (1902/3) a Heym-like youth is standing on top of a mountain peak, above the clouds, a motif which goes back to Caspar David Friedrich's famous self-portrait *The Wayfarer above a Sea of Mist* of 1818. *Night* (1890) is the first of Hodler's grandiose allegorical works and the first work in which he seeks to achieve intensification through repetition of the motif, here that of the sleeper; the central figure is a self-portrait, the dream by which he is startled representing death. *The Disillusioned* (1892) depicts a row of five men hopelessly awaiting death, the central figure once again being a self-portrait. Hodler's lifelong encounters with the nightmare figure of death,[23] so memorably depicted in *Night*, are comparable to Munch's and Ensor's similar experiences, but also to Heym's imaginative encounters of the same kind, particularly in his black tales. Hodler's *Night* may well have reminded Heym of *The Sleep of Reason Produces Monsters*, in which Goya showed himself being visited by the demons of his own imagination. Heym would have immediately identified with both artists, but particularly with Hodler, who depicted his own terrified encounter with death in the same way that Heym was to do in his stories 'Jonathan' and 'Das Schiff'. Heym is likely to have known Hodler's *Night* (which had been shown at the Second Künstlerbund Exhibition in Berlin in 1905 and had been mentioned in *Kunst und Künstler* that same year) by the time he came to write his poem 'Die Schläfer' ('The Sleepers') (*L* 177f.) in December 1910, for his poems 'Gruft I' (September 1910: *L* 126) and 'Der Abend' (27 September 1910: *L* 135) contain images of night reminiscent of the central figure in Hodler's *Night*. Shortly before December 1910, Simon Guttmann's article pointing to the affinity between Heym and Hodler had appeared (on 23 November), and Robert Jentzsch's poem 'Die Schläfer' (written in 1911) has a subtitle referring to Hodler;[24] Hodler's most famous painting was originally entitled *Le sommeil*. Similarly, *The Disillusioned* would have confirmed Heym in his own view of life. This is what he looked for in all the painters and poets he admired. For all his ebullience, he needed such reassurance.

Heym's interest in painting was not confined to Leonardo da Vinci, Van Gogh and Hodler. He also admired Altdorfer, El Greco, the greatest portrait painters – Rembrandt (the title of whose *The Three Trees* he uses) and Goya; Munch and Kubin. As in the case of literature (Alfred Dove, Gustav Renner), he also thought highly of the work of some now lesser-known artists, notably Martin Brandenburg. In contemporary reviews Heym's work was compared to Goya, Delacroix and Van Gogh, as well as to Rops, Pascin and – more important – Kubin. Like Van Gogh, Munch and Ensor, Redon and Kubin, Heym suffered the onslaughts of images whose hallucinatory reality was more real to him than the 'reality' of the outside world. Those who find his subject-matter (especially in the tales) rather strong should remember that he was a man with a powerful visual imagination and interest in art, living in the age of Rops, Redon and Kubin.

Edvard Munch, who lived in Berlin until 1908, was almost a generation older than Heym, yet occupied a similar historical position as a proto-Expressionist. Known and admired by poets of his own generation (Dehmel, Max Dauthendey and others), and by the editor of the *Berliner Tageblatt* from 1906 (Theodor Wolff), Munch became known in Germany in 1892 as a result of the scandal caused by the Munch exhibition staged by the Verein Berliner Künstler. His work was shown repeatedly by the Berlin Secession, of which he became a member in 1906. A number of his works on love and death were shown at the 1902 Secession. It is likely that Heym saw the exhibition, having been so impressed by the 1901 Secession. He may well have visited the Summer Salon of the Berlin Secession in 1905, which also included work by Munch.[25] The presence of what seem to be echoes of Munch in Heym's work – thus the line 'Das Zimmer schwankt um sie von ihrem Schrei' ('The room rocks around her from her scream') in 'Die Dämonen der Städte' (see Chapter VII) is reminiscent of *The Dead Mother* and *The Scream* – suggest that he knew Munch's work, but such echoes (and there are others) matter far less than the general parallel and affinity between the two men. Werner Haftmann has described Munch thus:

Munch thought in images. This manner of thinking requires the artist to discover the daemonic elements hidden in nature. Herein he relies on his psychic powers, the divining powers of the unconscious. Thus Munch does not, for example, paint a nude young girl; instead he paints *Puberty* because the antennae of his psyche go beyond visual perception ... Painting, for him, does not deal with definite points of nature or 'reality'. His optics is that of 'second sight', he discovers a 'second reality', seat of the essential life process, and this is what the artist experiences and reflects. Consequently Munch's work does not portray a fixed point of reality, but a cycle; he does not record the visible in the form of a definite landscape or figure, but rather in a sequence of images, 'a frieze of life', as he actually entitled the series of his large canvases. Such second sight is more especially the instrument of visually gifted poets.[26]

This is, without further ado, applicable to Heym, whose monumental poems represent just such a 'frieze of life' in the manner of Munch or Hodler. Besides, if a sense of terror in the face of a nature perceived to be fundamentally hostile is a feature of 'Northern' art, then Heym is as much a Northern artist as Munch. On the surface he is, admittedly, closer to Böcklin and Klinger. Thus the story 'Die Pest' is apparently indebted to Böcklin's and Klinger's depictions of Pestilence and Death (including Klinger's *Tod* of 1897 in which a dying woman is beckoned by her own death in the guise of a woman), and the poem 'Das Fieberspital' (*L* 166f.) has a parallel and possible source of inspiration in Klinger's *Vom Tode* of 1903. There is also Klinger's *Krieg* of 1898 (folio 5 of the cycle *Vom Tode*, Part II) which shows (lying down) a gigantic personification of war. One of Heym's dreams (*T* 181) may have been prompted by Klinger's drawing of a snake and a tiger fighting. There is no external evidence that Heym was familiar with Klinger's etchings, but such parallels suggest that he was; he had, after all, a keen interest in art, and Klinger's images were as memorable as any current at the time. However, the apparent echoes of Klinger suggest only that Heym was visually excited by some of Klinger's images, which left their mark thematically on his work; the parallel with Munch, on the other hand, reveals much more of the real Heym.

Among the painters whose work Heym admired were three relatively little-known figures: Heinrich Kley, Hans Baluschek and Martin Brandenburg. Heym's friend, the artist Ernst Moritz Engert, was the first to point to Heinrich Kley (1863–1945) as a likely influence on Heym. From 1908 Kley contributed to *Simplicissimus* a series of drawings involving gigantic devil-figures; these were reproduced in his *Skizzenbuch I* (Munich, 1909). Engert, who got to know Heym well in summer 1911, had an extensive collection of reproductions which included Kley and Kubin. A comparison of these figures with similar figures in Heym's later poetry shows that Kley probably helped to inspire Heym's demons, particularly in 'Die Dämonen der Städte' and 'Der Gott der Stadt',[27] although it should be added that these have more in common with the more robust demons portrayed by Goya, Max Slevogt and Alfred Kubin than with Kley's rather spindly figures.

Hans Baluschek (b. 1870) was best known for his Berlin paintings of urban scenes; Ernst Balcke pointed to the obvious parallel between Baluschek's *Laubenkolonie* and Heym's poem 'Laubenfest' (see p. 109 above), and it is possible that Baluschek gave Heym the starting-point for some of his other Berlin sonnets. Martin Brandenburg (1870–1919), a founder-member of the Berlin Secession, was described by Karl Scheffler as the 'Berlin poet of the bizarre, demonic and mysterious';[28] most of his work was fantastic in a way that would be unlikely to appeal to Heym, but – as we have seen – one painting of his, *Die Menschen unter der Wolke*, shown in the third exhibition of the Berlin Secession in summer 1901, impressed the then thirteen-year-old Heym so deeply that he described it as 'one of the few paintings I shall never forget' (*T* 131), no doubt because he recognized in the painting his own experience and view of life.

□ KUBIN

Heym's tale 'Die Bleistadt' (literally 'Town of Lead') puts one in mind of Alfred Kubin, not so much because the title is reminiscent of the far-from-ideal city of Perle in *Die andere Seite* (1909; *The Other Side*, translated by Denver Lindley, 1967), as because Kubin's *Death in the Desert* or *The Rider* (Death riding a skeletal camel) looks so much like an illustration to 'Die Bleistadt' that one is left wondering whether this striking image was known to Heym and fired his imagination. It certainly shows how close the two men's imaginations are. If it is true that Kubin's work exemplifies 'the more neurotic trends of German Expressionism',[29] then the same must apply to Heym's narrative work. Kubin, on his death-bed, asked the doctor not to take away the *Angst* which was the source of all his work; Heym, for his part, having spoken of 'the fear within me' (*T* 45), produced – in the story 'Das Schiff' – one of the most memorable studies of fear ever written. The world of both men was 'drenched with fear and horror';[30] 'Der Dieb' is no less a 'chamber of horrors' than Kubin's first portfolio. It is not chance that Kubin chose to illustrate Poe's tales, and that these evidently left their mark on Heym's black tales, for if Baudelaire, that earlier admirer of Poe, was preoccupied with what he called the monsters of his imagination so, too, were (among others) Kubin and Heym, both of whom depict a world of monsters, monstrosities and the monstrous; both, that is to say, create a vivid pictorial world of black visions and oppressive hallucinations, a disquieting, frightening world of hallucinatory realism. If 'grotesque realism' is to be seen anywhere in Heym's work, then it is here. What others repress, perhaps rightly so, is paraded *en plein jour* by both these men whose imaginations dwell on the 'other side', the 'night-side' of life.

Heym's gothic tales are remarkably close to Kubin's no less gothic novel, *Die andere Seite*; Kubin's nightmare vision (in the section of his novel entitled 'Die Hölle') of a decaying world in which archetypal terrors roam the streets is very much the world of Heym's 'Das Schiff'. Kubin's *Die Pest* parallels Heym's figure. Kubin's *Der Reiter*, as well as looking for all the world like an illustration for Heym's 'Die Bleistadt', is a probable source for a similar image ('wenn auf weissem Dromedar/Der Tod naht': 'when Death approaches on a white dromedary') in 'Grausame Zeit, da in des Krebses furchtbarem Zeichen' (June 1909: *L* 683). Kubin's *Der Rachen* is, as it were, the central image of Heym's 'Der fünfte Oktober'. There are other parallels, too, with Heym's poems. Thus Kubin's early *Der Krieg* parallels Heym's personification of war ('Einem Turm gleich tritt er aus die letzte Glut': 'Like a tower he tramples out the dying light') in his poem of the same title; Kubin's early *Hungersnoth* parallels Heym's 'Der Hunger'; the giant spiders of Kubin's *Die Hölle* (and elsewhere; they are a very common early motif) reappear in Heym's poem 'Die Irren' of June 1910.

Heym knew Kubin's early work and it seems that he occasionally quarried in it. Ernst Moritz Engert possessed 'some original Kubins, by which he [Heym] was very taken';[31] the evidence of the stories suggests that these Kubins came from the early *Facsimiledrucke nach Kunstblättern*. Engert said[32] that Heym drew inspiration from Kubin. Kubin's first exhibition was held at Paul Cassirer's in 1902, by which time Heym was already taking an active interest in art; there were further exhibitions of Kubin's work at the Kunstsalon Cassirer in 1904 and 1907. The 1902 exhibition led to the publication of Kubin's first portfolio, *Facsimiledrucke nach Kunstblättern*, published in Munich in 1903 by Hans von Weber. The 1903 portfolio includes a number of suggestive items: *Des Menschen Schicksal* (a Moira-figure), *Madame Mors*, *Der Krieg*, *Hungersnoth*, *Nach der Schlacht* and *Das Grausen*. It is virtually certain that Heym knew the portfolio and was influenced by the first four of these items, especially by Kubin's most famous image, his gigantic personification of war, which is altogether more powerful than Franz von Stuck's famous *Krieg* of 1894 or the similar works by Max Klinger and Arnold Böcklin. Kubin's early motifs also include: the world as Hell, the maws of Hell, 'gigantische und zerstörerische Schicksalsmächte' ('gigantic and destructive forces of destiny'), the Plague (*Seuche*, *Die Pest*), and so on. His second portfolio, *Sansara. Ein Cyclus ohne Ende* (1911), includes his version of Goya's *Saturn* (again cf. Heym's 'Der Krieg'). Kubin's *Die Fackel des Krieges* (1914), for its part, may reflect his knowledge of Heym's by then famous poem.

Other typical creatures of the gothic imagination abound in the work of graphic artist and poetic teller of tales alike. Heym, too, was a 'seer of doom'; his world, too, is one of 'harsh emptiness'. Both men's power lies in the evocation of 'a world suffused with horror',[33] and this world is evoked in a similar way, for both men had heads full of images; if Kubin had 'the visual imagination of a born storyteller',[34] Heym had the visual imagination of the born (but frustrated) artist. Like Kubin he is, imaginatively speaking, more at home among the dead than among the living; but this imaginative preoccupation masks a difference, for his horrified fascination with death (at a time when premonitions of his own early death were obsessing him) is the diametric opposite of Kubin's love of it. Heym loved the dead, but he loved them because they were victims of Death.

If Heym and Kubin are linked above all by their obsession with death and destruction,[35] they both belong with Goya. It was Alfred Lichtenstein who wrote a series of wayward satirical poems named after Goya's *Caprichos*, that series designed to illustrate the injustices, stupidities and barbarities of the age; but Heym's satires (e.g. 'Die Professoren') point in the same direction. When he visited Munich in

November 1911 he noted that he had seen a Goya – his diary entry, which refers to Goya's *Still-life; plucked turkey* in the Alte Pinakothek, clearly denotes an unknown work by an artist in whom he was interested; that interest probably had little to do with his portraits, and much more to do with Goya's ruthlessness and barefaced honesty, for Heym's ruthless formal rigidity is reminiscent of Goya. The work by Heym that most obviously invites comparison with Goya is 'Der Krieg', discussed in the next chapter. In saying that, I am thinking not only of the *Disasters of War* series, which goes further than Heym in depicting war as the very sign of man's bestiality, but also of Goya's famous oil painting *El gigante* (*The Giant*), which parallels Heym's 'Gott der Stadt' and 'Krieg' (I mean, of course, the figures as such); the parallel with 'Der Krieg' is particularly close, for Goya's *Giant* is also known as *Panic*. Heym's studies of madmen also invite comparison with Goya's, although they are probably not indebted to them. Finally, there is the parallel between the visionary *pinturas negras* of Goya's majestic final period, and Heym's demon-ridden 'black visions' (including the 'Schwarze Visionen' series of poems dating from January 1911), both of which stem from a realm of unreason beyond good and evil. Heym's imaginative world is similarly peopled with demons; there is a clear parallel between Goya's *Disparates* and Heym's black tales. If Kubin was an Austrian Goya, then Heym, on the evidence of the tales, was a Prussian one.

□ KIRCHNER AND MEIDNER

Heym was the poetic equivalent of the members of Die Brücke; they, among contemporary Germans, are his brothers: he has more in common with Ernst Ludwig Kirchner than with any member of the Neue Club. Kirchner, who never met Heym, recognized their affinity. It is a pity that Simon Guttmann's plan to bring together the members of Die Brücke and the Neue Club, and for them to produce a joint periodical (in which Heym's work would naturally have been to the fore), was overtaken by the dissolution of the club following Heym's death. Guttmann, who was student of art history, had got in touch with Emil Nolde in early 1911 and had championed him in *Der Demokrat*. When the members of Die Brücke moved to Berlin in autumn 1911, Guttmann established friendly relations with Karl Schmidt-Rottluff and Ernst Ludwig Kirchner. In 1912–13 he also got to know Erich Heckel, who produced a portrait of him, as did Kirchner. Guttmann drew the attention of both Heckel and Kirchner to Heym's poems, and Heckel's *Gläserner Tag* of 1913 may have been partly inspired by the poem 'Die Höfe luden uns ein' in Heym's *Umbra vitae* (1912).[36] Karl Schmidt-Rottluff designed the headpieces for the last two Neopathetisches Cabaret programmes on 16 December 1911 and 3 April 1912. Otherwise the only monuments to the kinship between the two groups are the proofs of the unpublished first and only number of the proposed joint journal (*Neopathos*), and, far more significant, Kirchner's portrait of Heym (dominated by those eyes whose look is no longer of this world; it was done from a photograph), and his illustrations for *Umbra vitae*.

It was because he identified with Heym that Kirchner illustrated *Umbra vitae*. The story begins with *Der ewige Tag*, which appeared in April 1911; a second impression appeared in March 1912, after Heym's death. In 1912, probably in March, Simon Guttmann (art critic of *Der Demokrat*) sent Ernst Ludwig Kirchner a copy of *Der ewige Tag*. Kirchner had moved to Berlin in October 1911, although he had been an increasingly frequent visitor to the city since Max Pechstein moved there in 1909. That Kirchner soon had contacts with the Neue Club is a matter of fact, but the statement that 'It was probably W. S. Guthmann [*sic*] who introduced Kirchner to Expressionist literary circles and also to Georg Heym'[37] appears to be only partly true. I am unaware of any evidence to support the idea that Simon Guttmann personally introduced Kirchner to Heym (Guttmann denied having done so), or indeed that Kirchner ever met Heym.

Guttmann probably gave Kirchner a copy of *Der ewige Tag* because he was thinking of publishing a posthumous volume of Heym's poetry illustrated by members of Die Brücke and others; the volume was to have included title-pages to the individual sections by Kirchner, Heckel and Schmidt-Rottluff, an engraved portrait of Heym by Nolde, a portrait by John Höxter and a silhouette by Ernst Moritz Engert. Unfortunately the plan came to nothing, but Kirchner acquired a copy of *Umbra vitae* on or shortly after its publication in June 1912. In the course of the next decade he proceeded to illustrate his copy of the book, using the blank lower half of most pages for this purpose. In a letter to Nele van de Velde dated 14 October 1919 Kirchner wrote of the 'free illustrations to the poems of *Umbra vitae*' which were keeping him busy; he described them as being 'like the accompanying melody to a song'.[38] On 27 February 1922 Hans Mardersteig (reader to the publisher Kurt Wolff and a friend of Kirchner) wrote to Wolff[39] suggesting that Kirchner should be asked to illustrate a reprint of *Umbra vitae*; he added that Kirchner had been making such illustrations off his own bat for years. By the beginning of 1923 Kirchner had completed the set of woodcuts and had decided to make an engraved two-colour portrait of Heym, which was inserted in the first ten (leatherbound) copies of the edition of 510 copies, which appeared in 1924 with forty-seven woodcuts.

Kirchner later wrote of 'the visionary richness in the smallest of formats' of his illustrations for Georg Heym's *Umbra vitae* as being 'unique'.[40] Others have agreed. The art historian Bernard Myers called them 'a triumph of modern book illustration',[41] and in an article on 'Die Holzschnitte von E. L. Kirchner zu Heyms *Umbra vitae*' Georg Schmidt drew attention to their originality:

Kirchner tries to hit each poem's particular note, which involves finding, from cut to cut, a new formal language, one could almost say a new technique. Kirchner's formal variations are inexhaustible; each woodcut is quite different, just as each poem is quite different – whereas most illustrators use the same formal language to the point of mannerism.[42]

Given his own very strong individuality, Kirchner was remarkably self-effacing, so that the illustrations are a monument both to his knowledge and love of Heym's work, and to the affinity between poet and painter. It is as well that Kirchner did most of the woodcuts in 1919–23; if he had done them in 1912 his very pronounced style might have caused him to ride roughshod over Heym's images, whereas in 1919–22, when he was recovering from his wartime breakdown, he was finding his way towards a new style and a new objectivity.

It was not until much later that Kirchner set down his attitude towards Georg Heym. On 17 April 1937, in a letter to Curt Valentin, he wrote:

Walt Whitman, that great poet, guided me in my view of life; in those grey days of poverty and hunger in Dresden the *Leaves of Grass* were my consolation and encouragement, as indeed they still are .. There is nothing in him for aesthetes, of course, for he smells of the earth, of life. He is free, free! ... We have someone who is his successor, Georg Heym, the poet of *Umbra vitae*, a German Whitman who foresaw what we have been through in the last two decades.[43]

Contemporary reviewers had occasionally mentioned Heym in the same breath as Whitman, but were right to conclude that he had rather more in common with Baudelaire.

Kirchner's comment does, however, make clear his veneration for Heym. The point has been made by the art historian Wolf-Dieter Dube:

If the poet Heym seemed to his friends in Berlin to be the incarnation of the new, Expressionist poetry, the same could be said of Kirchner in the field of the visual arts. His own relationship to Heym was perhaps the closest of any; he experienced an almost compulsive love and veneration for and an intense concern for his work, although he never actually met him.[44]

No less relevant is Dube's following point, that Kirchner had 'an astonishing way of penetrating to the heart of a matter', for the crux of the matter is that Heym and Kirchner were in a number of ways remarkably similar types responding to contemporary reality in comparable ways. Both were eccentrics, solitaries who lived for their work, single-mindedly pursuing a vision whose images filled their heads. They were both enthusiasts, vehement, impetuous, hypersensitive (and therefore easily offended), fatalistic. They were united in their enthusiasm for Woman, and for Byron, Baudelaire, Poe, Van Gogh and Nietzsche. Their tastes were similar; both had a predilection for the exotic. It is true that Heym's expressionism, unlike Kirchner's, developed from a romantic base; but this difference is less important than the fact that they both saw art as intensified life. They were both a prey to *Angst* and to a nervous exhaustion that was the inevitable result of their passionate approach to everything. Kirchner described his work as 'the life story of a paranoid'; Heym explored his own 'paranoia' in diaries and tales. Both were fatalists and, paradoxically, revolutionaries. Heym was no less radically anti-bourgeois than Kirchner. Their work is linked, as Salter has shown, by a sense of conflict which is expressed in comparable ways, so that leafing through the poems of *Umbra vitae* one can sense the affinity of the two men.[45] What Salter calls Heym's 'Streitformen', meaning the pointed, jagged vertical lines and forms which dominate his poetic images, above all in 1911,[46] have an obvious parallel in the similar lines and forms used by Kirchner in his Berlin paintings from 1911 to 1916. In both cases they are expressive of 'unresolvable conflict and existential crisis'.47 It was probably the sense of kinship revealed by such forms that led Kirchner to illustrate *Umbra vitae*.

Both appreciated the splendour of life (Kirchner was as much of a hedonist as Heym), but were obsessed by the isolation, alienation and desolation of life, particularly of city life. Heym's Berlin sonnets belong with Kirchner's Berlin paintings (as Kirchner himself reminds us in his illustration to Heym's 'Die Städte'), not least because poet and painter share a marked tendency to 'mythologize', in other words, to transform historically conditioned fact into timeless phenomena, so that their images of Berlin street life in 1911 are not only pictures of a collapsing society, but at the same time pictures of the human condition as such (Man as Nietzschean 'man-of-prey' [*Raubtier-Mensch*]). Had they met, Heym would surely have found in Kirchner his real 'brother'.

Ludwig Meidner (1884–1966) reacted to Heym's work earlier than Kirchner; he was himself influenced by Heym. Like Heym, Meidner came from Silesia; he studied fine art in Breslau (1903–5) and Paris (1906–7), and lived in Berlin in 1905–6 and from 1908 until well after Heym's death. Between 1908 and 1912 he immersed himself in Nietzsche's work, especially *Thus Spake Zarathustra*, in section LI of which ('On Passing By') he found verbal images of the urban apocalypse that was to be his own major theme from late 1911 to 1923: 'Woe to this great city! – I would that I already saw the pillar of fire in which it will be consumed.' In 1910–12 he took to frequenting the Café des Westens and to attending Neopathetisches Cabaret meetings, contexts in which Heym loomed large. Like Heym, he became a close friend of Jakob van Hoddis; later he described how he and van Hoddis would tramp through the suburbs of Berlin in the early hours of the morning, their heads full of similarly apocalyptic images. Heym, van Hoddis and Meidner were all 'Pathetiker', men of passionate temperament. In 1912 Meidner formed a group of painters called the Pathetiker, who first exhibited at the Sturm Gallery in November 1912; in taking its name from the Neopathetisches Cabaret, Meidner's group was expressing its solidarity with writers like van Hoddis48 and Heym. Heym was also known as a 'Pathetiker'. Had he lived, Heym would have found a natural home in the group around Meidner and in the periodical *Das Neue Pathos*.

Heym and Meidner moved in the same circles and had common friends in Jakob van Hoddis and Simon Guttmann. They apparently knew one another, though not particularly well, probably because Heym, in 1911–12, was so busy. Meidner admired Heym's work[49] and left a description of him at a Neopathetisches Cabaret reading: 'He looked uncommonly fit, with dark hair, and recited his poems in a manly voice and in a very confident and pleasing way.'[50] It was mainly after Heym's death that Meidner was influenced by him. Being men of not dissimilar temperament, with similar interests, preoccupations and obsessions, they were inevitably drawn, in part, to similar objects. Thus Meidner's *Gasometer in Berlin-Wilmersdorf* of October 1911 can be compared with Heym's 'Der Gastempel' (*L* 194) of January 1911; the fact that Heym's poem remained unpublished at the time does not mean that Meidner did not know it. The two works are, however, less interesting than the work which both men were shortly to produce.

Heym and Meidner were both fascinated by the megalopolis of Berlin, which so blatantly combined the great and the monstrous, vitality and corruption. Their feelings towards it were similarly ambiguous; Berlin was something they loved to hate. The whole idea of achieving spiritual renewal through an orgy of destruction spawned such ambiguity; Meidner's attitude towards the apocalyptic landscapes which he was shortly to produce is comparable to Heym's attitude to war. Heym's most famous (and most apocalyptic) poem, 'Der Krieg', was written in September 1911. Meidner may well have known it at this stage, for his own earliest apocalyptic painting, *Die Gestrandeten* of October 1911, can be seen as tantamount to an illustration of the last stanza of Heym's poem.[51] Meidner's *Schrecken des Krieges*, dating from about the same time, shows, as Heym's poem does, the destructiveness of war. In October 1911, then, Meidner began to produce his now famous series of apocalyptic paintings, partly in response to the poetry of van Hoddis and Heym.[52] This new development in Meidner's work was given a major boost in June 1912, when Heym's second collection, *Umbra vitae*, appeared posthumously. Meidner's attention was drawn to *Umbra vitae* by Guttmann and van Hoddis; it clearly acted as a catalyst and source of inspiration to him. In advancing the idea of a 'new pathos' in 1910, Stefan Zweig argued that the lyric poet was set to become the arouser of passions, the igniter of the sacred flame.[53] That is what Heym, in 1911–12, became for Meidner. His apocalyptic land-

scapes and city-scapes represent the most significant link between painter and poet. They are important, in the present context, because
Meidner was the first fellow-artist to respond creatively to Heym's
work.

VII

Poetry, 1910–1912

☐ WORD-PAINTING

In the last two years of his life Heym first produces work that is the summation of developments begun before 1910, and then, in June–November 1911, suddenly turns his back on it.

His earliest work, as we have seen, was neo-romantic; its images took the form of metaphors illustrating a mood, and the poetically primitive simile – so typical of *Jugendstil* or neo-romanticism – was as ubiquitous as it is in Rilke's earlier work; his use of colour was essentially impressionistic. During the years 1906–10 this neo-romantic impressionism gradually changes into something akin to post-impressionism. By 1910 the poet's ego has been largely suppressed; he has become a 'mirror of external reality'. The later poetry, which until June 1911 has little to do with moods, expresses the world of things or object-world; the means of expression (including the use of intensified colour and the fact that colours now tend to assume independence as nouns and adverbs instead of being mere epithets) are those of post-impressionist painting, the important models here being Vincent van Gogh and Ferdinand Hodler. Heym's later poems do not narrate; they depict; they show him perceiving reality visually and describing it in a painterly way – in a poem, 'Der Sonntag', he even writes of people and things as so many '[brush]strokes' (*L* 391). His work, which is now grounded in images rather than in thoughts or feelings, is primitive or 'naïve' in the sense of being the product of a non-rational form of perception. His poetic method is now 'word-painting' in the fullest and most precise meaning of the term; it is the optical registration of detail that gives the poetry of 1910 and early 1911 its famous 'impersonality'.

This 'word-painting' is exemplified in a poem which Heym sent to John Wolfsohn on 6 September 1910 in return for the 'very valuable' letter of 4 September in which Wolfsohn had compared him with Hodler and Van Gogh. The poem, written in July 1910, was as follows:

> Der weiten Buchen Tanzsaal zieht zu Tal
> Auf Silbersäulen von der Waldung Kamm.
> Im toten Laube glüht die Sonne fahl
> Aus Regenwolken fort, auf gelbem Stamm.
>
> Die grünen Halden ziehn, an Büschen reich,
> Und Dornenhecken, Feldern im Geviert,
> Ins Land hinaus, wo sich der Abend weich
> Das Götterhaupt mit blassen Kränzen ziert (*L* 104).

The distant beeches' dancing party moves valleywards from the crest of the woods on silver columns. Amid the dead leaves, on a yellow stem, the sun shines on palely out of rain-clouds.
The green hillsides, rich in bushes, and hawthorn hedges, and square fields, move out into the open countryside where evening gently adorns its god's head with pale wreaths.

The fact that the poem was written in July means that it was not written as a response to Wolfsohn's letter. At this time two painters were very much in Heym's mind, Van Gogh and the Berlin painter Hans Baluschek; in August Heym was to write 'Laubenkolonie' (inspired by Baluschek), and in September 'Die Gefangenen' (which, as we saw, has its starting-point in Van Gogh). However, if this helps to explain how Heym is now writing, it does not explain what he is writing. Thus the poem, quoted above, from the cycle 'Thüringen II', product of his visit to the Thüringer Wald in July 1910 (he had also been there with Ernst Balcke in May), is – quite specifically and concretely – a landscape poem, describing what he saw 'between Dreiherrensteinen and Inselsberg, looking towards Brotterode'.

This word-painting technique is further exemplified in a series of landscapes, 'Autumnus', 'Der Winter' and 'Printemps', the very titles of which indicate that we are faced less with 'poems' than with 'paintings'. 'Autumnus' was written in mid-September 1910:

Der Schwäne Schneeweiß. Glanz der blauen Flut.
Des breiten Strandes Gelb, das flach verläuft.
Gelärm der Badenden und Freude laut
Der braunen schlanken Leiber, die mit Zweigen
Sich peitschen blankes Wasser auf das Haupt.

Doch aufwärts steigt der Wald in blauen Farben
Des Nachmittags. Sein breites grünes Haupt
Ist sanft gerundet in den blassen Himmel
Der zitternd ausstreut frühen Herbstes Licht.

Weit an dem Stromtal zieht das Hügelland
Sich fern hinab, mit bunten Wäldern voll
Und voll von Sonne, bis es hinten weit
Verschwimmend tief in blaue Schatten taucht (*L* 129).

('Autumn') The snowy white of the swans. Brilliance of blue water. The yellow of the wide strand running flatly into the distance. Noise of bathers and joyful laughter of the slim brown bodies showering bright water over one another's heads with branches.

But the forest rises up in afternoon's blue colours, its broad green head gently rounded against the pale sky which trembles as it sheds early autumn light.

In the middle distance the hills descend the river valley, full of autumn-coloured woods and sunshine, until in the background they dissolve into blue shadows.

The poem opens with three colours, two of them carrying the weight of substantives, the third ('Glanz der blauen Flut') being no less a 'pure' colour (there is no contour to distract the eye from the colour as such). While the third line denotes sounds, the sounds in question serve only to conjure up a visual scene. Heym is therefore using colour as a painter uses it; his 'poem' is substantially a matter of light and colour effects.[1] The second stanza confirms this: the 'blue colours' are the blue shadows of the autumn afternoon as seen by a man with a painter's sense of inherent colour. The woods are rendered in purely visual terms: the green tree tops are seen against a pale sky radiating a thin autumnal light, their contour being rounded into a more immediately visible image. The background, described in the third stanza, is also seen as a painter would see it, leading the eye away into the blueness of infinity; this is at once a painterly phenomenon and a romantic one. What is new and remarkable about 'Autumnus' is the fact that Heym is no longer using nature to express his own mood, but is now simply concentrating on the natural objects in question, which he renders visually and in terms of colour.

A matter of weeks after 'Autumnus' Heym wrote another seasonal poem, 'Der Winter', which is again actual in origin:

Der blaue Schnee liegt auf dem ebenen Land,
Das Winter dehnt. Und die Wegweiser zeigen
Einander mit der ausgestreckten Hand
Der Horizonte violettes Schweigen.

Hier treffen sich auf ihrem Weg ins Leere
Vier Straßen an. Die niedren Bäume stehen
Wie Bettler kahl. Das Rot der Vogelbeere
Glänzt wie ihr Auge trübe. Die Chausseen

Verweilen kurz und sprechen aus den Ästen.
Dann ziehn sie weiter in die Einsamkeit
Gen Nord und Süden und nach Ost und Westen,
Wo bleicht der niedere Tag der Winterzeit.

Ein hoher Korb mit rissigem Geflecht
Blieb von der Ernte noch im Ackerfeld.
Weißbärtig, ein Soldat, der nach Gefecht
Und heißem Tag der Toten Wache hält.

Der Schnee wird bleicher, und der Tag vergeht.
Der Sonne Atem dampft am Firmament,
Davon das Eis, das in den Lachen steht
Hinab die Straße rot wie Feuer brennt (*L* 163).

('Winter') Blue snow lying on flat countryside which winter stretches. With arms outstretched signposts show one another the horizon's violet silence.

Four roads meet here on their way into emptiness. The stunted trees are beggar-naked. Red rowan berries glisten like bloodshot eyes. The roads

Linger briefly, speaking through their wayside branches. Then they wend their way into the solitude of North and South, East and West, where winter's short day blanches.

A tall broken basket was left behind in the field after harvesting: white-bearded, a soldier guarding the dead after the heat of the day and battle.

The snow turns paler still; daylight passes away. The sun's breath smoulders, making the ice in the potholes turn fiery red the length of the road.

One has only to look at the poem, however, to see that its interest lies not in its actuality, but in its use of colour: the blue snow (blue because of lack of light), the violet of the horizon (cf. Van Gogh), and – by contrast – the red berries standing as an enigmatic reminder of summer. No less painterly is the disposition of space in the form of the cross-roads with the roads radiating in all directions. It would, I think, have been better if the poem had finished at the end of the third stanza, for the last two stanzas arguably weaken the effect. The forgotten basket is theatrical (in a way reminiscent of Van Gogh), the simile somewhat contrived, and the fiery red of the setting sun (reflected in the frozen puddles) too close to mannerism to be justified here; it lacks any clear extension of meaning, vaguely apocalyptic though it is. The fact that the ending of the poem is so typical of him at this time, only underlines my point, which is that Heym, increasingly apocalyptic as his mood now is, is in danger of slipping into self-pastiche.

'Printemps' was written some seven months later, in late April/early May 1911:

Ein Feldweg, der in weißen Bäumen träumt,
In Kirschenblüten, zieht fern über Feld.
Die hellen Zweige, feierlich erhellt
Zittern im Abend, wo die Wolke säumt,

Ein düstrer Berg, den Tag mit goldnem Grat,
Ganz hinten, wo ein kleiner Kirchturm blinkt.
Des Glöckchen sanft im lichten Winde klingt
Herüber goldnen Tons auf grüner Saat.

Ein Ackerer geht groß am Himmelsrand.
Davor, wie Riesen schwarz, der Stiere Paar,
Ein Dämon vor des Himmels tiefer Glut

Und eine Mühle faßt der Sonne Haar
Und wirbelt ihren Kopf von Hand zu Hand
Auf schwarzem Arm, der langsam sinkt, voll Blut (*L* 261).

('Printemps') A footpath adream with white trees, with wild cherry blossom, crosses a field away in the distance, where a little church-tower catches the light. Pale branches, theatrically lit, tremble in the evening where the cloud,
    A dark mountain, gives the day a golden edge. In the gentle breeze the church bell spills its golden sound over the green corn.
    A ploughman walks, tall, on the horizon. In front of him, black as giants, the pair of oxen, a [janus-headed] demon against the deep red of the sky,

And over the black meadow a windmill catches the sun by the hair and as it revolves passes from blade to blade the head which slowly sinks, blood-red.

The poem is comparable to 'Autumnus', but goes beyond it in being not just a twelve-line poem à la Stefan George, but a sonnet, which means that the scene depicted is seen within an old-fashioned formal frame: it is a picture, but a picture of what? Is it the Parisian genre piece promised by the title? In the octave Heym describes a spring scene in a painterly, 'impressionistic' way; the emphasis is very much on colour and light, and therefore on life. The sestet is very different, for here the scene is darkened and intensified by being seen straight into the setting sun (which radically modifies the colour values), and by being seen through the eyes of Van Gogh (to whom the 'Ackerer ... groß am Himmelsrand' points). The silhouette effect now allows the horizon figures to appear as a demon, a kind of centaur (cf. Kley, Kubin), while the setting sun similarly takes on the appearance of a bloody head continually severed by the guillotine-blades of the windmill. Heym intensifies red into blood-red, as Van Gogh did, and then takes the blood-red colour for blood. What started as an apparently idyllic picture-postcard scene thus suddenly becomes ominous and indeed symbolical, for nature is not merely seen to be red in tooth and claw, but becomes the symbol of the revolution which is never far from Heym's mind at this time.

These three landscape seasons, to which Heym presently added a fourth, 'Der Sommer' (July 1911: L 302f.), are reminiscent of Brueghel's set of *Four Seasons*. There is some evidence that Heym admired Brueghel; in particular the poem 'Die Blinden' (October 1911: L 394) reads very much like a verbalization of Brueghel's famous *Parable of the Blind* of 1568; Heym has not one word of comment, but his image, like Brueghel's, conveys a tragic view of the human condition.

Heym's later poetry may also be distinguished from the earlier in many other ways according to many criteria. Thus it is marked by a concentration on objects and, for a time, on the realities of life in metropolitan Berlin; more fundamentally it is distinguished by a profound sense of alienation from the whole object-world as such, whether natural or man-made. But if Heym in 1910 and early 1911 concentrates much more than before on contemporary reality, most of his imagery continues to come from nature, which remains his main subject because of his obsession with death. At this time he writes about nature, about contemporary reality (including urban deprivation, though he sees this as part of a more fundamental malaise), about war and revolution, about purely imaginary things (e.g. his own wedding), about Greece (still), and so on; but linking all these, leitmotif of his work at this time, subject of most of his longest poems and the subject which most held his imagination, was Death. He may have given up neo-romantic emotional impressionism, but he is more of a romantic than ever; indeed, he has as good a claim to the title of 'last Romantic' as anyone.

From April 1910 he began to write more poems about contemporary urban reality. Given that he had already written some such poems, notably the 'Abende im Vorfrühling' series of sonnets in January 1910, and that the first two 'Berlin' sonnets were written before he joined the Neue Club, one can hardly ascribe to the club a decisive role in this respect. Indeed, it is more to the point to see Heym himself as one of the founders of Expressionist urban poetry. In 1910 contemporary urban reality was very much the coming theme. As we have seen, Heym had been influenced in this respect by the urban poetry of Baudelaire, Rimbaud and Dehmel, and had also seen the Berlin paintings of Hans Baluschek in the 1910 Secession. Urban poetry as such had, of course, existed in Germany before 1910. What is new is the 'expressionism' and, more important, the Baudelairean perception of the city, for Expressionist city poetry differs from the naturalist or impressionist variety in that the city is given a powerful extension of meaning, becoming the domain of demons. Heym will no doubt have been encouraged by his membership of the Neue Club to continue in the direction he was already taking, just as his example will have encouraged them to concentrate on the same subject. In terms of Heym's work the 'Berlin' series, dating from April 1910, is certainly a landmark in terms of quantity, but it could be argued that these famous poems are hardly 'expressionistic'; in purely aesthetic terms they are basically 'naturalistic' or 'impressionistic'. This applies to 'Berlin II' (*L* 58), the poem which, printed in Pfemfert's *Der Demokrat*, led to the publication of *Der ewige Tag*:

> Beteerte Fässer rollten von den Schwellen
> der dunklen Speicher auf die hohen Kähne.
> Die Schlepper zogen an. Des Rauches Mähne
> hing rußig nieder auf die ölgen Wellen.

Berlin

Beteerte Fässer rollten von den Schwellen
der dunklen Speicher auf die hohen Kähne.
Die Schlepper zogen an. Des Rauches Mähne
hing rußig nieder auf die öligen Wellen.

Zwei Dampfer kamen mit Musik Kapellen,
den Schornstein kappten sie am Brückenbogen.
Rauch, Ruß, Gestank lag auf den schmutzgen Wogen
der Gerbereien mit den braunen Fellen.

In allen Brücken, drunter uns die Zille
hindurchgebracht, ertönten die Signale
gleich wie in Trommeln wachsend, in der Stille.

Wir ließen los. Und trieben im Kanale
an Gärten langsam hin. In dem Idylle
sahn wir der Riesenschlote Nachtfanale.

Facsimile of a fair-copy made by Heym of his poem 'Berlin II'

Zwei Dampfer kamen mit Musikkapellen,
den Schornstein kappten sie am Brückenbogen.
Rauch, Ruß, Gestank lag auf den schmutzgen Wogen
der Gerbereien mit den braunen Fellen.

In allen Brücken, drunter uns die Zille
hindurchgebracht, ertönten die Signale
gleich wie in Trommeln wachsend, in der Stille.

Wir ließen los. Und trieben im Kanale,
an Gärten langsam hin. In dem Idylle
sahn wir der Riesenschlote Nachtfanale.

('Berlin II') Tarred barrels rolled from the doorways of dark warehouses on to tall barges. The tugs took the strain. The mane of smoke hung sootily over the oily waves.

Two steamers arrived with bands on board. Their funnels hit the arch of the bridge. Smoke, rust and a stench lay on the dirty water from the tanneries with their horseskins drying outside.

On all bridges beneath which the barge brought us, warning signals sounded in the stillness, growing louder like drums.

We let go of the barge and drifted slowly along a canal past people's gardens. In the midst of this idyll we caught sight of night's monster chimney-torches.

Concentrated and powerful though it is, the poem cannot be called 'expressionistic' in any sustainable sense; it is not even grotesquely realistic, just realistic.

The most impressive of Heym's sonnets about contemporary reality is 'Die Züge' of December 1910:

Rauchwolken, rosa, wie ein Frühlingstag,
Die schnell der Züge schwarze Lunge stößt,
Ziehn auf dem Strom hinab, der riesig flößt
Eisschollen breit mit Stoß und lautem Schlag.

Der weite Wintertag der Niederung
Glänzt fern wie Feuer rot und Gold-Kristall
Auf Schnee und Ebenen, wo der Feuerball
Der Sonne sinkt auf Wald und Dämmerung.

Die Züge donnern auf dem Meilendamme,
Der in die Wälder rennt, des Tages Schweif.
Ihr Rauch steigt auf wie eine Feuerflamme,

> Die hoch im Licht des Ostwinds Schnabel zaust,
> Der, goldgefiedert, wie ein starker Greif,
> Mit breiter Brust hinab gen Abend braust (*L* 189).

('The trains') Clouds of smoke, pink as a spring day, puffed out hurriedly by the trains' black lungs, drift down the river on which great rafts of ice crash together as they float away.

In the distance the wide winter's day of the low-lying land gleams like red fire and gold crystals on the snow and plains, where the fiery ball of the sun is sinking down on to forest and twilight.

The trains go thundering across the mile-long embankment which runs into the forest, day's tail. Their smoke rises like a fiery plume,

Which, high up in the light, tugs at the beak of the East wind which, golden-feathered, sweeps down towards evening with its powerful breast, like a great griffon-vulture.

This is, in the first instance, an admirably visualized early train-poem, at once realistic and visionary. By choosing the sonnet form Heym has implicitly renounced the onomatopoeia that is an important part of Ernst Stadler's better-known 'Journey over the Rhine-Bridge at Cologne by Night', but he partly compensates by the clarity and vividness of his imagery, which is the vehicle for what he would probably have thought of as the 'metaphysical' dimension of the poem, which, as in Stadler's, comes at the end. The trains are animated and indeed demonized by being given black lungs puffing out smoke which rises 'like a fiery plume'; they are thus dragonlike and therefore symbolic of evil, while the almost inevitable (blood-) red fireball of the setting sun gives the poem a characteristically apocalyptic dimension – all of this while remaining within the realm of vividly perceived reality, until, that is, we come to the most remarkable feature of the poem, its visionary ending. The east wind is animated or, better, demonized, into the lion-bodied eagle (*Greif*) or vulture (*Greifvogel*), which represents the monster Death and is a typical product of Heym's gothic imagination. The sonnet form, it has to be said, is an odd vehicle for such visions.

☐ THE DEMONS

Heym's best-known and in some ways most characteristic poems are those in which he conveys his view of the modern *cité maudite* as possessed by 'demons', that is, by uncontrollable forces of evil which corrupt and destroy man from within. Baudelaire wrote: 'Our minds are teeming with demons'; Heym conjures them into existence. A novel by Robert Saudek, published in Berlin in 1908, was entitled *Dämon Berlin*. Whether Heym knew of this title is not known, but the opening lines of 'Vorortbahnhof' (*L* 102) appear to echo a passage in another contemporary novel, Georg Hermann's *Kubinka* (1910).[2] In a review of his friend's work in *Die Aktion* for 8 May 1911, Ernst Balcke said that it was the 'demonic immensity' of Berlin that obsessed Heym; he added: 'And so the city is symbolized in the gigantic figure of Baal and in the form of evil demons (*D* 194).' He is referring to two of Heym's most famous poems, 'Der Gott der Stadt' and 'Die Dämonen der Städte'; his comment, interesting though it is, shows that he did not – as Heym knew – fully understand his friend's work. Let us now look at these two poems and at a closely related one, 'Der Krieg'.

The most ambivalent of these three memorable poems is 'Die Dämonen der Städte' (originally entitled 'Chimäre'), which shows a nameless city, inhabited by nameless human beings, being gradually taken over by equally nameless demons:

Sie wandern durch die Nacht der Städte hin,
Die schwarz sich ducken unter ihrem Fuß.
Wie Schifferbärte stehen um ihr Kinn
Die Wolken schwarz vom Rauch und Kohlenruß.

Ihr langer Schatten schwankt im Häusermeer
Und löscht der Straßen Lichterreihen aus.
Er kriecht wie Nebel auf dem Pflaster schwer
Und tastet langsam vorwärts Haus für Haus.

Den einem Fuß auf einen Platz gestellt,
Den anderen gekniet auf einen Turm,
Ragen sie auf, wo schwarz der Regen fällt,
Panspfeifen blasend in den Wolkensturm.

Um ihre Füße kreist das Ritornell
Des Städtemeers mit trauriger Musik,
Ein großes Sterbelied. Bald dumpf, bald grell
Wechselt der Ton, der in das Dunkel stieg.

Sie wandern an dem Strom, der schwarz und breit
Wie ein Reptil, den Rücken gelb gefleckt
Von den Laternen, in die Dunkelheit
Sich traurig wälzt, die schwarz den Himmel deckt.

Sie lehnen schwer auf einer Brückenwand
Und stecken ihre Hände in den Schwarm
Der Menschen aus, wie Faune, die am Rand
Der Sümpfe bohren in den Schlamm den Arm.

Einer steht auf. Dem weißen Monde hängt
Er eine schwarze Larve vor. Die Nacht,
Die sich wie Blei vom finstern Himmel senkt,
Drückt tief die Häuser in des Dunkels Schacht.

Der Städte Schultern knacken. Und es birst
Ein Dach, daraus ein rotes Feuer schwemmt.
Breitbeinig sitzen sie auf seinem First
Und schrein wie Katzen auf zum Firmament.

In einer Stube voll von Finsternissen
Schreit eine Wöchnerin in ihren Wehn.
Ihr starker Leib ragt riesig aus den Kissen,
Um den herum die großen Teufel stehn.

Sie hält sich zitternd an der Wehebank.
Das Zimmer schwankt um sie von ihrem Schrei,
Da kommt die Frucht. Ihr Schoß klafft rot und lang
Und blutend reißt er von der Frucht entzwei.

Der Teufel Hälse wachsen wie Giraffen.
Das Kind hat keinen Kopf. Die Mutter hält
Es vor sich hin. In ihrem Rücken klaffen
Des Schrecks Froschfinger, wenn sie rückwärts fällt.

Doch die Dämonen wachsen riesengroß.
Ihr Schläfenhorn zerreißt den Himmel rot.
Erdbeben donnert durch der Städte Schoß
Um ihren Huf, den Feuer überloht (*L* 186f.).

('The demons of the cities') They prowl through the night of cities cringing beneath their feet. Black palls of smoke and soot surround their chins like so many seamen's beards.

Their long shadows stagger through the sea of houses and extinguish the rows of street lights. On the pavements they creep forward like fog, feeling their way slowly forward, house by house.

One leg planted in a public square, the other kneeling on a tower, they tower up into the sky from which black rain is falling, playing their Pan's pipes into the darkening storm.

Round their feet revolves the massed cities' ritornello with its sad music, one great song for the dying. The tones rising up into darkness keep changing, are now dull, now shrill.

They roam beside the river which, black and broad as a reptile, its back flecked with yellow from the streetlamps, stretches sadly into the darkness which shrouds the sky in black.

They lean heavily against the side of a bridge and stick their hands into the crowd of people, like satyrs sticking their arms into the mud at the edge of a swamp.

One stands up. He hangs a black mask in front of the moon's whiteness. Night, falling like lead from the louring sky, presses the houses down into the shaft of darkness.

The cities' shoulders sap; a roof bursts open, red fire pouring out of it. They sit astride the ridge of the roof, yowling heavenward like cats.

In a room full of the powers of evil a woman in labour screams out in pain. Her huge stomach rises massively out of the bed round which the great demons stand.

Shaking, she holds on like grim death. The room rocks around her from her scream, then her fruit comes forth. Her womb gapes red and long and bleeding, is torn open.

The demons' necks grow as long as giraffes'. The child has no head. The mother holds it up. The frost-fingers of horror grasp her from behind as she falls back.

The demons for their part grow ever more gigantic. The horn on their forehead tears the red sky open. An earthquake rumbles through the cities around their hoofs, which are engulfed in flames.

'They' – the demons – are a vague and motley crew. They carry out a number of no doubt very demonic actions, but it is only in the last third of the poem that their power is shown, and even then it is shown in a strangely ineffectual way. One assumes that the house catching fire is as much their doing as the birth of the headless child, and yet it appears to catch them unawares. Only in the last two lines of the final stanza, as Richard Sheppard has said, 'is an apocalyptic event directly and unequivocally attributed to the demons' activity'.[3] Throughout the poem the poet's vantage-point is implicitly that of the demons, although – by comparison with 'Der Gott der Stadt' – Heym makes surprisingly little of the fact. It is not that the poem is less 'expressionistic' than 'Der Gott der Stadt'; it is simply less competently realized. If the demons are still learning their trade so, too, is Heym. Philip Thomson has suggested[4] that stanzas nine to eleven are overdone, so that an unintentional comic effect is produced; I do not agree – the comic effect comes in stanza eight, when the burning house makes the demons perched on its roof scream like so many scalded cats. The comedy here, which is surely deliberate and appears to involve self-pastiche, is quickly negated, for what remains in the mind is the birth of the headless child.

'Der Gott der Stadt', on the other hand, is one of Heym's most completely realized poems:

> Auf einem Häuserblocke sitzt er breit.
> Die Winde lagern schwarz um seine Stirn.
> Er schaut voll Wut, wo fern in Einsamkeit
> Die letzten Häuser in das Land verirrn.
>
> Vom Abend glänzt der rote Bauch dem Baal,
> Die großen Städte knien um ihn her.
> Der Kirchenglocken ungeheure Zahl
> Wogt auf zu ihm aus schwarzer Türme Meer.
>
> Wie Korybanten-Tanz dröhnt die Musik
> Der Millionen durch die Straßen laut.
> Der Schlote Rauch, die Wolken der Fabrik
> Ziehn auf zu ihm, wie Duft von Weihrauch blaut.
>
> Das Wetter schwelt in seinen Augenbrauen.
> Der dunkle Abend wird in Nacht betäubt.
> Die Stürme flattern, die wie Geier schauen
> Von seinem Haupthaar, das im Zorne sträubt.
>
> Er streckt ins Dunkel seine Fleischerfaust.
> Er schüttelt sie. Ein Meer von Feuer jagt
> Durch eine Straße. Und der Glutqualm braust
> Und frißt sie auf, bis spät der Morgen tagt (L 192).

('The god of the city') He is sitting astride an apartment block. The winds lie black about his brow. He glares angrily at where far away, in solitude, the last houses stray into the country.

Baal's red belly gleams with sunset; the great cities kneel around him. The prodigious number of church bells swell up to him out of a sea of black towers.

Like dancing Corybantes the music of the millions thunders noisily through the streets. The chimneys' smoke, factory-made clouds, rises up towards him like the scent of incense turning blue.

The storm smoulders in his eyebrows. Dark evening is stunned into night. Storm-winds stream, watching like vultures from the hair of his head which is standing on end in anger.

He raises his butcher's fist into the darkness. Shakes it. A sea of fire seethes through a street. And the fire and smoke roar and devour it, till at last day breaks.

The gigantic figure of Baal symbolizes the 'demonic immensity' of Berlin and, more generally, of life as such; the 'Weltstadt' is both a specific reference to Berlin and an allusion to the 'Stadt der Welt' (city of the world) in a more general sense, for – as we have seen – Heym, like Baudelaire, was obsessed by evil, which he projected as a 'crowd of demons'. At the same time this Baal, whose naming is delayed – a trick which Heym learnt from Hölderlin – until the second stanza, is a persona of Heym himself (Baal's Roman equivalent is Bacchus, and 'Bacchus' was one of Heym's nicknames among his *Saufbrüder*) looking out, 'voll Wut', over the demonically expanding Charlottenburg (the population of which rose from 20,000 in 1871 to 323,000 by 1919!) to where its last houses are lost in a hostile environment. This 'Gott der Stadt' is therefore, among other things, the twenty-three-year-old poet wishing death and destruction upon the philistine metropolis by which he was fascinated (in a letter he calls it the 'urbs lucis') and appalled.

Baal's belly gleaming red in the evening sun represents at once his appetite for death and Heym's appetite for life. That the monstrous noise of the church bells rises from a sea of black towers suggests that Heym is, with Nietzsche, seeing Christianity as life-denying. The poem contains a number of images which confirm that what Heym is describing here is both the real Berlin-Charlottenburg and, simultaneously, a symbolic monster city of the imagination, a place of myth. Baal is both a symbol of the deathly forces of life (specifically, of modern life) and a personification of Heym as rebel.

I find 'Der Gott der Stadt' more impressive than 'Die Dämonen der Städte' because in it Heym concentrates on one demon (for which, as we shall see, he probably had a visual model), one moment of appalling crisis, and the actions of that moment. The poem is accordingly far more concrete, specific, absolute ('verabsolutiert'); it is clear and revolutionary in its implications, and is also far more personal. It is written in iambic pentameters in those characteristic four-line blocks, with alternating rhymes; the iambics are as forceful as the trochaics of 'Der Krieg', and there are many other features which link the two poems. In both cases Heym uses personification to control the perspective and sharpen the focus of his vision. In 'Der Krieg' war is personified as a demon crushing the moon in his black hand; here the winds swirling around Baal's brow are as black as the night by which Heym was obsessed, as black as the destruction which Baal brings, and the wind is animated and demonized by the characteristic use of the plural which Heym inherited from Baudelaire.

Heym's demons represent, ultimately, the curse of existence in Schopenhauer's sense; there are cognate figures in Indian and Tibetan demonology. With these demons brooding over the cities whose evil they personify one can compare a series of drawings in *Simplicissimus*, including one by Max Slevogt which offers a close parallel to 'Der Gott der Stadt' and 'Der Krieg'; Heym is known to have read *Simplicissimus*, although there is no proof that he knew Slevogt's drawing, which appeared there in 1896. The horned devil (of 'Der Gott der Stadt') is a stock-in-trade of Heinrich Kley.[5] Slevogt and Kley both show a gigantic devil or demon standing over a chaotic scene. There is also Felicien Rops's figure *Satan semant l'ivraie* of c. 1887 (quite apart from being a strong influence on Kubin, Rops is an artist with whom Heym has not infrequently been compared), Arnold Böcklin's *Die Pest* of 1898 and Alfred Kubin's *Epidemie* of 1901. Such figures, commonplace in *fin-de-siècle* art, mostly go back to Goya's *The Giant* of 1808–10, which depicts a crowd fleeing from its fears, these being represented by a striding giant; as we have seen, Heym admired Goya's work. No doubt one or more of these works helped Heym to sharpen his own demon-image. There is also the image of Satan rising in the lines from Grabbe's *Herzog Theodor von Gothland* which Heym had used as a motto for his 'Die Hölle' cycle a few weeks earlier.

'Der Gott der Stadt' probably had a specific *point de départ*, maybe even in that famous occasion reported by David Baumgardt: 'In my flat in Charlottenburg he once sat on the outside windowsill and to the amazement of the passers-by sang the Marseillaise (D 11).' Whether that was the occasion or not (Baumgardt remembered the incident as having taken place in 1911; 'Der Gott der Stadt' was written on 30 December 1910), Baumgardt's flat probably provided Heym alias Baal with his vantage-point.

Closely connected with 'Der Gott der Stadt' is Heym's best-known poem, 'Der Krieg', which had an even more specific starting-point in reality:

Aufgestanden ist er, welcher lange schlief,
Aufgestanden unten aus Gewölben tief.
In der Dämmrung steht er, groß und unerkannt,
Und den Mond zerdrückt er in der schwarzen Hand.

In den Abendlärm der Städte fällt es weit,
Frost und Schatten einer fremden Dunkelheit,
Und der Märkte runder Wirbel stockt zu Eis.
Es wird still. Sie sehn sich um. Und keiner weiß.

In den Gassen faßt es ihre Schulter leicht.
Eine Frage. Keine Antwort. Ein Gesicht erbleicht.
In der Ferne wimmert ein Geläute dünn
Und die Bärte zittern um ihr spitzes Kinn.

Auf den Bergen hebt er schon zu tanzen an
Und er schreit: Ihr Krieger alle, auf und an.
Und es schallet, wenn das schwarze Haupt er schwenkt,
Drum von tausend Schädeln laute Kette hängt.

Einem Turm gleich tritt er aus die letzte Glut,
Wo der Tag flieht, sind die Ströme schon voll Blut.
Zahllos sind die Leichen schon im Schilf gestreckt,
Von des Todes starken Vögeln weiß bedeckt.

Über runder Mauern blauem Flammenschwall
Steht er, über schwarzer Gassen Waffenschall.
Über Toren, wo die Wächter liegen quer,
Über Brücken, die von Bergen Toter schwer.

In die Nacht er jagt das Feuer querfeldein
Einen roten Hund mit wilder Mäuler Schrein.
Aus dem Dunkel springt der Nächte schwarze Welt,
Von Vulkanen furchtbar ist ihr Rand erhellt.

Und mit tausend roten Zipfelmützen weit
Sind die finstren Ebnen flackend überstreut,
Und was unten auf den Straßen wimmelt hin und her,
Fegt er in die Feuerhaufen, daß die Flamme brenne mehr.

Und die Flammen fressen brennend Wald um Wald,
Gelbe Fledermäuse zackig in das Laub gekrallt.
Seine Stange haut er wie ein Köhlerknecht
In die Bäume, daß das Feuer brause recht.

Eine große Stadt versank in gelbem Rauch,
Warf sich lautlos in des Abgrunds Bauch.
Aber riesig über glühnden Trümmern steht
Der in wilde Himmel dreimal seine Fackel dreht,

Über sturmzerfetzter Wolken Widerschein,
In des toten Dunkels kalte Wüstenein,
Daß er mit dem Brande weit die Nacht verdorr,
Pech und Feuer träufet unten auf Gomorrh (*L* 346f.).

('War') He is risen now that was so long asleep, risen out of vaulted places dark and deep. In the growing dusk he stands, tall and unknown, and crushes the moon in his strong black hand.

In the evening noises of great cities fall frost and shadow of an unfamiliar pall. And the maelstrom of the markets turns to ice. Silence grows. They look around. And no one knows.

In side-streets something touches their shoulder lightly. Questions. There's no answer. Someone's face turns pale. Far away a peal of church-bells sounds plaintively, causing beards to tremble around their pointed chins.

On the mountains he's begun his battle-dance, calling: Warriors, up and at them. There's a rattling when he shakes his brute black head, round which hangs a chain loud with the skulls of a thousand dead.

Like a tower he tramples out the dying light. Rivers are brim-full of blood by fall of night. Legion are the bodies laid out in the reeds, covered white with the strong birds of death.

Over the blue sea of flame from burning towers he stands, over black streets full of clashing weapons. Over doorways blocked by the bodies of their sentinels, over bridges heavy with mountains of the dead.

Into the night he drives the fire across country, a red hound with the screaming of wild mouths. Out of the darkness springs the black domain of nights, edges sinisterly lit up by volcanic lights.

The dark satanic plains, flickering with fires, are covered with thousands of red pointed caps, and those milling around on the roads beneath him he sweeps into burning piles to make the flames more brightly burn.

And the flames, burning, consume forest after forest, yellow bats clawing jaggedly at the leaves; like a charcoal-burner he strikes his poker into the trees to make the fire burn properly.

A great city sank in yellow smoke, hurled itself soundlessly into the belly of the abyss. But gigantic over glowing ruins he stands, thrice brandishing his torch at the livid heavens,

Over storm-torn clouds' reflected glow, into the cold wastelands of dead darkness down below; that his fire may consume the night far and wide, he pours pitch and brimstone down on their Gomorrha.

'Der Krieg' was occasioned by the war-scare generated by the second Morocco crisis of 1911, which reached its peak in September.

More specifically, the poem, written between 4 and 10 September 1911, was inspired by an article entitled 'Die Hetzer' in the *Berliner Tageblatt* on 7 September, which began:

Great Pan ought not to be awoken when he is asleep; the ancient Greeks recognized that a long time ago. He might wake and inspire people with that fear which the Persians experienced at Marathon, that sudden, unexpected dread and horror which has since been given the name of panic ... Even today people still experience dread and horror of things which are unknown, inscrutable, and therefore particularly terrible.[6]

This does not mean that the poem is about a war which never actually materialized; on the contrary, the second Morocco crisis was so much a part of the prehistory of the First World War that, imaginatively speaking, the poem is more closely related to the events of 1914 than used to be realized. The poetic procedure – poem triggered by a newspaper article, which is quickly left far behind as his imagination takes over – is typical of Heym.

Heym will have been struck by the article in *Berliner Tageblatt* for two reasons, one visual and one personal. On the purely visual level he immediately linked great panic-inducing Pan with the Baal of his 'Der Gott der Stadt' (written nine months earlier) and thence with his likely models for that figure, which included Goya's *The Giant* and the first of his *Disasters of War* series ('Sad presentiments of what will happen'), Kubin's *Krieg* and works by Klinger, Slevogt and Rops; there was also the Hindu destroyer-god Siva, known to Heym from Schopenhauer's description of him. On a personal level, the article no doubt struck him because of its visual presentation of a subject by which his imagination was possessed. Heym was obsessed by a foreboding of war, and at the same time longed for it as a forceful interruption of the monotony of his young life and of the banality of the age. In his diary he wrote: 'I too can say: if only there would be a war, I should be cured. Every day is the same. No great joys, no great sorrows' (*T* 30 May 1907). The words 'if only there would be a war, I should be cured' ('Gäb es nur Krieg, gesund wär ich') are Grabbe's (they occur in a letter which Heym would have found in Rudolf von Gottschall's Grabbe biography, which appeared in that favourite series of the impecunious Heym, Reclams Universal-Bibliothek, in 1902); Heym took them over because he so wholeheartedly concurred – his whole view of war corresponds with

Grabbe's. After a number of similar entries he adds, on 15 September 1911: 'My enthusiasm having to lie fallow in this banal age of ours is stifling me.' Such was his longing for a heroic life – the most that man can hope for, according to Schopenhauer – that he even dreamt, in 1911, of taking part in great battles. The disparity between his dream of glory and his vision, in this poem, of the carnage to which the heroic leads, is striking. The form of the poem carries clear intimations of the heroic mode, but none whatsoever of the expected immortality. The pervasive enthusiasm is without any illusions; the 'heroic' line is wooden, so that the poem is like a dance of death. When Heym wrote it in early September 1911, 'Der Krieg' must have been a visualization of that great battle of which he dreamt; when it was read by others, however, it seemed a prophetic vision of the Great War for Civilization.

What strikes the reader at once is the monumental impersonality and barbaric grandeur of the poem, which aims to shock. It consists of juxtaposed explosive images which burst like shells in the reader's mind, a technique that was to be further developed in 1914/15, in poetry of a very different kind, by August Stramm. The heavy six-beat trochaic line makes the accent stalk through the poem like the incarnate demon of war through his apocalyptic landscape. The rhythm and imagery underline the extreme violence of the subject-matter, with occasional deviations from the metrical pattern giving the impression of violence continually erupting through the ordered surface of life: the old world represented by the trochaic metre is burst open by the violence of the anarchic subject-matter. The use of rhymed couplets throughout, with all the rhymes masculine ones, is highly appropriate since the rhyme scheme thus reflects and expresses the primitive, elemental quality of Heym's subject. The poem is 'lyrical' only in its Keatsian concentration.

The opening of 'Der Krieg', which may involve an allusion to the prediction that Friedrich Barbarossa will one day rise again from beneath the mountains of Thuringia,[7] is majestic in its barbaric grandeur. War is immediately personified into an infernal demon who rises from the collective unconscious. This, surely, is 'the great power which appears in our subconscious' of which Heym wrote in his diary in October 1911. In the poem war is personified in a figure of utter profanity whose obscene power is indicated by his ability to crush the moon in his brute black hand; the whole point and purpose of war is death. In his first draft Heym had written of War's 'Negerhaupt' ('nigger-head'), a reference (to the threat which French Moroccan troops were thought to pose to Germany) which was far too specific and topical to be allowed to stand, for while 'Der Krieg' documents Heym's desire for the destruction of the old order, it is poetically important to him that war should be mythologized by being treated in a way which transcends realism. This is partly achieved by means of painterly reminiscences (of Goya, Slevogt, Kley, Kubin and Rops; of Bosch and Brueghel; of Brandenburg; and so on). The demon War brings with him the chill of life-denying darkness. At first people are nonplussed; but then the uncanny, threatening atmosphere gets to them and puzzlement gives way to fear; the jerky, abrupt phrases punch home the confused reactions of men jerked out of their trivial routines who suddenly find themselves faced with the primeval violence which all the time had been lurking at the bottom of their own minds (*homo homini lupus*). The peal of bells is a *memento mori* which reduces the staid bourgeois to a figure of fun.

The scene now changes; from the city terrified by this sudden eruption of hitherto suppressed violence we see the demon War moving out into the landscape of war, which becomes increasingly a prophetic picture of the lunar waste of the Somme, until it finally assumes the proportions of myth, of something wholly uncontrollable. Personification is repeatedly used to add to the terror. Thus in the seventh stanza night, the abode of demons, is touched into independent existence by Heym's use of the plural, which implies a black world full of night-demons. Similarly, fire is animated into 'a red hound with the screaming of wild mouths', the mythical Hell-Hound itself carrying off the broken animal bodies of the dead, across the once-green fields, to eternal damnation; one thinks again of Van Gogh trying to express the terrible passions of humanity by means of red and green. The birds which cover the bodies of the dead after the battle are both reminiscent of Kubin's early *Nach der Schlacht* (*After the Battle*), which Heym must have known (he uses its title for a lesser poem), and repeat the familiar vulture-image of death. In the eighth stanza Death is again personified, this time as a monstrous stoker feeding the flames with the countless dead in their tall pointed caps (cf. the 'Pickelhauben' of the German war-dead in 1914, but also the world of Brueghel and of Bosch, who also portrays the Hell-Hound). The whole world is turned into a ghastly crematorium. In a brilliant nightmare-image which derives from Van

Gogh's bat painting *Stuffed Kalong*, the flames are described as 'Gelbe Fledermäuse zackig in das Laub gekrallt' ('Yellow bats clawing jaggedly at the leaves'); the purpose of this memorable metaphor is to be nightmarish; in one of his prose sketches Heym identifies the bat as 'the bat of death'. And while these brilliant images are being fired at the reader, the strutting mechanical rhythms go their incessant, senseless way.

All through the poem War is presented as the sign of evil, and at the end we see the original monster city destroyed by War, destroyed, that is, by the awakened evil within itself. Its fall is made to echo the Fall of Babylon the Great, but as the earth is reduced to a wasteland dominated by the gigantic figure of Death Triumphant, Christian iconography fails, for Death is, finally, reminiscent of the Hindu destroyer-god Siva Bhairava with his garland of a thousand skulls, and similar figures from Tibetan demonology. Heym's source for this image was probably Schopenhauer's *Die Welt als Wille und Vorstellung*, which he read in 1910 and which contains, in the famous Fourth Book (cap. 54), a reference to Siva with his necklace of skulls.

Given that Heym saw war through the eyes both of Goya and of Delacroix, both of Leonardo and of Michelangelo, it is not surprising that one of the most striking features of 'Der Krieg' is its ambiguity: war is seen as a terrifying and destructive power, and yet it is described with an unmistakable *frisson* of excitement. This Janus-headed view is found in Merezhkovsky's *Leonardo da Vinci*: for Leonardo war is 'the supreme folly of humanity, the "most bestial of madnesses"', whereas Michelangelo sees it as 'the struggle of heroes for ... greatness and glory'. For Heym it was both.

In 'Der Krieg' there is a tension not only between form and imagery, but between the moral and the aesthetic generally. The staid structure of the poem, which is blown apart by its violent imagery, simultaneously stands for the moral censure which is swept aside by the aesthetic excitement which the poem generates; it is the aesthetic that predominates. Heym had no illusions about war, but, as we have seen, he craved its excitement on a personal level. Ludwig Meidner's *Apocalyptic Landscapes* of 1912 were to be similarly ambivalent, for Meidner wrote: 'I feared such visions, yet the final results gave me an especially warm feeling of satisfaction, a slightly Satanic joy.'[8] Meidner's *Apocalyptic Landscapes* were influenced by 'Der Krieg' (first published in *Umbra vitae*), as was Max Slevogt's *Der Verantwortliche* (*Der Unbekannte, maskiert, watet mit einer Anzahl von Leichen auf dem Rücken durch ein Blutmeer*) (*The One Responsible, the Unknown, masked, wading through a sea of blood with a number of corpses on his back*) of 1917, but perhaps the most striking vindication of Heym's imaginative *tour de force* was Freud's *Zeitgemässes über Krieg und Tod* (1915), which links war to the stirrings of an unknown hidden self. Franz Marc, who had the same dreams as Heym and Meidner, lived just long enough to see where they led: 'I often think how in my childhood and teens I was sorry not to be living at a time when history was in the making – now it's upon us and is more terrible than anyone could have imagined.'[9]

Shortly after writing 'Der Krieg' Heym saw, on 15 November 1911, in the Alte Pinakothek in Munich, a work which he called 'Altdorfer: Krieg' (*T* 174). The painting in question is one of Altdorfer's most famous and brilliant works, the *Battle of Arbela*, which Heym's idol Napoleon so admired that he hung it in his bathroom at St Cloud. It is a brilliantly expressive and 'romantic' depiction of war, which is seen not merely as a duel between two heroes – Alexander the Great and Darius – but as a titanic struggle, a cosmic cataclysm in which nature itself is caught up; it is also a visionary landscape painting which points forward to the work of Caspar David Friedrich and William Blake. No doubt it caught Heym's eye because its subject-matter reflected the poem which he had written nine weeks earlier, but he will also have been deeply attracted to its intense, visionary treatment of its heroic–romantic theme. Here, if anywhere, was the great event in which he longed to be involved.

Heym wrote many other poems about war (the 'Marathon' cycle, the 'Mont St Jean' cycle, 'Nach der Schlacht', 'Marengo', etc.), including 'Der Krieg II'. 'Marengo' is discussed later. 'Der Krieg II' is a companion piece to 'Der Krieg'; its theme, like that of Kubin's famous work, to which it seems to owe nothing, is 'Nach der Schlacht' – the aftermath of war in the form of the aftermath of a particular battle, the field of battle, littered with the dead and dying, dominated by a gigantic personification of Death. Although on a more human scale than its famous predecessor, it lacks the power inherent in the latter's visionary, mythical treatment, as does 'Nach der Schlacht' (*L* 124), which owes its title to Kubin, but lacks the memorability of his image. More distinguished are the sonnet cycles, particularly the 'Marathon' cycle (*L* 23f.) (written in winter 1909/10, they were complete by March 1910).

What makes them interesting is not just their subject and the clear influence of Kleist, but the fact that they show Heym learning his trade as a sonneteer. As Karl Ludwig Schneider has said,[10] these sonnets are a formal experiment, complete with inevitable compromises for the sake of the form, in other words, for the sake of the rhyme. While it is true that the 'Marathon' sonnets laid the foundation for the success of the 'Berlin' ones, it is also important to stress that the 'Berlin' sonnets are better not because their subject-matter is different (those who write on Expressionism too often assume that it implies social criticism in the manner of Die Brücke, which is nonsense; what about the Blaue Reiter?), but because they are better sonnets.

□ MONUMENTAL FORMALISM

The tension between the explosive violence of Heym's imagery and his wooden verse forms produces the dance-of-death effect noted by Ernst Stadler in his review of Der ewige Tag in Cahiers Alsaciens in May 1912; there is also a high degree of alienation involved, for the explosive force of the imagery both mocks the form and is itself ridiculed by it. The central section of Stadler's review remains to this day the best single account of Heym's basic poetic technique at this time:

Of course in Heym one finds none of the passionate exuberance with which Verhaeren, say, has celebrated the greatness of the times in which we live and the wonders of our great cities. Heym's strong and solemn affirmation of life has been wrested from an awareness of the dangers and terrors of life. When he depicts the modern city, he gives us pictures of those in distress, the sick and down-and-out; he depicts hospitals in whose corridors diseases roam like phantoms; he depicts the hovels of the hopeless, the squalor and starvation of slum streets, in which ragged old men cower outside narrow doorways on summer evenings and noise can be heard coming from little rooms in which neglected children are penned up with their ailing parents. Heym is the high-priest of horrors. A visionary of the dreadful and the grotesque. A brother of Poe and Baudelaire (to whom he is also related through the strictness of his rhythms and metrical forms), and perhaps even more of Rops and Kubin. He is carried away by his own visions, paralysed as it were by their awfulness, though without perceptible emotional or lyrical response, fascinated by the sheer power of his images, whose outlines, often exaggerated to the point where they become crude or grotesque, he paints in with heavy, harsh, callous brushstrokes. The ruthless objectivity which piles image upon image, without ever losing sight of what he is doing; the rigid regularity of his rhythms, which lock a seething, raging chaos into a taut, tight form, combine with the outlandishness of his subjects to produce the strangest effect: a dance of death in all the trappings of courtly ceremonial. Poems like 'Louis Capet', 'Robespierre' and 'Ophelia' are of the highest artistic quality. With some others one is disturbed by a certain incongruity between the rigidity of the form and, on the other hand, the imagery which violently bursts out of those formal limits. If Heym had been allowed to develop his great potential, he would no doubt have discovered his own form, his own personal rhythm (*D* 237ff.).

Many of Heym's poems show not only this tension between conventional verse-form and a markedly unconventional imagery, but also a fundamental discord between his horrified visions and the sobriety with which they are described. There is a similar discord in Lichtenstein's work. In Heym's case, at least, the nonchalance is a mask.

'Having imagination is easy. What's difficult is shaping its images,' Heym wrote in his diary on 20 September 1908. Leaving aside the question of whether having imagination *is* easy, Heym uses a number of techniques to give his images force and dynamism, among them personification and verbal metaphor. Personification – a kind of aesthetic primitivism – is Heym's most basic technique. It is ironical that as man is increasingly depersonalized by the hostility of his environment, the abstractions of which this hostility consists are themselves personified. As a result, man's fears become more real than anything else about him; he is overshadowed by the megalopolis in which he lives, this being personified in a succession of monstrous 'deities' ('Die Dämonen der Städte', 'Der Gott der Stadt', 'Der Krieg') and of lesser demons typical of the gothic imagination (vampires, bats, etc.). It is the monstrousness of life, including the monstrous inhumanity of man, which such figures embody. Thus in 'Das Fieberspital' (*L* 166–9) fever is memorably animated into a 'yellow polyp'; it was probably a cloud which Heym saw at this time, 'a strange phantom, like a gigantic polyp with countless long thin arms' (*T* 30 November 1910), which gave him the fever-metaphor. We have seen, too, how brilliantly hunger is personified in the poem of that title.

Given the chaotic power with which Heym sees the monstrous as intervening in life, verb-metaphors are an important adjunct of his personification; it is what his demons *do* that makes them so appalling.

In the later poetry, the passive is used more and more as Heym sees man as the passive victim of a monstrous fate, which may appear in the guise of a mythical monster. The uncontrollable forces of nature are frequently given animal, monster or demon form; in his diary he wrote: 'Anguish arises in me like a great animal seeking to abandon me now that it has already sucked me dry' (*T* 5 September 1911). He is here reusing an image which he first used in 1905: 'Always there are these awful feelings of anguish which drain one of any higher potential, like so many ghastly spiders' (*T* 6 November 1905). As we have seen, in 'Die Züge' (*L* 189) there is a memorable final image in which the east wind is animated into a griffon (*Greif*) or vulture (*Greifvogel*). This image belongs together with a no less striking one in 'Die Schläfer' (*L* 177f.: 'Mit grünem Fittich ... flattert der Schlaf, der Schnabel dunkelrot': 'With crimson beak sleep flaps its green wings'), the effect of which is to link sleep with death. In each case the image takes us back to 'des Todes starken Vögeln' ('the strong birds of death') of 'Der Krieg', those imaginary but vulture-like creatures (cf. also the 'Totenvogel' of 'Die Morgue' (*L* 474–8) and the *Totenvogel* of German folklore). In 'Mors' (September 1910: *L* 130ff.), Death is personified in the same way:

> Doch auf dem Haufen weißer Schädel thront
> Der Tod im Dunkel, wie ein großer Vogel,
> Der nachts bebrütet einen großen Horst.
> Wie alt er ist. Wie stumm. Was mag er denken
> In seines großen Schädels weißem Dach.

But in the dark, enthroned on a pile of white skulls, sits Death, like some great bird hatching its brood by night. How old he is. How silent. What can he be thinking in the white vault of that great cranium?

In 'Was kommt ihr, weiße Falter' (*L* 311f.), the conventional baroque view of life is similarly given a sharp edge of nightmare:

> Ich höre oft im Schlaf der Vampire Gebell
> Aus trüben Mondes Waben wie Gelächter,
> Und sehe tief in leeren Höhlen
> Der heimatlosen Schatten Lichter.
>
> Was ist das Leben? Eine kurze Fackel
> Umgrinst von Fratzen aus dem schwarzen Dunkel
> Und manche kommen schon und strecken
> Die magern Hände nach der Flamme.

In my sleep I often hear the barking of vampires, coming like laughter from the dull moon's honeycombs, and see deep down in empty caverns the candles of the homeless shades.

What is life? A briefly burning torch, masks grinning all around it out of stygian darkness, some of them approaching and stretching out their skeletal hands towards the flame.

At such points Heym's visions must again be compared with those of Baudelaire, in whose menagerie of the vices in the guise of reptiles the vampires represent, as here, the agonies of the damned alive, and of Bosch. Viereck writes of Heym's 'horror that looks back to the pre-urban visions of Bosch',[11] which makes good sense in terms of the horrified visions of both men; but there the resemblance stops, for Bosch was a sectarian Christian depicting the sinfulness of the world as he saw it, whereas Heym is a pagan reduced to despair by what he sees as the mousetrap of life. Heym sees the world as the domain of demons, and indeed as the creation of demons.

The massivity of some of Heym's best poems, in which the images are crowded together in Bosch-like seeming confusion, and the animal dynamism of his imagery is reinforced by the power of his rhetoric, makes his poems 'glow with primitive energy and bypassed grammar'.[12] This is appropriate, for what meant most to him was imaginative passion, the brainstorm of the poem's gestation. At times, as we have seen, he was indifferent to the outcome. On the other hand, like any writer worth his salt, he was also plagued by the 'contrast between ambition and achievement' (T 25 May 1906). The very vividness of the images in his mind must have made him feel that he had not succeeded in capturing them, particularly when one remembers that he would have liked to be able to express them in a non-verbal medium. The most important feature of his imagery is its painterly quality; images of the moon as a 'rote Sichel' ('red sickle') or 'Geisterschiff' ('phantom ship') or 'ungeheurer Schädel, weiß und tot' ('huge skull, white and dead') are essentially visual and romantic, 'romantic' in the sense of 'horror–romanticism'. Over-emphasized though it may have been in the past, the visionary nature of Heym's later poetry remains a fundamental fact, recognized as such by his contemporaries. As we have seen, in terms of its pitiless clarity, his work has obvious affinities with the black visions of Redon, Kley, Kubin, Rops and Ensor, to say nothing of those of Bosch. The strongest feature of his poetry at this time is its imagery; there was much truth in the critic Anselm Ruest's comment (in a review of *Der ewige Tag*) that 'Heym's diamond quality, his wonderful visionary power and ability to express his vision, is totally without any idea of self-limitation, any concentration of its beams on one particular point' (*D* 428). This *Bilderwut* or 'firework-display' technique is typical of early Expressionist poetry – Alfred Lichtenstein was in his *Bilderbuch* (picture-book) phase at the same time (meaning that he was churning out strings of surreal images) – but it is also characteristic of Heym, whose problem was always how to articulate, concentrate and focus the amazing images in his head.

Since, therefore, there is a real danger of mistaking Heym for a kind of poet he was not, to say nothing of making false assumptions about his compositional method, some consideration of the genesis of his later poetry is necessary. In general terms it shows two things: that one needs to be very careful in drawing conclusions as to his method, which changes from poem to poem, and that his work was almost invariably subjected to a long and often laborious process of revision; often he was 'given', or found, no more than the opening or other key image. It must not be thought that Heym, being such an obviously 'inspired' poet, simply wrote down whole poems given to him by some 'angelic' voice, for the successive drafts of his work show very clearly that this was far from being the case. His starting-point was an image or images, a line or two, occasionally a stanza; but he was almost invariably left with a good deal to do – what this is differs greatly from poem to poem – and the successive revisions of his work show that he was extremely good at what Pater calls the labour of the file.

The word 'inspiration' therefore needs to be used with great caution. With Heym it is properly applicable to the initial image or line, which is often brilliant, and to the brilliance of the revisal itself, which often causes him to produce great (and sometimes massive) poems from small beginnings. Ernst Moritz Engert reported that Heym used to go around with his pockets full of poetic jottings and that he was in the habit of working on several poems at the same time; he would pace around Engert's apartment (or wherever) declaiming a line in maybe twenty different variations, until he eventually found the right one.[13] Judging by the extant manuscript versions of the poems, the whole process of revision was very different from what might be thought to happen. The only features common to Heym's revisals are those already mentioned. Otherwise he does not follow any particular pattern; different poems are written in different ways, and it is not infrequently a long time before the poem's seemingly 'inevitable' features emerge. Since truth, here as elsewhere, is concrete, I will illustrate this point, starting with some characteristic sonnets.

What Heym did not do was to stick to full sonnet form from the start. Thus while the first draft of 'Robespierre' (L 89; see below) was in sonnet form, and was indeed metrically correct, it was unrhymed! His skill in producing the properly rhymed second version is as obvious as the procedure itself is odd. There is an interesting contrast with 'Der Hunger' (L 158; see Chapter V); here Heym soon – from the second draft – worked from the rhyme, filling in the 'meaning' afterwards. The first draft of 'Printemps' (L 261; see Chapter VII), on the other hand, consisted of some twenty-two short lines/part-lines; there was no title, and no sign whatsoever of the sonnet that was to emerge, so that in this case the whole sonnet pattern was imposed by Heym at second draft stage, as a way of 'making something of' the first draft. What the first draft of 'Printemps' did have was two of the basic images of the later poem, the 'row of cherry trees in flower' and the 'ploughman seen against the horizon'. Initially Heym did not know what to do with these powerful images.

There are revealing differences of procedure in the case of two famous poems, 'Die Dämonen der Städte' and 'Der Gott der Stadt'. In the original draft of 'Die Dämonen der Städte' the first four stanzas (all of them drafted in full at that stage) were rhymed but not properly metricized, which obviously connects with a note on the first draft of the poem: 'Befürchtete, wahnsinnig zu werden und es wurde ein Gedicht' ('I was afraid of going mad, and a poem came to me'); at the time Heym's imagination was slipping out of control, leaving him close to insanity. The starting-point for 'Der Gott der Stadt' was just the title and the first line, with the rest having to be worked at; the second draft included all five stanzas, but was still inchoate, with a great deal of work needing to be done before the poem received its final form, which looks, of course, as though it had always been there.

In the case of the much more freely structured very late poems (discussed later in this chapter) the genesis is also revealing. Thus the first draft of 'Was kommt ihr, weiße Falter...' (L 311f.) lacked not only the all-important title-image, but many other key images, too; while the vampires were present from the beginning, it was only at second draft stage that 'der Vampire Schrein' ('the calling of vampires') became the far more powerful 'der Vampire Gebell' ('the barking of vampires'). With 'Träumerei in Hellblau' ('Reverie in Pale Blue') (L 337) it is the title that is so important in every sense, for the genesis of the poem, which records the changes of title in successive drafts, shows how long it sometimes takes for a poem's most outstanding feature (here the title) to emerge from the creative dross of gestation. The same applies to 'Letzte Wache' ('Last Vigil') (L 430ff.; see pp. 243–4 below) which had a particularly long and involved gestation. With the lapidary, absolute, once-and-for-all final version of 'Letzte Wache', compare the original note from which it grew:

> Willst Du nicht aufwachen
> Leer.
> Wie soll ich ohne Dich sein.

Won't you wake up [?]Empty. How can I live without you.

This original note is the 'poetic feeling', which most people have (cf. Gottfried Benn's comment in his *Probleme der Lyrik*: 'The contents of a poem, let's say sadness or intimations of mortality, are common to everyone, they are the human lot'); it only becomes a poem, and a great poem at that, when it has undergone a process of distillation and concentration. There could not be a clearer example of the truth of Benn's (to many people, alas, provocative) statement that 'The form *is* the poem'. The genesis of 'Mit den fahrenden Schiffen' (L 457) (see pp. 244–6 below) was longer and more complex, but essentially similar. The first note read:

> Ich suche Dich, Die ich verloren.
> Stehe unter der Städte Toren.
> In dem traurigen Licht.
> Hörest Du unsere Rufe nicht.

I look for you whom I have lost. Stand by the city gates. In the doleful light. You do not hear our calls.

It is the first line that is the basic feeling that remains to be elaborated, or, better, which awaits its classical expression. It took a further ten stages for that to be achieved.

It is therefore abundantly clear that what makes Heym's poetry is not just the *donnée*, which is normally a visual image, and not just that brilliant imagination (and, latterly, ear) which kept producing images and lines for him to try out, but – no less important – his willingness and ability to work so hard (often under appallingly difficult circumstances) to make his poems, for 'made' they certainly were. They become more 'absolute' in every sense as they are shaped. Naturally this involves the poem becoming more concentrated, which means getting rid of weak lines and images, and further distilling and strengthening the key ones; but it depends, ultimately, on the poet's vision becoming ever more sharply focused until it reaches a point of absolute or 'mythical' vision.

Many of Heym's poems are variations on a written or unwritten master-poem. Poems like 'Der Gott der Stadt' and 'Der Krieg' provide a pattern that is endlessly repeated by means of the same basic images and structures and the same rhetorical means, including – as we have seen – the all-important definite article which (as in Baudelaire) does so much to raise his imaginings to an archetypal or mythical level – the level of visions. If he were to be accused of unoriginality, it would have to be because – particularly in 1910 and early 1911 – he tends to copy himself; otherwise his originality is obvious. His painterly images, always vivid, sometimes lurid, 'crystallize and cluster around a central visionary focus'[14] in such a way that, like Kafka's images, they draw attention into themselves, away from the world, which they deny for the sake of art. And they are Kafka-like, too, in that the increasing suppression of the 'as if' element in Heym's metaphors is equivalent to Kafka's use of the 'intentional symbol' in which the first part of the metaphor in question is suppressed; in the poem 'Die Stadt' (*L* 452), for instance, the windows of the houses are described as animal eyes, not as being like them. We are presented with a challengingly, chillingly 'absolute' image: it is the reality of those animal eyes that remains in the mind's eye. The seemingly ruthless objectivity with which Heym piles images upon image like Ossa upon Pelion is the result of moral self-control, his way of keeping at bay the demons rampaging in his head. Until his last summer he must have been afraid of his visions, forced to put a brake on them lest they run away with him. For all its appearance of ruthless objectivity, his work is profoundly personal, as a comparison of the imagery of the poetry and the diary quickly reveals;

all his most memorable personifications (War, the God of the City, Hunger, etc.) are *personae*, masks, personifications of aspects of the poet.

To Heym the accumulation of images matters more than their sequence; it is generally a spatial impression that is conveyed, not a chronological or temporal one. This painterly emphasis on space reflects his view that life is not a meaningful sequence but a miasma, Schopenhauer's whirlpool of suffering. It was the obsessive nature of his vision that caused him to revert to the same basic forms; he was a painter of verbal images whose interest was in the canvas, not in the frame. For one form to be succeeded by another would imply a succession of different views, whereas there is in his view no such thing, for *plus ça change, plus c'est la même chose*. In his diary he made precisely this point: 'I think my significance lies in the fact that I have recognized that there is little chronological sequence. Most things take place in one dimension: everything exists simultaneously' (*T* 21 July 1910); this relates to Henri Bergson's concept of time and Robert Delaunay's and Guillaume Apollinaire's related ideas of simultaneity, and therefore underlines Heym's modernity.

None knew better than Heym that passion, of whatever kind, is a wilful mistress and will not always be controlled ('I feel as though I am in a strait-jacket. I'm coming apart at the seams mentally': *T* 29 November 1910). Certainly there are occasional failures of control in his work. If he uses personification to control his perspective, he uses Baudelairean forms in order to contain his visions. In 1910 he wrote a number of sonnet sequences, in addition to many single sonnets, and could be said to have been over-attached to the sonnet form, both in the sense that many of the poems in question could equally well have been Baudelairean sixteen-line ones, and in the sense that he is misusing a reflective verse form for descriptive and other purposes. Thus he uses it to describe a suburban station, an unpleasant November day and a tightrope-walker, to say nothing of using it to satirize a gaggle of professors or a Sunday boat-trip, to relate several series of battles, and to narrate a series of bloody executions ('Louis Capet', 'Danton', 'Robespierre') and attendant events ('Bastille', 'Le tiers état'). The poems in question are all outstanding ones. 'Robespierre' (*L* 90) is perhaps the best of all:

Er meckert vor sich hin. Die Augen starren
Ins Wagenstroh. Der Mund kaut weißen Schleim.
Er zieht ihn schluckend durch die Backen ein.
Sein Fuß hängt nackt heraus durch zwei der Sparren.

Bei jedem Wagenstoß fliegt er nach oben.
Der Arme Ketten rasseln dann wie Schellen.
Man hört der Kinder frohes Lachen gellen,
Die ihre Mütter aus der Menge hoben.

Man kitzelt ihn am Bein, er merkt es nicht.
Da hält der Wagen. Er sieht auf und schaut
Am Straßenende schwarz das Hochgericht.

Die aschengraue Stirn wird schweißbetaut.
Der Mund verzerrt sich furchtbar im Gesicht.
Man harrt des Schreis. Doch hört man keinen Laut.

('Robespierre') He is muttering to himself, staring down at the straw on the bottom of
the cart. His mouth is full of white saliva which he keeps gulping down. His bare foot is
hanging out of the side of the cart.
    With every jolt he flies up into the air. Then the chains on his arms rattle like bells.
One can hear the merry laughter of the children whose mothers are holding them up
over the heads of the crowd.
    Someone tickles his leg; he doesn't notice. The cart stops. He looks up and at the
end of the street, rising up black, he sees the scaffold.
    His ashen brow covers with sweat. His mouth contorts terribly. People wait for the
scream. But not a sound is heard.

Heym was fascinated by the French Revolution; he identified with
Robespierre as well as with Danton – on 30 May 1910 he ended a letter
to Erwin Loewenson: 'Your Georg Heym ... alias Robespierre on his
cart (*Thespiskarren*)' (*T* 203). His reasons for identifying with Robespierre
and Danton are made clear when he epitomizes them in his dramatic
fragment *Ludwig XVI*: 'Robespierre – Wollust', 'Danton – Enthusiast'.
Heym saw himself as both sensualist and enthusiast. In the sonnet,
Robespierre on his *Karren* represents Heym, who wrote of himself:
'Either the whole caboodle will be OK, or one day it will fall apart,
which I shall take absolutely calmly (*D* 513).' Robespierre is therefore
Heym, his *Karren* the *Karre* of Heym's life. It should perhaps be added
that, despite his self-identification, Heym had no sympathy for social-

democratic 'Robespierrchen' ('mini-Robespierres') (*PD* 177), whom he saw as futile; what Europe needed, he was convinced, was a *real* revolution. 'Robespierre' is an extraordinarily vivid and imaginative poem; the scene is absolutely realized whether the form be regarded as appropriate or not. The foot hanging out of the side of the cart is reminiscent of Géricault's *Cart Bearing Wounded Soldiers*.

The reader may well argue that the poet who uses the sonnet for so many different – and partly scurrilous or scandalous – purposes is showing a lack of formal range. Although the full range of Heym's poetry has not been widely known, his formal range has always been thought to be very limited. Of course, if one were to judge it by *Der ewige Tag* and *Umbra vitae* alone, or by the work produced in 1910 and early 1911, which amounts to much the same thing, then his range would certainly appear limited. From 1910 to early 1911 he writes mostly poems in iambic pentameter quatrains; they may have three stanzas (cf. George), or four (cf. Baudelaire) or rather more (his own characteristic monolithic form), or they may be a variation in the form of the sonnet (one of his favourite forms), but essentially they are written in iambic pentameters which tend to fall into four-line blocks. His monolithic form is paralleled by his liking for cycles (of sonnets or otherwise), some of them substantial – the 'Marathon' cycle of twenty-one sonnets (*L* 23f.), the 'Mont St Jean' sonnet cycle (*L* 42f.), the 'Berlin' sonnets (*L* 56 *passim*), the 'Verfluchung der Städte' cycle (*L* 220f.), 'Die Irren' (*L* 253.), 'Schwarze Visionen' (*L* 212f.), and so on. There is also the interesting satirical cycle of 'Das Grundbuchamt (*L* 265f.). For all the differences of many kinds, his work in 1910 and early 1911 is uniform, massive, monotone, monolithic. It is lyrical mainly in its concentration; it has little of the lightness of his early and his final work, and little of the formal and tonal variety of his prime model (Hölderlin). Its formal limitations are as obvious as the rhymes are – often – slapdash.

It would, however, be quite wrong to think that that was the end of the matter, for since his collected poems have been published it has become clear that his formal range is far wider than had been thought, and that his early and very late work has a lightness and a delicacy of touch which is lacking from much of the work written between 1909 and 1911. We may regret that he wrote so many stereotyped poems, just as we may regret that he wasted so much time trying to produce dramatic work, but we may no longer speak of an overall lack of formal range.

In considering the uniformity of his 1910–11 work it is important to realize that he is all the time playing with fire in the form of that brilliant, wayward imagination. The occasional failures of control in his poetry have been well described by Philip Thomson:

Heym takes grim, horrifying or repulsive subjects and, by imposing on them a high-powered lyrical treatment, draws them into a poetic world ... Heym subsumes the horrifying and the ugly into a lyrical dimension ... His best poems succeed because he is able to use violent and extreme subject-matter and style with sensitivity and control. Where the pathos and power are not sustained, however, where he lapses into clumsy and contrived diction, his poetry is grotesque [in the sense that] one's sense of the ludicrous is aroused by the clumsiness of treatment. [The] discrepancy between intention and result is comical.[15]

Such failures are, however, few and far between; much more significant is the fact that here, too, Heym can generally match Baudelaire, of whom Swinburne said that 'even of the loathsomest ... putrescence and decay he can make some noble use'.[16]

The other type of 'failure' paradoxically involves too much control, for Heym arguably failed for too long to escape from what he himself came to call the 'lie' of iambics and the 'blasphemy' of fixed rhymes. His implied self-criticism sounds like an expression of his exasperation with himself for producing iambics in conventionally rhymed four-line blocks when he could have been writing more personally and in some ways more effectively in other forms.

There are several possible reasons for the relentless formalism or monotone of so much of his work. He may have found it difficult to escape from the example of the coffee-house poets, who almost invariably wrote in iambic pentameters, or of Baudelaire, or he may have been afraid to break the mould, but there is also much to be said for the view that it was the obsessive nature of his cyclopic vision that caused him to revert to the same basic form(s). Indeed, it has been well argued that the practically unchanging pattern of his work from early 1910 to mid-1911 is one of the most significant features of it:

Thus the poet forces everything into his idiosyncratic view of things, which is imperiously fixed and rarely changes; the poetic form remains as unchanging as the vision in terms of language (impersonal vocabulary, monumental syntax) and verse and metric forms (five-beat iambics, held together in four-line blocks by the same rhymes). The basic mood of these verses with their growling monotone, their dreadful sense of desolation, and diabolical ennui, has on the reader the effect of a nightmare.[17]

In other words, what kept coming into Heym's mind were iambic pentameter lines in four-line blocks, and not only did his obsessive, cyclopic vision leave him with little time or inclination to break the mould of his work; it left him with no incentive for doing so since that formally primitive monotone is the necessary expression of the monotony of life. This argument would have been more convincing if Heym had *not* broken the mould in September 1911. The most likely explanation is therefore quite different: that Heym found Wolfsohn's and Guttmann's comparison of himself with Hodler so flattering that this caused him to continue to produce 'monumental' poetry for longer than would otherwise have been the case, particularly since what is in question is the form of his favourite poem, Rimbaud's 'Le bateau ivre'.

☐ ELEGIAC RELEASE

Whatever the reason, it is a fact that until the last few months of his life Heym refused to let his imagination run away with him formally and rhythmically speaking. So far as his best-known work is concerned, that written between December 1909 and September 1911, there is both a relative lack of any 'personal rhythm' (as Stadler noted) and relatively little rhythmic variation. It is, however, important to distinguish between the rhythmic monotone of his most typical work, and the rhythmic lightness of touch and variety of his early and very late work. With reference to his work as a whole it is not true to say that his 'ear is better than his eye; his pulsations are truer than his pictures';[18] what is true is that some of his last poems show him to have been acquiring a marvellous ear.

The bulk of Heym's poetry (some two-thirds of his entire output) dates from the last two years of his life, and half of that was produced in his last eight months. This was both a time of extraordinary fertility, in which presentiment was the spur, and – from July to November 1911 – the time that saw him produce his best poetry ever (all of it in the

'Hölderlinian' short line of his earlier manner), including the half-dozen consummate pieces that are (if Gottfried Benn was right) the poet's lot, in the sense of being the most for which he has any right to hope. The best spell of his life began in July with 'Deine Wimpern, die langen', and ended in November with 'Mit den fahrenden Schiffen' and 'Still sind die Tage' (all quoted below); the high point of his entire life in poetic terms was September–November 1911 (in human terms it was April–August 1908). Not all his final work was good, of course, and not all his late revisions were to the point (thus the first version of 'In die Nacht' (L 410) is better than the second), but this is only to be expected; what is surprising is that while producing such consummate short-line lyrics he continued to produce so much long-line dross.

When he wrote, on 27 September 1911, that 'Iambics are untrue ... I have come full circle; I'm back where I began ... Rhyme for its own sake is a blasphemy; I am back to my earliest poems', he was speaking no more and no less than the truth. He was sick of iambics and mindlessly predictable rhymes, and for the past three months had been writing in a marvellously matured version of his earliest manner. These are, therefore, the words of a poet who has, for two years, written poems of one kind, only to discover, when it is too late, that he should have been writing a different sort of poem altogether. Up to December 1909 his work is metrically very varied; from December 1909 to September 1911 he wrote few poems that were not in iambic pentameters, and then, in September 1911, he had only three months left to return to the metrical freedom and variety of his teenage poems. Tragically, and ironically, he died just at the moment when his imagination, including his aural imagination, had begun to revolt: 'Now I've got a fight on my hands, for my imagination has turned against me and will no longer do as I wish. My imagination and my soul are afraid and are as it were running desperately around their cage. I can no longer control them' (T 20 November 1911). The upshot was both that he found himself writing more freely and personally and beautifully than ever before, in poems like 'Deine Wimpern, die langen' and 'Mit den fahrenden Schiffen', and that his imagination was now prepared to assert itself to break the monotone, as it does so dramatically in the crumbling final lines of 'Die Morgue' and the broken cadences of 'Letzte Wache'.

The release from mannered iambic pentameters in monolithic form ('carmen maximum' he called it) comes, quite suddenly, in late

May or early June 1911, towards the end of 'Die Morgue'. Suddenly, after twenty-three quatrains, the seemingless endless succession of inflexible iambic pentameter quatrains crumbles, in the most dramatic way, and is replaced first by a brilliantly varied and imaginative and startingly new form of dactylic verse, which is still rhymed, and then by eight trimeter lines which show the poet's imagination suddenly breaking free of the last constraint of rhyme in the extremity of his personal horror and premonition of death. He has never written more brilliantly than this:

> Werden wir Blumen sein? Werden wir Vögel werden,
> Im Stolze des Blauen, im Zorne der Meere weit?
> Werden wir wohnen in den tiefen Erden,
> Maulwürfe stumm in toter Einsamkeit?
>
> Werden wir auf den Locken der Frühe wohnen,
> Werden wir blühen im Baum, und schlummern als Frucht?
> Oder Libellen blau, auf den See-Anemonen
> Zittern im Mittag in schweigender Wasser Bucht?
>
> Werden wir schweifen, wo strahlende Äther sind,
> Ewig hinauf und hinab im unendlichen Raum?
> Werden wir Wolken sein? Oder der Wälder Wind?
> Vielleicht nur ein Lied, und ein Kuß, und ein Traum.
>
> Oder – wird niemand kommen?
> Und werden wir langsam zerfallen
> Zu dem Gelächter des Monds,
> Der hoch über Wolken saust,
> Zerbröckeln in Nichts,
> Daß ein Kind kann zerballen
> Unsere Größe dereinst
> In der dürftigen Faust? (L 290).

Shall we one day be flowers? Shall we be birds in the proud blue sky, over faraway raging seas? Shall we dwell deep down in the earth, silent as moles in their lifeless solitude?

Shall we dwell in Aurora's locks, shall we come to flower in a tree and slumber on as fruit? Shall we be blue dragonflies trembling on sea-anemones [sic] in silent bays at noontide?

Shall we roam in the radiant beyond, rising and falling eternally in infinite space? Shall we be clouds? Or the wind in the woods? Or maybe just a song, or a kiss, or a dream?

Or – will no one come? And shall we slowly pass away, mocked by the moon flying high above the clouds, shall we merely crumble away to nothing, so that one day a child can hold our former glory in its hand?

It is as though something suddenly snapped, and can be heard to snap to this day; it is as though he suddenly realized that he was writing predictably at a time when this was the last thing that was called for. Whatever the reason, he suddenly began to sing with a voice of angelic sweetness, or, rather, in a voice in which beauty and tragedy are no longer mutually incompatible, but have, together, become the voice of human destiny.

This sudden release was caused, in part, by the tension of the subject-matter, which had to break, but it owes much to the example of three other poets, one (Hölderlin) his oldest model, and the other two (Albert Samain, Paul Verlaine) his latest discoveries. The emotional surge of the dactyls is pure Hölderlin (as well as pure Heym), while the lightness of the final trimeters (and, elsewhere, dimeters) reflects his reading of Samain and Verlaine.

Heym's indebtedness to Hölderlin is not necessarily expressed in formal terms, and when it is, the form is not necessarily that of Heym's final manner. There is, for instance, the poem 'Marengo' (L 165), written in December 1910, at which time he was under other formal influences, which must be quoted because it is steeped in Hölderlin and illustrates Heym's imaginative preoccupation with the Napoleonic wars:

Schwarzblau der Alpen, und der kahlen Flur,
Die Südsturm drohn. Mit Wolken tief verhangen
Ist grau das Feld. Ein ungeheures Bangen
Beengt den Tag. Den Atem der Natur

Stopft eine Faust. Hinab die Lombardei
Ist Totenstille. Und kein Gras, kein Baum.
Das Röhricht regt kein Wind im leeren Raum.
Kein Vogel streift in niedrer Luft vorbei.

Fern sieht man Wagen, wo sich langsam neigt
Ein Brückenpaar. Man hört den dumpfen Fall
Am Wasser fort. Und wieder droht und schweigt

Verhängnis dieses Tags. Ein weißer Ball,
Die erste der Granaten. Und es steigt
Der Sturm herauf des Zweiten Prairial.

Blue-black of Alps and bare pasture-land threatened by a storm from the south.
Beneath a blanket of cloud the field [of battle] is grey. A gigantic foreboding pens in the
day. Nature's breath.

Has been stopped by a fist. The length of Lombardy there is a deathly silence. Not
a tree, not a blade of grass moves. There is not a breath of wind in the reeds. Not a bird
is about in the lower air.

In the distance carts can be seen where a pair of bridges slowly collapse. The dull
sound is carried away by the water. Once more there is a threat and then a silence.

From the day's destiny. A white ball, the first of the shells. And the storm of the
Second Prairial has begun.

As Walter Schmähling has said,[19] 'Marengo' may or may not be based
on Hölderlin's hymn to Napoleon, 'Dem Allgenannten', in which
Napoleon (who is not named there either) stands on top of the Alps,
'Hinsehend über Italien und Griechenland – Mit dem Heer um ihn –
Wie der Gewitterwolke...' ('Eyes fixed on Italy and Greece, with his
army around him, like a thundercloud'); what is certain is that
'Marengo' is the work of a young poet who is steeped in Hölderlin, and
that the first tercet of the sonnet at least was shaped by a process of
verbal association triggered by the rhyme words.[20] Marengo is the
village in Piedmont, scene of Napoleon's victory over the Austrians in
1800. That Heym's description of the battle is ahistorical should not
surprise anyone: the notion of historical truth was unimportant for
him.

'Marengo' notwithstanding, it is true to say that Hölderlin's poetic
impact on Heym was strongest in the early and last poetry. He was
returning to Hölderlin when death intervened. The marvellous series of
elegies written in his last few months, which constitute his greatest
claim to fame, are not so much 'influenced' by Hölderlin as imbued
with and worthy of comparison with his work. The point was made by
contemporary critics. Kurt Pinthus, for instance, reviewing Umbra vitae
in 1912, wrote:

The external form of these posthumously published poems is freer than that of
the earlier work ... In some poems of shattering beauty and delicacy ... the
rhythm becomes so free and light, the images so bright and clear, that it is as
though Hölderlin has returned from the dead (D 265).

In 1922 Pinthus returned to the same point: 'The presentiment of his early death brought release both to his feelings and to the form of his work; his last poems are bathed in a propitiatory chiaroscuro, and he wrote some poems about love and death which possess a mournful tenderness and gentle musicality which had not been heard since the death of Hölderlin (*D* 150).' Eugen K. Fischer, also in 1922, commented similarly on the fact that some of Heym's late poems, such as 'Deine Wimpern, die langen', possess the simplicity and musicality of truly great poetry, and are thus related to Hölderlin (*D* 159). The rhythmical freedom and the clarity of the images in Heym's last poems are fully worthy of their ultimate inspiration. That Heym attains this Hölderlinian 'Gestaltungsform' is all the more remarkable in that he is, on the face of it, the very opposite of Hölderlin: 'Heym was certainly no Hölderlin, no weightless, ethereal, star-like celestial spirit. He was the opposite of the late Hölderlin, a vigorous, vital, full-blooded son of the earth (Wolfsohn in *D* 148).' However, although Heym said that John Wolfsohn was a good judge of him, this comment takes him too much at face value, for he was 'angel' as well as 'rowdy', and the angel spoke with the voice of Hölderlin.

Most of the best of Heym's last poems are written in his newly rediscovered Hölderlinian manner. A good example is 'Herbstliche Tetralogie, IV':

Herbstliche Zeit
Und der Nebel streicht
Und der Nebel wächst
Über die Wälder weit,
Zwischen verdorrter Bäume Fluch
Ist er gespannt wie ein Leichentuch.

Die Welt ist ganz nahe,
Einsam und leer,
Wie eine Insel
Im grauen Meer.

Die Felder sind öde
In traurigem Einerlei
Krähen streichen manchmal vorbei
Oben im Himmel
Und schreien schnöde

Wie irrende Seelen
In dunklem Ort.
Eh man sie sah
Sind sie im Nebel fort.

Selten ein Baum
Mit hungrigen Ästen
Wie ein Schatten im Feld
Frierend im grauen Raum
In schweigender Unterwelt.

Alles ist tot und kalt
Wie ein endloser Traum.
Manchmal nur schreitet
Eine Gestalt,
Riesig verzerrt,
Hinten am Ackersaum (*L* 376f.).

('Autumn tetralogy, IV') Autumn days, and the mist is sweeping and spreading over the woods; between blasted trees it is stretched like a shroud.

The world is so close, lonely and empty, like an island in a grey sea.

The fields are deserted, clad in sad monotony; once in a while crows pass overhead, crying out scornfully like lost souls in a dark place. No sooner are they seen, than they vanish in the mist.

But seldom is a tree to be seen, with starving branches, like a shadow in the field, freezing in a grey space, in a silent limbo.

Everything is cold and dead, like an endless dream. Just occasionally a gigantically distorted figure is to be seen in the background, walking along the edge of the field.

This perfectly exemplifies what Heinrich Eduard Jacob must have had in mind when he said: 'An anapaestic/dactylic form, hesitating between the two in Hölderlin's way, a gentle sense of release, is what the last poems reveal (*D* 70).' 'Herbstliche Tetralogie' was first published in the collected poems; this final poem in the cycle was written on 26 September 1911.

On 8 October Heym wrote another, very different (and formally less perfect) poem entitled 'Die Bäume Knarren', which is of particular interest because it involves a direct echo of the poem by Hölderlin that had most formal influence on him at this time, 'Hälfte des Lebens':

Mit gelben Birnen hänget
und voll mit wilden Rosen
Das Land in den See,
Ihr holden Schwäne

Und trunken von Küssen
Tunkt ihr das Haupt
In's heilig nüchterne Wasser.

Weh mir, wo nehm ich, wenn
Es Winter ist, die Blumen, und wo
Den Sonnenschein, und Schatten der Erde?
Die Mauern stehn
Sprachlos und kalt, im Winde
Klirren die Fahnen.

('Mid-Life') With yellow pears and full of wild roses the land hangs down into the lake, you graceful swans, and drunken with kisses you dip your heads into the holy yet sober water.

Woe is me, for where shall I find the flowers when winter comes, and where the sunshine and shade? The walls are speechless and cold; in the wind weathercocks clatter.

It is to this that Heym's poem alludes:

Die Bäume knarren, wirr betäubt.
Sie wissen nicht, was sie auseinandertreibt,
Ihre haarlosen Schöpfe.

Und die Raben, über den Wäldern gesträubt,
Streifen in das Verschneite weit,
Eine klagende Herde.

Die Blumen starben in der goldenen Zeit
Und Winter jagt uns über dunkle Erde (L 408).

The trees are creaking, confused and benumbed. Their bare tops do not know what is driving them apart.

And the ravens over the woods, feathers ruffled, roam the snow-covered land, a mournful band.

The flowers died in the golden age and winter drives us across a dark world.

The first six lines are an elaboration and continuation of the last three lines of 'Hälfte des Lebens'. The trees and the crows are clearly affected by the winds of which Hölderlin writes; Heym's 'knarren' echoes Hölderlin's 'klirren'. It is, however, the last two lines of Heym's poem that are most interesting, for they both allude very specifically to the 'Winter' and 'Blumen' of Hölderlin's second image, and at the same time refer to Hölderlin's time – the age of the French Revolution – as the 'goldene Zeit' which it unquestionably was for Heym.

It was in June 1911, in other words, at the time of writing 'Morgue', that Heym wrote to Hildegard Krohn: 'Read Rimbaud, Baudelaire, Samain, Keats. These are men with something to show for themselves (*D* 507).' The reference to Albert Samain is particularly significant. Heym's notebooks show that Samain was on his mind in winter 1910–11; there are three references to Samain, two apparently dating from December 1910,[21] and another dating from March 1911.[22] In the first two cases Samain's name appears together with that of Villiers de l'Isle Adam; in each case it is only Samain's name that appears – there is no indication of the nature of Heym's interest in the French poet. There was little in the life of Samain with which Heym would have been at all likely to identify, so he presumably has the work in mind. Samain was best known for his first collection, *Au jardin de l'infante* (1893); his *Gedichte* (translated by Lucy Abels) appeared in Berlin in 1911 and may well have been the occasion of Heym's comment. There are no noticeable thematic echoes of Samain in Heym, who would hardly have been impressed by the French poet's rather over-sensitive subject-matter, but it does seem likely that he was encouraged by short-line poems like 'Chanson violette' and 'Silence' to do a volte-face and return to his own earliest manner. Hölderlin's 'Hälfte des Lebens' pointed in the same direction, as did Verlaine.

If the ending of 'Die Morgue' marks the sudden change in Heym's work, the first great poem in this new manner is 'Deine Wimpern, die langen' (*L* 315f.), written in late June or early July 1911 and dedicated to Hildegard Krohn; it probably goes back to early June 1911, when he wrote to her: 'Be my Alissa and Clara, then even in the grave we will think of one another on winter nights.' Seven months later she was attending his funeral. When the poem first appeared in *Die Aktion* on 12 February 1912, it bore the title 'An Hildegard K.', to which the by then dead poet's father had objected.

Deine Wimpern, die langen,
Deiner Augen dunkele Wasser,
Laß mich tauchen darein,
Laß mich zur Tiefe gehn.

Steigt der Bergmann zum Schacht
Und schwankt seine trübe Lampe
Über der Erze Tor,
Hoch an der Schattenwand,

Sieh, ich steige hinab,
In deinem Schoß zu vergessen,
Fern, was von oben dröhnt,
Helle und Qual und Tag.

An den Feldern verwächst,
Wo der Wind steht, trunken vom Korn,
Hoher Dorn, hoch und krank
Gegen das Himmelsblau.

Gib mir die Hand,
Wir wollen einander verwachsen,
Einem Wind Beute,
Einsamer Vögel Flug.

Hören im Sommer
Die Orgel der matten Gewitter,
Baden in Herbsteslicht,
Am Ufer des blauen Tags.

Manchmal wollen wir stehn
Am Rand des dunkelen Brunnens,
Tief in die Stille zu sehn,
Unsere Liebe zu suchen.

Oder wir treten hinaus
Vom Schatten der goldenen Wälder,
Groß in ein Abendrot,
Das dir berührt sanft die Stirn.

Göttliche Trauer,
Schweige der ewigen Liebe.
Hebe den Krug herauf,
Trinke den Schlaf.

Einmal am Ende zu stehen,
Wo Meer in gelblichen Flecken
Leise schwimmt schon herein
Zu der September Bucht.

Oben zu ruhn
Im Hause der durstigen Blumen,
Über die Felsen hinab
Singt und zittert der Wind.

Doch von der Pappel,
Die ragt im Ewigen Blauen,
Fällt schon ein braunes Blatt,
Ruht auf dem Nacken dir aus (*L* 315f.).

Your lashes, your long lashes, your eyes' dark waters, let me plunge into them, let me fathom their depths.

As the miner goes down the shaft and swings his dim lamp over the ores' gateway, high up on the shadowy rock face,

So do I descend into you, seeking to forget what can be heard rumbling overhead, the brightness and suffering and daylight.

In the fields where the wind stands still, drunken with the corn, tall thorns grow together, tall and ailing against the blue sky.

Give me your hand, let us grow together, prey to the wind, the flight of solitary birds,

Let us listen together in summer to the organ notes of distant storms. Let us bathe together in autumnal light at the blue day's edge.

Let us sometimes stand at the edge of the dark well, looking deep into its stillness, looking for our love.

Or let us leave the cover of the golden forest, tall, in a sunset which gently touches your brow.

Divine sorrow, say nothing of eternal love. Raise up your tankard, drink sleep.

One day to stand at the end, where the sun-speckled sea is already quietly entering the September bay.

To lie up above it among the thirsty flowers, the wind singing and trembling over the rocks.

But from the poplar reaching up into the eternal azure a brown leaf is already falling, coming to rest on your neck.

On the face of it, this is a love-poem inspired by Hildegard Krohn; but if one reads it slowly and, above all, if one *listens* to it, it is revealed to be something more. Ostensibly a lyrical celebration of love's desire, it is in reality a masked elegy. Most of the poem is present or prefigured in that marvellous opening stanza, which goes way beyond an earlier treatment of the motif in a scene of the early dramatic fragment *Arnold von Brescia* ('Das Auge taucht hinein/In deines Auges blaue Wogen': 'My eye plunges into the blue waters of your eye') (*PD* 443) and its ultimate source in Baudelaire's 'Le Chat' ('laisse-moi plonger dans tes beaux yeux': 'let me plunge into your beautiful eyes'). The imagery of Heym's poem flows with its rhymes, so that the symbolisms of the poem intermingle. The miner goes down in his shaft in an action that parallels the lover's descent into his beloved. Both separately and together the actions are symbolical, as rhythm and interlaced imagery show. But, ultimately, the two visible symbolic planes flow into a third, invisible one, for the falling cadence of the poem contains enough of elegiac metre to leave one in no doubt that the poem is simultaneously a love-poem and a poem about death. The leaf which falls on the beloved's neck at the end is a *memento mori* which stands for the shadow under which man lives and the rapidly lengthening shadow under which Heym was living. The leaf is preceded by other shadows, but the most telling of these is the shadow cast on the near-perfect beauty of the poem by the falling cadence which makes this lyrical celebration of love's desire into a masked elegy. Heym rarely, if ever, wrote more delicately than this. On 2 July 1910 he had what was clearly a precognitive dream about his own death eighteen months later. Many of his poems show that he was obsessed with death; his best poems on the subject are those which are simultaneously love-poems. 'Deine Wimpern, die langen' is such a poem; so, more obviously, are two other late poems in trimeters, 'Letzte Wache' and 'Mit den fahrenden Schiffen'.

In 'Deine Wimpern, die langen' there was a marvellous tension between the images of love and the cadences of death. 'Letzte Wache' (*L* 342), written on 4 September, is wholly elegiac but breathes love. Here is what Gottfried Benn called[23] one of the three greatest love-poems ever written:

> Wie dunkel sind deine Schläfen.
> Und deine Hände so schwer.
> Bist du schon weit von dannen,
> Und hörst mich nicht mehr.
>
> Unter dem flackenden Lichte
> Bist du so traurig und alt,
> Und deine Lippen sind grausam
> In ewiger Starre gekrallt.
>
> Morgen schon ist hier das Schweigen
> Und vielleicht in der Luft
> Noch das Rascheln von Kränzen
> Und ein verwesender Duft.

> Aber die Nächte werden
> Leerer nun, Jahr um Jahr.
> Hier wo dein Haupt lag, und leise
> Immer dein Atem war.

('Final Vigil') How dark your temples are, and your hands so heavy. You are already faraway and can no longer hear me.

Beneath the flickering light you seem so sad and so old; your lips are cruelly contorted in eternal numbness.

Tomorrow there will already be silence here and perhaps still a rustling of wreaths and a breath of decay in the air.

But the nights will become emptier now, year by year. Here, where your head lay and your gentle breathing was always to be heard.

The two central stanzas explain Peter Viereck's view that this is 'the most bluntly powerful elegy ever written in German',[24] but what stands out even more is the perfect and delicate beauty of the stanzas by which that blunt power is framed. The first and last stanzas have the kind of beautiful simplicity achieved after Heym's death first by Bertolt Brecht (in his most beautiful elegy, 'Jahr für Jahr') and then by Johannes Bobrowski. It seems almost incredible that the man who produced the iambic monotone of all those black visions should suddenly have proved capable of writing some of the best trimeters in the German language.

The difference between the two versions of 'Mit den fahrenden Schiffen...' (L 456ff.), both of them written in early November, illustrates Heym's new-found freedom and sureness of touch. The first version of the poem – it is an elegy – was written in what could be called a loosely 'elegiac' pattern; the predominantly dactylic lines started by being mostly pentameters, and ended by being mostly hexameters. In rewriting the poem Heym has given his metrical imagination its head, but has cut the six-beat lines in half (cf. Rilke's procedure with the sonnet form), so that again we have a poem in the by now familiar, basically dactylic trimeter pattern. The result is a revelation, a poem which is lighter, more lucid, and deeply elegiac:

> Mit den fahrenden Schiffen
> Sind wir vorübergeschweift,
> Die wir ewig herunter
> Durch glänzende Winter gestreift.

Ferner kamen wir immer
Und tanzten im insligen Meer,
Weit ging die Flut uns vorbei,
Und Himmel war schallend und leer.

Sage die Stadt,
Wo ich nicht saß im Tor,
Ging dein Fuß da hindurch,
Der die Locke ich schor?
Unter dem sterbenden Abend
Das suchende Licht
Hielt ich, wer kam da hinab,
Ach, ewig in fremdes Gesicht.

Bei den Toten ich rief,
Im abgeschiedenen Ort,
Wo die Begrabenen wohnen;
Du, ach, warest nicht dort,
Und ich ging über Feld,
Und die wehenden Bäume zu Haupt
Standen im frierenden Himmel
Und waren im Winter entlaubt.

Raben und Krähen
Habe ich ausgesandt,
Und sie stoben im Grauen
Über das ziehende Land.
Aber sie fielen wie Steine
Zur Nacht mit traurigem Laut
Und hielten im eisernen Schnabel
Die Kränze von Stroh und Kraut.

Manchmal ist deine Stimme,
Die im Winde verstreicht,
Deine Hand, die im Traume
Rühret die Schläfe mir leicht;
Alles war schon vorzeiten.
Und kehret wieder sich um.
Gehet in Trauer gehüllet,
Streuet Asche herum.

On journeying ships we have passed by, we who have wandered eternally through gleaming white winters. We always went further afield, dancing in the islanded sea, the tide passing us by and the sky resounding with emptiness.

Name me the city in whose gateway I have not sat, wondering whether your footstep had not passed through, you whose lock of hair I cut off. In the dying light of nightfall I held my questing lamp to see who came by, but alas it always shone into an unfamiliar face.

I called your name among the dead in secluded places, where the buried dwell; alas, you were not there. And I walked across fields, and the trees fluttering overhead stood before a freezing sky and were leafless for winter.

Ravens and crows I sent out [to look for you], and they flew through sunless skies over the land passing below them. But at night they fell like stones with a sad sound, holding in iron beaks their wreaths of straw and leaves.

Sometimes I hear your voice in the wind, feel your hand gently touching my brow in a dream. Everything that once was now returns again. Walk in mourning, scatter ash about you.

In a number of other very late poems Heym goes even further in the direction of lightness and insubstantiality by using the dimeter (in the modern sense) pattern of his very first poem, 'Die Quelle' (July 1899); it is a development that gives a very precise meaning to his words: 'I am back where I began (T 166).' At almost exactly the same time he was writing 'Der Abend' (L 386f.), which both illustrates his point and is another example of an elegy that breathes the evanescence which is its theme.

Es ist schon spät.
Wartet. Der Frühmond geht
Bald hinter den Brücken.
Die Masten im Hafen
Der ruhigen Schiffe
Sinken in Rauch.
Die Häuser am Wasser,
Die rundum schlafen,
Wachsen in Nebel
Höher und blasser.

O Dämmerstunde.
Vergeßt nicht.
Wer euch begegnet
In stillen Gassen
Ist bleich im Gesicht
Und erkennet euch nicht.

Alle Fenster sind tot
Wie bleiche Augen in letzter Not.
Die Wege sind endlos
Und krumm
Und das Dunkel kriecht
Um euch herum.

Hört ihr hinten den Schritt.
Jemand wandert euch mit.
Wenn ihr hinter euch seht
Und in traurige Winkel späht,
Ist niemand da,
Niemand mehr,
Alles einsam und leer.

Haltet fest euer Herz.
Hütet euch sehr.
Wolken ziehen herauf vom Meer.
Nacht beginnt
Und der Sterbewind
Ächzt in des Dunkels Grunde.

O traurige Stunde
Wo Böses erwacht,
Ihr werdet weinen
Zu Mitternacht.

It is already late. Wait. The early moon will soon be passing beyond the bridges. The masts of the silent ships in the harbour are vanishing beneath a pall of smoke. The houses by the river, which are all asleep, are growing taller and paler in the mist.

O twilight hour. Do not forget. Anyone you meet in the silent streets is pale-faced and does not recognize you.

All windows are lifeless, like pale eyes in the hour of their ultimate need. The paths are endless and winding, and the darkness is creeping up on you.

Do you hear the footsteps behind you? There is something following you. Yet when you glance back and peer into every sad corner, there is no one there, no longer anyone there; everywhere is empty and deserted.

Keep a firm hold on your heart. Take great care. Clouds are rising from the sea. Night is falling and the undertaker's wind is moaning in the heart of the darkness.

Oh, sad is the hour when evil awakes; by midnight you will be weeping.

Heym rarely, if ever, surpassed those lines. I wish to end, however, by quoting a poem written two months later, in November 1911, 'Still sind die Tage' (L 461):

Still sind die Tage
Im fallenden Herbste.
Kaum noch gerühret
Von schläfrigen Winden
Stehet der Baum,
Mit goldenen Blättern
Trocken und dorrend,
Und still wie Wandrer,
Mit dünnen Ästen
Im grauen Raum.

Kurz ist das Leben
Und wenige Sterne.
Immer voll Trübem
Wolkige Jahre
Nehmen uns auf.
Wir aber lägen
Lieber begraben,
Oder verschüttet,
Dort wo die Träne
Rinnet zuhauf.

(Still are the days') Still are the days as autumn falls. Barely touched by sleepy winds the tree stands there with its golden leaves dry and dying, still as a wayfarer with its skeletal branches against a leaden sky.

Life is short and few are its stars. Cloudy years full of sorrows engulf us; but we prefer to be buried (whether dead or alive) where our tears gather.

This may well serve as Heym's epitaph. 'Kurz ist das Leben/Und wenige Sterne' ('Life is short and few are its stars') was his experience of life. A poem like this shows again that Heym's best poetry has little to do with Expressionism. The only word that properly describes the best of his last poems is 'classical'. There is nothing more tragic than the fact that Heym died just when he did. Had he lived longer, his formal range would have become wider as his despair deepened or as his experience of life widened. We have seen that Emmy Ball-Hennings commented that Heym was half-rowdy, half-angel. The poems for which he has become known (and which have received most critical attention) are the work of the brilliantly gifted rowdy; the marvellous series of short-line elegies and near-elegies dating from his last six months are the work of the angel. In the long run these poems will be regarded as his major contribution to German poetry, for they show beyond all possible doubt that he is one of the greatest German elegiac poets. He always wrote better on the down-beat of passion than on the up-beat, but he has now become an elegiac love-poet of immense power. No one has charted the landscape of sorrow and loss more beautifully.

VIII

The Tales

Unlike his dramatic pieces, Heym's tales deserve to be far better known. They are at present little known and therefore underrated and misunderstood. It was typical of him that he chose to label them 'Novellen', for the genre is as old-fashioned and conventional as his other chosen genres, although there is no need to dwell on the point, for what matters is not so much the frame as the image it contains (and apropos content one might similarly ask whether it is not egregiously old-fashioned to write, in 1911, tales containing bucentaur, dragon and kraken, to say nothing of the Evil Eye). Whether some of Heym's tales are exemplary novellas or not is less important than the fact that they are related as closely as may be to the poems, in the sense that they revolve around the same images. Like the poems, the tales are, without exception, about their author. This, the most fundamental point about them, was made by Kurt Kersten in 1913:

These *Novellen* are not so much *Novellen* as poems in prose; people rarely confront one another; there is no sign of the short-story writer's superiority vis-à-vis his characters, just one individual crying his anguish into an empty world – and that individual is invariably Heym.[1]

This is basic to any understanding of these tales, which are not 'prose poems' as such, but 'lyrical tales' or – if one is thinking of the view of life which they express – black tales. Another contemporary reviewer, Monty Jacobs, made the point:

The posthumously published *Novellen* are informed by the rhythm of his poetry: the voice is that of a poet, but a poet whose rigorous sense of style protects him from the danger of destroying the *Novelle*-form altogether. In the interplay of its images and metaphors an originality and power of language thus enhances the art of narrative instead of swamping it.[2]

However, while it is right to emphasize the power of Heym's language, these stories cannot usefully be termed *Novellen* as such. This point, too, was made by a contemporary reviewer, in this case Alfred Wolfenstein:

What is good about these prose pieces is the fact that they are, as it were, unrhymed Heym poems; what is less good about them is their prose. He calls them *Novellen*, but they are really sketches of the products of his imagination ... These tales are occasions for grandiose fantasias of unheard-of power: full of overwhelming torrents of colour and spectral spasms, like pictures by Delacroix.[3]

We therefore come back to the same basic point: that these tales are as much 'black visions' as Heym's poem cycle of that title, or as Goya's *pinturas negras*. That Heym[4] called them 'poems in prose' is not surprising.

The best of the tales were written in January–October 1911. It was on 27 October 1911 that Heym wrote to Rowohlt: 'I am now on another path. The path of the *Novelle* is not my path (*T* 274).' By then he knew, with absolute certainty, that what constituted what was left of his 'way' was the elegy; but he also recognized that the *Novelle* as such was not his thing, and no doubt also recognized in his own mind that he had been using the *Novelle*-form as a guise under which to write a species of poetry. Heym himself recognized their monologic nature when he wrote to Rowohlt on 6 December 1910: 'My *Novellen* are not really *Novellen* at all, but monologues or dialogues about love (*Erotik*) (*T* 225).' To say that they are 'Dialoge' and 'über die Erotik' is nonsense; no doubt Heym was trying to 'sell' them to Rowohlt by describing them thus. That he needed to do so is shown by Rowohlt's reluctance to publish them. The time-scale speaks for itself, as does Rowohlt's letter to Heym of 25 November 1911:

Quite apart from the fact that the stories which I have so far received hardly amount to a book, as a publisher I also have the most serious reservations about bringing them out as a volume of stories. However much I like the stories personally, I am firmly convinced that there is no chance of winning over even a small body of readers and customers for a book which is solely concerned with delirious madmen, cripples and corpses (*T* 271f.).

Heym responded to this by pointing to the success of Octave Mirbeau's *Le jardin des supplices*, which thus becomes a kind of model. Another model in terms of subject-matter may have been Hanns Heinz Ewers's *Das Grauen* (1907). Heym knew Ewers at least from December 1910 and admired him.

Heym saw his *Novellen*, as we should do, in terms of images: 'Last night I dreamt a whole *Novelle*,' he wrote in his diary on 8 August 1910; he proceeded to describe four 'Bilder'. His images, and the visions which they form, are variously reminiscent of Kubin, of Goya, and of the Book of Revelation. The world of his stories is very much an *orbis pictus*.

These *Novellen*, which are so very closely related to Heym's dreams, are waking nightmares. They have a common theme: the sense of terror in the face of a nature perceived to be fundamentally hostile – a feature of Northern or gothic art; such a view of nature is characteristic of Heym's work from 1910.

The world which Heym depicts in his tales is a hellish one. But this, and the fact that he has not a little in common with the 'Satanic school' (Southey) of English late Romanticism, does not mean that he is himself a Satanist:

In the blessed abundance of our literature we already have Satanists who ... seem very demonic to themselves. But in the case of Heym the reader is disturbed by the spectacle of someone whose fancy grew charnel as a result of a personal impulse or Fate which would not be denied.[5]

Heym is no Satanist, for he is far from worshipping the evil by which he is obsessed. For him the greatest evil, the most hideous and terrifying of all demons, is Death, and the greatest fear the fear of death:[6] 'One thing drove him to write, that thing being Death ... In almost all his *Novellen* Death is on the rampage.'[7] Ernst Blass saw this imaginative struggle with death as giving the *Novellen* an intensity and immediacy which even the poems lack:

I believe that they surpass the poems. I believe that the most intense, universal, vital and inescapable experience a human being can have, namely the realization that tomorrow he may cease to exist ... is experienced more intimately in these tales than it is in most of the poems.[8]

This is both true and hardly surprising, for the *Novellen* were written at a time when Heym was wrestling with Death – his own approaching death – for all the world like a man of God wrestling with the Devil. For him the *Novellen* served their purpose in enabling him to come to terms with this spectre and achieve a balance and an acceptance which in turn made possible his greatest poetry, that of the final months of his life. They had served their purpose; his way lay elsewhere.

In spring 1910, Heym took to writing 'city' poems and stopped trying to write 'historical' romances. The following year he wrote most of his *Novellen*, only one of which ('Der fünfte Oktober') has a 'historical' setting ('Die Novella der Liebe' has a pseudo-historical setting). It does not follow, however, that his work from now on is concerned with contemporary society. In particular, it is misleading to say that 'Most of the *Novellen* treat contemporary events',[9] for in the best of them contemporary events provide no more than the starting-point for a self-related vision, as in 'Der Dieb', which goes far beyond the theft of the *Mona Lisa* in August 1911; Heym's very spelling ('Monna Lisa') shows that he is concerned less with the unknown thief than with the man who identified with Leonardo da Vinci as described by Dmitry Merezhkovsky: himself. This personal element is what makes the difference between a vivid sketch such as 'Die Pest' (based on press reports of the outbreak of cholera in Manchuria in winter 1910/11), and a grandiose tale such as 'Das Schiff', which has more to do with *l'horreur de la vie* than with any real events in Harbin or elsewhere. Heym despised contemporary society too much to dwell on it; it was himself in whom he was engrossed, himself on whom he dwelt.

One of the main questions posed by these *Novellen* is whether they are more than mere self-expression. One has to be careful, for while the revolutionary enthusiasm enshrined in 'Der fünfte Oktober' has clear implications for the Wilhelmine society which Heym detested, it is also true to say that his revolutionary enthusiasm is largely an end in itself, a moral good, something which is existentially necessary to him. It is not for nothing that he was known as a *Pathetiker*, for what matters to him is intensity of experience, to burn always with a hard, gem-like flame. His attitude towards contemporary society, and indeed towards everything else, is always coloured by self-awareness and a fierce subjectivity. His characteristic art is monologic.

It has been said that Heym's prose pieces can hardly be understood without reference to their supposed aim of criticizing modern society: 'There is more to them than that alone, but in every case they are more than the mere expression of personal distress. In his intuitive way Heym was a penetrating diagnoser of his age's ills.'[10] This is weighted in the wrong way, for while it is true that Heym's *Novellen* are more than mere expressions of personal distress, that personal distress, representative of the human condition, is their primary significance. They are, above all, expressions of a state of mind, personal and human documents rather than social ones. While Heym's 'personal distress' is tied up with his view of the age and the society in which he had the misfortune to live, he is far too exceptional a character for it to be true to say that his work makes little sense without reference to its supposed aim of criticizing modern society. On the contrary, it makes complete sense without such an aim. To see Heym's tales as less subjective than they are is to misunderstand them; to see them in quasi-sociological terms is to diminish them. No less than the poems, the tales have to do with the human condition as such, metaphysical rather than social issues.

The main *Novellen* were all written after the decisive second turning-point in his poetic career in late 1910, after which, in K. L. Schneider's words: 'The urban background takes on ghastly, frightening features; again and again what is seen has superimposed on it elements of a visionary reality, the picture space being gradually filled with figures born of a dark imagination.'[11] His reading in 1910 of Baudelaire and – surely – of Poe and Verlaine, has left a profound mark, although the change is also the result of a spell of mental hyperactivity which for a time threatened his stability.

The best of Heym's *Novellen* self-evidently transcend the grotesque realism of their surface in that this is the expression of an inner reality. Yet conventional descriptions of the changes in his style are not particularly helpful or relevant, partly because in stylistic terms these stories arguably belong to his second phase (the phase of 'grotesque realism'), and partly because the question of the grotesque is in any case rather more momentous than that of any notional phases. Philip Thomson has said that Heym is 'only on rare occasions truly or consistently grotesque' because he 'subsumes the horrifying and the ugly into a lyrical dimension'.[12] From this it would follow that the stories, which, for all their poetic nature, lack a lyrical dimension in this sense, must be more truly 'grotesque'. This is, however, not the case; the 'grotesque' is not an appropriate category in which to place them, given that they are totally lacking in the comic constituent of the 'grotesque' in a literary sense; that many of their details are grotesque, horrifyingly so, is another matter. I would therefore argue that they exemplify not the 'grotesque', but the 'gothic' with its inherent emphasis on the macabre. In other words, Heym's essential romanticism, which has many different faces, includes the 'horror-romanticism' of Edgar Allan Poe.

It is a striking fact that contemporary reviewers, in linking Heym with Poe, invariably linked him with Poe *and* Baudelaire (see *D* 102, 224, 238, 271). What Poe and Baudelaire have in common is, above all, a sense of *l'horreur de la vie* and a 'gothic' preoccupation with death; in the cases of Baudelaire and Heym at least there is, moreover, a link between the carnal and the charnel. The evidence of his *Novellen* suggests that Heym read Poe in 1910, when a complete German edition of the tales appeared (*Die Abenteuer Arthur Gordon Pym's und andere Erzählungen*, new complete edition, translated by H. Eiler, Berlin, 1910). Baudelaire's translation (*Histoires extraordinaires*) appeared in the same year. There had, of course, been many earlier German editions, including a number of recent ones (*Werke*, in 10 volumes, edited by Hedda and Arthur Moeller-Bruck, Minden, J. C. C. Bruns, 1901–4; *Novellen der Liebe*, translated by Gisela Etzel, Berlin, F. Schulze, 1908; *Die Novellen von der Liebe*, translated by Gisela Etzel, Munich and Leipzig, G. Müller, [1909]; and two Reclam volumes [*Seltsame Geschichten*, 1909; *Ausgewählte Novellen*, translated by J. Möllenhoff, n.d.]), but what is so very striking is the fact that no less than five different editions appeared in 1910 (the 'new complete edition', translated by H. Eiler, Berlin, A. Weichert; *Das Feuerpferd und andere Novellen*, translated by Gisela Etzel, Munich, G. Müller; *Ausgewählte Novellen*, translated by Hedda and Arthur Moeller-Bruck, Berlin, F. Schulze; *Der Goldkäfer und andere Novellen*, translated by Gisela Etzel, illustrated by Alfred Kubin, Munich, G. Müller; and *Das schwätzende Herz und andere Novellen*, translated by Gisela Etzel, illustrated by Alfred Kubin, Munich, G. Müller). The evidence of Heym's *Novellen*, which are suddenly so Poe-like, makes it likely that it was an edition appearing in the bookshops in 1910 that caught his eye and prompted him to produce his own black tales; with the exception of 'Der fünfte Oktober', all his best tales (which date from 1911) are Poe-like; previously none had been. With five editions of the Poe tales appearing in the Berlin bookshops in 1910, two of them from Berlin publishers, Heym could not have possibly have missed them; given that two of the five were illustrated by Kubin, whose work he knew and admired, he would have noticed them at once. The evidence may be deductive, but it is very strong.

Before going any further, let us remember what Monty Jacobs said in 1913: 'There is no need to trouble the French and the Americans, who are always invoked whenever the expert experiences a *frisson*. For Georg Heym rode his own horse.'[13] Of course, Heym 'rode his own horse', and a powerful beast it was; originality is the most obvious thing about the man and his work. But he would have been a fool not to learn from others – and, for all his impetuous, head-strong nature and impatient anti-intellectualism, he was no fool. He learned from a number of earlier writers, who appear to have included Poe. His affinity with Poe is important because of the new light which it throws on the tales; but let us not forget that he also has an affinity with Kafka, whose work is far removed from Poe's.

Georg Theodor Franz Arthur Heym, like Poe's Arthur Gordon Pym, was blessed with an 'enthusiastic temperament, and [a] somewhat gloomy, although glowing, imagination'. An early reviewer wrote of Poe's 'recoil from the haunting phantasms of death and annihilation'.[14] Heym knew those phantasms all too well; in his work they are terrifyingly real. Of his tales we may indeed say what Poe said of his own *Tales of the Grotesque and Arabesque* (1840), that their terror is 'not of Germany, but of the soul'. By 1910/11 Heym's imagination had become genuinely 'gothic', so that he is never more himself than when he is closest to Poe and Baudelaire. He shares not only some of Poe's gothic trappings, but also his use of the unnamed and tormented narrator; indeed, he goes further than Poe, for while Poe may not be 'always and everywhere his own biographer',[15] that is precisely what Heym is in tale after tale. We are told that Poe's major figures 'rarely have a social context', and that when they do, it is usually incidental.[16] The same applies to Heym, and for much the same reason: that his figures belong not in a social context, but in his own mind, for they represent his own fears and obsessions. There is a similarity here with Kafka's figures. Poe makes repeated use of extraordinary states of consciousness, including insanity and nightmare; so, too, does Heym. Roderick Usher, whose moods are alternately vivacious and sullen, is not only like Poe himself;

he is like Heym, who described himself as two persons in one. Heym's 'heroes' are possessed by that same 'sense of gloom, misery and decay'[17] conveyed by the narrator of 'The Fall of the House of Usher'. Above all, Heym shares Poe's single great obsession; what Allen Tate said of Poe, that 'he is progressively mastered by one great idea ... until at last he is engulfed by it. It is his own descent into the maelstrom'[18] emphatically applies to Heym, whose nightmare, drawn by Kubin, came true. Is it any wonder, then, that Heym, too, described men *in extremis*, facing archetypal terrors? Like Poe in 'The Fall of the House of Usher', Heym – in 'Das Schiff' – succeeds in building up an unsurpassable atmosphere of impending horror, and the ending of 'Das Schiff' is every bit as unforgettable as that of 'The Masque of the Red Death'. Whatever the precise facts of Heym's debt to Poe, in several of his tales he has equalled Poe in his own genre.

The first story in Heym's posthumously published *Der Dieb. Ein Novellenbuch* (September 1913) is 'Der fünfte Oktober'. It is in two main ways the odd one out: in being an ostensibly historical *Novelle*, and in being ostensibly positive; there are as yet few signs of Heym having discovered Poe. On the face of it, it retells an incident from the French Revolution which loomed so large in Heym's imagination. Peter Kropotkin's *Die französische Revolution, 1789-1793* provided the starting-point.[19] Heym takes over from Kropotkin the idea of the French mob being motivated by hunger caused by a shortage of bread, although he is not interested in the details of history, or in political or social theory, or even in the French Revolution for its own sake. His interest in history as such, and in the French Revolution, is purely subjective: he identified with the historical figures of the time because that time embodied the enthusiasm and excitement and greatness which his own time lacked, and which he craved. That craving and that enthusiasm are what 'Der fünfte Oktober' is about. The mob's hunger for bread, which in retrospect is a hunger for action, is Heym's own 'Hunger nach einer Tat' (*T* 17 June 1910), his 'craving for life' ('Gier nach Leben', *T* 29 September 1909). Unlike Kropotkin, Heym is not interested in what will follow the Revolution; he is interested in a moment of history for the sake of the intense feeling which it embodied, because he identifies that intensity of feeling with life. A story which appears to be about the French Revolution is therefore in reality about Georg Heym, whose almost obsessive use of the metaphoric 'like' or 'as' ('wie') in this particular story underlines the fact that the whole thing is a metaphor.

Gottfried Benn argued that the use of simile is, poetically speaking, a somewhat primitive technique: 'This "as" always interrupts the poet's vision, it drags something else in ... it is not a primary form ... [it] always [represents] an incursion of the epic into the lyric, a slackening of the linguistic tension, a weakness in the creative process.'[20] That Heym uses simile so much more in his narrative than in his poetic work tends to confirm the truth of Benn's assertion, but more interesting is the fact that a technique which, if found in lyric poetry, seems to represent 'ein Einbruch des Erzählerischen' ('an incursion of the epic') is precisely the opposite when it occurs in a narrative text; in Heym's tales, at least, the extensive use of simile is – among other things – part of their poetic nature, part and parcel of the vision in question, and therefore a continual reminder of their symbolic nature.

'Der fünfte Oktober' (PD 6f.) is related to a number of poems written between June 1910 and September 1911 which are either about the French Revolution or use related imagery; they include 'Bastille', 'Le tiers état', 'Vom Schanktisch her', the first version of 'Gebet', and so on. The most telling parallel is with that marvellous sonnet, 'Der Hunger' (November 1910) (discussed in Chapter V above), in which Heym writes about himself and his hunger for life under the guise of a starving dog, 'Ich armer Hund'. Here it is a starving mob, but the meaning is the same. 'Der fünfte Oktober' is not a 'prose poem', but it is poem-like in that Heym is describing his own emotions and emotional needs, and in that he is, here too, a 'Monteur von Bildern': the whole text is conceived in visual terms, is indeed essentially a series of memorably vivid images, most of which are linked with similar images in the poems. In both senses of the term it is a brilliant piece of work.

The tale has two related themes and turns on two related images. In the first half the basic image is that of the mouth; in the second half the 'Menschenstrom' ('stream of humanity') image predominates. The mouth, gaping open like the maws of Hell, is reminiscent of Kubin's Der Rachen and, more obviously, of Heym's own 'Der Hunger', written only a short time before; here that same extreme hunger possesses the mob: 'The mob drifted around all day as though it were at the gateway to a new and fabulous revelation. Starved to the point of emaciation, it dreamt of paradises of repletion.' The ovens are not only personified; they are animalized and demonized; by using the word 'Maul' Heym transmogrifies them into animals reminiscent of his starving dog and of the mob itself, which only becomes human when it puts behind it the animal apathy and obsession of its hunger. At the beginning of the story the mob dreams of 'Paradiese der Sättigung' ('paradises of repletion'), that is, dreams of the bread which will free it from the 'Burg des Elends' ('stronghold of wretchedness') in which it is trapped. Their minds are totally obsessed by the thought of bread: 'they waited for the carts, searching the skyline like a gaggle of astronomers looking for a new star' (an image which Heym was to re-use shortly afterwards in the poem 'Die Menschen stehen vorwärts in den Straßen'). It is as though they are waiting for a divine revelation, as indeed they are.

As the pangs of their hunger become sharper, and they grow weaker, a great wave of apathy settles on them 'wie eine grosse Decke' ('like a great blanket') (this is, as it were, the negative counterpart of the longed-for white layer of flour covering the city), while across the central plain ghostly mills line the horizon like so many giant corn-gods. Over the mills thus personified hover the mob's dreams, animated into great black birds. The mob itself is described as consisting of 'flocks of beggars, herds of outcasts': they are animals without hope. They stand there motionless, frozen in their apathy, like so many 'innumerable Lots cast into eternal immobility by the flame of some hellish Gomorrah'. The whole story being envisaged in antithetical terms, once the mob is fired by enthusiasm, it begins to flow like molten lava; it is the 'Menschenstrom' image that dominates the second half of the story.

The turning-point of the *Novelle* is the appearance of Maillard, which is significantly described: 'From the whitish sky at the far end of the road a black speck appeared, which rapidly increased in size.' This is not just a typically vivid and dramatic way of putting it; it also strongly suggests that Heym has already been reading Poe, in whose 'The Thousand-and-Second Tale' we read: 'At length, on the edge of the horizon we discovered a black speck, which rapidly increased in size.'[21] The use of the word 'Malstrom' ('maelstrom') three pages later probably also derives from Poe. As yet these are incidental borrowings in a story which is not Poe-like.

With the arrival of Maillard instead of the longed-for bread, the situation is transformed. That the mob's craving for bread was in reality a craving for action, and that what it needed was inspiration, is soon shown. Maillard is described as being like a great black bird (hitherto the symbol of the mob's dreams); he climbs up into a tree in order to address the crowd, and his words literally move them. What follows is one of the most memorable passages in the entire story:

His words were drowned in the cry of rage. A great wave of clenched fists was shaken in the air. The masses began to sway, like a great maelstrom, around his tree.

And the tree rose up out of the sea of shouting faces, out of the eddying oaths from those distorted faces, out of the echo of their anger which came back from the heavens like an enormous black whirlwind and began to blow him from side to side ... like the clapper of a giant bell.

The tree rose up like a dark flame which some chthonic demon had caused to shoot up.

High up in his bare branches Maillard hung like a gigantic black bird, moving his arms round in circles, as though about to fly away into the evening over the sea of faces, a demon of despair, a black Belial, the god of the mob, scattering black fire from his hands (*PD* 15–16).

The most remarkable thing about this passage is the style in which Heym's meaning is clothed. Maillard, whose words unleash the demons of anger and revolution, may thus appropriately have the appearance of a 'black Belial' (Belial here having the apocalyptic connotation of Satan), but in fact he is also a god-like figure, for the enthusiasm with which he fires the mob is the stuff of life and therefore the staff of life. For Heym, as for his beloved Hölderlin, enthusiasm is divine.

Enthusiasm: this is the real theme and the real point of the story, and it is this that makes it so personal. In the last analysis Heym doesn't give a damn about post-revolutionary society; it is quality of life, intensity of experience (Pater's 'high passions') that is his concern. The eternal dream of greatness by which the crowd, human now in its idealism, is moved, is Heym's own most personal and insistent dream.

The story ends with the memorable, if ambiguous, image of the setting sun. Earlier the absence of the sun had (*pace* Hölderlin) signified despair and death; now it is present, identified with life, enthusiasm, greatness, fame, those *summa bona* of the poet Georg Heym, to whose love of Van Gogh the poplars like burning flames point. The story, always personal, thus ends on a highly personal note. It also ends ambiguously, for while all the emphasis is on the sun and what it symbolizes, that sun is setting. Instead of the dreamt-of 'Morgenröte' there is the 'Abendröte'. Is this 'le coucher du soleil romantique'? Does it imply that the world is entering a period of Hölderlinian Night? Or that enthusiasm is giving way to despair, life to death? We cannot be sure. Not quite. On the other hand, there is no doubt as to Heym's basic message, which is that enthusiasm is life, and apathy death.

We have seen how far Heym's so-called 'Novelle' goes beyond Kropotkin, who gave him no more than a starting-point which he quickly transcended. Heym's story is more vivid, more romantic, more heroic than anything in Kropotkin; it has more in common with the work of Delacroix. Nor, as I have said, is Heym remotely concerned with the same things as Kropotkin. He is a poetic revolutionary, not a revolutionary theorist. His story is about the French Revolution only in the sense that he regarded revolution as he regarded war: as a source of personal excitement. No, the story is really about Heym's hunger for life and about the enthusiasm – in its original Greek and Hölderlinian sense of being possessed by a god, that god being, for Heym, Helios – which he identified with life and on which he utterly depended to burn up the despair into which he was always liable to sink; for him it was the vital spark of life itself. The first half of the story shows, negatively, that man depends on it. In a real sense the mob receives the bread which it craves, in the form of the inspiration which enables it to transcend its animal limitations and its subhuman apathy.

The extent to which 'Der fünfte Oktober' is, or is not, a *Novelle*, is neither here nor there. What matters is that the story, with its rhetorical, quasi-biblical style ('High overhead in the cold October sky passed Time's iron plough, tilling its fields with Worry and sowing them with Want, that one day the flame of revenge might rise up from them') and continual similes, is self-evidently an allegory or parable.

The second story in *Der Dieb*, 'Der Irre' ('The Madman') (*PD* 19f.) is very different, but no less remarkable and no less subjective. It is based on one of Heym's 'expeditions through Berlin' (*T* 157), in this case a walk from the asylum ('Nervenheilanstalt') in Wittenau (in the northern outskirts) to the department store Kaufhaus Wertheim in the Leipziger Platz. Having said that, one has said very little, for what matters is not Heym's poetic treatment of the Berlin background, but the meaning of his tale, which is again not so much a 'story' or 'Novelle', as a highly subjective poetic study, this time of the poet's own state of mind in late 1910/early 1911, when he felt he was in danger of going mad.

Its very subject makes it a variation on his poetry, in which 'no theme is treated so often and in so many variations, as that of the madman'.[22] More specifically, this story of a discharged mental patient's horrifying last hours parallels several poems written between June 1910 and May 1911 (L 91, 253–8, 262), as well as three others written in October/November 1911 (L 402, 430, 449), which form a pendant to the story. Of these poems it is the first ('Die Irren', L 91), written in June 1910, that is the most interesting, for it contains an image ('like big spiders sticking to walls') which links it with 'Der fünfte Oktober', where Heym wrote of the mob: 'They were hanging from the railings like hideous spiders'; thus showing that the spider is a self-image, maybe an image of self-loathing (one wonders whether Heym knew Redon's unforgettable spider image and/or the giant spider in Kubin's *Die Hölle*). The motif of the broken skull also links the poem with the present story.

More directly revealing, however, are a number of diary entries which show 'Der Irre' to be a self-study. As early as 15 March 1908 Heym had written: 'I know my fate now. To go mad like Hölderlin. But differently: after a life without love.' It is on 5 May 1910 that the most relevant and revealing entries begin, for on that day Heym wrote: 'Facing me I see a poor madman. In my head there is a spark of genius; in his there is only darkness. And yet I have much in common with him.' His point is developed on 1 August 1910: 'That genius is some-how allied with disease, is proved by the case of my own family ... When all is said and done genius really does seem to be a kind of degeneration [or mental disease].' His wording suggests that he had been reading 'Genius and Madness', in which Poe quotes the line 'Great wit to madness nearly is allied', and argues that 'genius' is 'a result of mental disease'. Heym writes as though Poe's finding is confirmed by his own experience. If he has not been reading Poe, then he must have had Max Nordau's *Degeneration* in mind.

Basic to the meaning of 'Der Irre' is the diary entry for 5 November 1910: 'I derive a good deal of amusement from observing myself. I, the madman, observe my symptoms with pleasure and satisfaction.' On 29 November he writes: 'I feel as though I am wearing a strait-jacket'; it is an imaginary (and foredoomed) 'escape' from this situation that the story develops. And there is more to come. On 20 December, as we have seen, he explains why he is so near to going crazy:

Ye gods, I am practically going out of my mind. Snowed under with work of a particularly ghastly sort, having to learn shoals of stuff by rote so that my head is at bursting point (*daß mir der Schädel kracht*), bogged down with all sorts of minor troubles – Elsa K. insists on having her 10 M. back, – the agony, the misery of it, and all the time the poetic images are coming out of my ears instead of being got down on paper. – Stuffed full of pills. Hideous dreams ... Sexual repression. In short, on the threshold of a nice bout of hysteria.

His overwrought condition is hardly surprising. The present story is probably, at least in part, one of those 'Hideous dreams'. His use of the phrase, 'so that my head is at bursting point' points to the most horrific incident in the story, when the anonymous autobiographical 'hero' bangs the children's heads together as though they are cymbals. In fact they are symbols, for the murders are a reflection of the murderous frustration which Heym felt at the time; some of them are probably also a sheer poetic elaboration of the phrase 'mir kracht der Schädel'.

On 28 May 1911 the diary records: 'My brain is going round in circles, like a prisoner banging on his prison door.' Both the 'Irrenanstalt' ('asylum') and the outside world of the story represent the prison of life from which Heym escaped only in death; a sketch dating from 1911, which begins: 'That afternoon the poet had undertaken one of his expeditions', goes on to compare the world to 'an enormous prison'. By summer 1911, Heym tells us, he was regarded as mad (he had always been regarded as 'crazy').

These diary entries leave one in no doubt that Heym is himself his madman. His text shows him exploring the insanity to which he now felt himself close; it shows him trying to break out from his situation and failing to do so (the 'Irrenanstalt' stands for the world as he experienced it). The story ends, as most of them do, in the death of the Heym-like hero.

'Der Irre' is linked with 'Der fünfte Oktober' by several images, the most important being that of the great bird. Maillard was described as being like a great black bird; the madman, shortly before his death, fancies himself to be a great white bird:

He was a great white bird over a lonely ocean powered by an eternal brightness, high up in the blue sky. His head nudged the white clouds, he was neighbour to the sun, which filled the sky overhead, a great golden bowl which was beginning to emit a loud booming noise (*PD* 32).

Of course, in this second story *being* a bird is also an embodiment of 'einen Vogel *haben*' ('to be crazy'). The murderous madman who sees himself as a great bird is what Albrecht Schaeffer called Heym's 'Dämon mit dem Geierkopf' (*D* 113), which probably derives from Goya's *Caprichos*. The great white bird, Baudelaire's symbol of the poet, is for Heym the symbol of his poetic destiny: Death.

Despite such linked images, 'Der Irre' lacks the wealth of imagery of the previous story, just as it lacks those insistent similes. The quasi-biblical overwriting of 'Der fünfte Oktober' has given way to a clinical style which is reminiscent – given the horror of what is being thus described – of Poe. In 'The Tell-Tale Heart', we remember, a murder is committed by a madman, but there are details in Heym's story which suggest that it may have been his reading of Poe's 'The Murders in the Rue Morgue' that gave him the idea of exploring and developing his own potential psychosis in this particular way. In Poe's tale the deed is thought to have been done by 'some raving maniac, escaped from a neighboring *Maison de Santé*', but turns out to have been done by an orang-utan; in Heym's story the madman is explicitly – and quite unnecessarily – compared to 'a huge orang-utan'. The most likely explanation is that Heym is alluding to the most famous of Poe's stories. Be this as it may, 'Der Irre' is the first of his black tales in the manner of Poe, although there is an important difference between Heym and Poe, as Allan Blunden has pointed out:

Poe's narrative manner [in 'The Murders in the Rue Morgue'] is quite different, for he is generally talking *with* his readers, dictating that his perspective shall also be theirs. Poe's narrative voice registers the shock and horror of a sensitive mind confronted by the ghastly; he anticipates our own reactions – fashions them, rather – and when we read Poe we are consoled, ultimately, by a common consent as to what is and what is not acceptable among civilized men. Not so with Heym. 'Der Irre' is more horrible than Poe's tales because Heym himself has deserted us, because Heym himself no longer believes in the civilization which the madman offends.[23]

There follows another memorably macabre study, 'Die Sektion' (*PD* 35f.). This is linked with the poem 'Morgue' (May/June 1911; second version, November 1911), but its origin lies elsewhere, for it shows Heym identifying with the first dead person he ever saw (T 5 June 1908), imagining himself dead (he was haunted by that premonition of early death), his head still filled with his 'Jahr der Liebe' (T 107) for Hedi, with whom he associated red poppies (see T 111: 'Roten Mohnes Blüten nahmst du viele'). The story therefore combines the two things that were most real for him: his love(s) and his approaching death. The idea of the dead man's mind being still filled with the dream of love may have been put into his mind by another story by Poe, 'The Colloquy of Monos and Una' ('I appreciated the direful change now in operation upon the flesh, and, as the dreamer is sometimes aware of the bodily presence of one who leans over him, so sweet Una, I still dully felt that you sat by my side').[24]

Hermann Korte may be right to say: 'The dream of the dead man on the dissecting table is a grotesque travesty of the Utopian ideal of the "beautiful life", and at the same time a parody of the morbid, decadent, "aesthetic" cult of death at the turn of the century';[25] but such an overly 'literary' interpretation is as little to the point as a purely psychoanalytical one would be; what counts is the imagination which has gone into this brilliantly morbid study of the self. The power of Heym's imagination will by now be clear, for we have already seen him identify with the mob in the French Revolution, with a madman, and now with a corpse which he foresees as his own.

Perhaps 'Jonathan' (*PD* 38f.) should have preceded 'Die Sektion' instead of following it, for it is a study of sickness unto death. Jonathan, 'poor little Jonathan', is, of course, Heym himself: Heym without the 'greatness' of which he dreamt, Heym as the would-be hero destroyed by his own 'sickness', by philistine society (represented by the doctors) and by the demon Death. The story is paralleled by the poem 'Das Krankenhaus, I–II' (May 1911) and, more important, by the many references in Heym's diaries to his own 'sickness'. It belongs together with 'Der Irre' and 'Die Sektion', for it shows the autobiographical hero-victim finding it impossible to make the existential leap which he longs to make, and going, instead, to a humiliating and degrading early death after an unfulfilled existence. It is hideously prophetic. There is a melancholy, tragic contrast between poor little Jonathan (particularly when his stature has been halved by the removal of his legs) and the great, heroic sense of adventure which, once it comes to nothing, leaves him with nothing for which to live. The story – it is again a 'study' – is antithetical, being based on the contrasts between the sick individual and his vital dreams; the constricted room and the dreamt-of open spaces; the bourgeois world and the world of heroism, adventure, poetry and love; the individual and society; life and death; and so on. The basis for these contrasts is not merely the disparity between muscular 'rowdy' and 'sick' mind, but that between Heym's life and the life he would have liked to live.

Jonathan's *Aufbruch* five years previously, which ends so tragically, refers to Heym leaving Neuruppin for Berlin, only to find himself being ground down and slowly destroyed by society and by the Furies by which he felt pursued. Jonathan's travels in the South Seas are a reflection of Heym's feeling of being 'far better suited to living in remote regions, in the further reaches of Asia, than to living at home' (*D* 502). Like Jonathan, Heym also continually found himself deprived of 'den weiten Himmel der Liebe' ('the wide open skies of love'). Jonathan's later travels in Africa reflect Heym's wish to cross Africa (*T* July 1909) as a cure for his 'sickness'.

The story, with its repeated references to Jonathan's 'Qualen' ('sufferings') and a reference to the 'Garten des Lebens', presumably reflects Heym's reading of Octave Mirbeau's *Le jardin des supplices* (1899: *Der Garten der Qualen*, 1901), to which he refers in a letter to Rowohlt; he also uses the word in relation to his own sufferings (e.g. *T* 162: 'suffering rears up within me like a great beast'). The story is cross-linked with the previous ones by some notable images, in this case that of the maws of life/death waiting to devour the individual ('the bed ... standing wide open, like a mouth about to swallow a new patient'; 'the crater of his fever devoured him forever'; etc.). This echoes Baudelaire's 'Le temps mange la vie', but also his 'Le coucher du soleil romantique', from which Heym's 'trembling heart' motif may well come: for Jonathan, for whom love is a pathetic flash in the pan of his dreadful death, the sun of romanticism sets with a vengeance. There is also the death of the pit in Poe. Then there is 'terror like a great white bird', that great white bird which we have already seen and which is reminiscent of the 'Great Bird' of which Merezhkovsky makes Leonardo da Vinci dream all his life, and which finally comes to him at the moment of his death, symbol of his Destiny coming home to him at last.

There is a terrible contrast between Jonathan's wretched death, which Heym is imagining himself suffering, and the heroic death for which Heym longed in vain. Jonathan is, as it were, choked by the apathy with which Heym fought a running battle, which is why he clearly identified with the mob even in the first half of 'Der fünfte Oktober'. In the last analysis 'Jonathan' is about what Heym called 'our terrible inscrutable destiny' (*T* 76), and the 'infinite cruelty' of God (*T* 141). The style of the piece combines the styles of 'Der fünfte Oktober' and 'Die Sektion', but despite the clinical detail necessitated by the subject, the story is for the most part realized in painterly terms: Death standing on the roof of the house, Death as 'a man in a grey shroud'. With Heym's tales it is the visual detail that etches itself into the memory.

'Das Schiff' (*PD* 52f.), the next story in *Der Dieb*, is another version of the previous one, in which 'Jonathan' first sailed the South Seas in a 'Korallenschiff', this being the first stage of his unsuccessful attempt to evade his destiny, which ended in death. In 'Das Schiff' (the ship is a 'Korallenschiffer') something similar happens. The story, originally entitled 'Pest auf dem Schiff', is a study of the fear of death. It is reminiscent of Poe's 'The Masque of the Red Death' and 'The Fall of the House of Usher', for Heym's story, like Poe's, is concerned with the 'grim phantasm, FEAR'. 'Das Schiff' is a vivid, Poe-inspired visualization of what Heym called 'the fear within me' (*T* 45), that is to say, his own fear of death. There are also parallels between 'Das Schiff' and Poe's 'The Narrative of Arthur Gordon Pym' – the South Seas, Desolation Island (Poe's name fits Heym's island), the mysterious hieroglyphs (which reappear on the skins of Heym's plague victims!) and the gigantic white bird(s). It is, however, the differences that are ultimately more significant, for Poe's 'romance' is an adventure story, whereas Heym's is every inch a 'gothic tale'.

Heym once again identifies with his main character, in this case the Frenchman, who is the last to die and whose fear is therefore the most prolonged. No doubt the Frenchman's nationality reflects Heym's romantic dream of serving as a hussar officer in Napoleon's Grande Armée, and indeed his predilection for all things French (notably Delacroix, whose paintings seem to have inspired his heroic self-image; but also, as we have seen, Stendhal, Baudelaire and Rimbaud, Verlaine, Villiers de l'Isle Adam and Octave Mirbeau). However, the ship itself also represents Heym (cf. *T* 148: 'I am drifting around like a ship...' – a Flying Dutchman image – and also Baudelaire's 'Maximes consolantes sur l'amour': 'Northern man, ardent navigator lost in the mists'), as does, therefore, the 'Flying Dutchman' (see the poems of that title: *L* 195ff., 201ff.), to which Heym alludes in this story. Poe's 'Pym' is probably in the background here, for it includes (in Chapter X) a memorably gruesome description of 'that fated vessel'. The form taken by the plague in 'Das Schiff' is reminiscent of Poe's Red Death, which left scarlet marks on the body of its victims, whom it killed within half an hour. The figure of Death, which recalls the dying figure of Madeline Usher in Poe's famous story, is here a personification of Heym's 'Schicksal' and represents the Furies or Erinyes (daughters of Night and Darkness) by whom he felt hounded; he must have seen them pushing him back into the icy water in 1912 – unless what then crossed his mind was a passage in the last of Villiers de l'Isle-Adam's *Contes Cruels*: 'When the forehead alone contains a man's existence, that man is illumined only from above, and his jealous shadow, falling straight behind him, will drag him down by the feet into the Invisible.' Villiers de l'Isle Adam, whose mind, like Heym's, was possessed by glory, love and death, was also a 'brother of Poe'; his *Contes Cruels*, vivid, vision-full, occasionally lurid, had also served Heym as a model (*T* 256). The dragon in 'Das Schiff' is possibly another gratuitous allusion to Poe, in this case to 'The Fall of the House of Usher'.

In general terms, this most vividly gruesome of all Heym's tales is a nightmare version of the premonitory dream by which he was obsessed. Thus the ship, which he associated with adventure and glory, has here become the Ship of Death, the Flying Dutchman (Heym saw *himself* as the Flying Dutchman, manned by Death), while the heroic death of which he dreamt has become a wretched, terrifying end; even Woman has assumed her negative aspect of 'La Mort' (cf. Böcklin's *Die Pest* for Pestilence as a woman). The story therefore shows Heym's deepest fears coming true: that, far from allowing him to experience heroism and glory in love and war, his personal Destiny will lead him to a terrible end that will make a mockery of his life. Which is precisely what it did, so that the ghastly, Poe-like story is very much a premonitory one; yet even without that final irony, it would have been unforgettable.

More particularly now, the ash-grey figures of those about to die are a reflection of Heym's sense of being 'consumed by grey misery' (*T* 6 July 1910). He dreamt about the plague in August 1910, and also wrote a short prose piece entitled 'Die Pest' (*PD* 114), based on reports of the outbreak of cholera in Manchuria in winter 1910/11, which is, however, little more than a piece of brilliantly impressionistic (or Kubinesque) reportage; beside 'Das Schiff' it is insignificant. When writing about the plague, especially in 'Das Schiff', he very likely also had in mind the death of Cesare Borgia as described by Merezhkovsky (it occurs just before the death of Leonardo da Vinci in Merezhkovsky's book, which he read at least ten times). The ending of 'Das Schiff', in which the Frenchman smashes his skull (as in 'Der Irre'), can be seen as an echo and enactment of Heym's diary for 20 December 1910: 'I am practically going out of my mind ... my head is at bursting point.' The final image ('the terrible bright light') also goes back to the diary, with its reference to the 'hellish, lonely light' (*T* July/August 1911); in other words, life, symbolized by the sun, finally reveals itself as death. Heym would probably have seen with grim satisfaction the man-made hole in the ozone layer which threatens to transform the life-giving Sun into the very agent of Death.

A story which seemed far removed from reality is therefore once again seen to be a visualization or externalization of Heym's morbid inner world. Like the three preceding stories, it deals with a subject in which Poe had specialized, the destruction of a human being. It is striking that in this story everything is described as 'terrible' ('schreck-lich'). This alone would put the reader in mind of Poe. Heym once more makes heavy use of simile in his attempt to bring to terrible life a phantom or phantasm of the mind, and he certainly succeeds in this, for the story is a macabre *tour de force* as a depiction of a man driven to the very extremity of mindless terror by his fear of death. It is a remarkably consequential development of a few basic images from the diaries, notably that in his dream of 19 June 1909: 'Wearing some crazy costume I am leaving my room, chased by a terrifying phantom. With my very last strength I am just able to bolt the door in its face (*T* 183).'

Interrupting the sequence of stories in *Der Dieb*, it will be useful at this point to look briefly at a story, also dating from 1911, which was not included in *Der Dieb*. The piece in question, which is entitled 'Die Bleistadt' (*PD* 115f.), is linked with 'Das Schiff' both thematically and by the 'leaden atmosphere' of that story and the 'Kraken' of this. The atmosphere of 'Die Bleistadt', too, is positively apocalyptic; it shows the extent to which the Book of Revelation, quoted in *Der Dieb*, caught Heym's imagination. The burning sky of the present tale is more than a cliché; it belongs together with the black sun and blood-red moon of the Apocalypse.

But if 'Die Bleistadt' belongs very much in the context of the stories that we have been discussing, it differs from them in that there is not a single protagonist with whom Heym identifies; this may be why he did not include it in *Der Dieb*, for otherwise it is more impressive than 'Ein Nachmittag' (which he did include). The manner in which the story is narrated suggests that its implications are more general, in other words, that those whose brows bear 'the white seal of horror' are simply men faced with the human condition. However, these men also represent Georg Heym, who by 4 September 1911 was writing: 'I have fought an heroic battle, but suddenly I feel as though I cannot go on (*T* 162).' 'Die Bleistadt' is a visualization of that state of mind. This time his defeat at the hands of life is transposed into that 'Crossing of Africa' ('Durchquerung Afrikas') that was another of his romantic pipe-dreams.

'Die Bleistadt' would, I think, have been a better choice for inclusion in *Der Dieb* than 'Ein Nachmittag' (*PD* 65f.), a very slight piece which shows that Heym regarded his first experience of being deceived by a girl as symptomatic of the way in which 'life presents itself to us as a continual deception'.[26] The 'little boy', like 'little Jonathan', is accordingly a *persona* of Georg Heym. As a tragic story of love 'Ein Nachmittag' is a good deal less impressive than the very early 'Die Novella der Liebe' (1907) (*PD* 100f.), which is interesting in that it is as personal as the later stories, but with the Renaissance setting which Heym favoured at the time.

The title-story 'Der Dieb' ('The Thief') (*PD* 72f.), with its motto from one of Baudelaire's 'Poésies de circonstance' ('Aux sots je préfère les fous/Dont je suis, chose, hélas, certaine': 'To fools I prefer madmen, of whom, alas, I am surely one'), is yet another highly personal work, although this is not immediately apparent. Heym's starting-point is both certain and concrete enough: the theft of the *Mona Lisa* from the Louvre on 22 August 1911, with attendant press reports and speculations, to say nothing of the poet Guillaume Apollinaire being arrested on suspicion of the theft. This will have attracted his attention because he knew the *Mona Lisa* so well from Merezhkovsky's fictionalized life of Leonardo, which we have seen was quite simply his favourite book. His spelling – 'Monna Lisa' – signals his debt to Merezhkovsky, whose novel is as full of visions and portents as his own tale was to be. Before discussing the identity and motivation of the thief, let us recall Walter Pater's celebrated description of *La Gioconda*:

La Gioconda is, in the truest sense, Leonardo's masterpiece, the revealing instance of his mode of thought and work. In suggestiveness, only the *Melancholia* of Dürer is comparable to it; and no crude symbolism disturbs the effect of its subdued and graceful mystery. We all know the face and hands of the figure, set in its marble chair, in that circle of fantastic rocks, as in some faint light under sea. Perhaps of all ancient pictures time has chilled it least. As so often happens with works in which invention seems to reach its limit, there is an element in it given to, not invented by, the master ... the unfathomable smile, always with a touch of something sinister in it ... is expressive of what in the ways of a thousand years men had come to desire. Hers is the head upon which all 'the ends of the world are come', and the eyelids are a little weary. It is a beauty wrought out from within upon the flesh, the deposit, little cell by little cell, of strange thoughts and fantastic reveries and exquisite passions. Set it for a moment beside one of those white Greek goddesses or beautiful women of antiquity, and how they would be troubled by this beauty, into which the soul with all its maladies has passed! All the thoughts and experience of the world have etched and moulded there, in that which they have the power to refine and make expressive the outward form, the animalism of Greece, the lust of Rome, the mysticism of the Middle Age with its spiritual ambition and imaginative loves, the return of the Pagan world, the sins of the Borgias. She is older than the rocks among which she sits; like the vampire, she has been dead many times, and learned the secrets of the grave; and has been a diver in deep seas, and keeps their fallen day about her...[27]

Even if he did not know this famous passage (Pater's *The Renaissance* appeared in German in 1902), a young man in love with Beauty could not be indifferent to the *Mona Lisa*, could not but speculate on the motivation of the man who had carried her off.

Heym's imaginary thief is mad, so that the story is linked with 'Der Irre' and with all the references already quoted to Heym's own near-madness at this time. Numerous connections show that the thief, like the madman in 'Der Irre', is Heym himself, who wrote in his diary on 28 May 1911 that he was going crazy ('Ich bin am verrückt werden'). Both he and his thief are alienated from their early friends; both pursue a variety of interests in order to keep melancholy at bay – in studying biology, astronomy and archaeology, the thief is following Heym's vitalism, sun-worship (and the study of cloud patterns) and immersion in history. Both see visions (the thief's drawings are comparable with Heym's poems, produced only because he could not draw); they share a love of clouds, and what they see in them is comparable to the religiously inspired visions of Bosch, Patinir and (Pieter) Brueghel; thus the thief sees the Devil standing over a bevy of black bodies who are kneeling before him. Like Heym himself, the thief sees clouds in terms which vary from the mythological to the pseudo-mythological to the merely portentous. Thus one evening, after the burning of 'the book', he hears a storm which 'drove the crimson bucentaur of a cloud across the sky'; that is when he starts hearing voices. The bucentaur is a characteristic inhabitant of Heym's imagination: a monster, half-man and half-bull, it symbolizes the duality of man, but with the emphasis on the baser part. The 'bucentaur of a cloud' is, however, essentially a ship image, probably deriving from Byron's 'Childe Harold's Pilgrimage' (IV, xi); the 'bucentaur' was the ceremonial barge in which, from 1311 to 1789, the Doge of Venice used to ride out annually to reaffirm his allegiance with the sea and therefore his sea-power; later a hulk, it here becomes a symbolical barque-of-death (cf. 'Das Schiff').

The thief's burning of what he calls 'the book' parallels and stands for Heym's ritual burning of his law books and his destruction of a legal file (see Chapter IV above). Both feel themselves possessed by the Devil (Heym: 'Fate, this Satan, is evidently my enemy': T 157: 28 May 1911). Both hear voices (see Heym's diary entry for 14 November 1910). It is significant that Heym makes the theft happen not on 22 August (1911), but on 17 August (1910), the day on which he wrote in his diary: 'Indeed, if a god existed, he would have to be dragged to the gallows ... for his cruelty.' The state of mind is notably similar to that of the thief. The theme of this story, and of all the others, is ultimately this arbitrary and endless cruelty. The thief's view of life and of Christ ('He had recognized the terror of death as the ultimate truth') is Heym's. The thief's reading of the Book of Revelation reflects Heym's. And so on. What all this means is that the thief, too, is a particularly close personification of Heym. This is why

Heym introduces the narrative with the thief's prayer, and continues it by alternating between direct speech, interior analysis, interior monologue and external description in such a manner that the reader no longer knows where to draw the line between the author's and the character's viewpoint.[28]

The point is that author and character are essentially one.

Like his creator, the thief records his visions, one of the most remarkable of which, 'an enormous bat which seemed to be fixed to the sky with its wings outstretched', may derive from Merezhkovsky's description of Leonardo's flying-machine as resembling an enormous bat. By means of this machine, man was to be able to make himself lord of the winds, conqueror of space (which he has subsequently done, though still overmanned by Death). For Heym this became an Icarus image, for he saw man's every attempt at transcendence as being crushed by the grim laws of human destiny. More generally, bats are as ubiquitous a part of Heym's gothic world as of Goya's, from which they probably derive. The Christian symbol around which women gather is the Cross on which the Son of Man met Death. When the thief first sees the Devil, it is with a woman's face and, on the brow, the signs which Death wore in 'Das Schiff'. Death and Devil are thus identified. There are 'she-devils' in Poe and Baudelaire, but Heym's 'Teufelin' ('she-devil') comes straight from Merezhkovsky, whose novel the 'White She-Devil' dominates. Heym used the figure in 'Jonathan' when he referred to 'this Satan of a nurse, this withered old devil', but at that stage he had not developed the figure via Merezhkovsky. The reasoning that lies behind the thief's perception of the *Mona Lisa* as a she-devil is found in Heym's diary: 'I see that there is nothing worse for me than love' (*T* 26 October 1910. Cf. here 'Yes, Woman was the original Evil').

The thief in Heym's story is not just an imaginary version of the real thief who stole the *Mona Lisa* in 1911; he is based on Leonardo's disciple, Giovanni Boltraffio, for Heym gives him Giovanni's attitude towards the White She-Devil of earthly beauty, goddess of earthly love. In other words, Heym has used his knowledge of Merezhkovsky's novel to motivate the thief. Boltraffio regarded Leonardo as the precursor of the Antichrist because of his worship of Aphrodite; Heym's madman's infatuation with *La Gioconda* is based on Boltraffio's seduction by *La Diavolessa bianca* in the person of the comely witch Cassandra; disciple and madman are moved by a similar religious mania symbolized in the Great Swan, which stands both for the Son of Man and for Aphrodite (*La Diavolessa bianca*). In more general terms, Beauty and Religion are seen as diametrically opposed. In Merezhkovsky's novel there is a connection between Aphrodite, *La Diavolessa bianca*, Madonna Lise Gioconda, and the death of Leonardo da Vinci, who finally associates *La*

Gioconda with Death. I don't think that this means that Heym is blaming himself for *his* 'sinful enthusiasm for heathen beauty', rather that he is seeing his love of beauty as a fundamental part of the destiny which is to destroy him.

That the story transcends its point of departure in the press is evident. It seems to be an imaginative study (via Merezhkovsky's novel) of the possible motivation of the unknown thief, but, via that same novel, it goes far beyond that, for Heym identifies with the unknown thief (whom he assumes to have been motivated by an obsession with beauty comparable to his own obsession with it), with Giovanni Boltraffio, and with his idol Leonardo da Vinci (the examplar of the artist as hero). The story seems to be about Beauty being destroyed by a madman, but in reality it is, much more, about a mad man (and with him other men) being destroyed by Beauty, which he loves. In other words, Heym sees himself being destroyed by his 'Schicksal' in the form of his passion for Beauty. The story is closely linked with 'Der Irre' and with 'Das Schiff', but more generally it is in line with all the other stories except the first, in that in it Heym is seeing himself being destroyed by life. The real thief is therefore Death, which 'comes as a thief' in the Book of Revelation (XVI, 15), so that the story is not about a theft which took place on 22 August 1911 (or even 17 August 1910), but about one which was to take place on 16 January 1912. Influenced as it is by the Book of Revelation, by Poe and by Schopenhauer, to say nothing of the pervasive influence of Dmitry Merezhkovsky, 'Der Dieb' is a last vivid example of Heym's gothic tales. That his 'fancy grew charnel'[29] in summer/autumn 1911 is obvious. Most of his tales are about death. That his premonition was both real and came true must be allowed to temper our view of their morbidity. Dead men, it is said, tell no tales; but this one did, and terrible tales they are. The firemen burning like torches, at the end of this last story, form a shocking image of the insensate cruelty of life.

Heym's tales owe their impact to the fact that he writes dramatically, making frequent use of antithesis, and that he deploys a wealth of vivid images and makes frequent use of personification. Thus, while he does not eschew abstract words, his work is concrete, and therefore memorable. These black tales bear comparison with the *Novellen* of Kleist (another of Heym's favourite authors), for here, too, are power and vividness of expression and a nightmare quality resulting from men being driven to the limits of human endurance, those hallmarks of one of the greatest of all German story-tellers. Heym's *Novellen* and Kleist's express a fundamentally similar view of life, doing so in a controlled style strikingly at odds with the lack of control which they portray. 'Kleistian' is an honourable epithet, and it fits these tales, which are the product of a brilliant, sometimes wayward imagination.

Postscript:
Georg Heym and
Expressionism

Georg Heym is a member of the 'Expressionist' generation, that brilliant generation which included the painters Alexei Jawlensky, Wassili Kandinsky, Ernst Ludwig Kirchner, Paul Klee, August Macke, Franz Marc, Paula Modersohn-Becker and Emil Nolde (and many others scarcely less gifted), and the poets Gottfried Benn, Alfred Lichtenstein, Ernst Stadler, August Stramm and Georg Trakl (and many other lesser talents). Kafka, though hardly an Expressionist, was a member of the same generation. Because Heym belonged to that generation, has things in common with some of those named (notably Kirchner and Trakl), was a member of the Neue Club and published in Expressionist periodicals, he has come to be known as an 'Expressionist'. In his own day, when there was hardly any such thing as 'Expressionism', he was known as a 'Pathetiker' or 'man of feeling', a far better label than the one he has worn posthumously.

The term Expressionism is problematical in that it denotes both a movement in German art and literature (to say nothing of music, film and architecture) lasting from the foundation of the group of painters known as Die Brücke in 1905 to the currency reform of 1923/4, and a stylistic tendency or quality of expressive emphasis and distortion which is normally associated with Northern or gothic art in times of stress (for example, in the work of Matthias Grünewald), but may be found in any time and place (e.g. in Late Renaissance Mannerism in Italy; in El Greco; in Japanese art); when Ludwig Tieck wrote in his novel *Sternbald* (1798) that he wished to describe not trees and mountains, but his own feelings at the sight of them, he was describing a form of Expressionism. This twofold meaning of the term, which is unfortunate, is only the starting-point for further problems, for modern German Expressionism has come to mean all things to all men.

If one takes a sufficiently magisterial view, there is much to be said for the view that twentieth-century German Expressionism, which, as in Heym's case, grew out of the neo-romanticism of the *fin-de-siècle*, itself constitutes the tragic phase of Romanticism. We have seen how many Romantic features Heym possesses. On a more mundane level, Expressionism is, as the word *Ausdruckskunst* implies, the art of self-expression; it involves a high degree of expressive intensification and distortion and a significant degree of abstraction. In practice it began as an aesthetic revolution against naturalism (realism), and ended by being associated with a political revolution (the Bolshevik revolution of 1917, the German revolution of 1918). This fact complicates the issue, for some critics identify Expressionism with the early anti-mimetic movement which gave rise to abstract art, while others associate it with its later socially revolutionary content. Early Expressionism, which is what is in question here, is notable for its mishmash of old and new elements (e.g. in poetry, the new 'stringing together' of images within conventional poetic forms; in painting the combination of expressive colour and conventional line). Heym lived only just long enough to get beyond that mishmash, which is characteristic of his best-known poetic work.

Expressionism involves the expression of a new mood, a new attitude to life. That mood is often ecstatic, often deeply pessimistic; it invariably involves a passionate response to life; it is the new 'Rausch-kunst' for which Nietzsche called. It is marked by anti-naturalism, passion, a 'gothic' view of life (demons similar to those which haunted Heym are to be found in Grünewald) and a political radicalism which eventually led to political engagement and activism. In a general sense 'Expressionism' denotes any art which is expressive rather than mimetic: '*Expressionism* ... recognizes that the chief object of a good picture is to convey the expression of an emotion of the artist, and not his impression of something he sees.'[1] Thus Van Gogh's *Night Café* is an expressionist painting in that his concern was not to render exactly what he had before his eyes, but to 'express the terrible passions of humanity by means of red and green'.[2] Wilhelm Worringer put it more generally when he argued, in 1908, that 'the impulse to imitation has nothing to do with art'.3 The era of non-representational art had begun; Expressionism was, especially for some members of the Blaue Reiter group of painters (Kandinsky, Jawlensky, Marc) a staging-post on the way to abstraction. What matters for the Expressionist is inner reality (according to some contemporary philosophers the only reality there is), not visual but visionary experience; as Paul Klee said, art does not reproduce what is already visible, it makes things visible for the first time. Art is therefore not reproduction, but creation, imagination. All this applies in a less immediately obvious way to poetry or verbal expressionism, so that words tend to be important for their 'vibrations' or associations or sounds. Expressionist poetry is non-representational poetry, concerned not with description of outer reality, but with expression of inner reality (cf. the Futurist aim of painting states of mind); its concern is simply to be expressive (of, say, Heym's *Angst*). This brings us back to Heym's tales, which are nothing if not expressive.

When these so-called *Novellen* rise to the surface of public awareness, it is as examples of 'Expressionist prose' – a fearsomely various beast. The very fact that there is radical disagreement as to what 'Expressionist prose' is, and that most definitions apply only to one or two writers, ought to make anyone pause before using the term, which is as meaningless as it is misleading. When it is argued that 'it is exactly the unlimited variety of styles and moods which is characteristic of the movement',4 then the obvious conclusion is that, in that case, 'Expressionist prose' does not exist, for 'Expressionism' has outgrown its critical usefulness as a label. In his lifetime Heym was known as a 'Pathetiker' because of the vehemence of his feelings and expression.

By and large it has been assumed that Heym, as a major poet of the Expressionist era, is *ipso facto* an Expressionist. Whether he can properly be described as an Expressionist is a matter of definition. As a painter *manqué* with a strongly visual style he is, like the typical Expressionist painter, concerned with 'the visual projection of his emotional experience'.5 The trouble is that this criterion is by no means exclusive to Expressionism; it applies to all expressive art – and 'expressive' and 'expressionistic' are not synonymous. Likewise, the passion and intense subjectivity of Heym's work are characteristic of, but by no means exclusive to, Expressionism. Although his work gives that impression of almost manic creativity which is also found in Expressionism, it is simply not expressionistic in the most essential way, namely as regards form. His work may encapsulate both the grotesque and the tortured, anguished awareness of Northern (Expressionist) or 'gothic' art, but its form is unambiguously that of the opposite, classical tradition; there is a parallel with his beloved Hölderlin, whose work is romantic in content, classical in form. Heym's work may be expressionistic in that he conveys emotions rather than recording visual impressions, but if by Expressionism is meant art in which traditional ideas of naturalism are abandoned in favour of distortion and exaggeration in order to express the artist's emotion, then we cannot label Heym an Expressionist without one serious reservation: that his work is not so much anti-mimetic (which is the most fundamental characteristic of Expressionism) as simply increasingly imaginative. He has, it is true, an individual style which conveys his own particular tensions, but by that criterion virtually all poets are 'expressionists'. Everything that he wrote is self-expressive, but so, too, in the final analysis, is all art, particularly since the Romantic era. The dynamic use of imagery and syntax – absolute metaphor and radical simplification of syntax – which typifies his style is common to all forms of modernism. His poetry certainly parallels early Expressionist painting in combining traditional verse forms (line) with non-traditional imagery (colour). A sense of the unreality of the world of objects has been seen as characteristic of Expressionism; the trouble is that it is no less certainly characteristic of all visionary art, most of which is not expressionistic but expressive. And in Heym's case it is, paradoxically, combined with its opposite: an overwhelming sense of the physical reality ('Dinglichkeit') of the world. Heym shares with self-styled Expressionists a sense of historical crisis and a profound pessimism; neither quality is, however, peculiar to the years 1905 to 1912. The fact that Heym's main creative period corresponds so precisely with early Expressionism only makes the temptation to indulge in imprecise labelling all the more insidious. In the last analysis, however, it does not greatly matter whether he is deemed an Expressionist or not; his style and his attitudes are better described than labelled. As man and poet Heym is nothing if not original.

I do not think that Heym's tales can usefully be termed 'Expressionistic'. The fact that they are expressive of their author's existential condition, notably of his obsession with and fear of death, does not make them Expressionistic. There is no point in attributing to such memorably idiosyncratic (and therefore eccentric) works a label which would not only link them with other works with which they have little in common, but which would be a denial of Heym's considerable individuality and obvious nonconformity even in things artistic (he was known for 'riding his own horse'). To place his 'Novellen' beside examples of 'Expressionist prose' is not only to emphasize their vigour and vitality; it is also to emphasize their difference and their complete lack of an 'Expressionistic' style as such. This is the crux: that these stories are simply not written in an Expressionist style, and no amount of discussion of their 'expressiveness' should be allowed to disguise that fact. In purely stylistic terms they are as old-fashioned as they are powerful; both their *Novelle*-form and their style (the frequent similes, the preponderance of attributive adjectives, the tendency to overwriting within the limits of apparent realism and of conventional syntax) are non-Expressionist characteristics. The heavy use of certain recurrent adjectives and adverbs (notably 'schwarz' and 'schrecklich') points in the direction of Edgar Allan Poe and, more generally, of the stylistic melodramatics of the 'gothic tale'. In literary historical terms there is a good case for regarding these tales as belonging to the gothic tradition; is it chance that one of the last books Heym read (in December 1911) was Wilhelm Worringer's *Formprobleme der Gotik* (1911)? It is probably not chance that his favourite English poets – Keats, Byron and Shelley – were all more or less predisposed towards the gothic, none more so than Shelley in his 'Alastor' (to which Heym frequently appears to allude) and *The Cenci* (which he copied). Several of his favourite French writers (Baudelaire, Mirbeau, Villiers de l'Isle Adam) belong to that same tradition, while the contemporary painters with whom he is linked by his morbid, visionary imagination (Van Gogh, Munch, Hodler, Ensor, Kubin) are either close to it or part of it. If one must apply labels – and the perceived need to do so is the denial of criticism – then I would say that while Heym's imagination marks him out as what Herbert Read calls a 'Northern Expressionist', the tales belong to the genre of the gothic tale (while also being psychological self-studies, versions of his defeat at the hands of life), and the style to 'expressive realism'. But the labels are unimportant. The reader is left torn between compassion for the man whose view of the human condition was so black, and admiration for the way in which he expressed that vision. Heym knew perfectly well that there is – or should be – more to life than the blank terror of these tales; but in so far as *l'horreur de la vie* is part of the range of human responses to life, he must be given credit for giving it such memorable expression. That he has done this in a genre which is 'not his' is a singular achievement.

In retrospect it seems clear that Heym sought, like Shelley, to turn himself into a mythical figure by fictionalizing his life, although the manner of his death contributed more to his reputation than his life had done (cf. the case of Van Gogh). More than anything else, however, it is the reception of Expressionism as such that has dominated his reception and reputation alike, for he is known today as 'an Expressionist poet', known above all for two poems, 'Der Krieg' and 'Der Gott der Stadt'; 'Der Krieg', written in 1911, was influential in 1914, not so much because it combined heroic and post-heroic views of war, as because of its rhetoric. Nowadays the poem is read in the context of Expressionism in poetry. The poet who should be known as one of the greatest elegiac poets to have written in German is belittled by being taken as a literary historical exemplar.

It was in the decade following his death that Heym was best known in Germany, for his memory was kept alive by his friends and the tributes they went on publishing, and, of course, by posthumously published works, notably the *Dichtungen* of 1922 (edited by Kurt Pinthus and Erwin Loewenson) and the new edition of *Umbra vitae*, illustrated by Ernst Ludwig Kirchner, which came out in 1924. The *Dichtungen* led directly to the first study of his life and work, by Helmut Greulich (1931). During the Nazi period, when Expressionism was banned as 'degenerate', Heym and his fellow Expressionist poets were semi-forgotten. Since 1945 there has been an explosion of first scholarly and then general interest in Expressionism, as the dates in the Bibliography show, and not a little important work has been done on Heym; in this context no one deserves more credit than the late Karl Ludwig Schneider. This does not mean, however, that Heym's work has been fully researched, or that his reputation has been fully established, for neither is the case. Looking back, it is now clear that all the emphasis on Expressionism in the past generation of scholarship has been to the detriment of the individual poets and painters who have come to be grouped under the Expressionist umbrella. Public and critics alike want 'overviews', which, in the case of the Expressionist poets and painters means ignoring not only their highly individual talents, but, ironically, their very expressionism, for if Expressionism means anything it means doing one's own thing – something for which Georg Heym was famous.

By the time of his death Heym had already outgrown Expressionism. He died, as we have seen, at a time when he had just written poems which he would have been most unlikely to better, and before he had found an appropriate career other than writing poetry. Had he not died in 1912, he would probably have shared the fate of his friend Robert Jentzsch (1890–1918), who fell on the Western front, although there can be no certainty that he would not have gone the same way as Jakob van Hoddis (1887–c. 1942), who suffered from prolonged mental instability and eventually died in a concentration camp. Of his other friends and associates, David Baumgardt (1890–1963) became Professor of Philosophy in Berlin before emigrating to the United States in 1939; Erwin Loewenson (1888–1963), who saved Heym's manuscripts for posterity, devoted his life to Zionism and died in Tel Aviv; John Wolfsohn (1889–1936) worked as a lawyer before emigrating to Palestine; Simon Guttmann (1891–1989) became one of the founders of photo-journalism and emigrated to London; Hildegard Krohn (1892–?) died in a concentration camp. It is impossible to speculate as to what would have happened to Heym and his reputation if he had not died in 1912. All the statistics suggest that he would have died in 1914–18. No comparable poets survived the war (Gottfried Benn is hardly comparable). Speculation is futile; his achievement is there for all to see, provided, that is, they have what he called 'Optik' (in English, eyes to see).

Notes

(Place of publication is London unless otherwise stated.)

I: LIFE, 1887–1909

1. Quoted from Nina Schneider, *Katalog II*, p. 23.

2. ibid. Cf. the first paragraph of Rider Haggard's *Allan Quatermain*: 'The great wheel of Fate rolls on like a Juggernaut, and crushes us all in turn, some soon, some late – it does not matter when, in the end it crushes us all ... we cry for mercy; but it is of no use, the black Fate thunders on and in its season reduces us to powder.' Heym may conceivably have known *Allan Quatermain*, available in German in an English-language edition.

3. On *Le Monde où l'on s'ennuie*, see my *George Moore and German Pessimism*, Durham, 1988, pp. 15f.

4. SUB Hamburg, Nl. Heym, Inv. Nr. 93/1, fol. 8.

5. SUB Hamburg, Nl. Heym, Inv. Nr. 26, fol. 118.

6. Quoted from Nina Schneider, *Katalog II*, p. 31.

7. *Leonardo da Vinci* appeared in an anonymous English translation as *The Forerunner* in 1902; the German title is retained in the text as being less misleading.

8. *Modern German Poetry 1910–1960*, edited by Michael Hamburger and Christopher Middleton, 1962, p. xxvi.

9. W. H. Sokel, *The Writer in Extremis*, Stanford, 1959, p. 98.

10. ibid.

11. Gabriele D'Annunzio, *The Child of Pleasure*, translated by G. Harding, 1898, p. 45; Heym knew the novel and clearly identified with Andrea Sperelli, cf. *T* 114.

12. Dmitry Merezhkovsky, *The Forerunner*, 1902, p. 351.

13. Hermann Korte, *Georg Heym*, Stuttgart, 1982, p. 18.

14. Kafka, in 'A Report to an Academy'.

II: ROMANTIC HERO

1. Helmut Greulich, *Georg Heym (1887–1912). Leben und Werk*, Berlin, 1931, p. 15.

2. Hans Bethge, *Hölderlin*, Berlin and Leipzig, 1904, pp. 12, 14–15, 20, 24, 27f., 29, 32, 34–5, 39f., 44 and 82.

3. ibid., pp. 12f.

4. ibid., p. 36.

5. ibid., p. 31.

6. ibid., p. 57.

7. The Reclam volume was Hölderlin, *Gedichte*, edited by Georg Jäger, Leipzig, n.d. (Universal-Bibliothek, no. 510). The line quoted is the first line of 'Die Heimat'.

8. Plato, *Phaedrus*, 279B.

9. Alfred Dove, *Caracosa*, Berlin, 1894, vol. II, p. 190. The enthusiasm of the mob in Heym's story 'Der fünfte Oktober' calls to mind the phrase 'die Begeisterung des Hungers' and the behaviour of the flagellants in the final chapter of Dove's novel.

10. *Columbia Dictionary of Modern European Literature*, New York, 1947, pp. 200f.

11. Paragraph 5.

12. Schopenhauer, *Parerga and Paralipomena, II*, paragraph 172 bis.

13. Dmitry Merezhkovsky, *Julian Apostata*, translated by Carl von Gütschow, Leipzig, 1903, p. 227.

14. SUB Hamburg, Nl. Heym, Inv. no. 24, fol. 16r.

15. Merezhkovsky, *Michelangelo*, Leipzig, 1905, p. 13.

16. With *T* 56 and *PD* 172, cf. Merezhkovsky, ibid., pp. 85f.

17. Merezhkovsky, *Peter der Große und sein Sohn Alexei*, translated by Carl von Gütschow, Leipzig, 1905, p. 279.

18. R. A. Nicholls, *The Dramas of Christian Dietrich Grabbe*, The Hague, 1969, p. 14.

19. See Bernd W. Seiler, *Die historischen Dichtungen Georg Heyms*, Munich, 1972, p. 151.

20. In the projected invasion of England in 1804; see Joachim Maass, *Kleist. A Biography*, translated by Ralph Manheim, 1983, pp. 92f.

21. Kleist, *Hinterlassene Schriften*, edited by Ludwig Tieck, Berlin, 1821, vol. II, p. 202.

22. See *D* 297.

23. *D* 181.

III: EARLY POETRY AND DRAMA

1. Julius Bab, *Richard Dehmel*, Berlin, 1926, p. 64.

2. Jakob van Hoddis, *Dichtungen und Briefe*, edited by Regina Nörtemann, Zurich, 1987, p. 186.

3. Peter Viereck, 'Ogling through the Ice. The Sullen Lyricism of Georg Heym', in *Books Abroad*, no. 45, 1971, p. 236.

4. Hoddis, op. cit., p. 156; Alfred Lichtenstein, *Gesammelte Gedichte*, edited by Klaus Kanzog, Zurich, 1962, p. 151.

5. Quoted from Nina Schneider, *Katalog II*, p. 139.

6. *Jahrbuch für die geistige Bewegung*, edited by Friedrich Gundolf and Friedrich Wolters, vol. I, February 1910; vol. II, April 1911.

7. Ludwig Klages, *Stefan George*, Berlin, 1902.

8. Friedrich Wolters, *Melchior Lechter*, Munich, 1911.

9. *Maximin. Ein Gedenkbuch*, edited by Stefan George, Berlin, 1907.

10. Gustav Renner, *Gedichte* (Gesamtausgabe), Berlin, 1904, p. 20.

11. Ronald Salter, 'Gustav Renner – ein vergessenes Vorbild Georg Heyms', in *Schlesien*, vol. 22, 1977, p. 86.

12. ibid, p. 88.

13. cf. Hermann Korte, *Georg Heym*, Stuttgart, 1982, p. 33.

14. ibid.

15. Richard Sheppard, *Die Schriften des Neuen Clubs, 1908–14*, II, Hildesheim, 1983, pp. 495f.

16. ibid., p. 496.

17. *Caracosa*, Berlin, 1894, vol. I, p. 80.

18. Bernd W. Seiler, *Die historischen Dichtungen Georg Heyms*, Munich, 1972, p. 93.

19. *The Last Days of Pompeii*, Book II, Chapter 4.

20. ibid., Book III, Chapter 11; Book IV, Chapter 3.

21. Simon Guttmann's words are quoted from his letter to Nina Schneider of 7 September 1988. I am grateful to Nina Schneider for permission to quote from this letter.

22. Ursula Mahlendorf, 'Georg Heym's Development as a Dramatist and Poet', in *Journal of English and Germanic Philology*, vol. 63, 1964, p. 66.

23. Hoddis, *Weltende*, edited by Paul Pörtner, Zurich, 1958, p. 33.

24. Goethe, *Faust I*, lines 2710–16 and 3534.

25. Korte, op. cit., p. 92.

26. ibid., p. 91.

27. ibid., p. 89.

28. In the 'Nachwort' to *Georg Heym – Auswahl*, edited by Karl Ludwig Schneider and Gunter Martens, Munich, 1971, pp. 263f.

IV: LIFE AND DEATH, 1910–1912

1. This paragraph is based on information contained in a letter from Simon Guttmann to Nina Schneider dated 7 September 1988. I am grateful to Nina Schneider for permission to reproduce this information.

2. Letter from Simon Guttmann to Nina Schneider of 7 September 1988.

3. Helmut Greulich, *Georg Heym (1887–1912). Leben und Werk*, Berlin, 1931, p. 15.

4. This story is based on the transcript of a discussion between Karl Ludwig Schneider and Kurt Hiller which took place in Schneider's Oberseminar on Georg Heym on 1 June 1961, and which was kindly placed at my disposal by Nina Schneider.

5. Quoted from Nina Schneider, *Katalog II*, p. 78.

6. ibid., pp. 84, 137.

7. Simon Guttmann, in conversation with Nicholas Jacobs.

8. In 1902/3 Heym wrote in an autobiographical sketch that 'frohe Zukunfts-träume umgaukelten mich' (Nina Schneider, *Katalog II*, p. 23). This implies that dreams of a happy future took on the appearance of leering animal masks, cf. the passage which he found in Merezhkovsky's *Peter der Große* (translated by Carl von Gütschow, Leipzig, 1905, p. 104) in 1907: 'The human faces took on the appearance of animal masks.'

9. Cf. *D* 501f.

10. Greulich, op. cit., p. 33.

11. SUB Hamburg, Nl. Heym, Inv. Nr. 24, fol. 16r.

12. Cf. Greulich, op. cit., p. 39.

13. See *Katalog der 3. Kunstausstellung der Berliner Sezession*, Berlin, 1901, cat. no. 27. Brandenburg's painting is reproduced in Nina Schneider, *Katalog I*, p. 17.

14. Letter from Simon Guttmann to Nina Schneider of 7 September 1988.

15. Greulich, op. cit., p. 37.

16. SUB Hamburg, Nl. Heym, Inv. Nr. 20: Kladde für Vorlesungsmitschriften, WS 1911/12.

17. SUB Hamburg, Nl. Heym, Inv. Nr. 24.

18. His note about the *Pantschatantra* may derive from a reading of Schopenhauer's *Die Grundlage der Moral*.

19. SUB Hamburg, Nl. Heym, Inv. Nr. 89, fols 1 and 2. Scattered throughout the *Nachlaß* are similar drawings, all of them childish in execution.

20. SUB Hamburg, Nl. Heym, Inv. Nr. 24, fol. 18r.

V: TRAGIC POET

1. SUB Hamburg, Nl. Heym, Inv. no. 15, fols 3v and 4.

2. *Selected Poems and Letters of Keats*, edited by Robert Gittings, 1966, p. 8.

3. ibid., p. 9.

4. ibid., p. 16.

5. ibid., p. 17.

6. Arthur Symons, *Charles Baudelaire. A Study*, 1920, p. 23. The words 'load every rift ... with ore' were used by Keats in a letter to Shelley dated August 1820.

7. Patricia Clements, *Baudelaire and the English Tradition*, Princeton and Guildford, 1985, p. 6.

8. Martin Turnell, *Baudelaire. A Study of his Poetry*, 1953, p. 305.

9. Michel Butor, quoted in Clements, op. cit., p. 10.

10. Turnell, op. cit., p. 228.

11. Baudelaire, *The Painter of Modern Life and Other Essays*, translated and edited by Jonathan Mayne, 1964, p. xiv.

12. Baudelaire, *Selected Poems*, edited by Joanna Richardson, 1975, pp. 18f.

13. August Wiedmann, *Romantic Art Theories*, Henley-on-Thames, 1986, p. 17.

14. Baudelaire, *The Painter of Modern Life and Other Essays*, p. 59.

15. Van Gogh, *Briefe*, translated by Margarethe Mauthner, n.d., pp. 58f.

16. *The Journal of Eugène Delacroix*, translated by Lucy Norton, 1951, pp. 33f., 39.

17. ibid., p. 38.

18. Baudelaire, *Art in Paris 1845–1863*, translated and edited by Jonathan Mayne, 1965, p. 65.

19. ibid., p. 66.

20. ibid., p. 65.

21. Baudelaire, *The Painter of Modern Life and Other Essays*, p. 45.

22. ibid., p. 48.

23. Arthur Symons, *The Symbolist Movement in Literature*, New York, revised edition, 1919, p. 115.

24. Baudelaire, *The Painter of Modern Life and Other Essays*, p. 63.

25. Baudelaire, 'Semper eadem' (cf. Schopenhauer's 'Sufferings of the World', in his *Studies in Pessimism*, translated by T. B. Saunders, 1906, p. 12).

26. Symons, *Charles Baudelaire. A Study*, p. 37.

27. Baudelaire, 'Le Voyage'.

28. Schopenhauer on Dante in *The World as Will and Idea*, translated by R. B. Haldane and J. Kemp, vol. 1, seventh edn, n.d., p. 419.

29. T. S. Eliot, 'Baudelaire', in *Selected Prose*, 1953, p. 189.

30. Quoted from Clements, op. cit., p. 29.

31. Eliot, op. cit., p. 189.

32. Turnell, op. cit., pp. 238f.

33. Eliot, op. cit., p. 191.

34. Rimbaud, letter to Paul Demeny of 15 May 1871.

35. Nina Schneider, *Katalog II*, p. 138.

36. Symons, *The Symbolist Movement in Literature*, second edn, 1908, p. 65.

37. ibid., p. 72.

38. Pater, in his 'Winckelmann' essay in *The Renaissance*.

39. Heym's Stendhal quotations (*T* 160, 163) come from Book II, Chapters 13, 14, 19, 42 and 44; and Book I, Chapter 1, of the novel.

VI: PAINTER MANQUÉ

1. In an interview with Peter Hasubek in 1964, the tape of which Nina Schneider kindly made available to me.

2. Dmitry Merezhkovsky, *The Forerunner*, reprinted 1929, pp. 291f.

3. Heym can be shown to have attended some exhibitions of (or including) Van Gogh's work, and in some other cases may reasonably be assumed to have done so. In what follows I keep to the facts, e.g. that he could have attended a certain exhibition. When an image from a work in that exhibition appears in Heym's poetry of the time, readers will draw their own conclusion. Care does need to be exercised here.

4. Quoted from Richard Sheppard, *Die Schriften des Neuen Clubs 1908–14*, 2 vols, Hildesheim, 1980–3, vol. II, p. 153.

5. ibid., p. 502.

6. Vincent van Gogh, *Briefe*, translated by M. Mauthner, n.d., p. 45.

7. ibid., p. 51.

8. G. Albert Aurier, *Oeuvres posthumes*, Paris, 1893, p. 261.

9. Quoted from J. B. de la Faille, *The Works of Vincent van Gogh*, Amsterdam and London, 1970, p. 20.

10. Quoted from Jean Leymarie, *Van Gogh*, translated by James Emmons, 1978, p. 152.

11. ibid., p. 172.

12. ibid., p. 166.

13. Werner Haftmann, *Painting in the Twentieth Century*, translated by Ralph Manheim, 2 vols, New York and London, 1965, vol. I, p. 26.

14. Carl Einstein, *Die Kunst des 20. Jahrhunderts*, third edn, Berlin, 1931, p. 23.

15. The diary entry suggests that Heym may have known Hofmannsthal's 'Farben', published under the title 'Das Erlebnis des Sehens', in *Kunst und Künstler* in 1908; see Hofmannsthal, *Prosa* II, Frankfurt, 1951, pp. 353f.

16. cf. 'Water Mill at Kol, near Nuenen' (F 48a).

17. See Ronald Pickvance, *Van Gogh in Saint-Rémy and Auvers*, New York, 1986, p. 61.

18. F. Elgar, *Van Gogh*, 1958, p. 234. Heym knew the words 'Life is probably round' from Vincent van Gogh, *Briefe*, p. 75.

19. The poem also seems to have had a verbal starting-point in Zarathustra's words 'Verily, I would not be like the rope-makers: they spin out their thread and themselves go backwards all the time' (Nietzsche, *Thus Spake Zarathustra*, Part I, Chapter XXI).

20. Ronald Salter, *Georg Heyms Lyrik*, Munich, 1972, pp. 217ff.

21. ibid., p. 223.

22. In Nina Schneider, *Katalog II*, pp. 105f.

23. Sharon L. Hirsh, *Ferdinand Hodler*, 1982, p. 49.

24. See Nina Schneider, *Katalog II*, pp. 108f.

25. P. J. Lewis, *Georg Heym's Optical Sense* (D.Phil., Oxford, 1989), p. 132. On parallels between Heym and Munch see Chapter 3 of this thesis.

26. Haftmann, op. cit., p. 59.

27. In his interview with Peter Hasubek (see note 1 above), Engert mistakenly referred to Kley's *Der Krieg* and its influence on Heym's poem of that title. In fact Kley's *Pfui Deifel* influenced poems like 'Der Gott der Stadt', while Heym's 'Der Krieg' was influenced rather by Kubin.

28. *Kunst und Künstler*, January 1910.

29. *The Oxford Companion to Art*, Oxford, 1970.

30. G. Sebba, in his Introduction to Kubin's *Dance of Death*, New York, 1973, p. v.

31. Interview with Peter Hasubek (see note 1 above).

32. ibid.

33. Sebba, op. cit., p. viii.

34. ibid.

35. Salter, *Georg Heyms Lyrik*, p. 238.

36. Nina Schneider (*Katalog II*, p. 95) first mooted the possibility of Heckel's *Gläserner Tag* being influenced by Heym.

37. C. Z. von Manteuffel, in *E. L. Kirchner, Drawings and Pastels*, edited by R. N. Ketterer, New York, 1982, p. 120.

38. Quoted from Heym, *Umbra vitae*, reprinted in Munich, 1969, Nachwort.

39. See Kurt Wolff, *Briefwechsel eines Verlegers*, Frankfurt, 1966, p. 391; see also *Umbra vitae*, op. cit., p. 9.

40. E. L. Kirchner, *Davoser Tagebuch*, edited by L. Grisebach, Cologne, 1968, p. 87.

41. Bernard Myers, *Expressionism*, 1963, p. 111.

42. *Das Werk*, XII, No. 8, Zurich, 1925, p. 241.

43. Quoted from *Umbra vitae*, p. 13.

44. Wolf-Dieter Dube, *The Expressionists*, 1972, translated by Mary Whittall, p. 37.

45. Willi Grohmann, *E. L. Kirchner*, Stuttgart, 1958, p. 79.

46. Salter, *Georg Heyms Lyrik*, p. 163.

47. Donald E. Gordon, *Ernst Ludwig Kirchner*, Cambridge, Mass., 1968, p. 79.

48. Gordon, *Expressionism. Art and Idea*, New Haven and London, 1987, p. 100.

49. Ludwig Meidner, *Im Nacken das Sternemeer*, Leipzig, 1918, p. 77.

50. Quoted from Nina Schneider, *Katalog II*, p. 100.

51. Carol S. Eliel, *The Apocalyptic Landscapes of Ludwig Meidner*, Los Angeles and Munich, 1989, p. 31.

52. ibid.

53. Quoted in Gordon, *Expressionism. Art and Idea*, p. 101.

VII: POETRY, 1910–1912

1. Ronald Salter, *Georg Heyms Lyrik*, Munich, 1972, p. 75.

2. See K. Brösel, *Veranschaulichung im Realismus, Impressionismus und Frühexpressionismus*, Munich, 1928, pp. 43f.

3. Richard Sheppard in *New German Studies*, vol. III, no. 2, 1975, p. 107.

4. Philip Thomson, *The Grotesque in German Poetry 1880–1933*, Melbourne, 1975, pp. 71f.

5. Particularly in his *Skizzenbuch I* of 1909 ('Diaballeteuse', 'Pfui Deifel', 'Sabotage'), but also in *Skizzenbuch II* of 1910. See *The Drawings of Heinrich Kley*, New York, 1961.

6. Inevitably my account of the origins of 'Der Krieg' is indebted to Günter Dammann, Karl Ludwig Schneider and Joachim Schöberl, *Georg Heyms Gedicht 'Der Krieg'* (Heidelberg, 1978) to which acknowledgement is made and to which the reader is referred.

7. P. J. Lewis, *Georg Heym's Optical Sense*, D.Phil., Oxford, 1989.

8. Quoted from Donald E. Gordon, *Expressionism. Art and Idea*, 1987, p. 24. See also Carol S. Eliel, *The Apocalyptic Landscapes of Ludwig Meidner*, Los Angeles and Munich, 1989.

9. Franz Marc, *Briefe aus dem Felde*, second edn, Berlin 1941; reprinted 1948, p. 25.

10. See Nina Schneider, *Katalog II*, p. 67.

11. Peter Viereck, 'Ogling through the Ice. The Sullen Lyricism of Georg Heym', in *Books Abroad*, no. 45, 1971, p. 233.

12. ibid., p. 238.

13. Engert, interview with Peter Hasubek (see Chapter VI, note 1), with acknowledgement to Nina Schneider.

14. Michael Hamburger and Christopher Middleton (eds), *Modern German Poetry 1910–1960*, 1962, p. xxvii.

15. Thomson, op. cit., pp. 69–72.

16. Quoted from *Swinburne as Critic*, edited by Clyde K. Hyder, 1972, p. 30.

17. Heinz Rölleke, in *Expressionismus als Literatur*, edited by Wolfgang Rothe, Berlin and Munich, 1969, p. 356.

18. Viereck, op. cit., p. 240.

19. In the Afterword to his Reclam edition of Heym, *Dichtungen*, Stuttgart, 1964.

20. See Günter Dammann's valuable article, 'Theorie des Stichworts', in *Texte und Varianten*, edited by Gunter Martens and Hans Zeller, Munich, 1971.

21. SUB Hamburg, Nl. Heym, Inv. no. 9, fols 25r, 188.

22. ibid., Inv. no. 26, fol. 164.

23. *Lyrik des expressionistischen Jahrzehnts*, edited by Gottfried Benn, 1962, pp. 8f. In the anthology *Verse der Liebe* (Wiesbaden, n.d.) Benn named the two other poems: Richard Dehmel's 'Helle Nacht' and Goethe's 'Nachtgesang'. By the same token, in a letter to Max Niedermayer dated 15 January 1951 Benn described Heym's 'Mit den fahrenden Schiffen' as the most beautiful poem of the twentieth century.

24. Viereck, op. cit., p. 240.

VIII: THE TALES

1. *Berliner Tageblatt*, 26 February 1913.

2. *Der Tag*, 19 June 1913.

3. *Der Gegenwart*, 5 July 1913.

4. On the front cover of the MS of 'Ein Nachmittag'; SUB Hamburg, Nl. Heym Inv. no. 34.

5. Monty Jacobs, in *Der Tag*, 19 June 1913.

6. cf. Schopenhauer's 'On Death', which Heym read in 1906 or earlier (in *The World as Will and Idea*, translated by R. B. Haldane and J. Kemp, seventh edn, n.d., vol. III, p. 252).

7. Kurt Kesten, in *Berliner Tageblatt*, 26 February 1913.

8. *Die Argonauten*, May 1914.

9. Bernd W. Seiler, *Die historischen Dichtungen Georg Heyms*, Munich, 1972, p. 12.

10. *Handbuch der deutschen Erzählung*, edited by K. K. Polheim, Düsseldorf, 1981, p. 440.

11. Karl Ludwig Schneider, *Zerbrochene Formen*, Hamburg, 1967, p. 51.

12. Philip Thomson, *The Grotesque in German Poetry 1880–1933*, Melbourne, 1975, pp. 67, 69.

13. *Der Tag*, 19 June 1913.

14. Quoted from G. Rans, *Edgar Allan Poe*, 1965, p. 66.

15. ibid., p. 85.

16. ibid., p. 71.

17. ibid., p. 80.

18. Allen Tate, *The Man of Letters in the Modern World*, 1955, p. 129.

19. Peter Kropotkin, *Die französische Revolution, 1789–1793*, translated by Gustav Landauer, 2 vols, Leipzig, 1910; see vol. I, pp. 40, 86, 143f., 148f.; vol. II, p. 279.

20. Gottfried Benn, *Probleme der Lyrik*, Wiesbaden, 1951, p. 16.

21. Poe, *Works*, edited by J. H. Ingram, 1899, vol. I, p. 220.

22. K. L. Schneider, op. cit., p. 57.

23. Allen Blunden, 'Notes on Georg Heym's Novelle "Der Irre" ', in *German Life and Letters*, vol. XXVIII, 1974–5, pp. 117f.

24. Poe, *Works*, vol. II, p. 202.

25. Hermann Korte, *Georg Heym*, Stuttgart, 1982, p. 77.

26. Schopenhauer, op. cit. (note 6 above), p. 382.

27. From Pater's essay, 'Leonardo da Vinci', in *The Renaissance*.

28. Ursula Mahlendorf, *Germanic Review*, XXXVI, no. 3, 1961, pp. 191f.

29. Poe, op. cit., vol. I, p. 244 (quotation from 'The Premature Burial').

POSTSCRIPT

1. Rupert Brooke, 'The [Second] Post-Impressionist Exhibition at the Grafton Galleries', *The Cambridge Magazine*, 23 and 30 November 1912.

2. The Letters of *Vincent van Gogh*, edited by Mark Roskill, 1963; reprinted 1982, p. 288.

3. Wilhelm Worringer, *Abstraktion und Einfühlung*, Munich, 1908, *passim*.

4. Armin Arnold, in *Expressionism as an International Literary Phenomenon*, edited by U. Weisstein, Paris and Budapest, 1973, p. 81.

5. Peter Selz, *German Expressionist Painting*, Berkeley, 1957; reprinted 1974, p. vii.

Bibliography

In English

Allan, Roy F., *Literary Life in German Expressionism and the Berlin Circles*, Göppingen, 1974.

Bick, Judith, 'Cross or Judas-Tree. A Footnote to the Problem of Good and Evil in Georg Heym', *German Quarterly*, 46, 1973, pp. 22–30.

Blunden, Allan, 'Beside the Seaside with Georg Heym and Dylan Thomas', *German Life and Letters*, 29, 1975/6, pp. 4–14.

Blunden, Allan, 'Notes on Georg Heym's Novelle "Der Irre"', *German Life and Letters*, 28, 1974/5, pp. 107–19.

Bridgwater, Patrick, *The Expressionist Generation and van Gogh*, Hull, 1987.

Bridgwater, Patrick, *The Poet as Hero and Clown. A Study of Heym and Lichtenstein*, Durham, 1986.

Bridgwater, Patrick (ed.), *The Poets of the Café des Westens*, Leicester, 1984.

Bridgwater, Patrick (ed.), *Twentieth-Century German Verse*, second edn, Harmondsworth, 1968.

Cook, Frances E. B., *The Dream Image in the Poetry of Georg Heym*, Diss., Berkeley, 1970.

Eliel, Carol S., *The Apocalyptic Landscapes of Ludwig Meidner*, Los Angeles and Munich, 1989.

Feilchenfeldt, Walter, *Vincent van Gogh and Paul Cassirer. The Reception of Van Gogh in Germany from 1901 to 1914*, Zwolle, 1988.

Furness, R. S., *Expressionism*, London, 1973.

Gordon, Donald E., *Expressionism. Art and Idea*, New Haven and London, 1987.

Gordon, Donald E., *Ernst Ludwig Kirchner*, Cambridge, Mass., 1968.

Hamburger, Michael, *Reason and Energy. Studies in German Literature*, London, 1957.

Hamburger, Michael and Middleton, Christopher (eds), *Modern German Poetry 1910–1960*, London, 1962.

Jung, Claire, 'Memories of Georg Heym', in *The Era of Expressionism*, edited and annotated by Paul Raabe, translated by J. M. Ritchie, London, 1974.

Krispyn, Egbert, *Georg Heym. A Reluctant Rebel*, Gainesville, 1968.

Krispyn, Egbert, *Georg Heym and the Early Expressionist Era*, Diss., University of Pennsylvania, 1963.

Krispyn, Egbert, 'Sources and Subject Matter in two Short Stories by Georg Heym', *AUMLA*, 12, 1959, pp. 52–7.

Lehnert, Herbert, 'Alienation and Rebellion in the German Bourgeoisie. Georg Heym', in *Expressionism Reconsidered, Relationships and Affinities*, ed. G. Bauer Pickar and K. E. Webb, Munich, 1979, pp. 25–34.

Lewis, P. J., *Georg Heym's Optical Sense. The function of painterly elements in the lyrical work*, D.Phil., Oxford, 1989.

Liptzin, S., *Shelley in Germany*, New York, 1924.

Mahlendorf, Ursula R., 'The Myth of Evil. The Reëvaluation of the Judaic-Christian Tradition in the Work of Georg Heym', *Germanic Review*, XXXVI, 3, October 1961.

Mahlendorf, Ursula R., 'Georg Heym's Development as a Dramatist and Poet', *Journal of English and Germanic Philology*, 63, 1964, pp. 58–71.

Myers, Bernard S., *Expressionism*, London, 1963.

Pasley, Malcolm (ed.), *Germany. A Companion to German Studies*, second edn, Oxford, 1982.

Price, L. M., *The Reception of English Literature in Germany*, London, 1968.

Sgroi, Celia Ann, *Georg Heym's Metaphysical Landscape*, Diss., Ohio, 1975.

Sheppard, Richard, 'From Grotesque Realism to Expressionism: A Linguistic Analysis of the Second Turning-Point in Georg Heym's Poetic Development', *New German Studies*, III, 2, Summer 1975, pp. 99–109.

Sokel, Werner, *The Writer in Extremis. Expressionism in Twentieth-Century German Literature*, Stanford, 1959.

Thomson, Philip, *The Grotesque in German Poetry 1880–1933*, Melbourne, 1975.

Viereck, Peter, 'Ogling through the Ice. The Sullen Lyricism of Georg Heym', *Books Abroad*, no. 45, 1971, pp. 232–42.

Vordtriede, Werner, 'The Expressionism of Georg Heym', *Wisconsin Studies in Contemporary Literature*, 4, 1963, pp. 284–97.

Willett, John, *Expressionism*, London, 1970.

In German

Adams, Marion, 'Die Helden in Georg Heyms Dramen. Identifikation und Distanzierung des Autors', in *Rezeption der deutschen Gegenwartsliteratur im Ausland*, ed. P. Papenfuß and J. Söring, Stuttgart, 1976, pp. 345–52.

Balcke, Ernst, 'Georg Heym. Der ewige Tag', *Die Aktion*, I, 1911, cols. 375–77.

Bartsch, Kurt, *Die Hölderlin-Rezeption im deutschen Expressionismus*, Frankfurt, 1974.

Brösel, K. *Veranschaulichung im Realismus, Impressionismus und Frühexpressionismus*, Munich, 1928.

Brown, Russell E., *Index zu Georg Heym 1910–1912*, Frankfurt and Bonn, 1970.

Cosentino, Christine, *Tierbilder in der Lyrik des Expressionismus*, Bonn, 1972.

Dammann, Günter, 'Theorie des Stichworts. Ein Versuch über die lyrischen Entwürfe Georg Heyms', in *Texte und Varianten. Probleme ihrer Edition und Interpretation*, ed. Gunter Martens and Hans Zeller, Munich, 1971, pp. 203–18.

Dammann, Günter, 'Untersuchungen zur Arbeitsweise Georg Heyms an seinen Handschriften. Über die Entstehung der Gedichte "Mortuae", "Totenwache", "Letzte Wache"', *Orbis Litterarum*, 26, 1971, pp. 42–67.

Dammann, Günter, Schneider, Karl Ludwig and Schöberl, Joachim, *Georg Heyms Gedicht 'Der Krieg'*, Heidelberg, 1978.

Durzak, Manfred, 'Nachwirkungen Stefan Georges im Expressionismus', *German Quarterly*, 42, 1969, pp. 393–417.

Ellermann, Heinrich, *Georg Heym, Ernst Stadler, Georg Trakl. Versuch einer geistesgeschichtlichen Bibliographie*, Hamburg, 1934.

Eykman, Christoph, *Die Funktion des Häßlichen in der Lyrik Georg Heyms, Georg Trakls und Gottfried Benns*, second edn, Bonn, 1969.

Greulich, Helmut, *Georg Heym (1887–1912). Leben und Werk*, Berlin, 1931.

Heselhaus, Clemens, *Deutsche Lyrik der Moderne*, Düsseldorf, 1962.

Heydebrand, Renate von, 'Georg Heym, Ophelia', in *Gedichte der 'Menschheitsdämmerung'. Interpretationen expressionistischer Lyrik*, ed. H. Denkler, Munich, 1971, pp. 33–55.

Heym, Georg, *Dichtungen*, ed. K. Pinthus and E. Loewenson, Munich, 1922.

Heym, Georg, *Gesammelte Gedichte*, ed. C. Seelig, Zurich, 1947.

Heym, Georg, *Dichtungen und Schriften*, ed. K. L. Schneider, 4 vols, Hamburg and Munich, 1960–8.

Heym, Georg, *Gedichte 1910–1912. Historisch-kritische Ausgabe aller Texte in genetischer Darstellung*, 2 vols, ed. Günter Dammann, Gunter Martens and Karl Ludwig Schneider, Tübingen, 1992.

Heym, Georg, *Der Athener Ausfahrt. Trauerspiel in einem Aufzug*, Würzburg, 1907.

Heym, Georg, *Der ewige Tag*, Leipzig, 1911.

Heym, Georg, *Umbra vitae*, ed. Baumgardt *et al.*, Leipzig, 1912.

Heym, Georg, *Der Dieb*, Leipzig, 1913.

Heym, Georg, *Marathon*, ed. Balduin Möllhausen, Berlin-Wilmersdorf, 1914.

Heym, Georg, *Umbra vitae*, with 47 woodcuts by E. L. Kirchner, Munich, 1924 (facsimile reprint, with Nachwort by Elmar Jansen, Munich, 1969).

Hirschenauer, Rupert, 'Georg Heym, Tod des Pierrots', in *Interpretationen moderner Lyrik*, ed. R. Hirschenauer, Frankfurt, 1962, pp. 48–59.

Höxter, John, *Ich bin noch ein ungeübter Selbstmörder*, Hanover, 1988.

Ihekweazu, E., 'Wandlung und Wahnsinn. Zu expressionistischen Erzählungen', *Orbis Litterarum*, 37, 1982, pp. 327–44.

Korte, Hermann, *Der Krieg in der Lyrik des Expressionismus*, Bonn, 1981.

Korte, Hermann, *Georg Heym*, Stuttgart, 1982.

Kubin, Alfred, *Das zeichnerische Frühwerk bis 1904*, ed. H. A. Peters, Baden-Baden, 1977.

Lehnert, Herbert, 'Das romantische Erbe und die imaginäre Gegenwelt. Georg Heym: "Deine Wimpern, die langen"', in Herbert Lehnert, *Struktur und Sprachmagie*, Stuttgart, 1966, pp. 67–78.

Leistner, Gerhard, *Idee und Wirklichkeit. Gehalt und Bedeutung des urbanen Expressionismus in Deutschland, dargestellt am Werk Ludwig Meidners*, Bern, 1986.

Loewenson, Erwin, *Georg Heym oder Vom Geist des Schicksals*, Hamburg, 1962.

Mahlendorf, Ursula, R., *Georg Heym. Stil und Weltbild*, Diss., Brown University, 1958.

Majut, Robert, 'Erinnerungen an Georg Heym, Erwin Loewenson und das neopathetische Cabaret', *German Life and Letters*, 24, 1970/1, pp. 160–74.

Martens, Gunter, '"Im Aufbruch das Ziel." Nietzsches Wirkung im Expressionismus', in *Nietzsche. Werk und Wirkungen*, ed. H. Steffen, Göttingen, 1974, pp. 115–66.

Martens, Gunter, *Vitalismus und Expressionismus. Ein Beitrag zur Genese und Deutung expressionistischer Stilstrukturen und Motive*, Stuttgart, 1971.

Martens, Gunter, 'Umbra vitae und Der Himmel Trauerspiel. Die ersten Sammlungen der nachgelassenen Gedichte Georg Heyms', *Euphorion*, 59, 1965, pp. 118–31.

Martens, Gunter, 'Georg Heym und der "Neue Club"', in Georg Heym, D 390–401.

Martini, Fritz, 'Georg Heym, "Die Sektion"', in Fritz Martini, *Das Wagnis der Sprache*, Stuttgart, 1954, pp. 260–86.

Mautz, Kurt, *Mythologie und Gesellschaft im Expressionismus. Die Dichtung Georg Heyms*, Frankfurt, 1961.

Meckel, Christoph, 'Allein im Schatten seiner Götter. Über Georg Heym', *Der Monat*, 20, 1968, pp. 63–70.

Motekat, Helmut, 'Georg Heyms "Umbra vitae"', *Deutschunterricht für Ausländer*, 7, 1957, pp. 65–72.

Raabe, Paul (ed.), *Expressionismus. Der Kampf um eine literarische Bewegung*, Munich, 1965.

Recknagel, Rolf, 'Georg Heym — Der den Weg nicht weiß', *Neue Deutsche Literatur*, 12, 1964, Heft 10, pp. 74–96.

Regenberg, Anton, *Die Dichtung Georg Heyms und ihr Verhältnis zur Lyrik Charles Baudelaire's und Arthur Rimbaud's*, Diss., Munich, 1961.

Roebling, Irmgard, *Das Problem des Mythischen in der Dichtung Georg Heyms*, Bern and Frankfurt, 1975.

Rölleke, Heinz, *Die Stadt bei Stadler, Heym und Trakl*, Berlin, 1966.

Rölleke, Heinz, 'Georg Heym', in *Expressionismus als Literatur*, ed. W. Rothe, Bern and Munich, 1969, pp. 354–73.

Rölleke, Heinz (ed.), *Georg Heym Lesebuch*, Munich, 1987.

Rothe, Wolfgang (ed.), *Expressionismus als Literatur*, Berlin and Munich, 1969.

Rüesch, Jürg Peter, *Ophelia. Zum Wandel des lyrischen Bildes im Motiv der 'navigatio vitae' bei Arthur Rimbaud und im deutschen Expressionismus*, Zurich, 1964.

Salter, Ronald, 'Gustav Renner – ein vergessenes Vorbild Georg Heyms', *Schlesien*, 22, 1977, pp. 85–96.

Salter, Ronald, *Georg Heyms Lyrik*, Munich, 1972.

Salter, Ronald, 'Georg Heym und Ferdinand Hodler', *Orbis Litterarum*, 31, 1976, pp. 134–59.

Saudek, Robert, *Dämon Berlin*, Berlin, 1907.

Schmähling, Walter, *Die Darstellung der menschlichen Problematik in der deutschen Lyrik von 1890–1914*, Diss., Munich, 1962.

Schmähling, Walter, 'Nachwort', in Georg Heym, *Dichtungen*, ed. Walter Schmähling, Stuttgart, 1964, pp. 75–84.

Schneider, Ferdinand Josef, *Der expressive Mensch und die deutsche Lyrik der Gegenwart*, Stuttgart, 1927.

Schneider, Karl Ludwig, *Der bildhafte Ausdruck in den Dichtungen Georg Heyms, Georg Trakls und Ernst Stadlers*, Heidelberg, 1961.

Schneider, Karl Ludwig, 'Das Bild der Landschaft bei Georg Heym und Georg Trakl', in *Der deutsche Expressionismus. Formen und Gestalten*, ed. H. Steffen, Göttingen, 1965 (also in Karl Ludwig Schneider, *Zerbrochene Formen*).

Schneider, Karl Ludwig, 'Georg Heym', in *Deutsche Dichter der Moderne*, ed. Benno von Wiese, Berlin, 1965.

Schneider, Karl Ludwig, *Zerbrochene Formen. Wort und Bild im Expressionismus*, Hamburg, 1967.

Schneider, Karl Ludwig, 'Die Menschen unter der Wolke', *Philobiblon*, XXV, 1 February 1981, pp. 4–6.

Schneider, Nina (ed.), *Georg Heym: Der Städte Schultern knacken* [= *Katalog I*], Zurich, 1987.

Schneider, Nina, *Georg Heym 1887–1912* [= *Katalog II*], Berlin, 1988.

Schneider, Nina, '"Dieser seltsame Dichter..." Zur Entdeckung Georg Heyms', *Auskunft. Mitteilungsblatt Hamburger Bibliotheken*, vol. 10, no. 3, 1990, pp. 233–41.

Schwarz, Georg, *Georg Heym*, Mühlacker, 1963.

Schwarz, Waltraut, 'Von Wittenau ins Kaufhaus Wertheim. "Der Irre" von Georg Heym', *Neue Deutsche Hefte*, 26, 1979, pp. 70–88.

Seelig, Carl, 'Leben und Sterben von Georg Heym', in Georg Heym, *Gesammelte Gedichte*, ed. Carl Seelig, Zurich, 1947, pp. 201–37.

Seiler, Bernd W., *Die historischen Dichtungen Georg Heyms*, Munich, 1972.

Sheppard, Richard (ed.), *Die Schriften des Neuen Clubs, 1908–1914*, 2 vols, Hildesheim, 1980–3.

Soergel, Albert, *Dichtung und Dichter der Zeit*, Leipzig, 1911 (new edn, 1925).

Stadler, Ernst, 'Georg Heym. Der ewige Tag', *Cahiers Alsaciens*, I, 3, 1912, p. 144 (extract in George Heym, *D* 237–9).

Steigmaier, Edmund, 'Kreis und Vertikale als strukturtragende Elemente in der Dichtung Georg Heyms', *Deutsche Vierteljahreschrift*, 47, 1973, pp. 456–66.

Uhlig, Helmut, 'Vom Ästhetizismus zum Expressionismus', in *Expressionismus. Gestalten einer literarischen Bewegung*, ed. H. Friedmann and O. Mann, Heidelberg, 1956, pp. 96–106.

Wiesinger, Walther, 'Georg Heym, "Robespierre"', in *Wege zum Gedicht*, ed. R. Hirschenauer and A. Weber, II, Munich/Zurich, 1968, pp. 527–33.

Zech, Paul, 'Wie Georg Heym den Krieg sah', *Die Hilfe*, XXII, 1916, pp. 364f.

Zimmermann, Werner, 'Georg Heym, "Jonathan"', in Werner Zimmermann, *Deutsche Prosadichtungen unseres Jahrhunderts*, vol. I, Düsseldorf, 1966, pp. 165–76.

In French

Colombat, R., *Rimbaud, Heym, Trakl*, 2 vols, Bern, 1987.

Schiller, Ingeborg, *L'influence de Rimbaud et de Baudelaire dans la poésie préexpressioniste allemande*, Diss., Paris, 1968.

Index

Page references in **bold** indicate poems by Georg Heym which appear in full in the text.